UTOPIA'S AVENGER

Volume 2

Created by
Oh Se-Kwon

TOKYOPOP®

HAMBURG // LONDON // LOS ANGELES // TOKYO

Utopia's Avenger Vol. 2
Created by Oh Se-Kwon

Translation - Woo Sok Park
English Adaptation - Jai Nitz
Copy Editor - Peter Ahlstrom
Retouch and Lettering - Star Print Brokers
Production Artist - Jennifer Carbajal
Graphic Designer - Fawn Lau

Editor - Bryce P. Coleman
Digital Imaging Manager - Chris Buford
Pre-Production Supervisor - Erika Terriquez
Art Director - Anne Marie Horne
Production Manager - Elisabeth Brizzi
Managing Editor - Vy Nguyen
VP of Production - Ron Klamert
Editor-in-Chief - Rob Tokar
Publisher - Mike Kiley
President and C.O.O. - John Parker
C.E.O. and Chief Creative Officer - Stuart Levy

A  Manga

TOKYOPOP Inc.
5900 Wilshire Blvd. Suite 2000
Los Angeles, CA 90036

E-mail: info@TOKYOPOP.com
Come visit us online at www.TOKYOPOP.com

ISBN: 978-1-59816-671-2

First TOKYOPOP printing: April 2007
10 9 8 7 6 5 4 3 2 1
Printed in the USA

UTOPIA'S AVENGER

Oh Se-Kwon

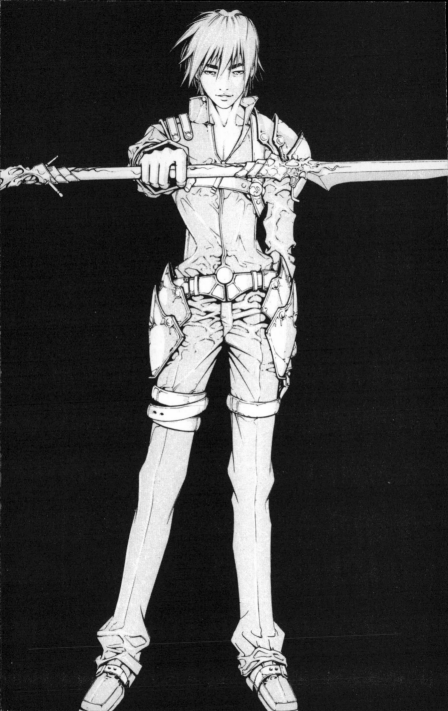

UTOPIA'S AVENGER

Story So Far

ONCE, THERE WAS A LEGENDARY
KINGDOM CALLED YULDO,
AN IDEAL COUNTRY IN WHICH PEACE AND
PROSPERITY FLOURISHED FOR YEARS.
THE HEROIC WARRIOR HONG GIL-DONG
CREATED THIS UTOPIAN LAND--
AND THEN SUDDENLY DISAPPEARED
WITHOUT A TRACE.
BUT TIME PASSED, AND A BAND OF
RUTHLESS WARRIORS INVADED
THE KINGDOM, LEAVING IT IN UTTER RUINS.
NOW, HONG GIL-DONG HAS RETURNED, AND
ALONG WITH HIS FAITHFUL COMPANION,
DANU, HE IS DETERMINED TO RAISE HIS VILLAGE
FROM THE ASHES. BUT EVIL FORCES LURK
IN THE SHADOWS, OBSERVING OUR HERO'S
EVERY MOVE--WAITING FOR THE OPPORTUNITY
TO STRIKE DOWN UTOPIA'S AVENGER...

UTOPIA'S AVENGER

Contents

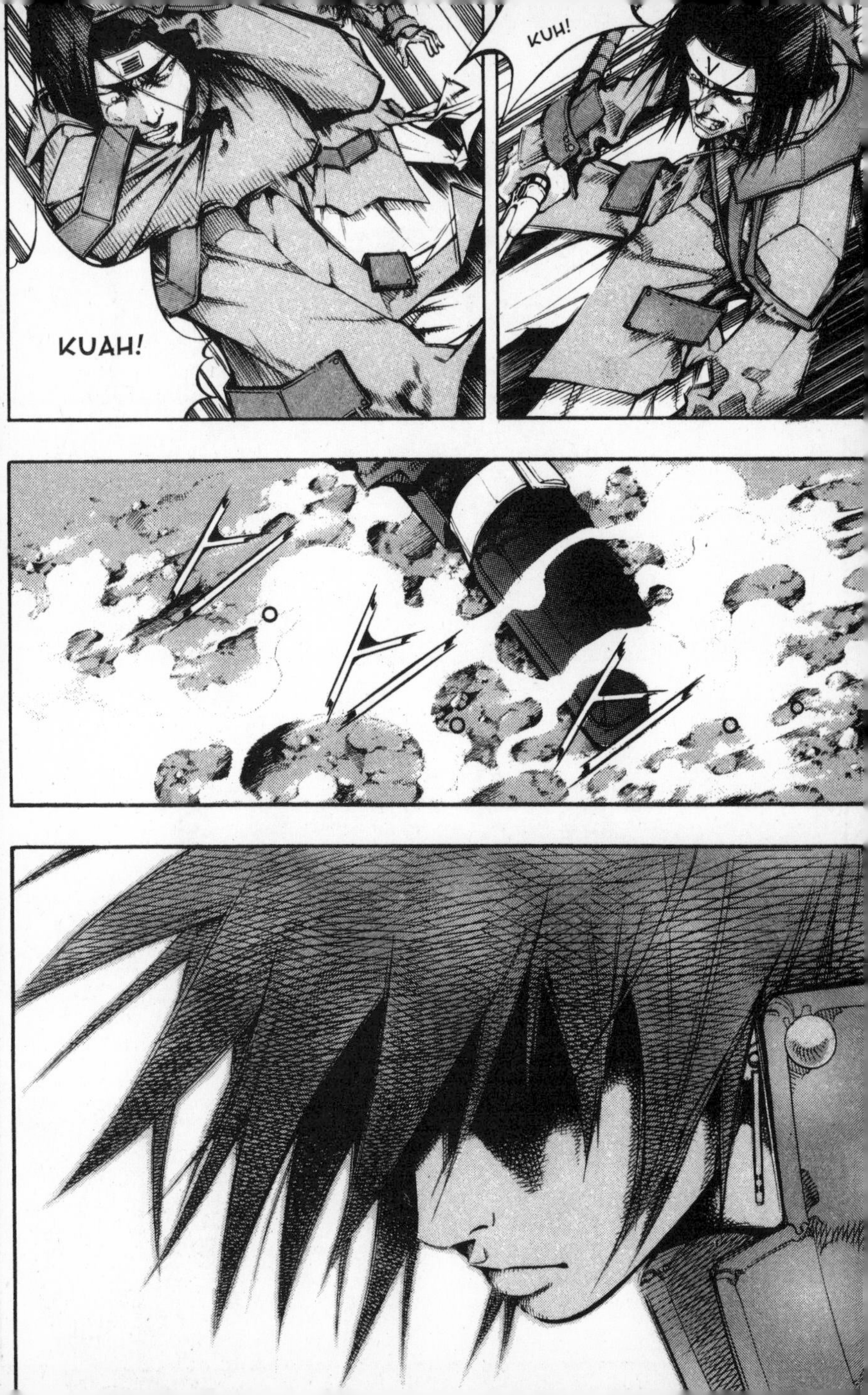
KUH!
KUAH!

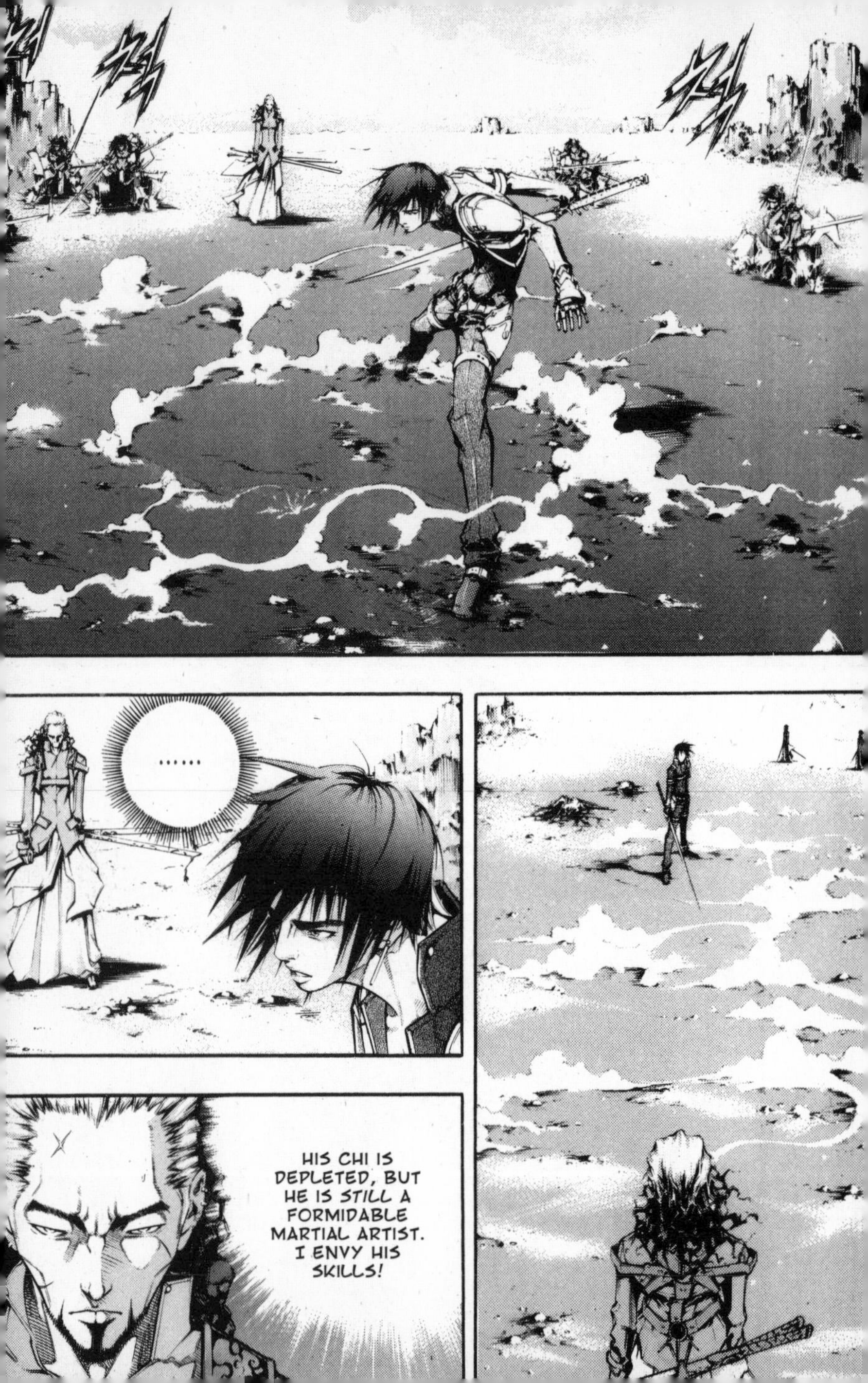
......
HIS CHI IS DEPLETED, BUT HE IS *STILL* A FORMIDABLE MARTIAL ARTIST. I ENVY HIS SKILLS!

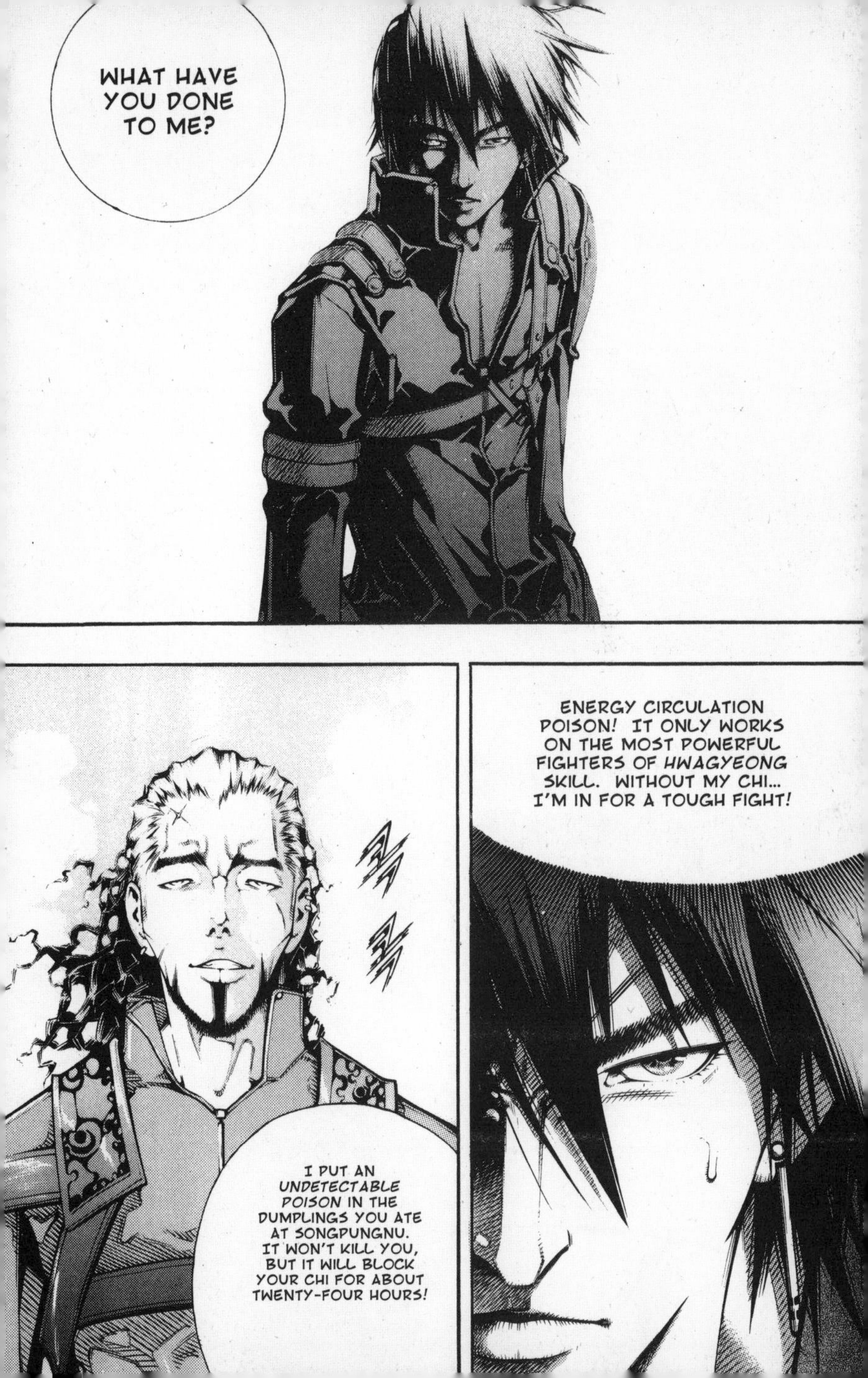
WHAT HAVE YOU DONE TO ME?
I PUT AN UNDETECTABLE POISON IN THE DUMPLINGS YOU ATE AT SONGPUNGNU. IT WON'T KILL YOU, BUT IT WILL BLOCK YOUR CHI FOR ABOUT TWENTY-FOUR HOURS!
ENERGY CIRCULATION POISON! IT ONLY WORKS ON THE MOST POWERFUL FIGHTERS OF HWAGYEONG SKILL. WITHOUT MY CHI... I'M IN FOR A TOUGH FIGHT!

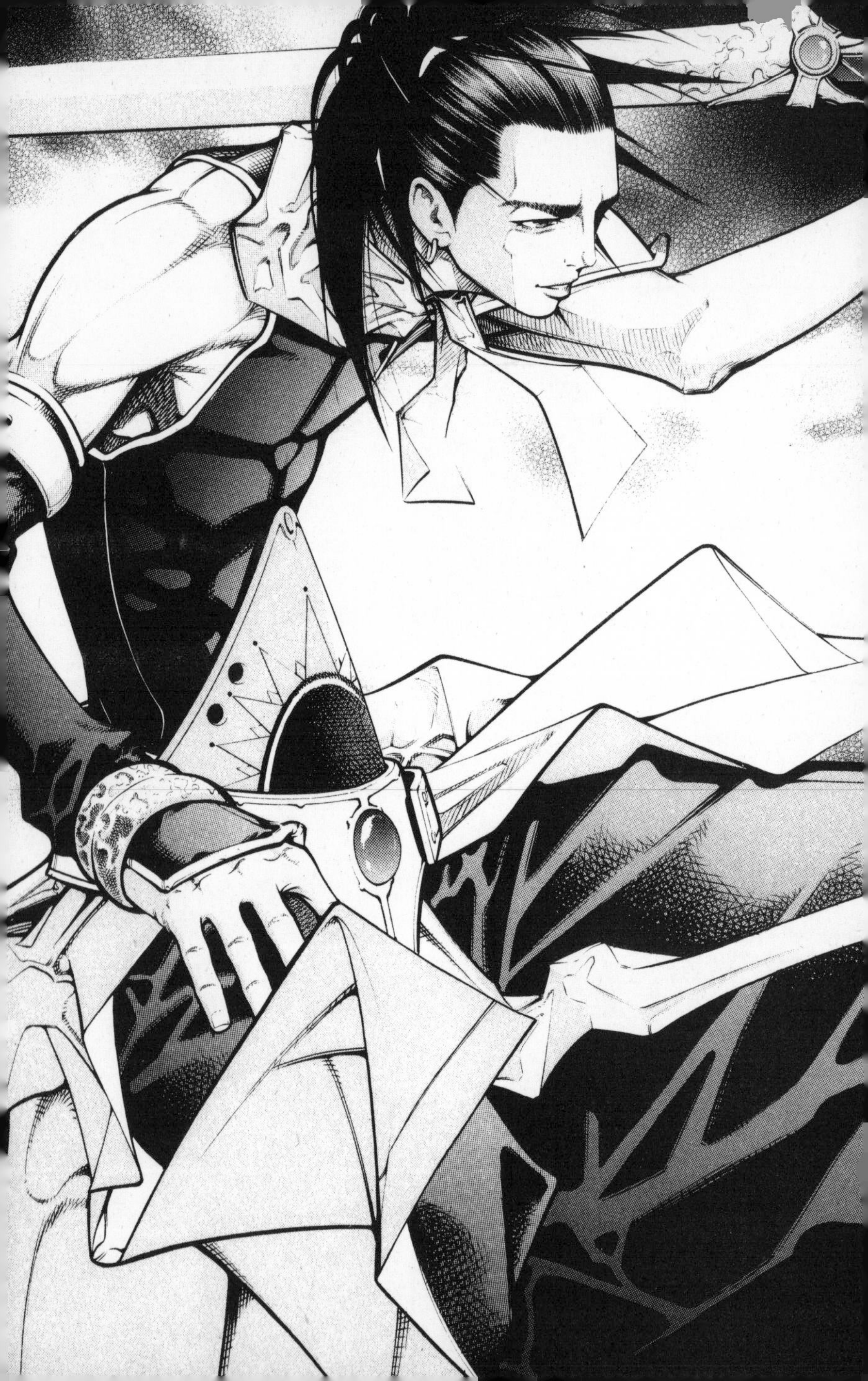

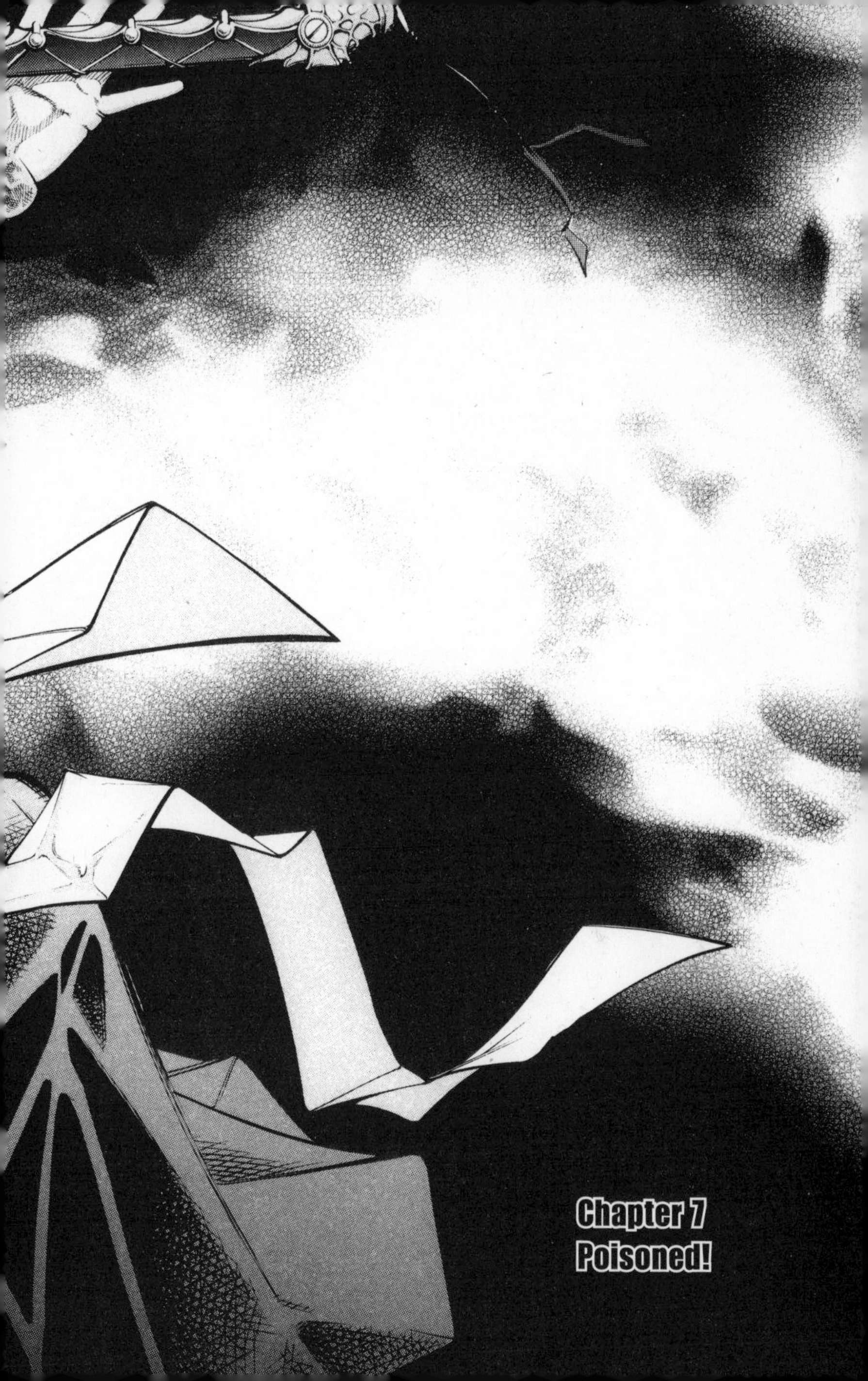
Chapter 7
Poisoned!

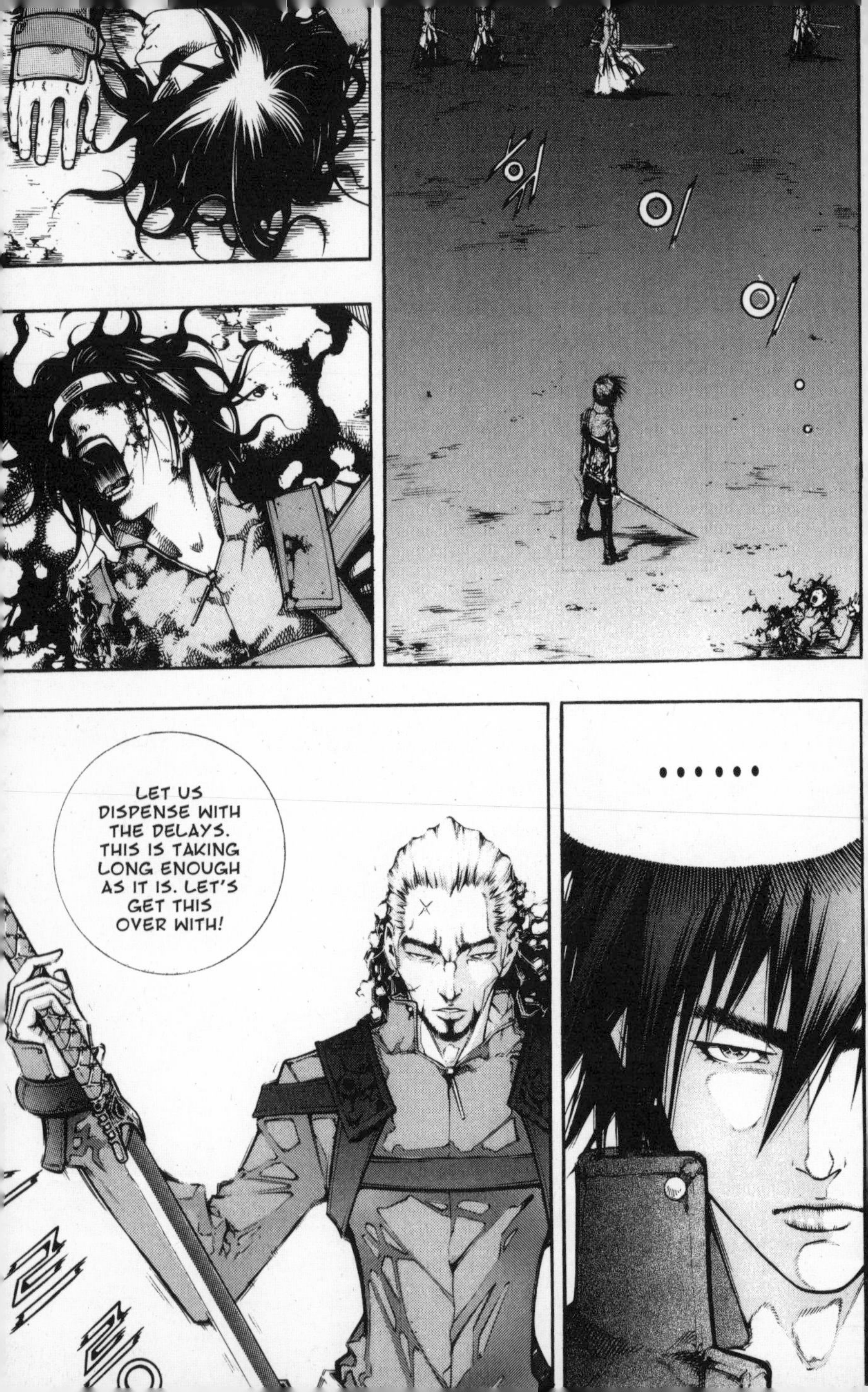
LET US DISPENSE WITH THE DELAYS. THIS IS TAKING LONG ENOUGH AS IT IS. LET'S GET THIS OVER WITH!
......

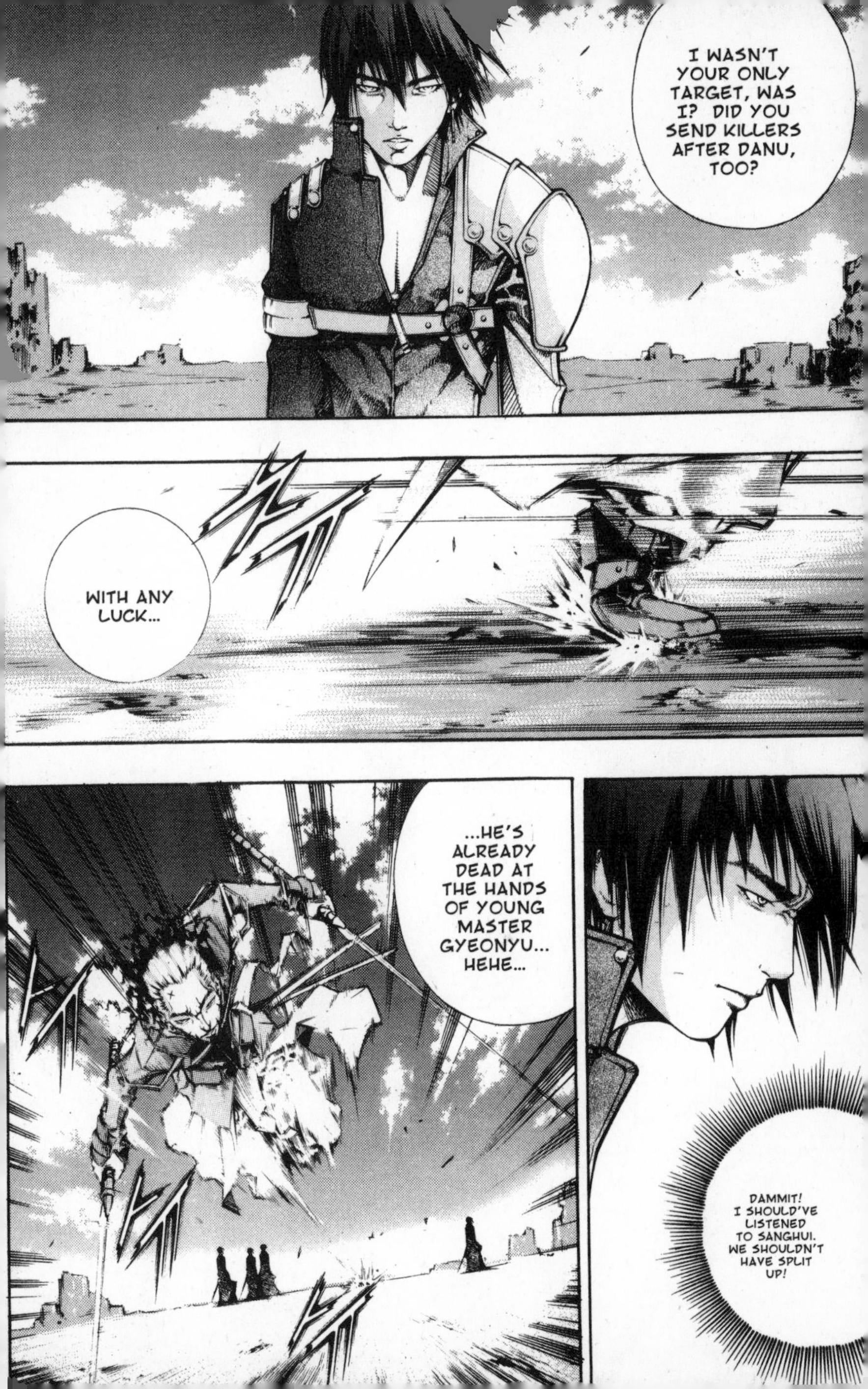
I WASN'T YOUR ONLY TARGET, WAS I? DID YOU SEND KILLERS AFTER DANU, TOO?
WITH ANY LUCK...
...HE'S ALREADY DEAD AT THE HANDS OF YOUNG MASTER GYEONYU... HEHE...
DAMMIT! I SHOULD'VE LISTENED TO SANGHUI. WE SHOULDN'T HAVE SPLIT UP!

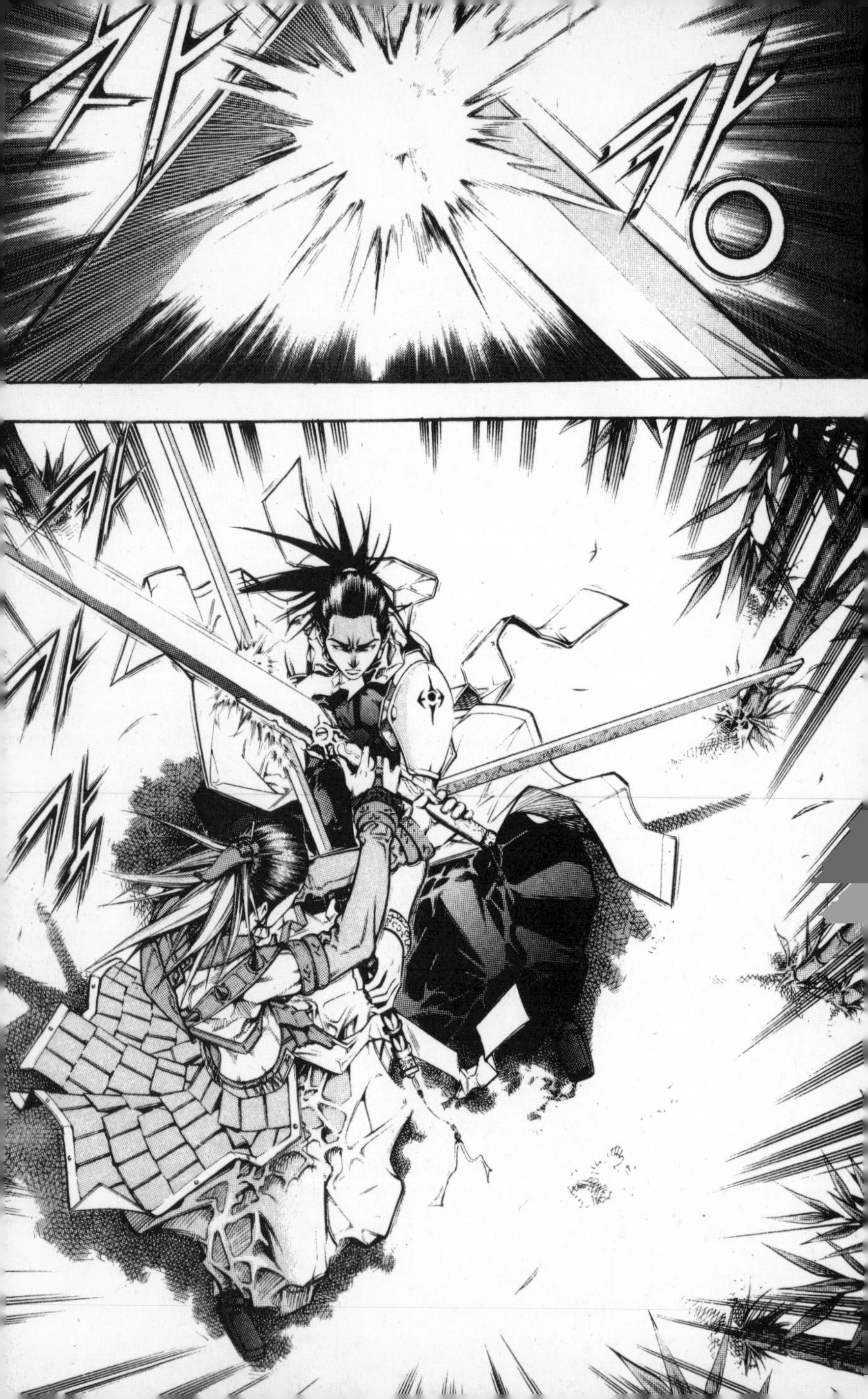

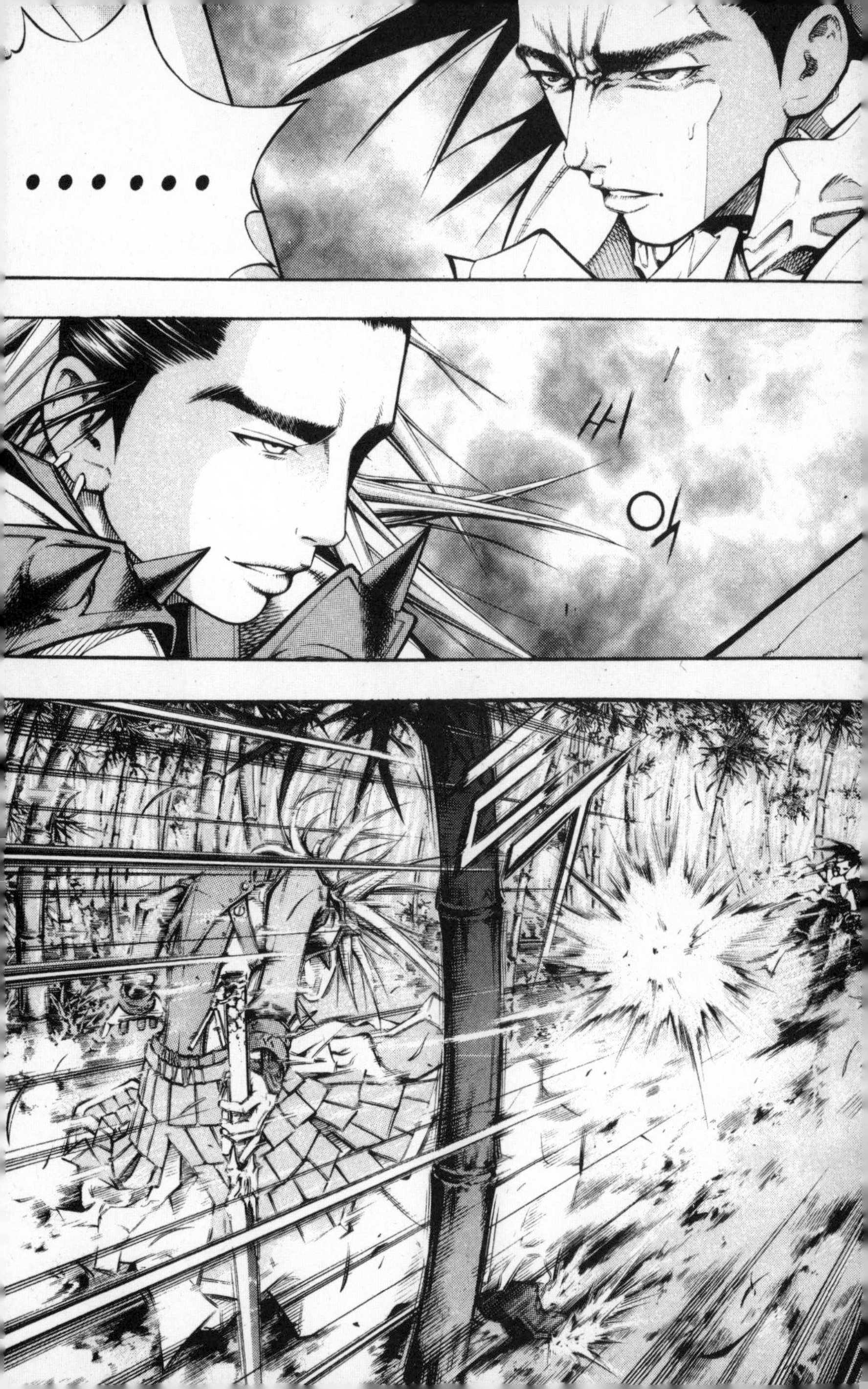
......

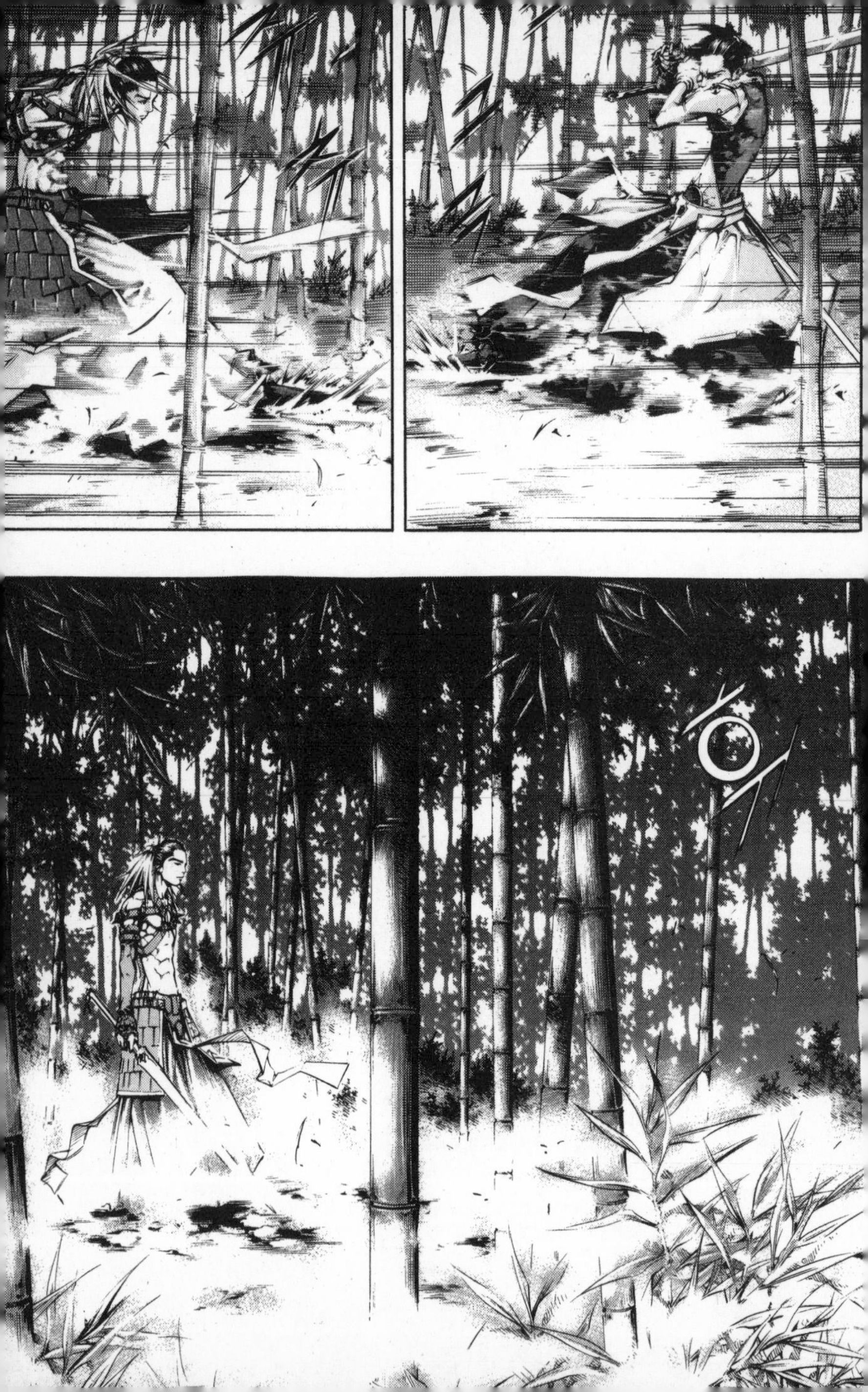

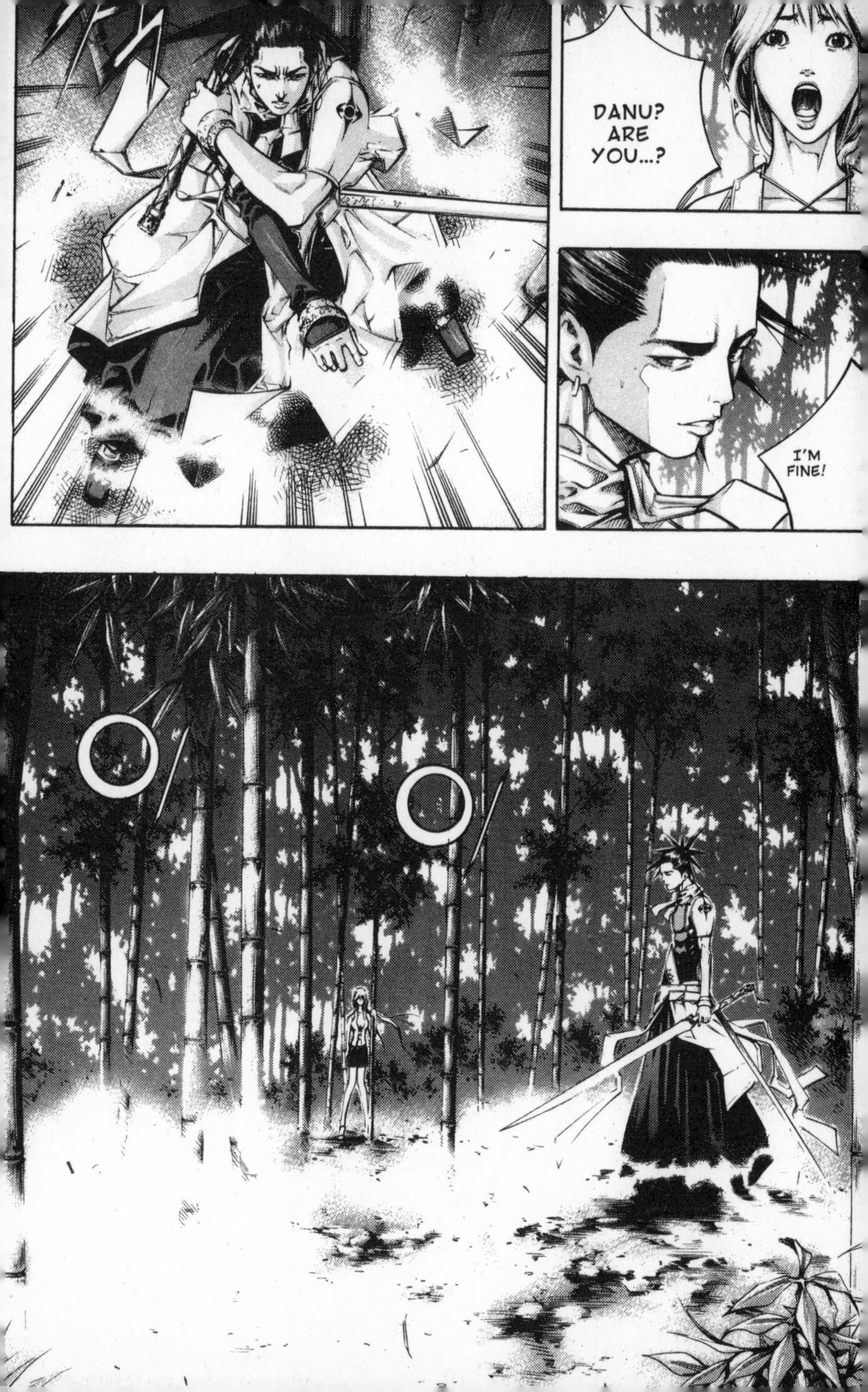
DANU? ARE YOU...?
I'M FINE!

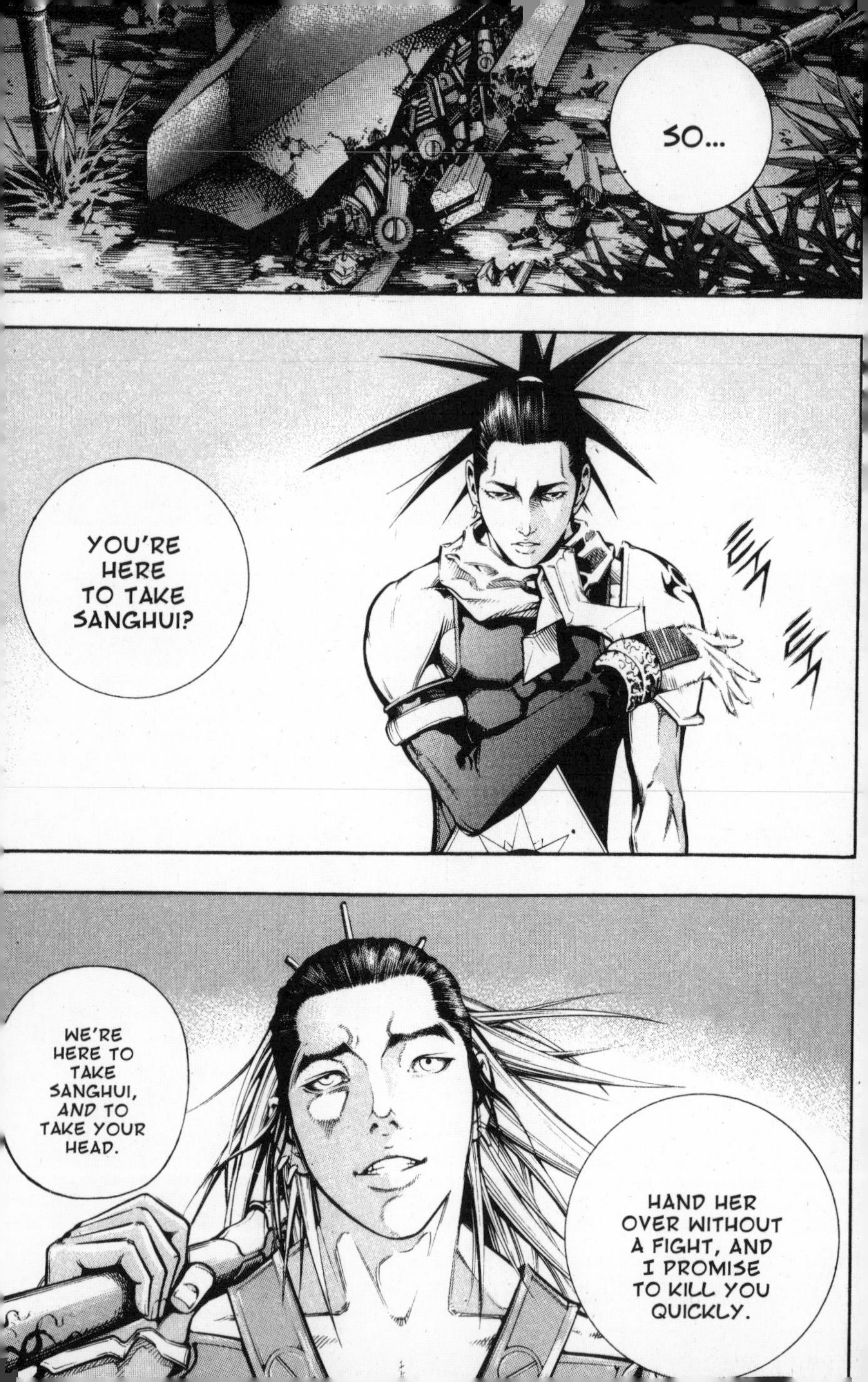
SO...
YOU'RE HERE TO TAKE SANGHUI?
WE'RE HERE TO TAKE SANGHUI, AND TO TAKE YOUR HEAD.
HAND HER OVER WITHOUT A FIGHT, AND I PROMISE TO KILL YOU QUICKLY.

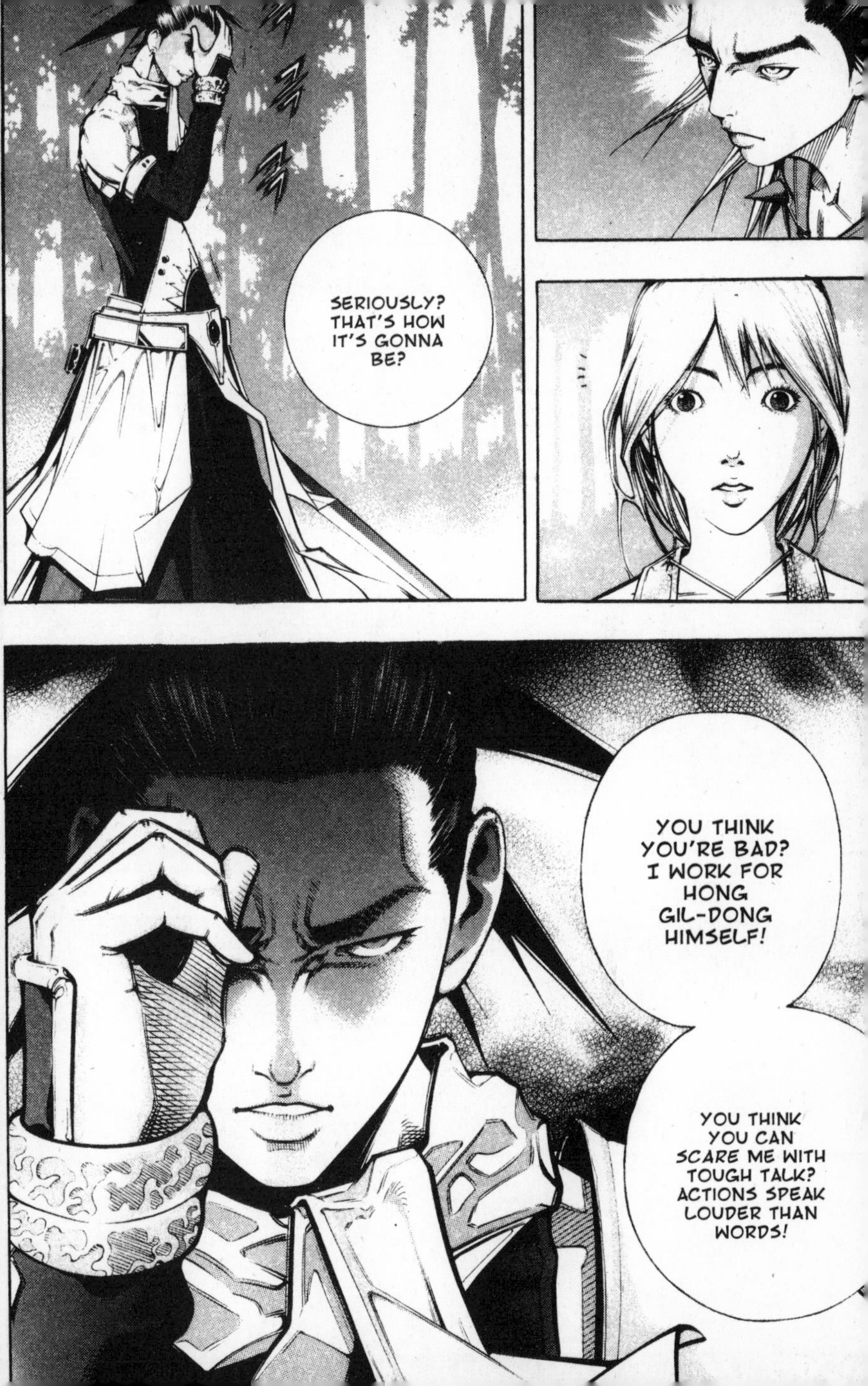
SERIOUSLY? THAT'S HOW IT'S GONNA BE?
YOU THINK YOU'RE BAD? I WORK FOR HONG GIL-DONG HIMSELF!
YOU THINK YOU CAN SCARE ME WITH TOUGH TALK? ACTIONS SPEAK LOUDER THAN WORDS!

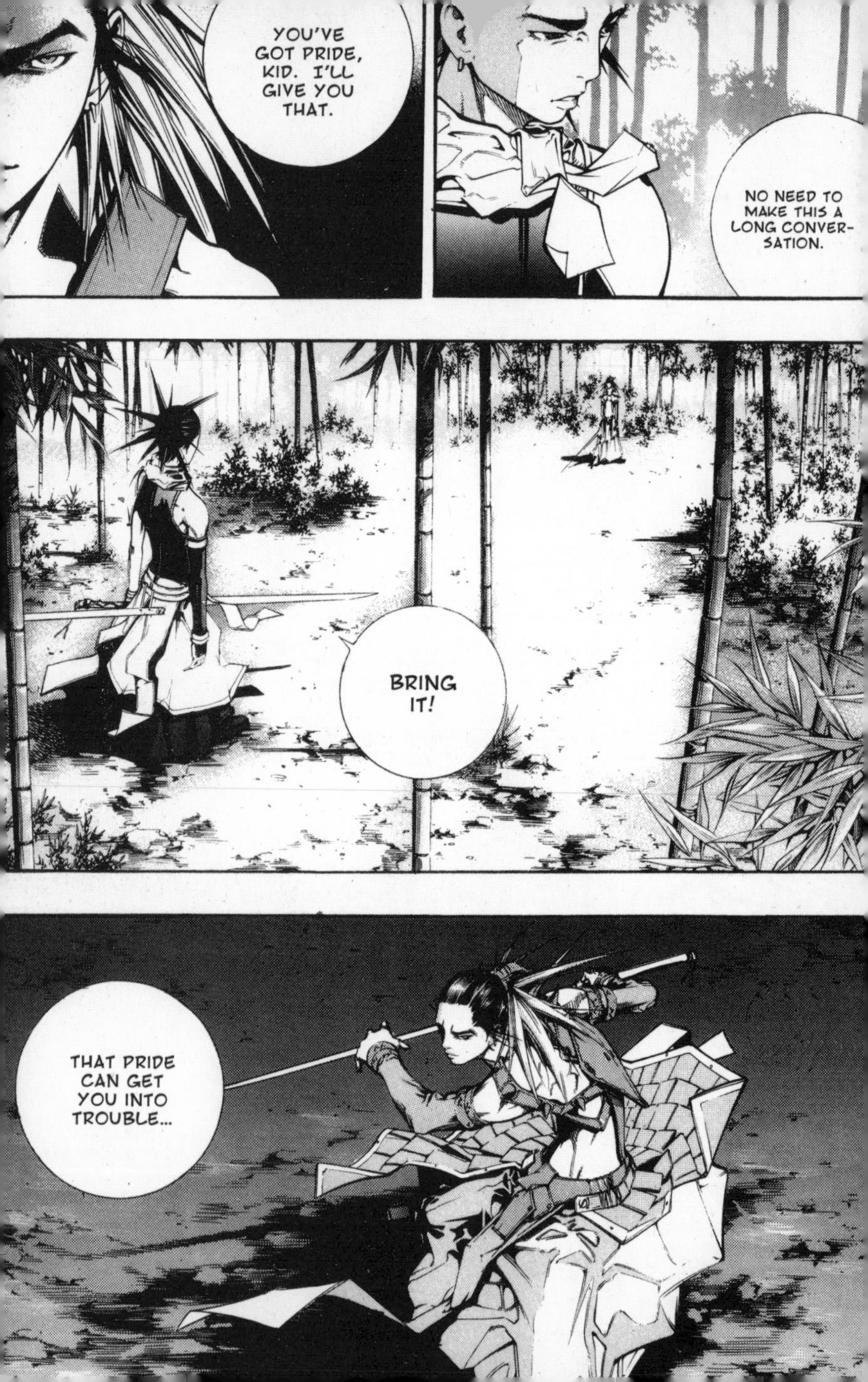
YOU'VE GOT PRIDE, KID. I'LL GIVE YOU THAT.
NO NEED TO MAKE THIS A LONG CONVER-SATION.
BRING IT!
THAT PRIDE CAN GET YOU INTO TROUBLE...

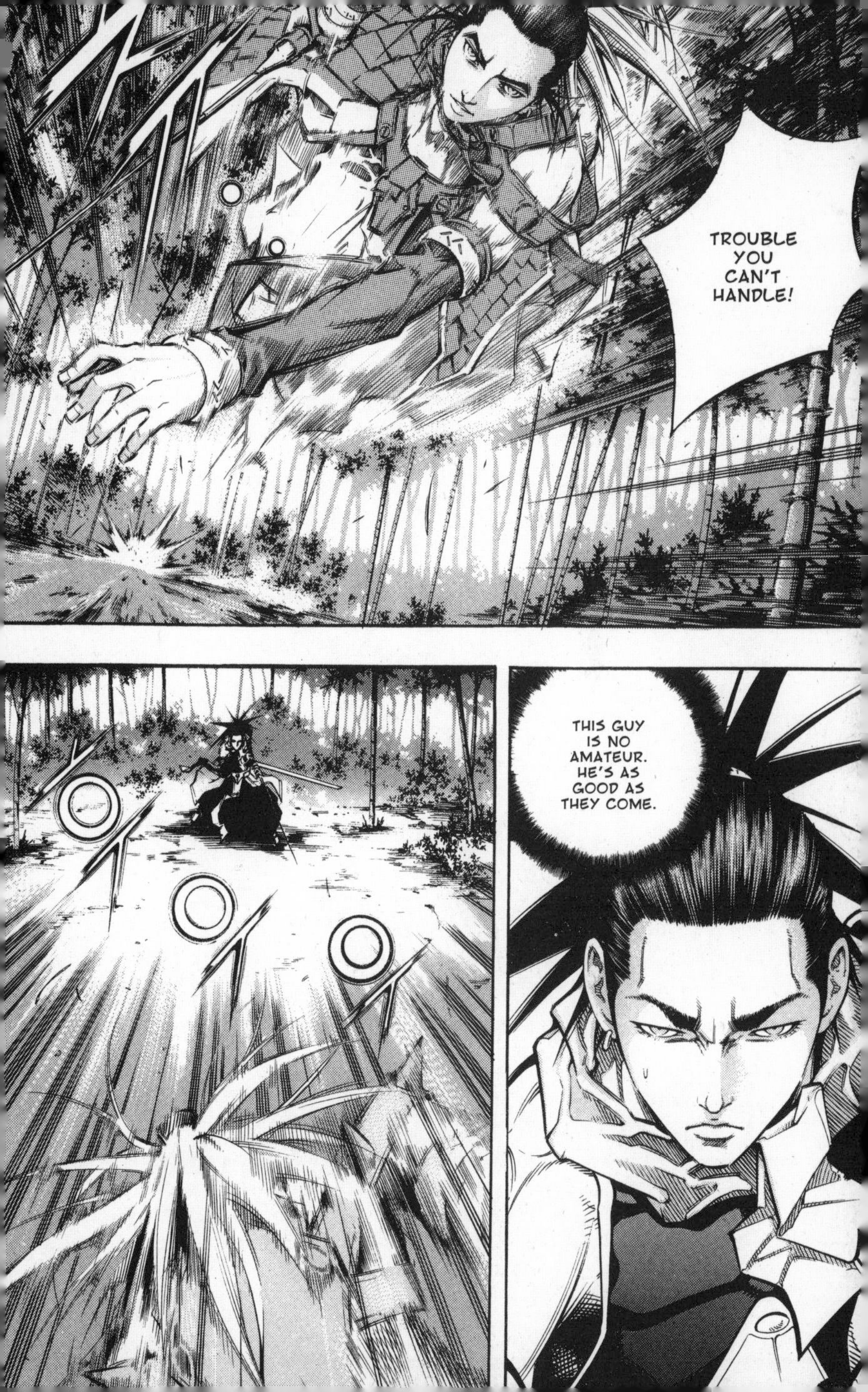
TROUBLE YOU CAN'T HANDLE!
THIS GUY IS NO AMATEUR. HE'S AS GOOD AS THEY COME.

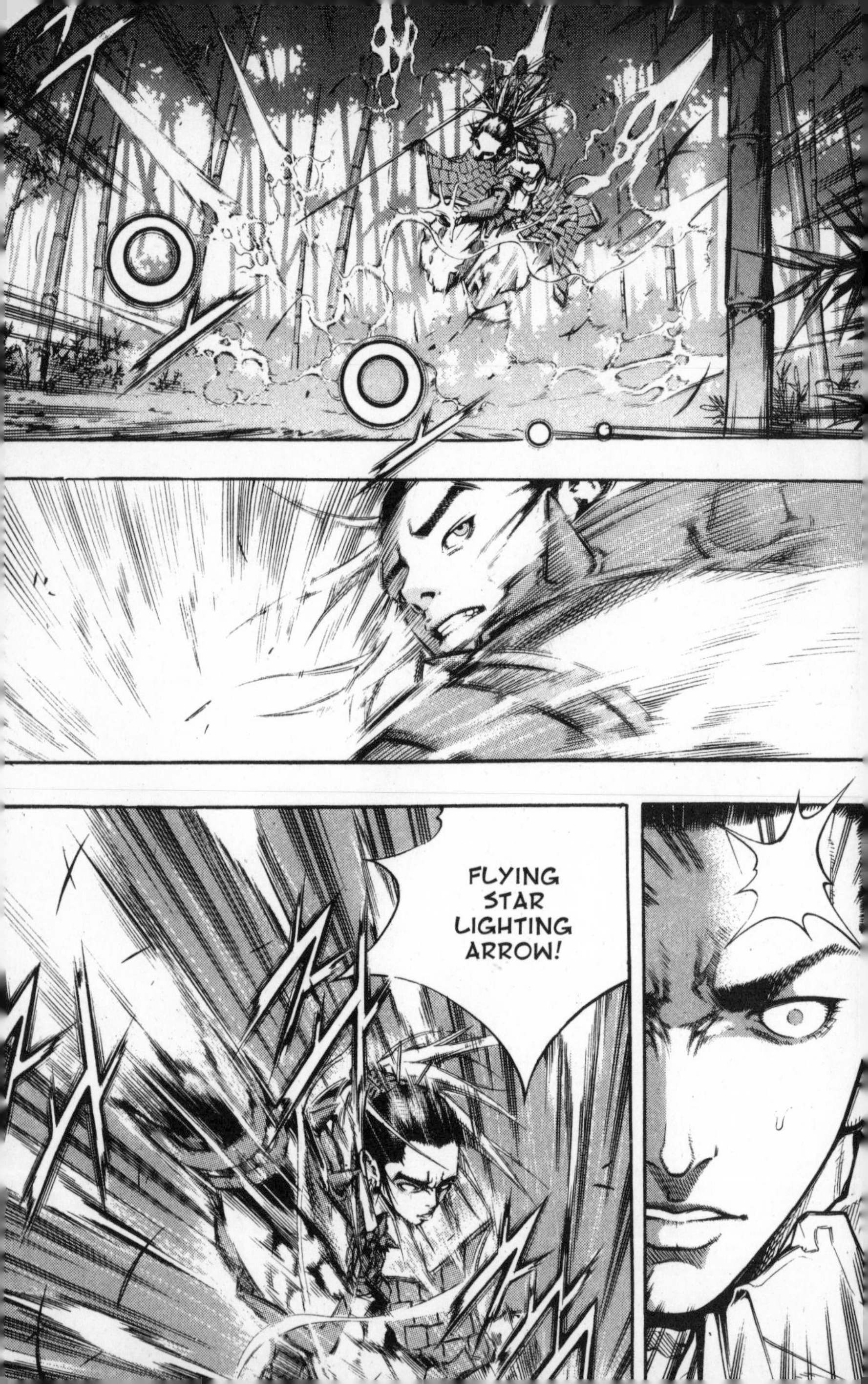
FLYING STAR LIGHTING ARROW!

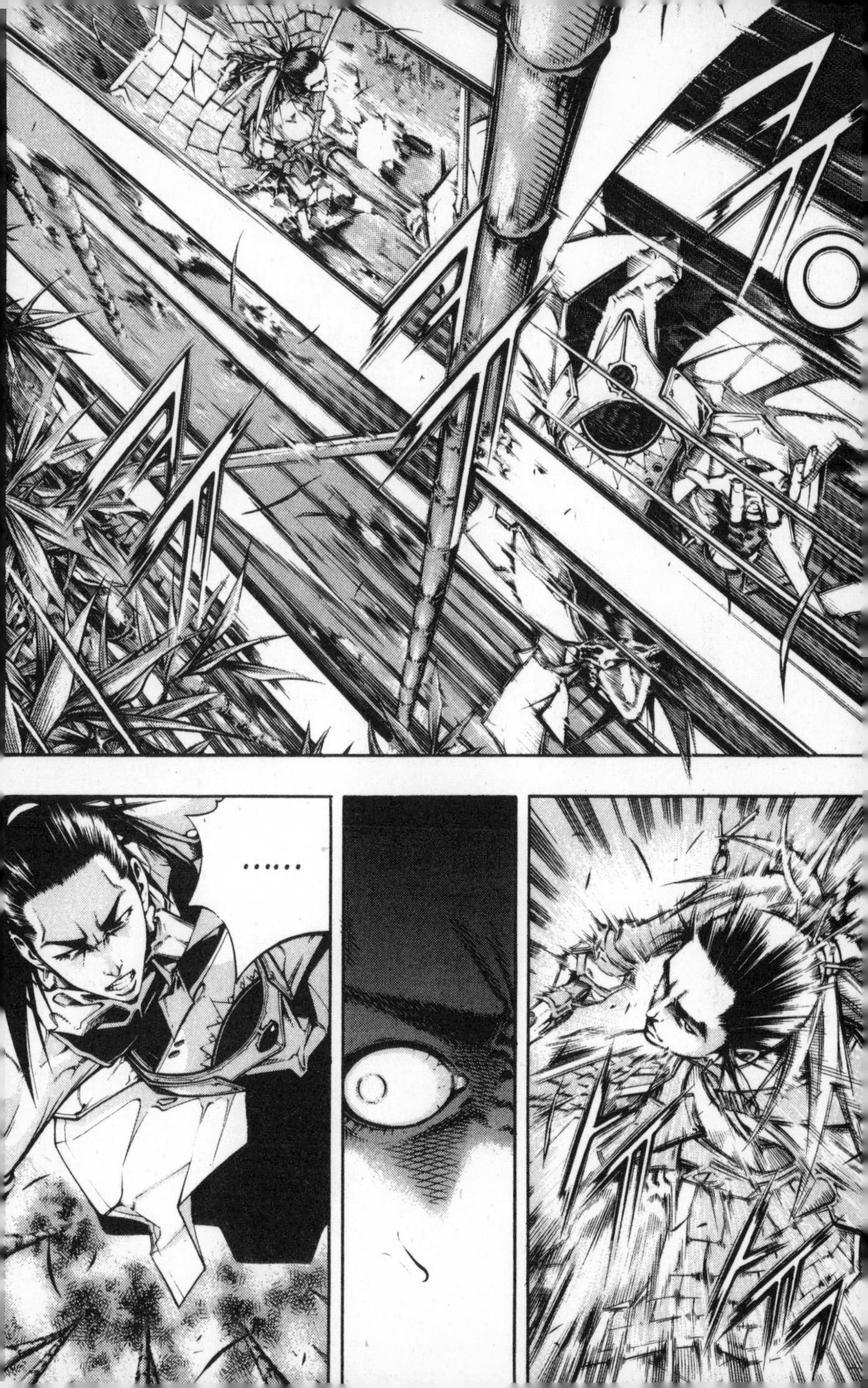
......

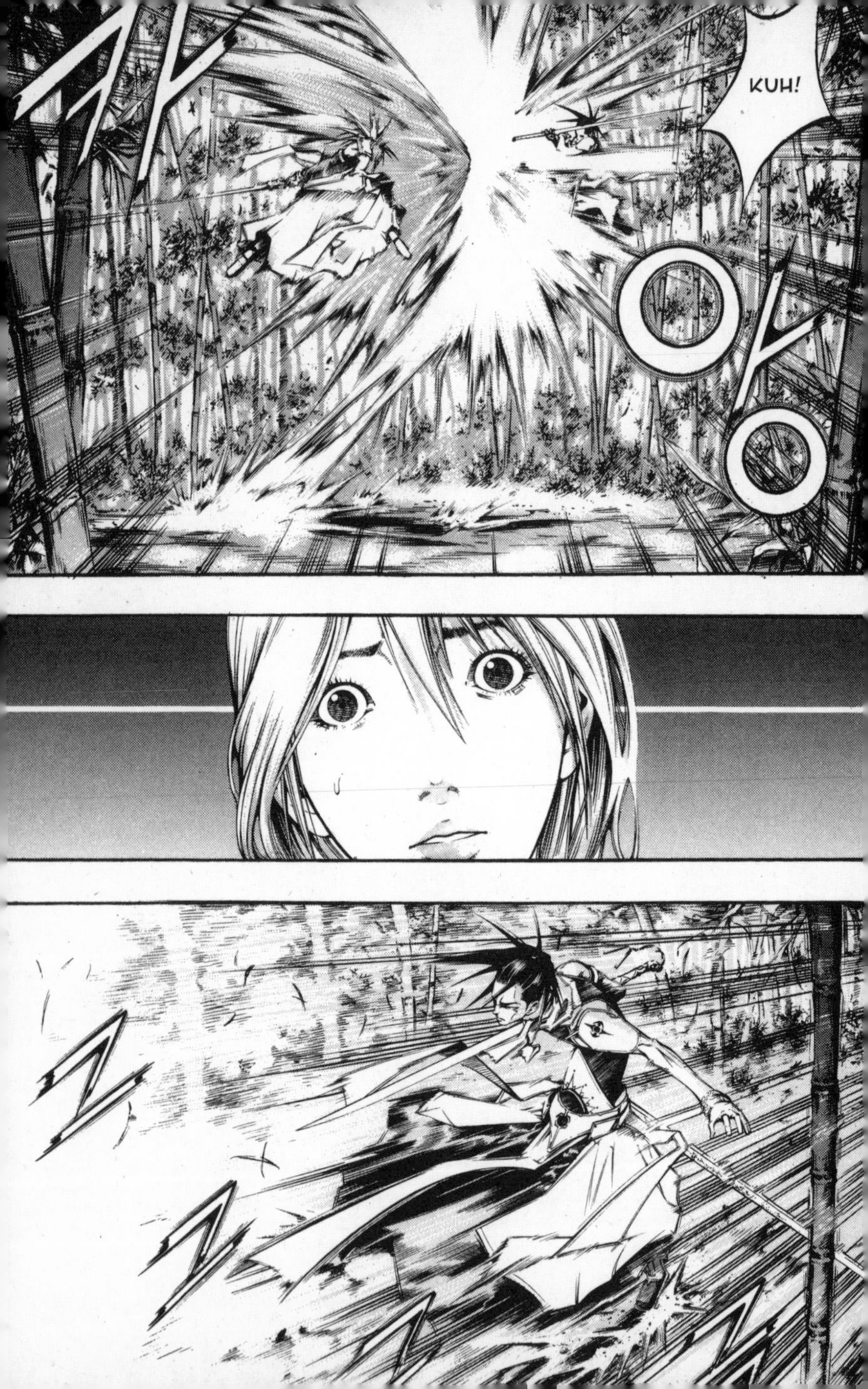
KUH!

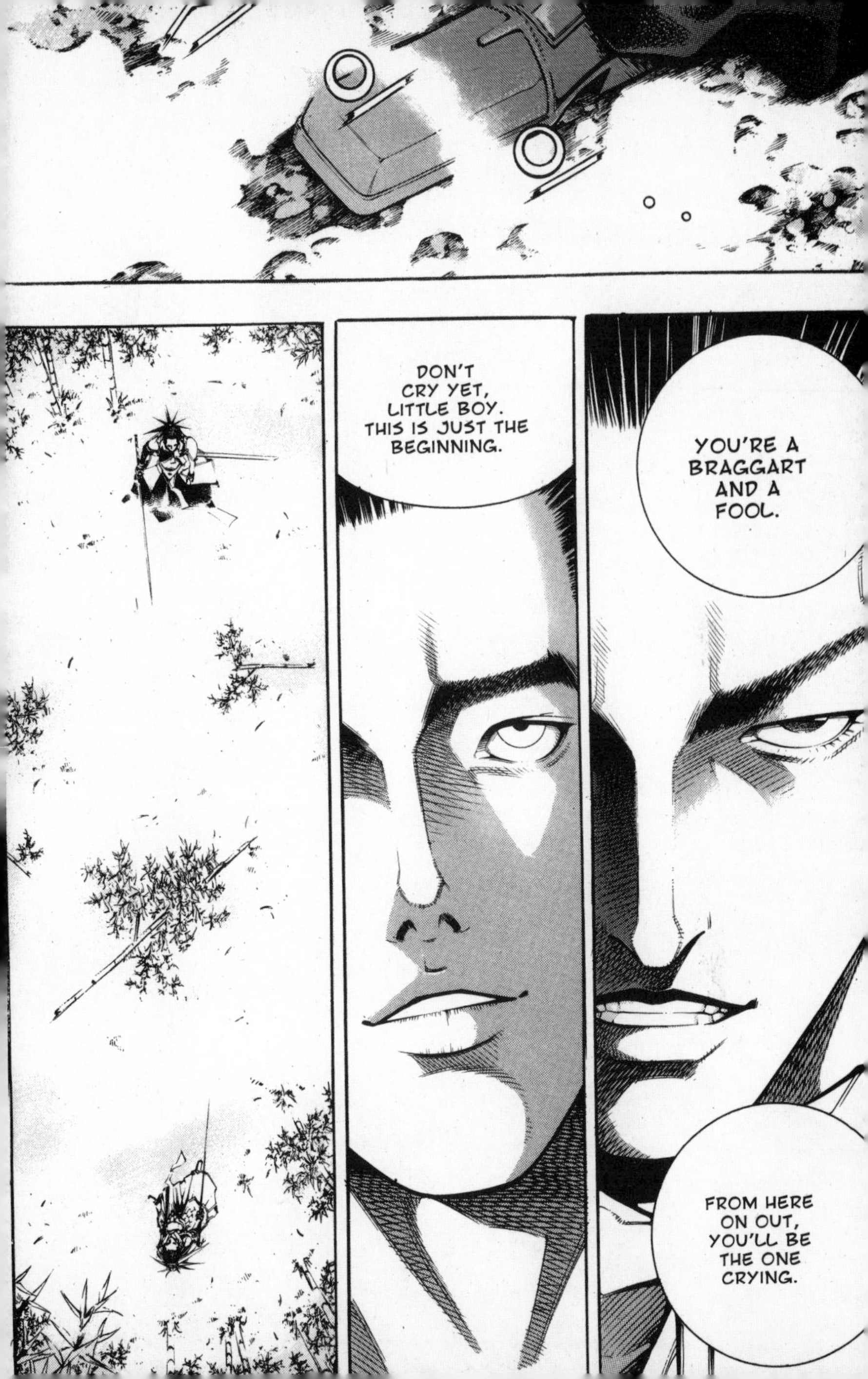
YOU'RE A BRAGGART AND A FOOL.
FROM HERE ON OUT, YOU'LL BE THE ONE CRYING.
DON'T CRY YET, LITTLE BOY. THIS IS JUST THE BEGINNING.

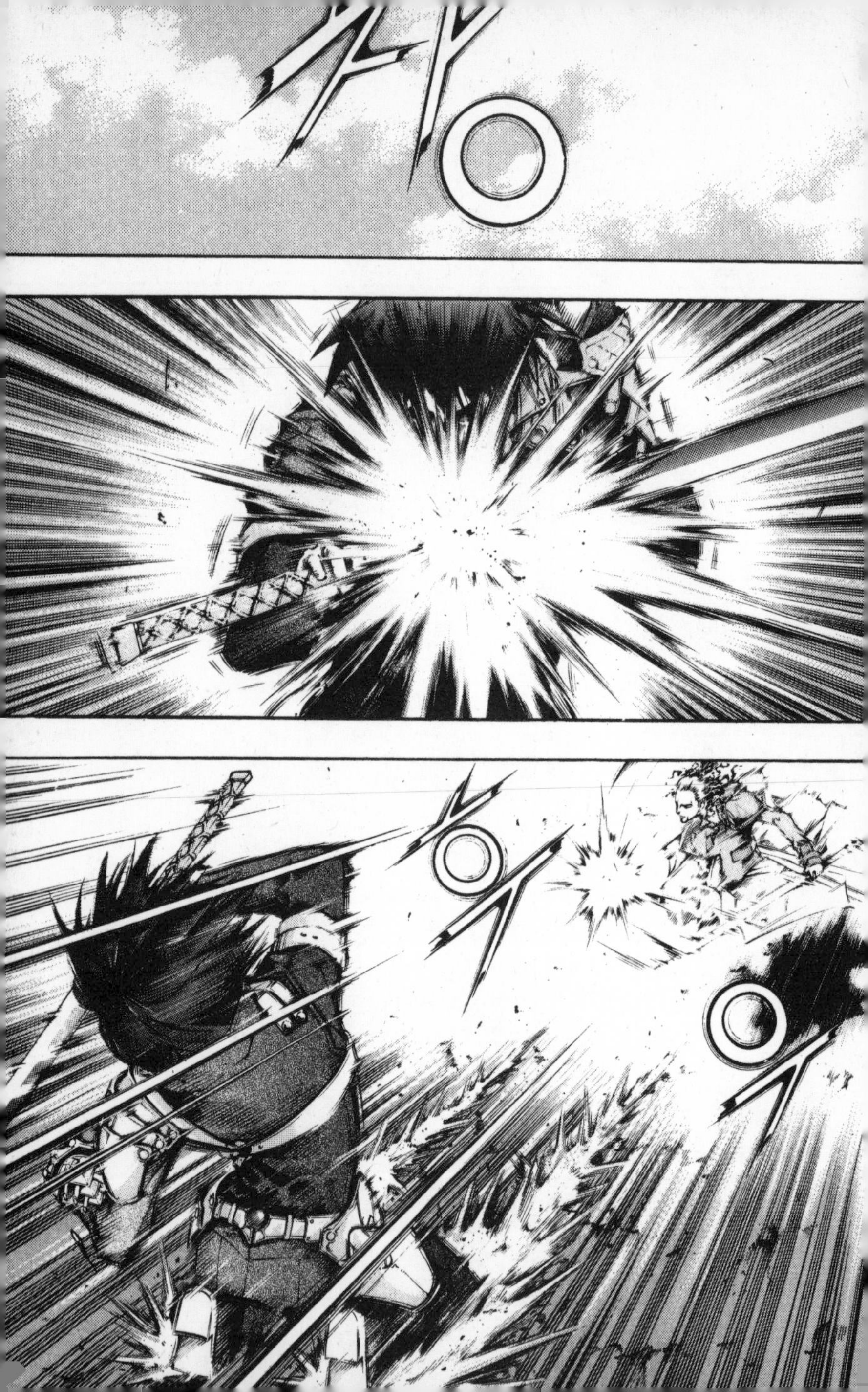

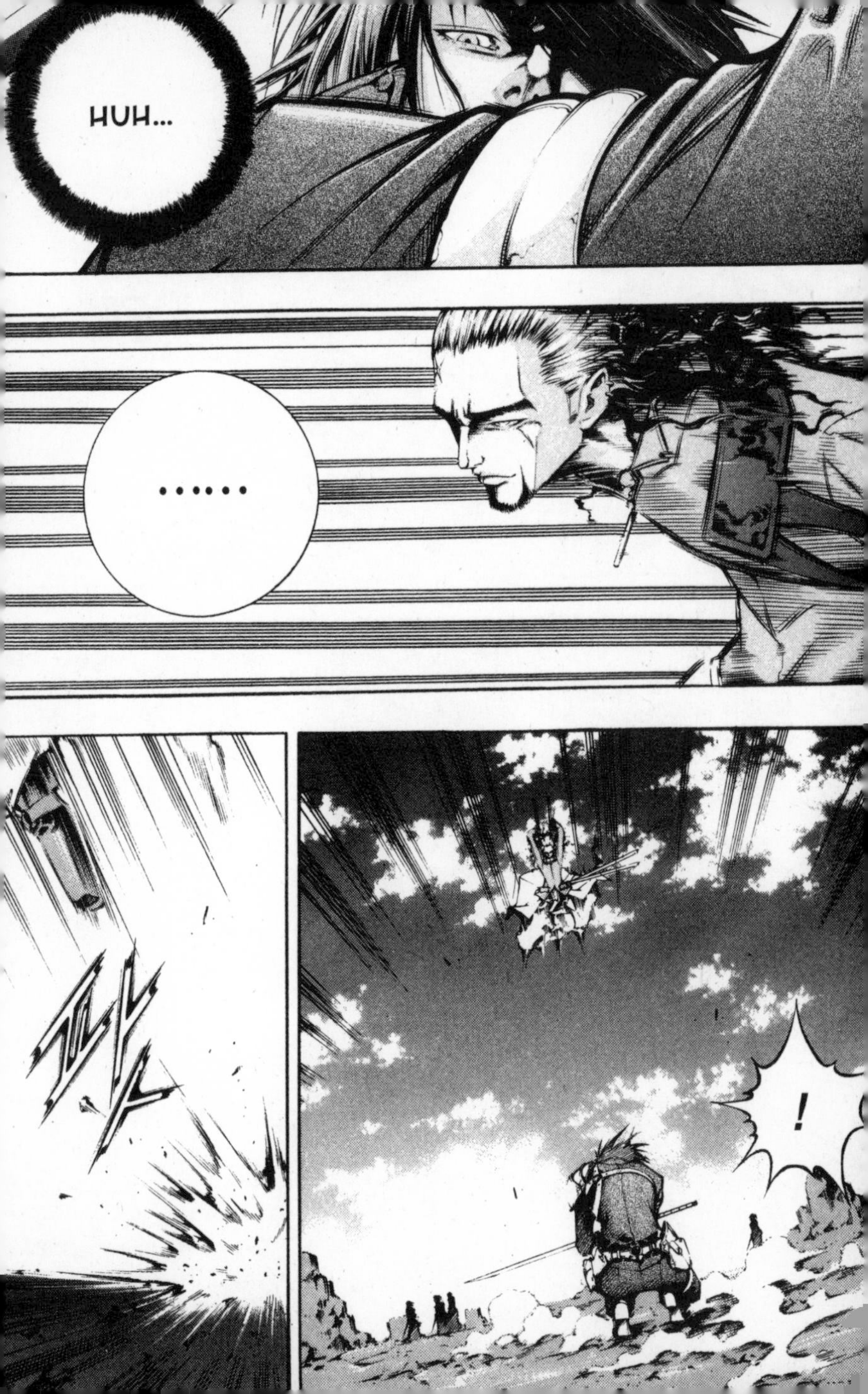
HUH...
......
!

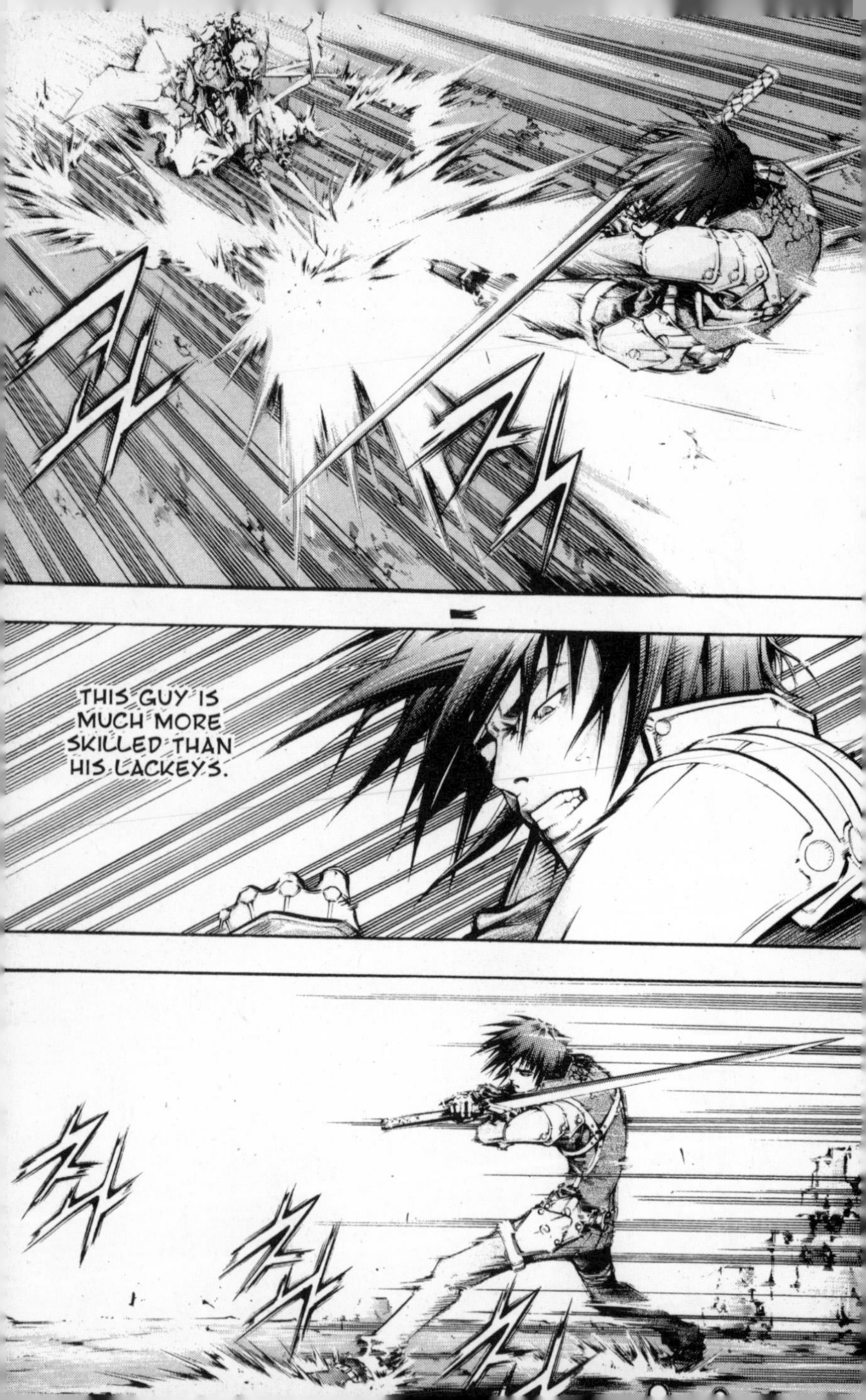
THIS GUY IS MUCH MORE SKILLED THAN HIS LACKEYS.

HEH.

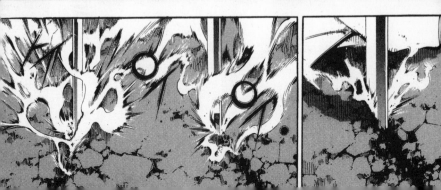

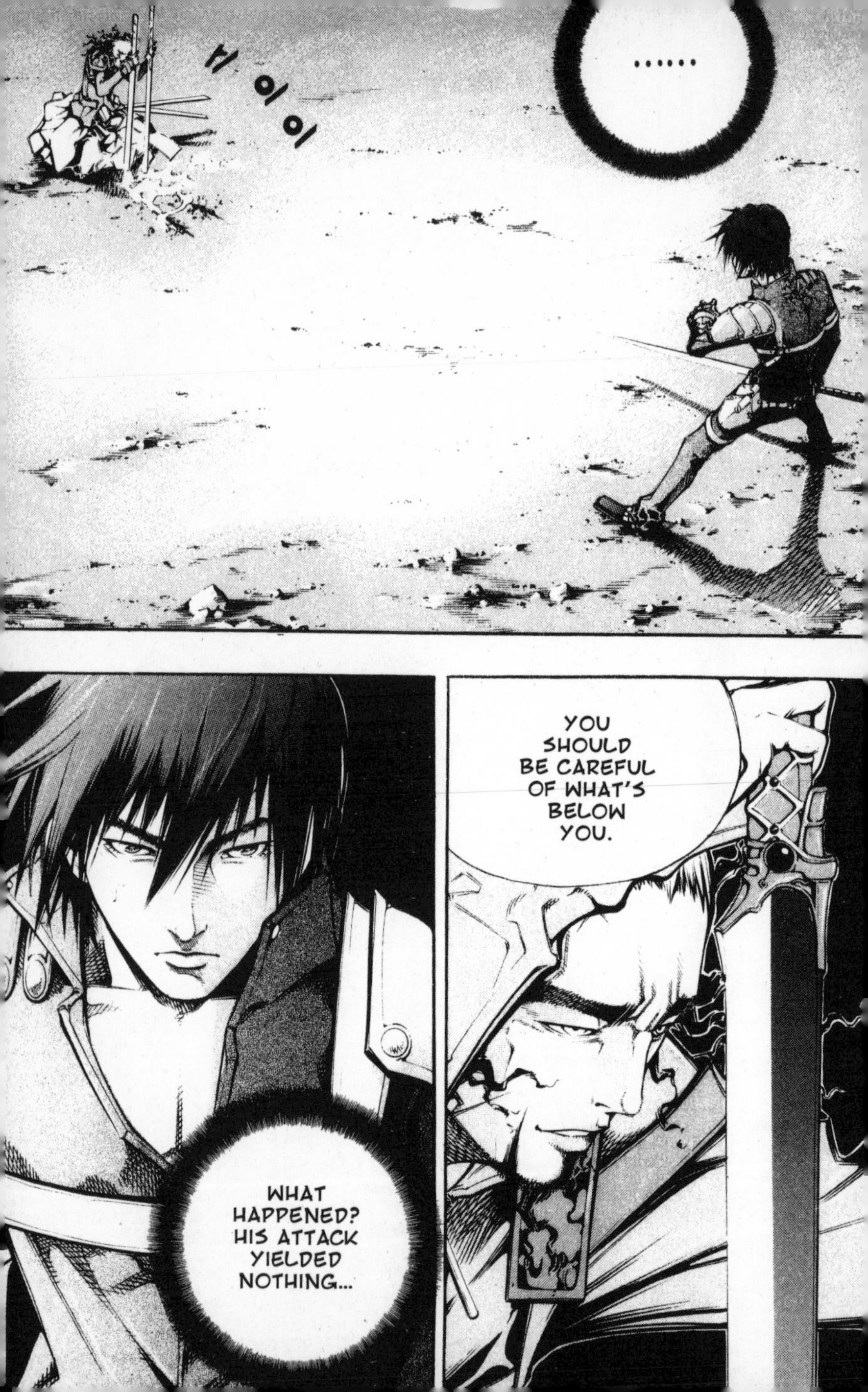

......
YOU SHOULD BE CAREFUL OF WHAT'S BELOW YOU.
WHAT HAPPENED? HIS ATTACK YIELDED NOTHING...

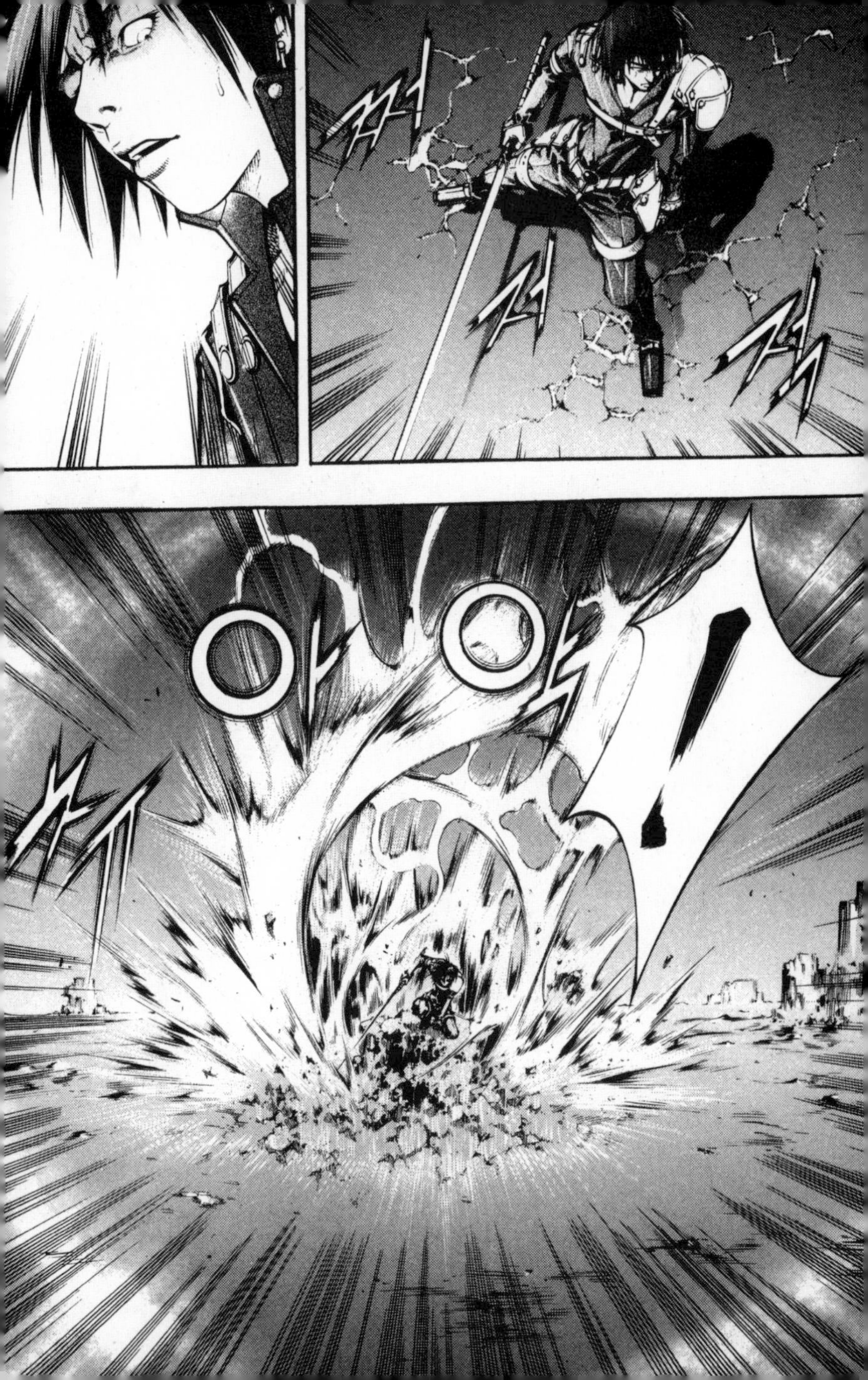

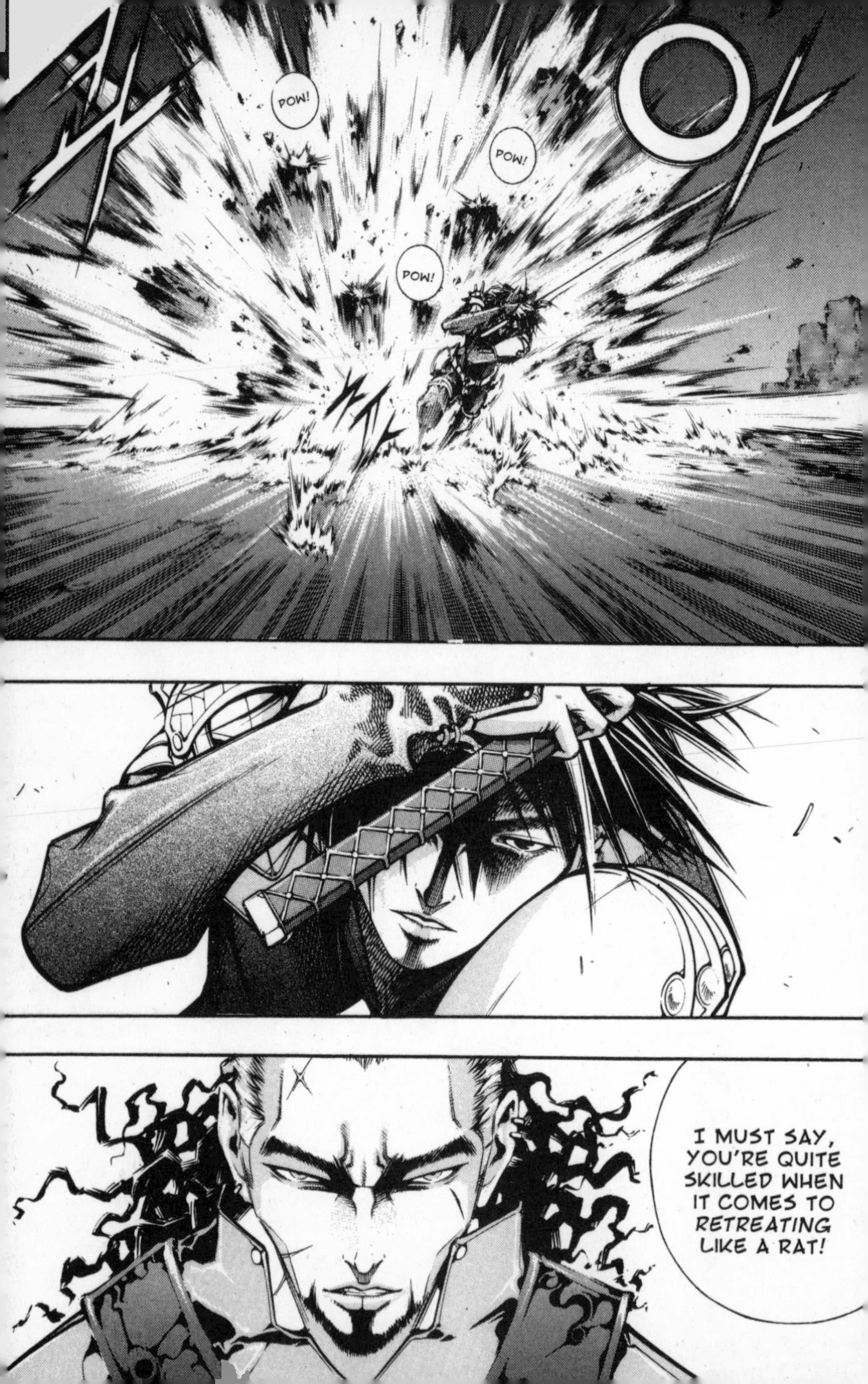
POW!
POW!
POW!
I MUST SAY, YOU'RE QUITE SKILLED WHEN IT COMES TO RETREATING LIKE A RAT!

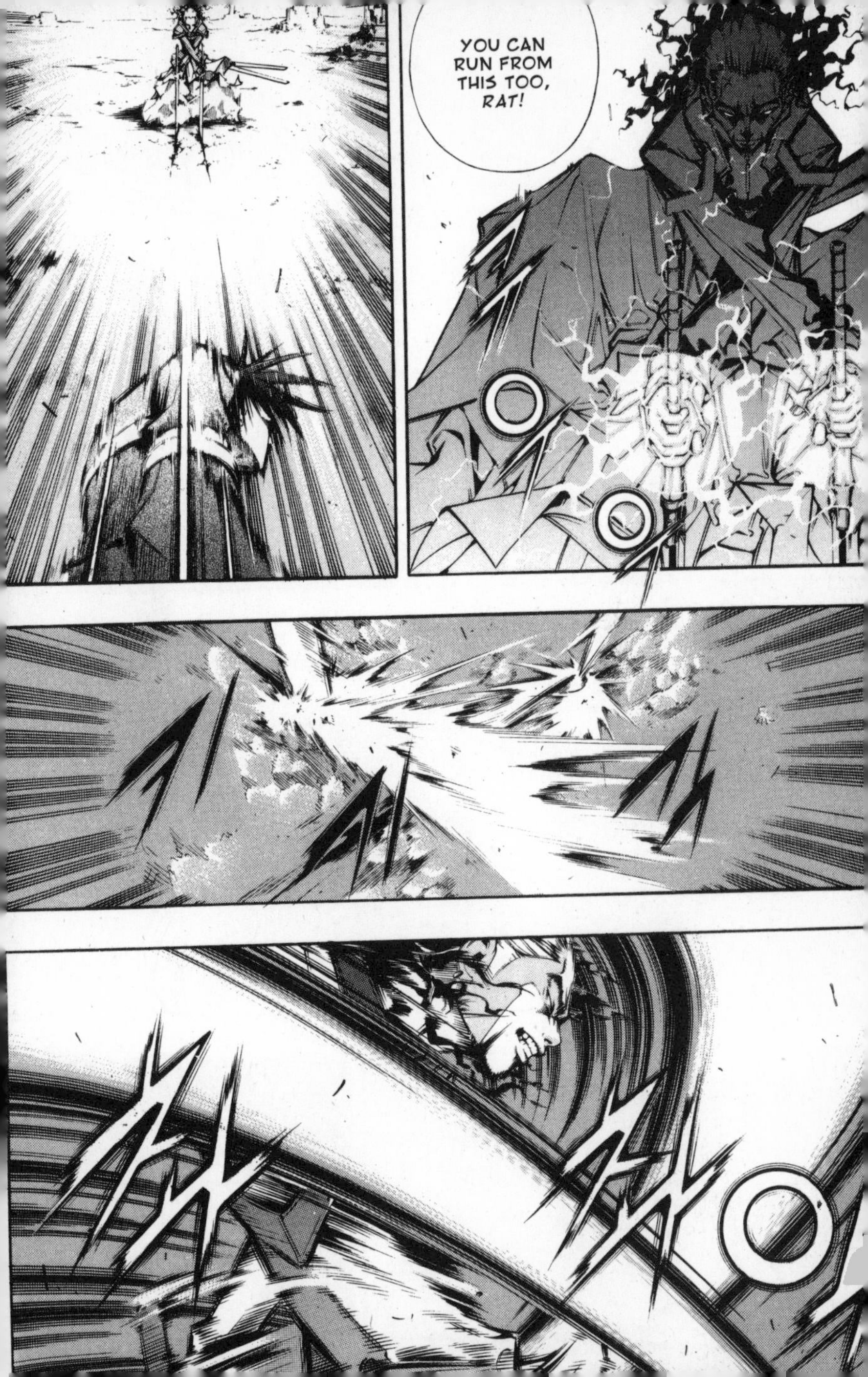
YOU CAN RUN FROM THIS TOO, RAT!

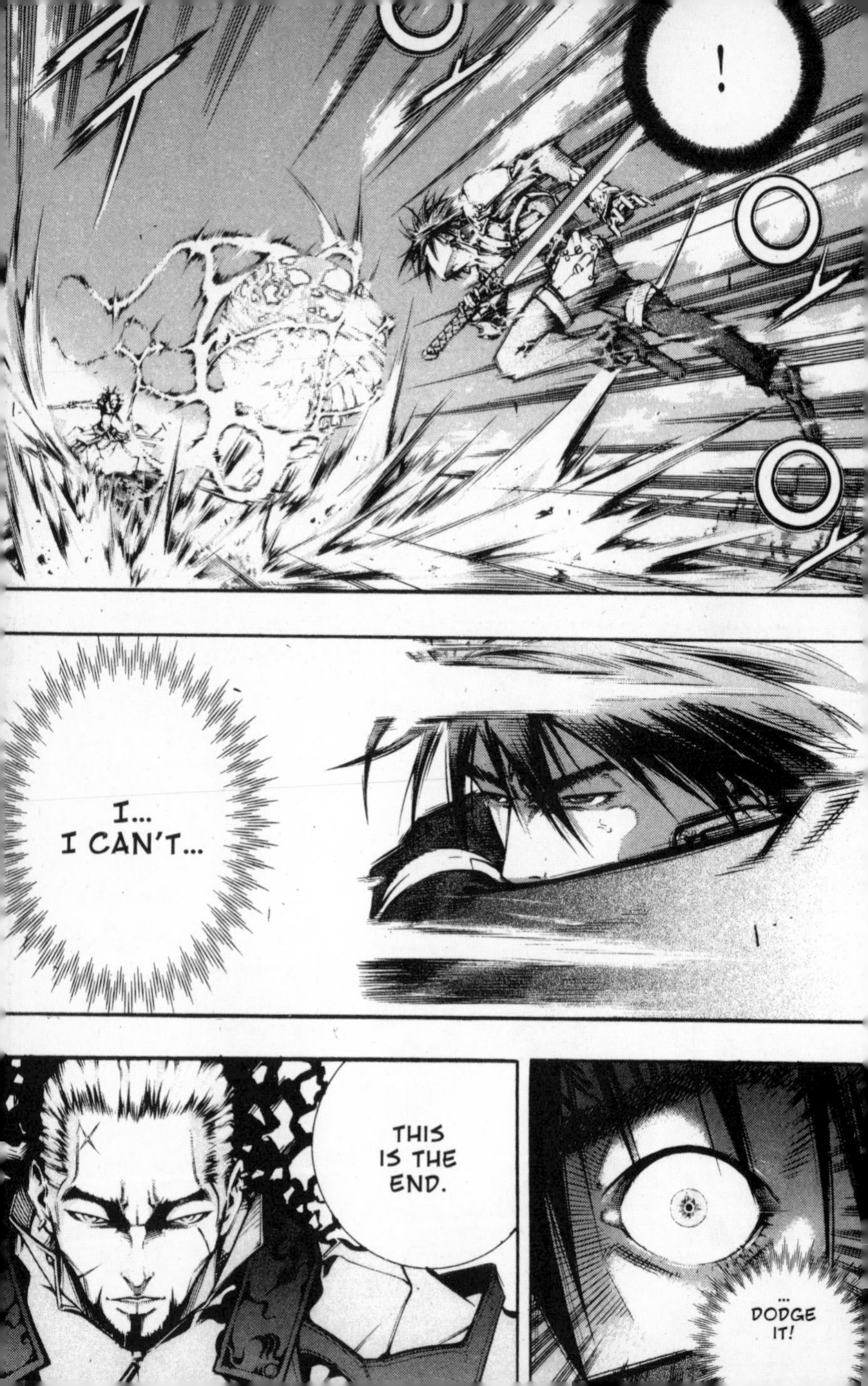
!
I...
I CAN'T...
THIS IS THE END.
...DODGE IT!

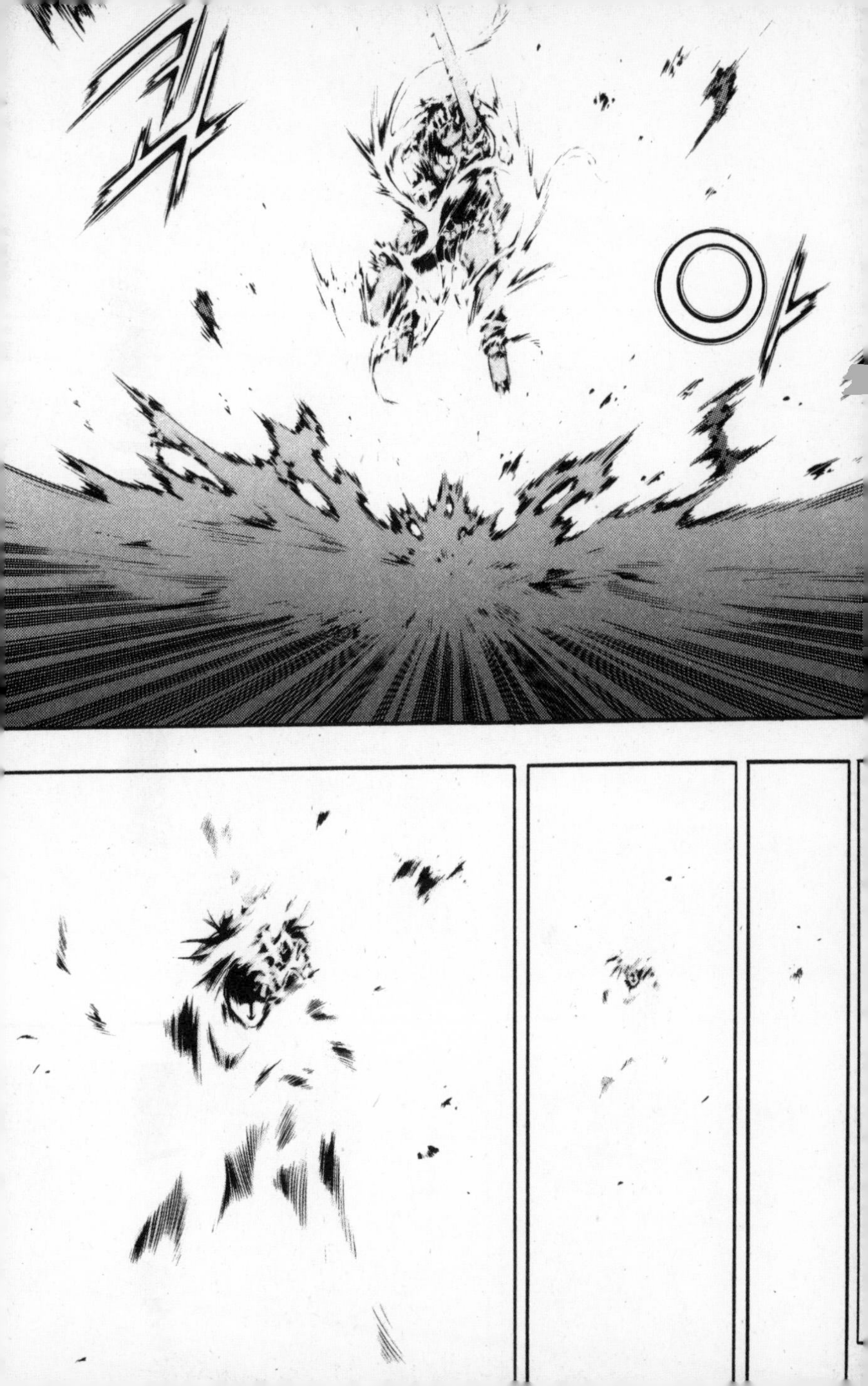

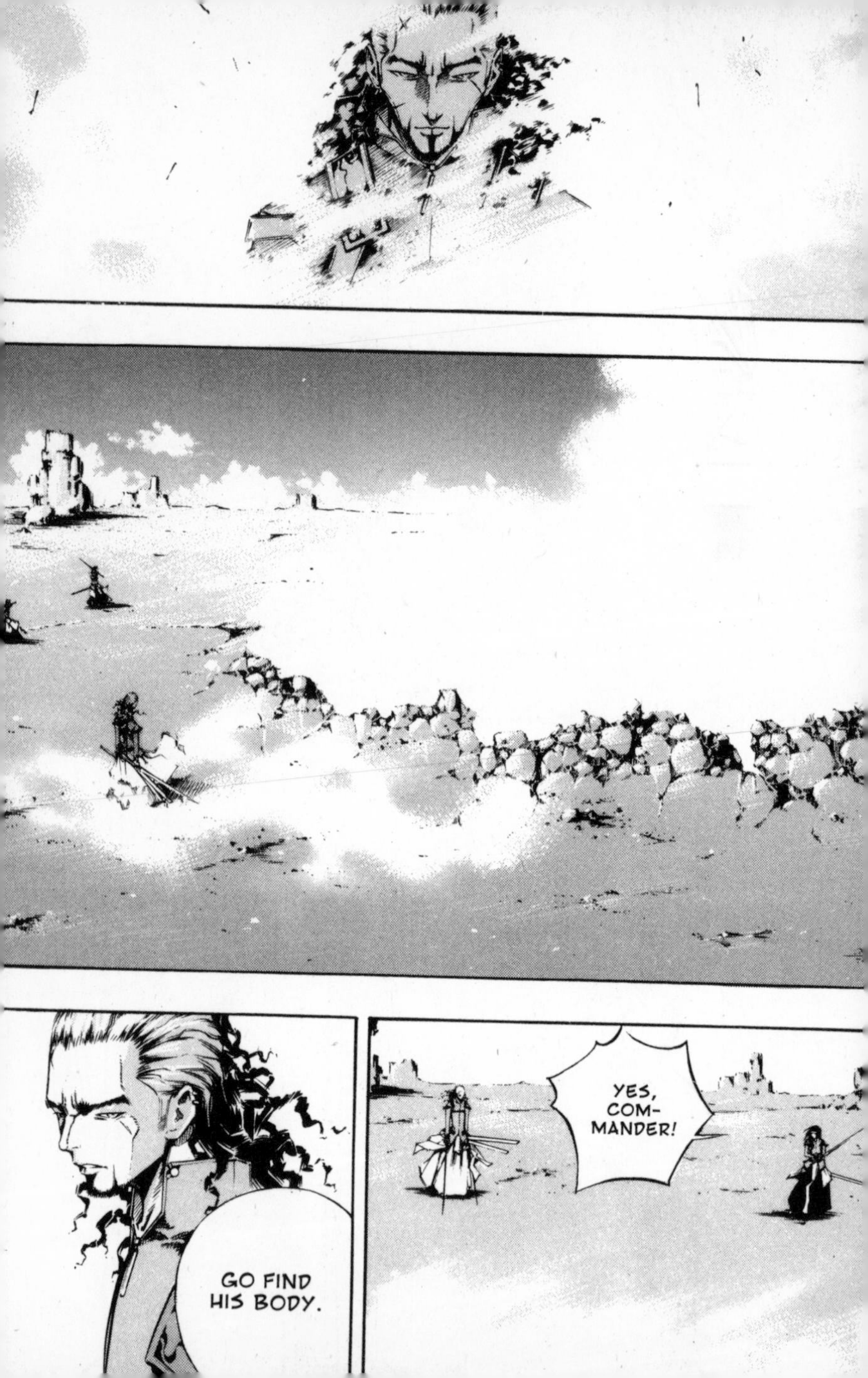
GO FIND HIS BODY.
YES, COM-MANDER!

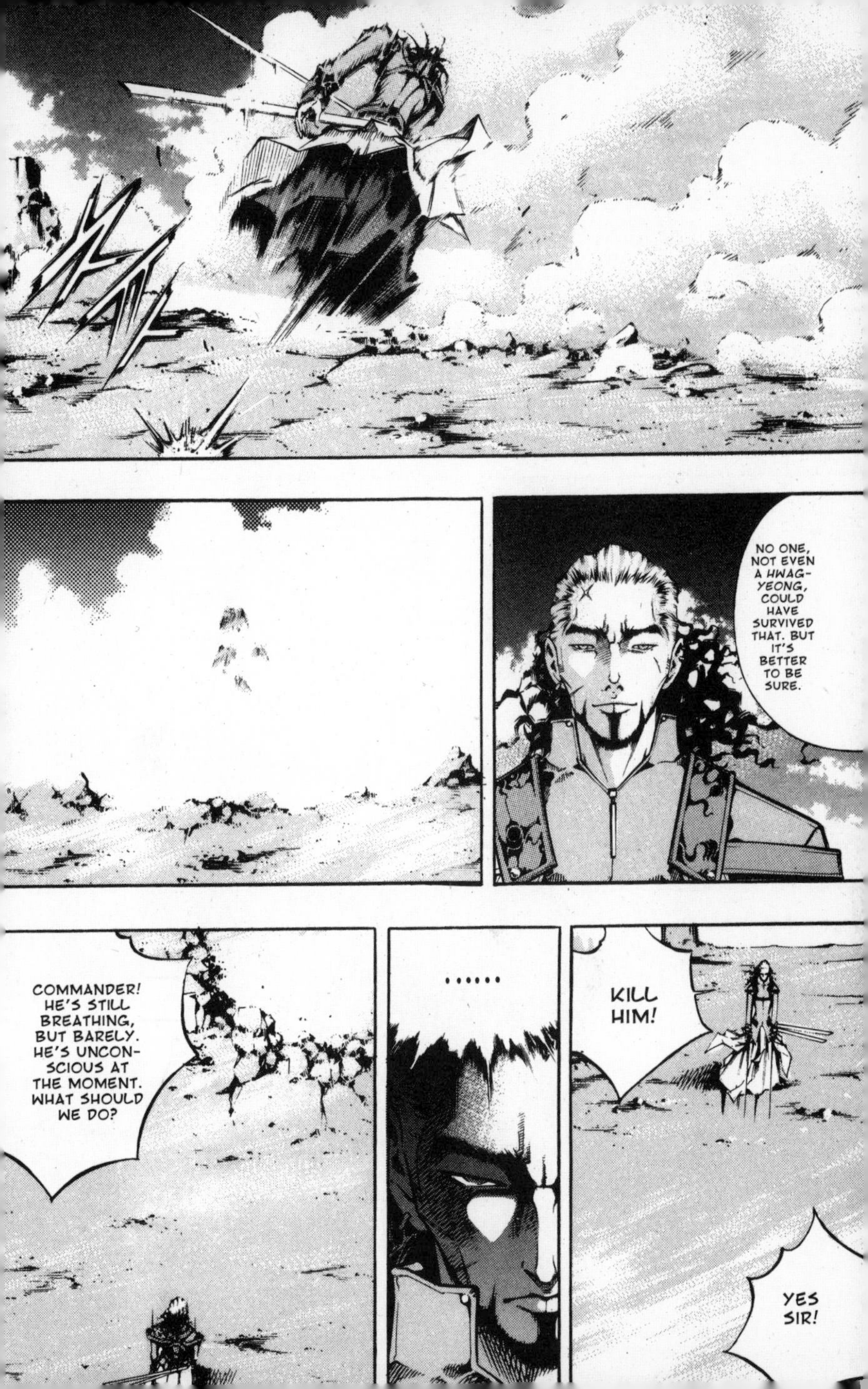
NO ONE, NOT EVEN A HWAG-YEONG, COULD HAVE SURVIVED THAT. BUT IT'S BETTER TO BE SURE.
COMMANDER! HE'S STILL BREATHING, BUT BARELY. HE'S UNCONSCIOUS AT THE MOMENT. WHAT SHOULD WE DO?
......
KILL HIM!
YES SIR!

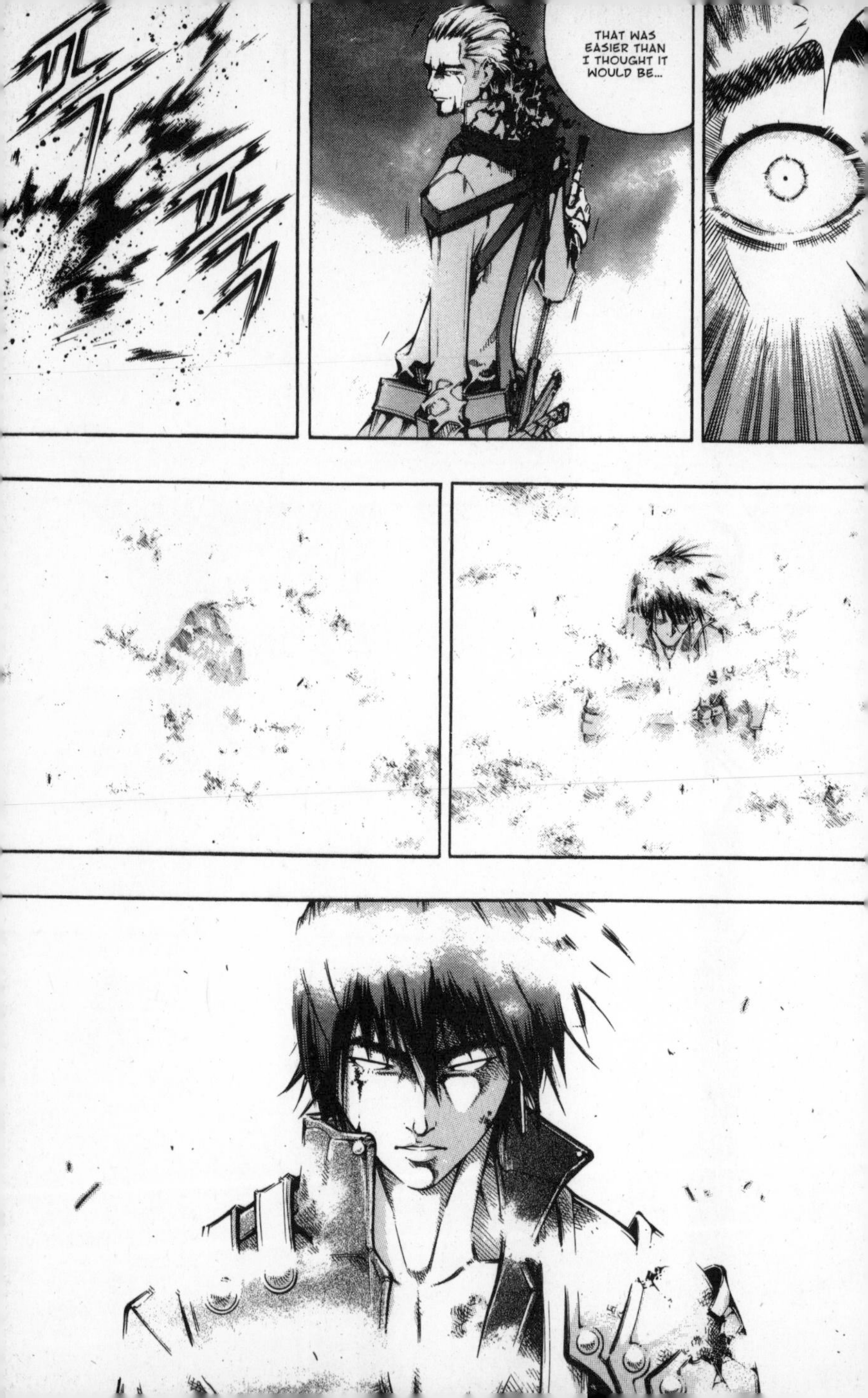
THAT WAS
EASIER THAN
I THOUGHT IT
WOULD BE...

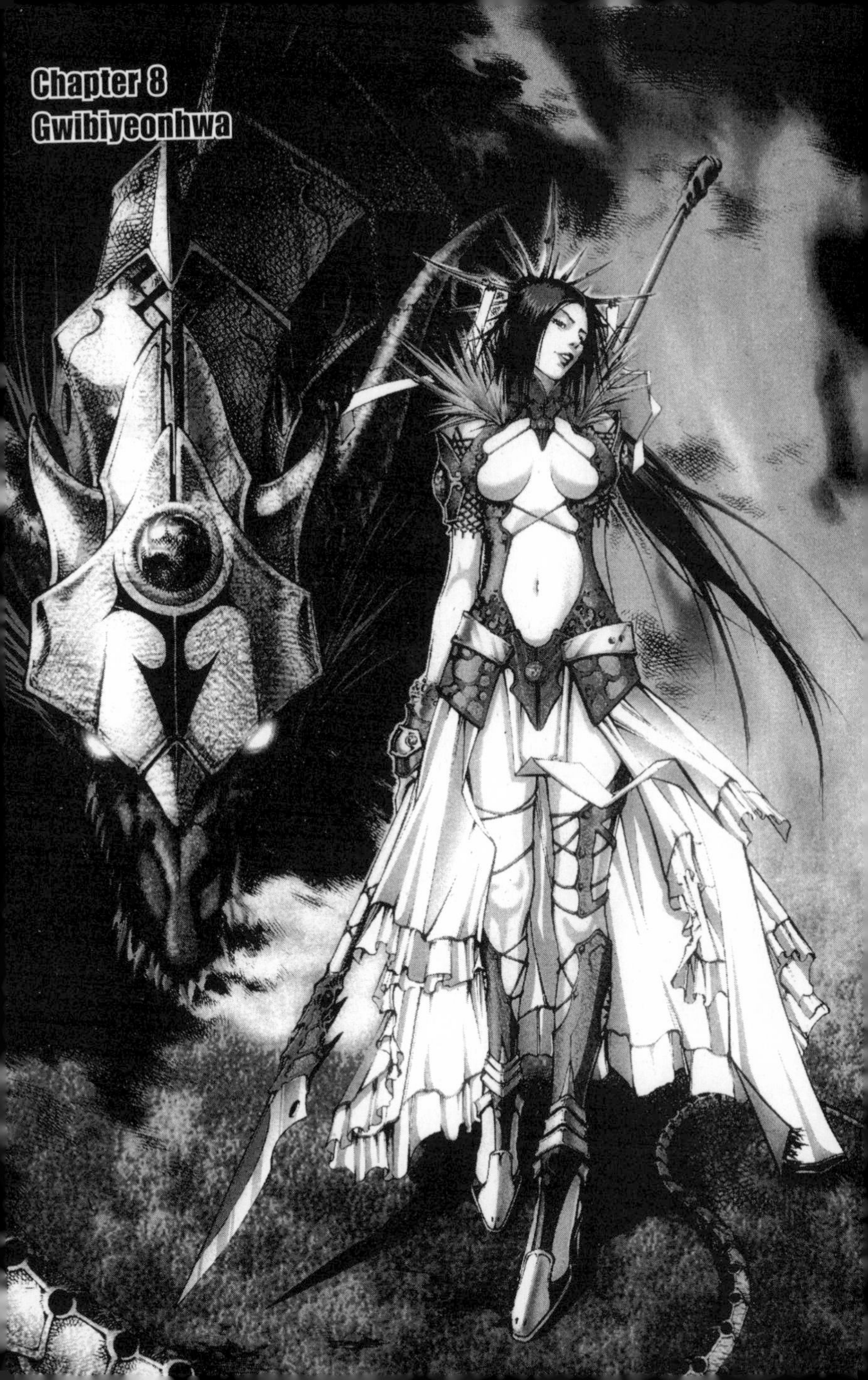
Chapter 8
Gwibiyeonhwa

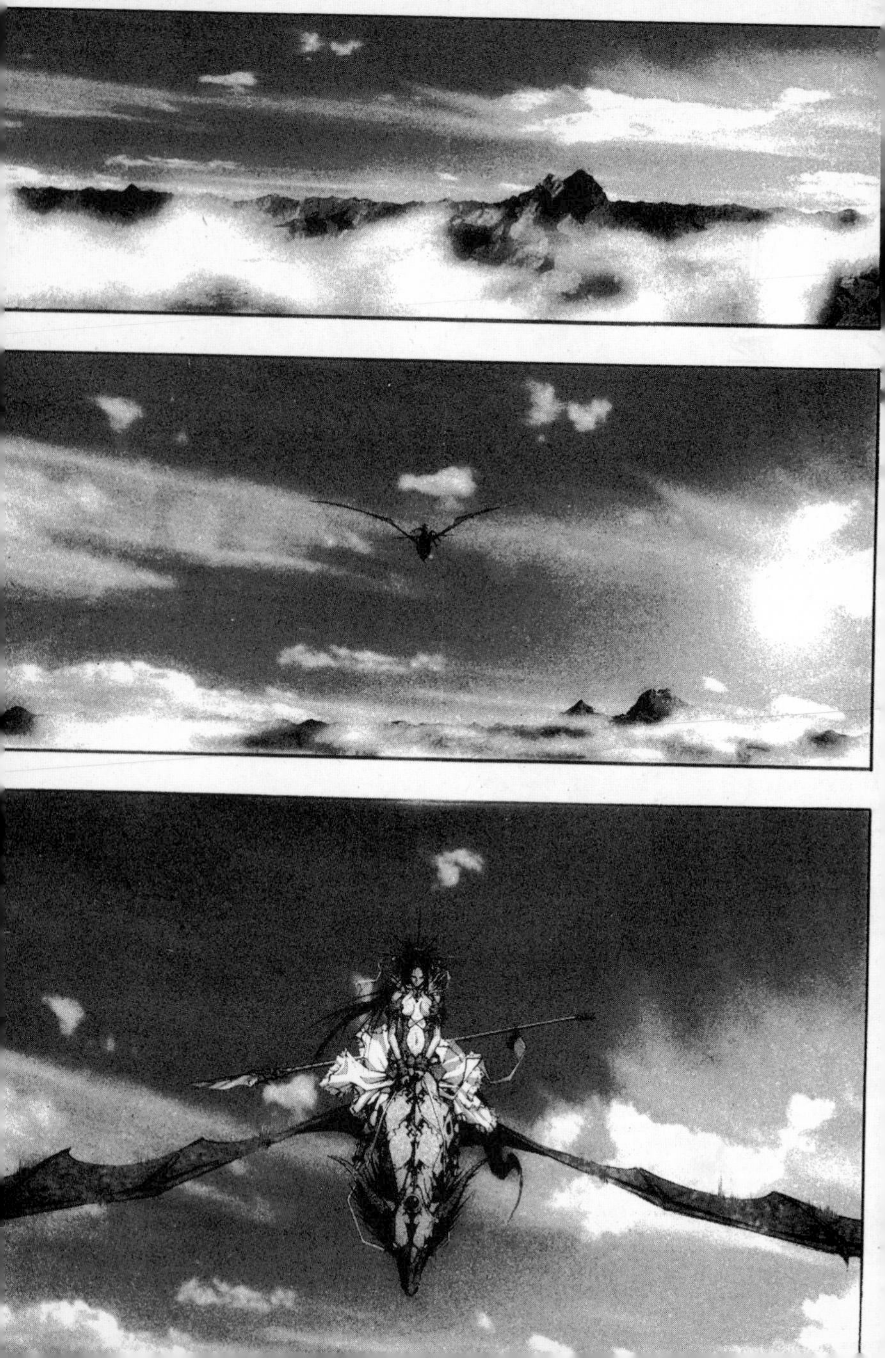

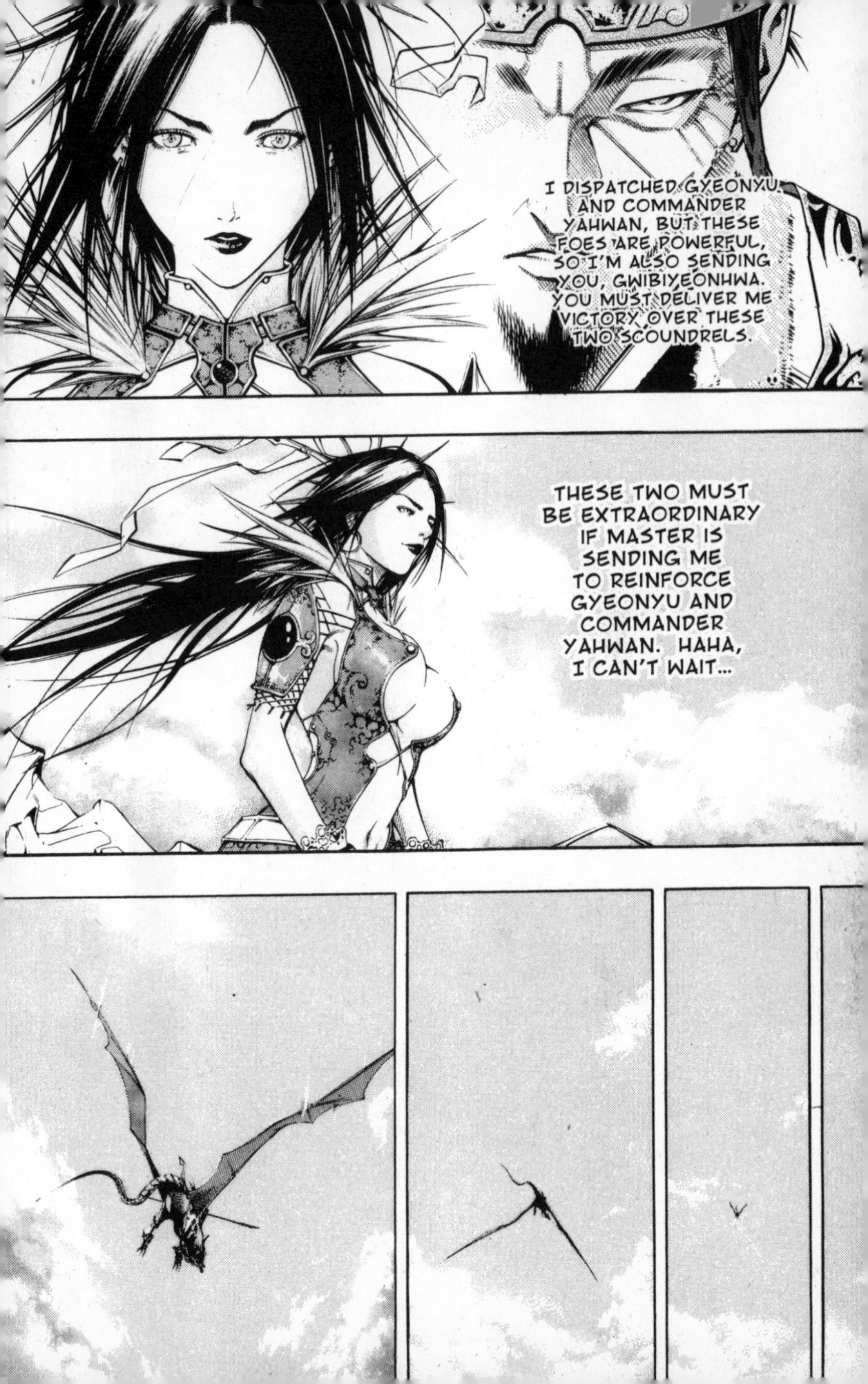
I DISPATCHED GYEONYU AND COMMANDER YAHWAN, BUT THESE FOES ARE POWERFUL, SO I'M ALSO SENDING YOU, GWIBIYEONHWA. YOU MUST DELIVER ME VICTORY OVER THESE TWO SCOUNDRELS.
THESE TWO MUST BE EXTRAORDINARY IF MASTER IS SENDING ME TO REINFORCE GYEONYU AND COMMANDER YAHWAN. HAHA, I CAN'T WAIT...

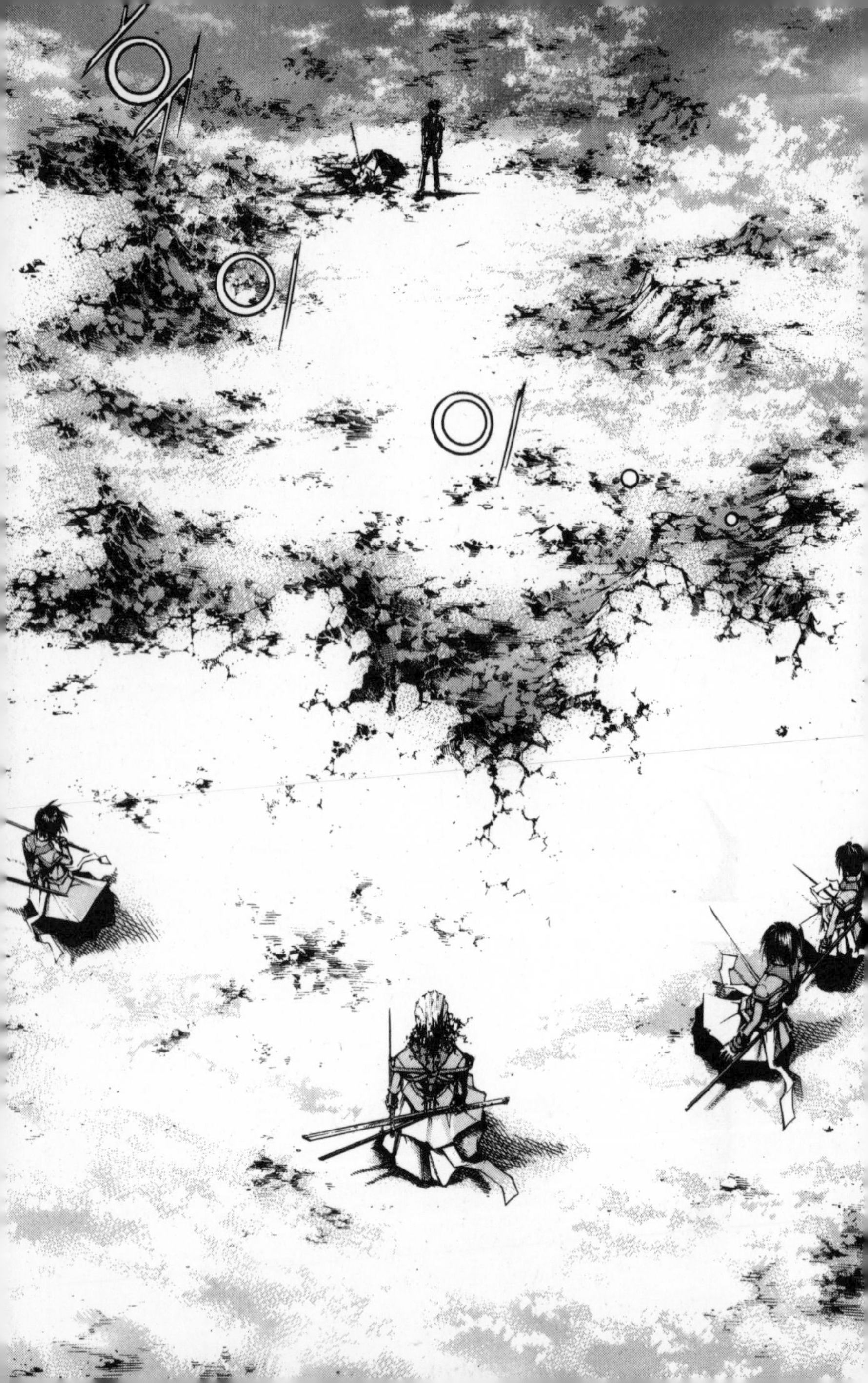

SOMETHING'S WRONG.

COULD IT BE? NO.

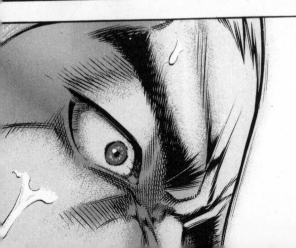

DID HE REGAIN HIS CHI?

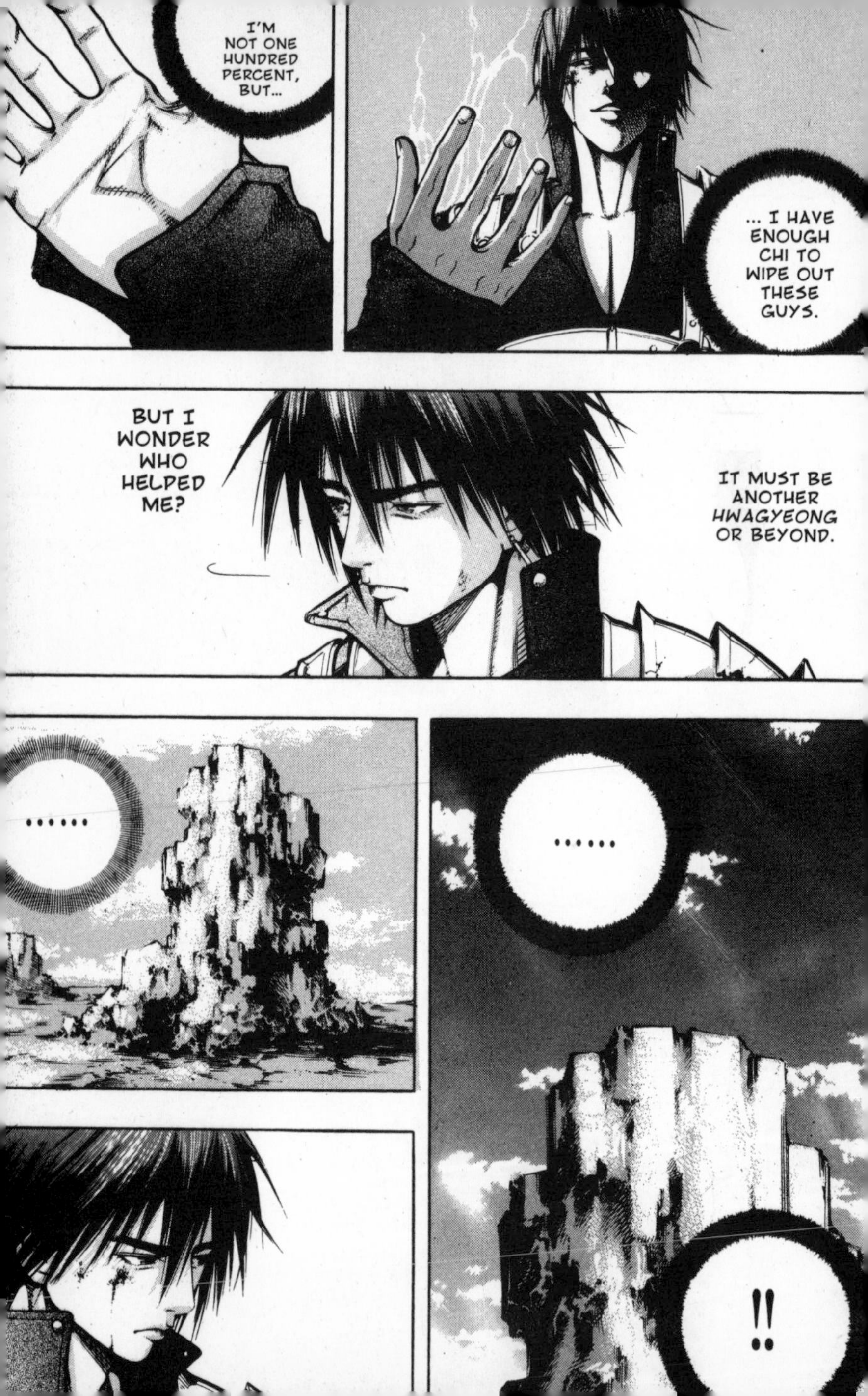

I'M NOT ONE HUNDRED PERCENT, BUT...
... I HAVE ENOUGH CHI TO WIPE OUT THESE GUYS.
BUT I WONDER WHO HELPED ME?
IT MUST BE ANOTHER HWAGYEONG OR BEYOND.
......
......
!!

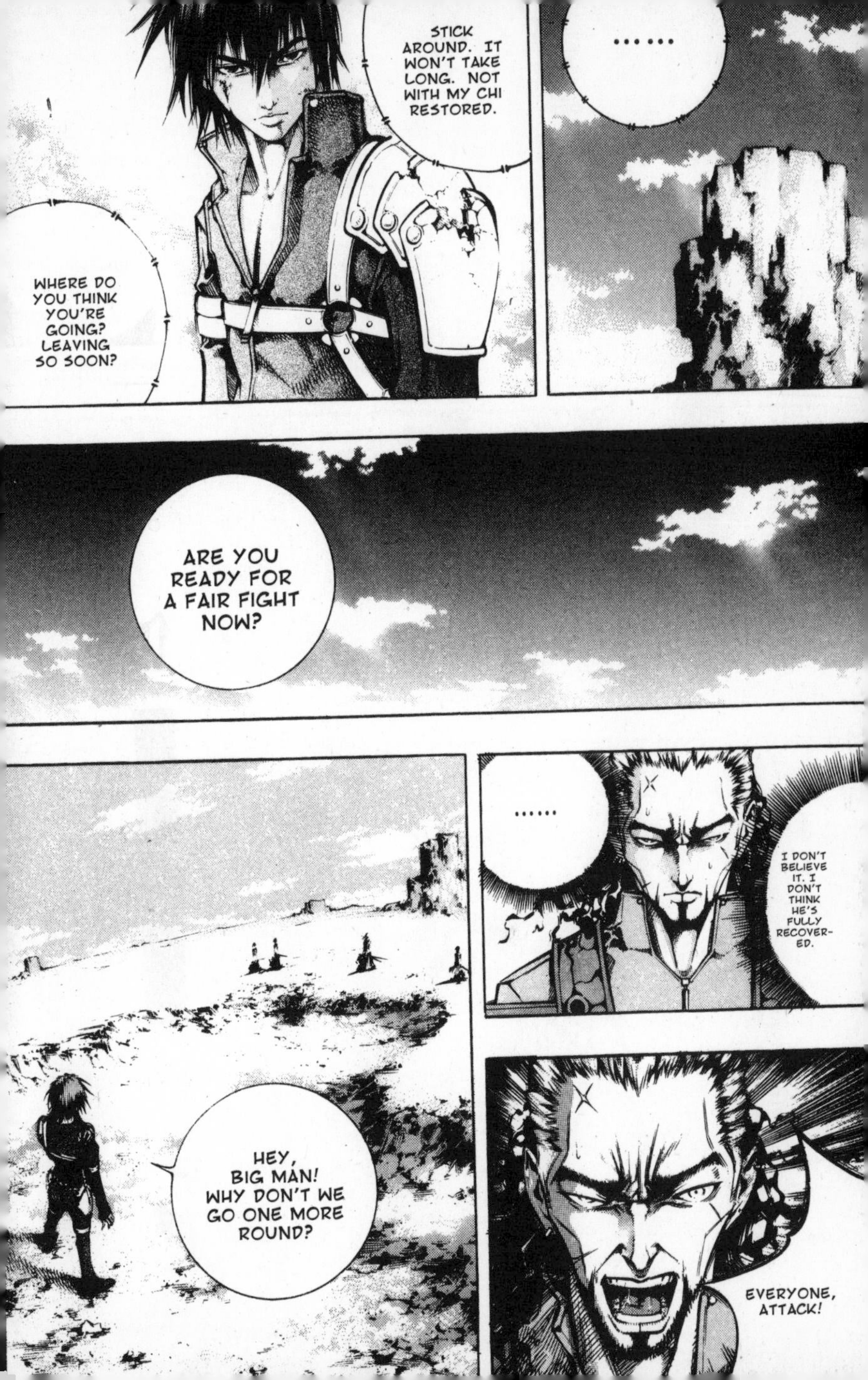
WHERE DO YOU THINK YOU'RE GOING? LEAVING SO SOON?
STICK AROUND. IT WON'T TAKE LONG. NOT WITH MY CHI RESTORED.
......
ARE YOU READY FOR A FAIR FIGHT NOW?
HEY, BIG MAN! WHY DON'T WE GO ONE MORE ROUND?
......
I DON'T BELIEVE IT. I DON'T THINK HE'S FULLY RECOVERED.
EVERYONE, ATTACK!

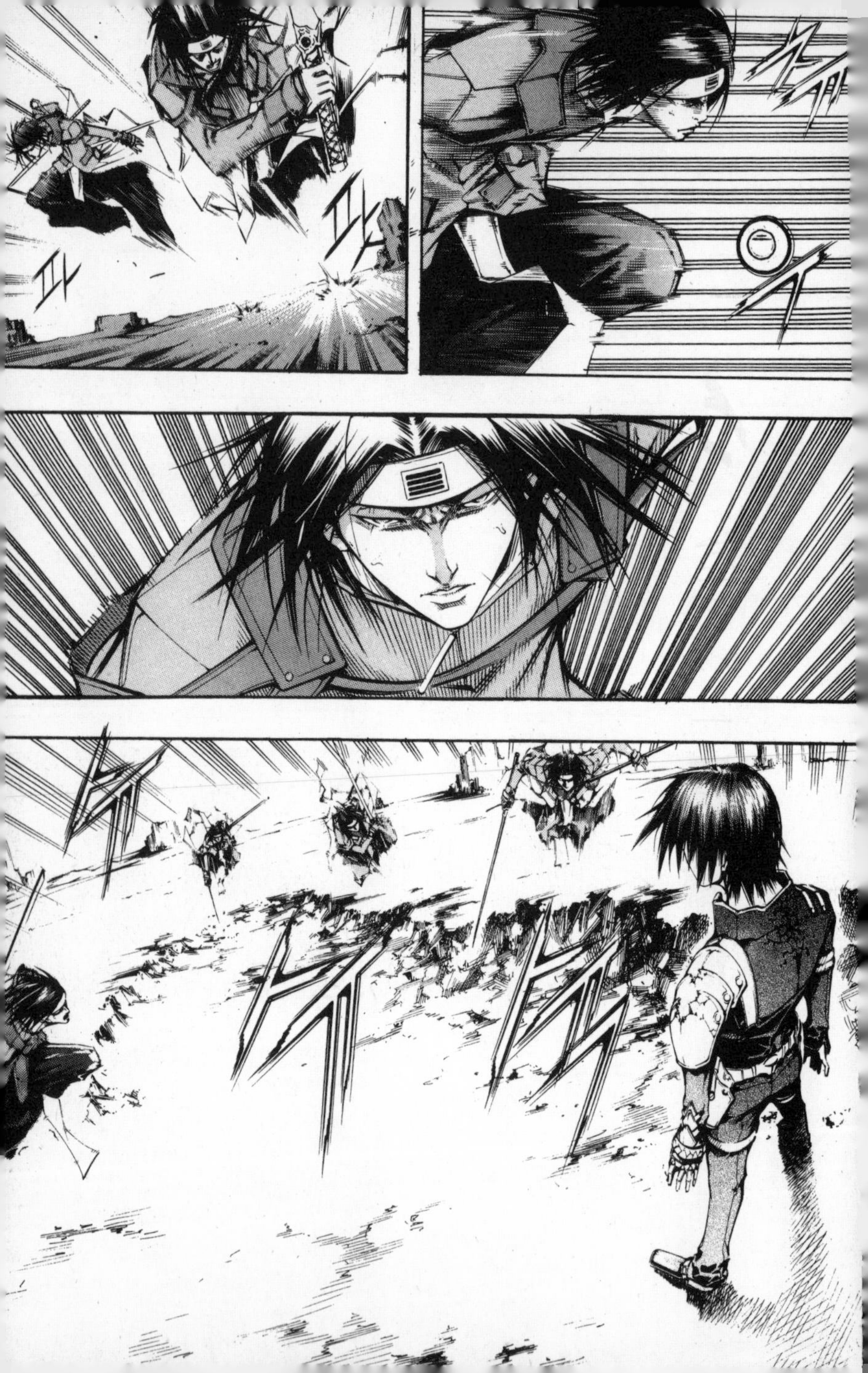

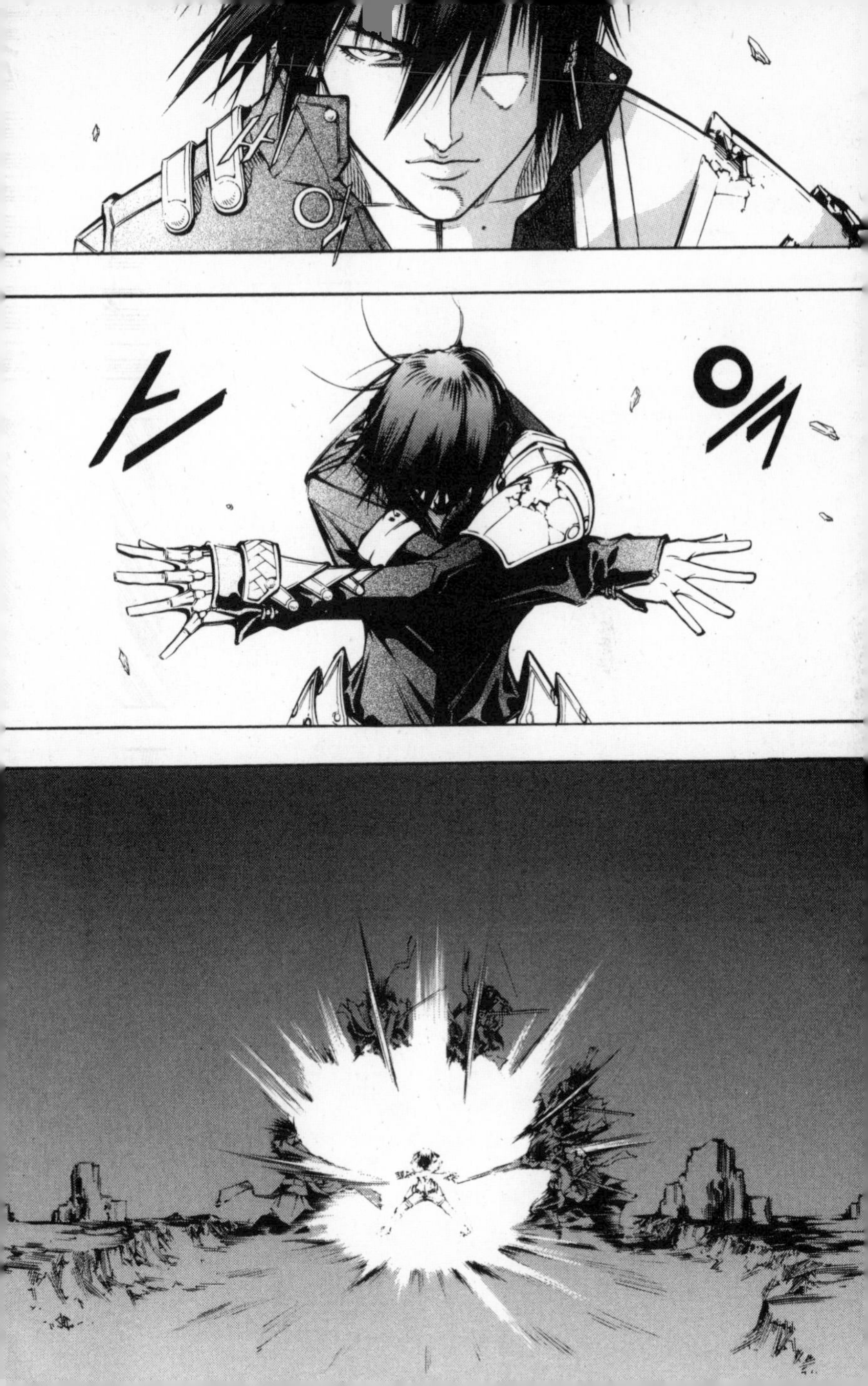

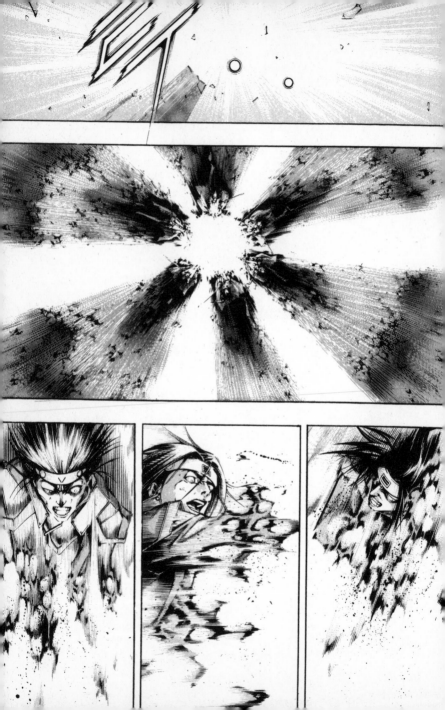

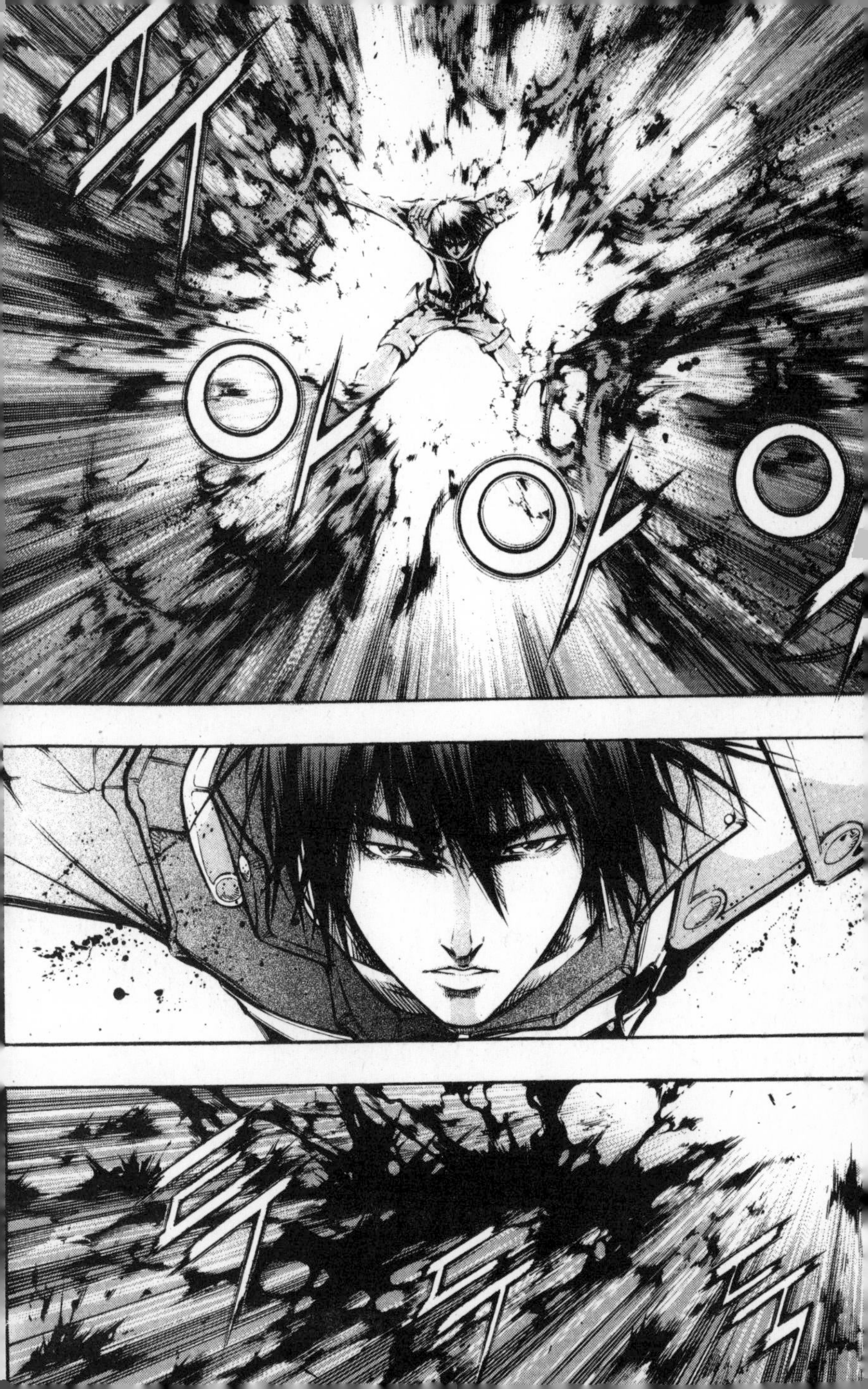

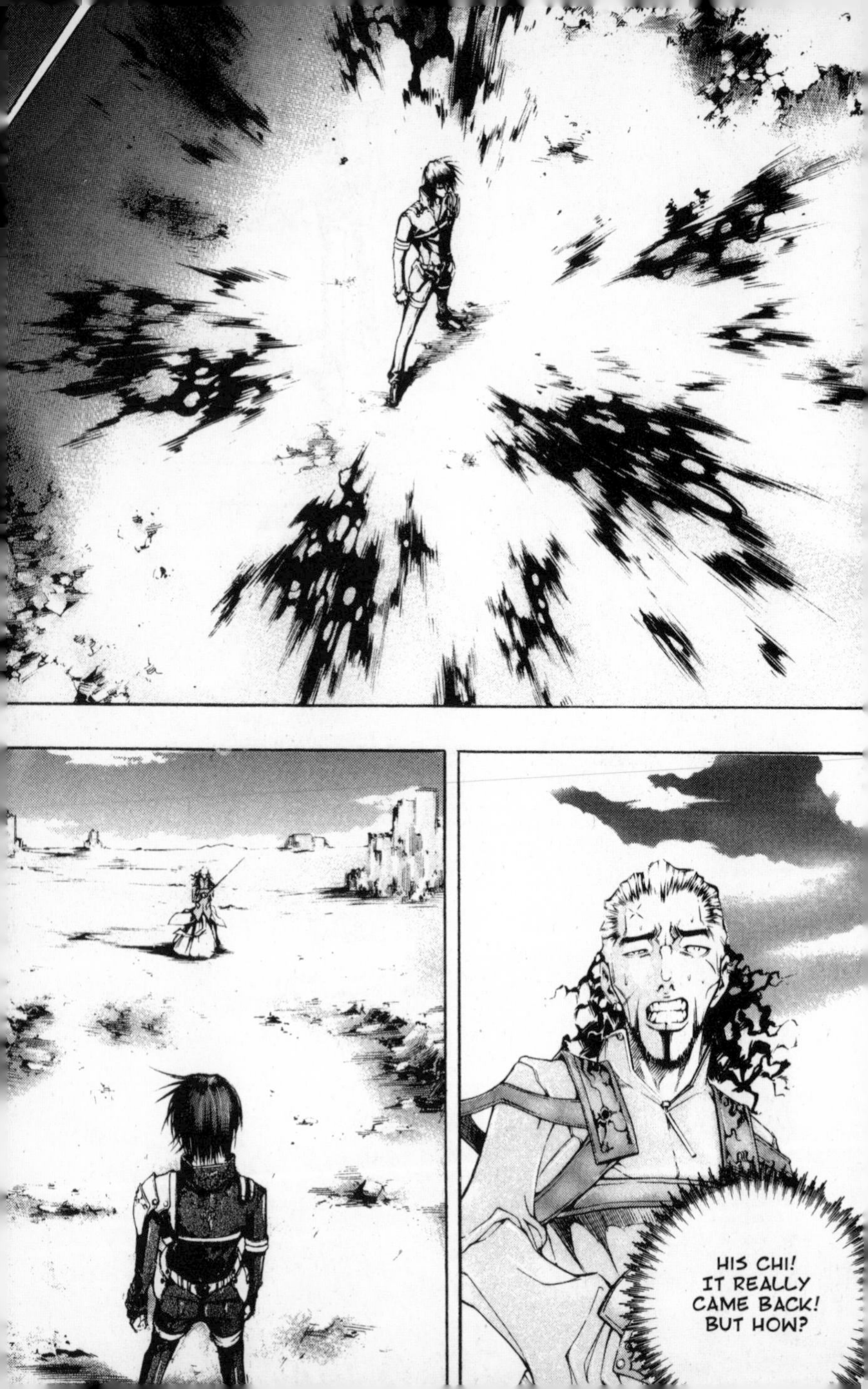
HIS CHI!
IT REALLY
CAME BACK!
BUT HOW?

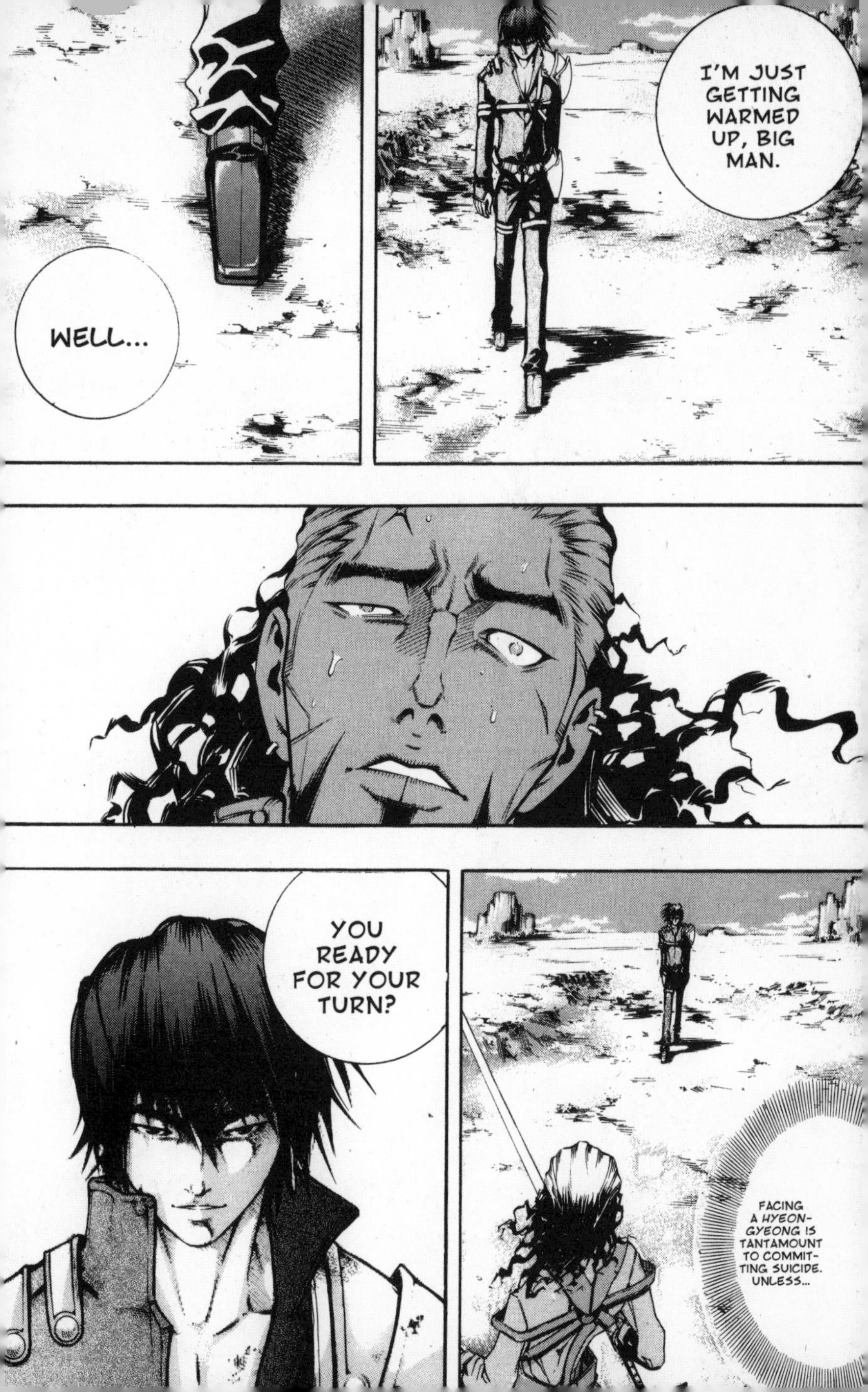

WELL...
I'M JUST GETTING WARMED UP, BIG MAN.
YOU READY FOR YOUR TURN?
FACING A HYEON-GYEONG IS TANTAMOUNT TO COMMIT-TING SUICIDE. UNLESS...

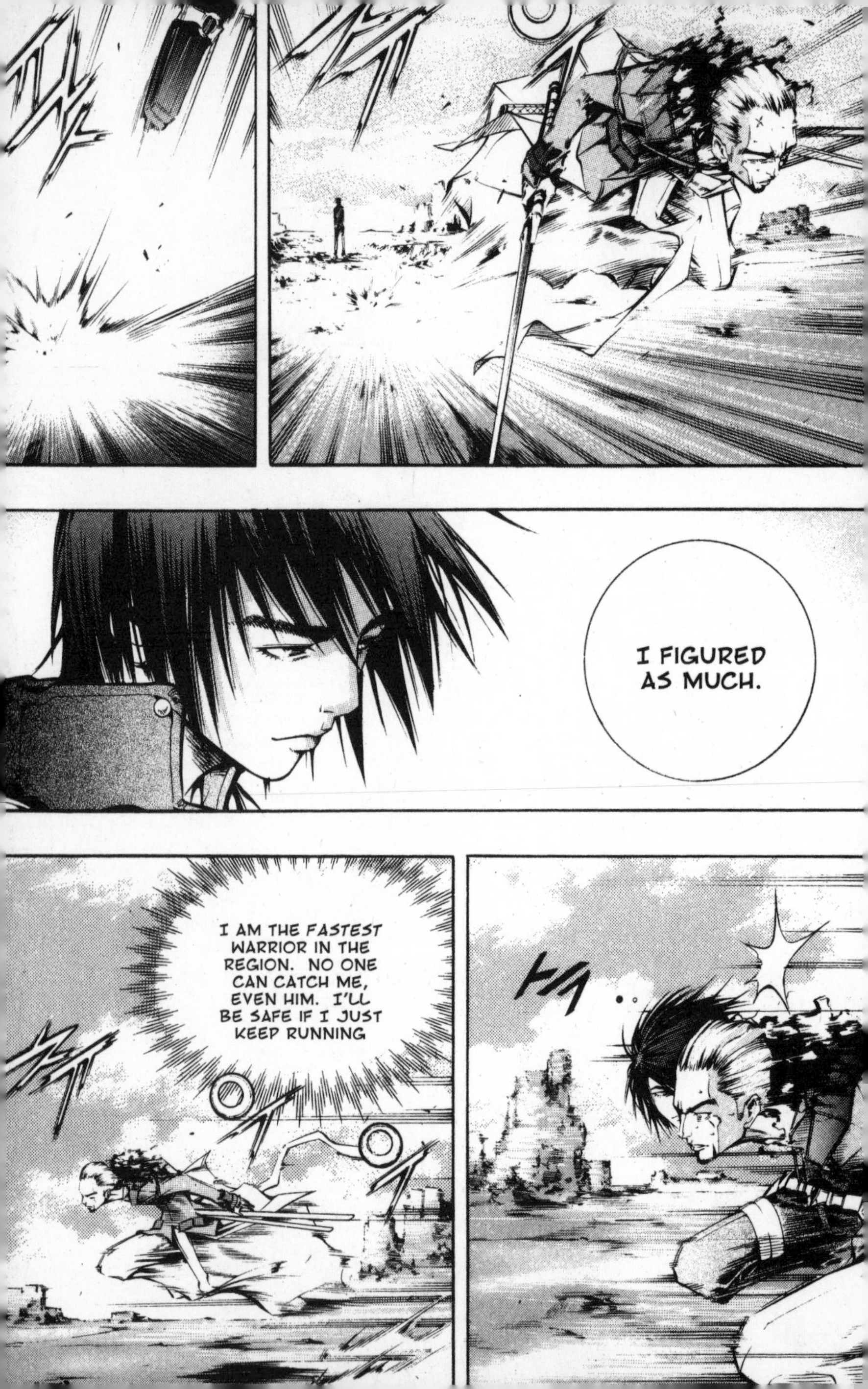
I FIGURED AS MUCH.
I AM THE FASTEST WARRIOR IN THE REGION. NO ONE CAN CATCH ME, EVEN HIM. I'LL BE SAFE IF I JUST KEEP RUNNING

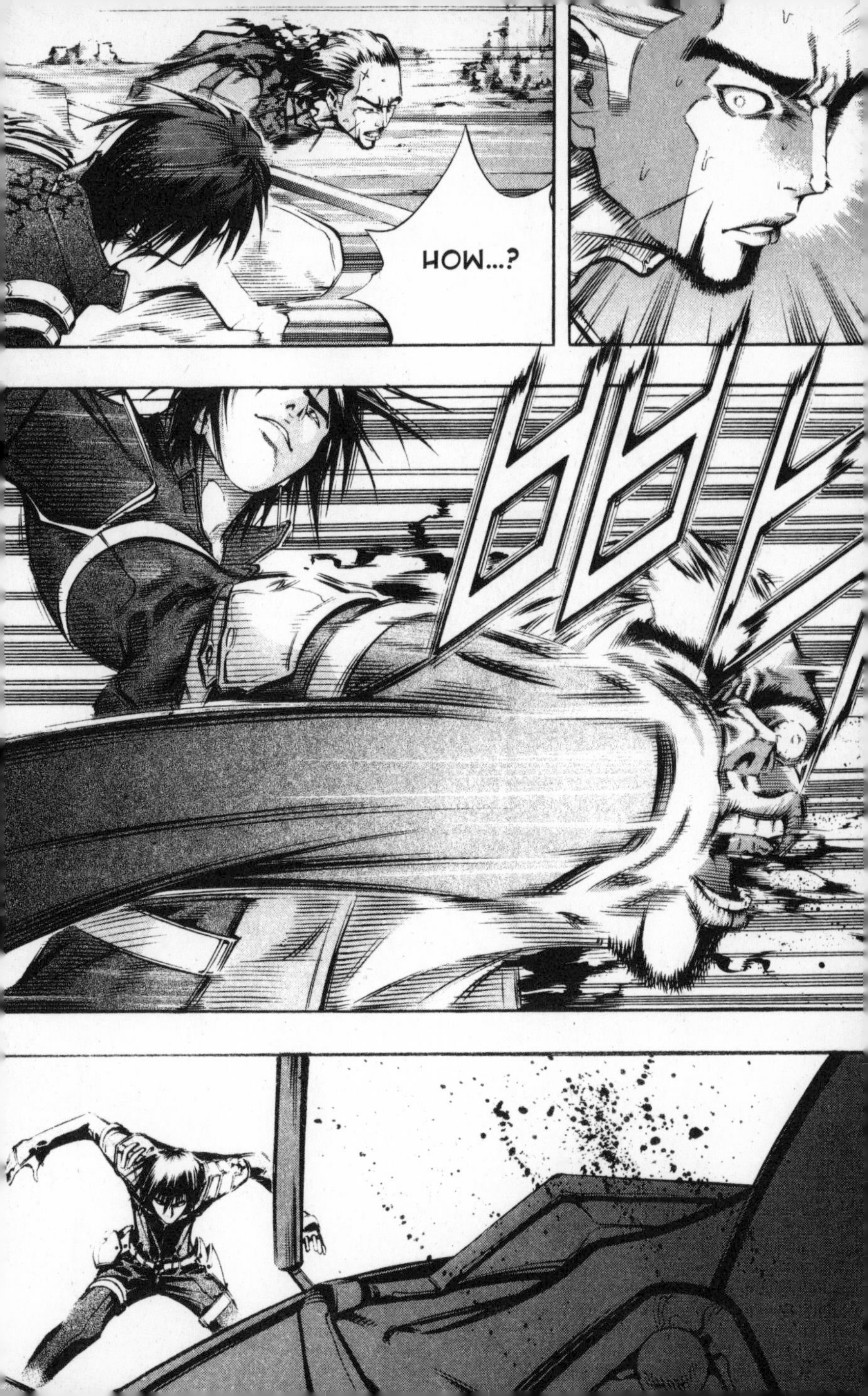
HOW...?

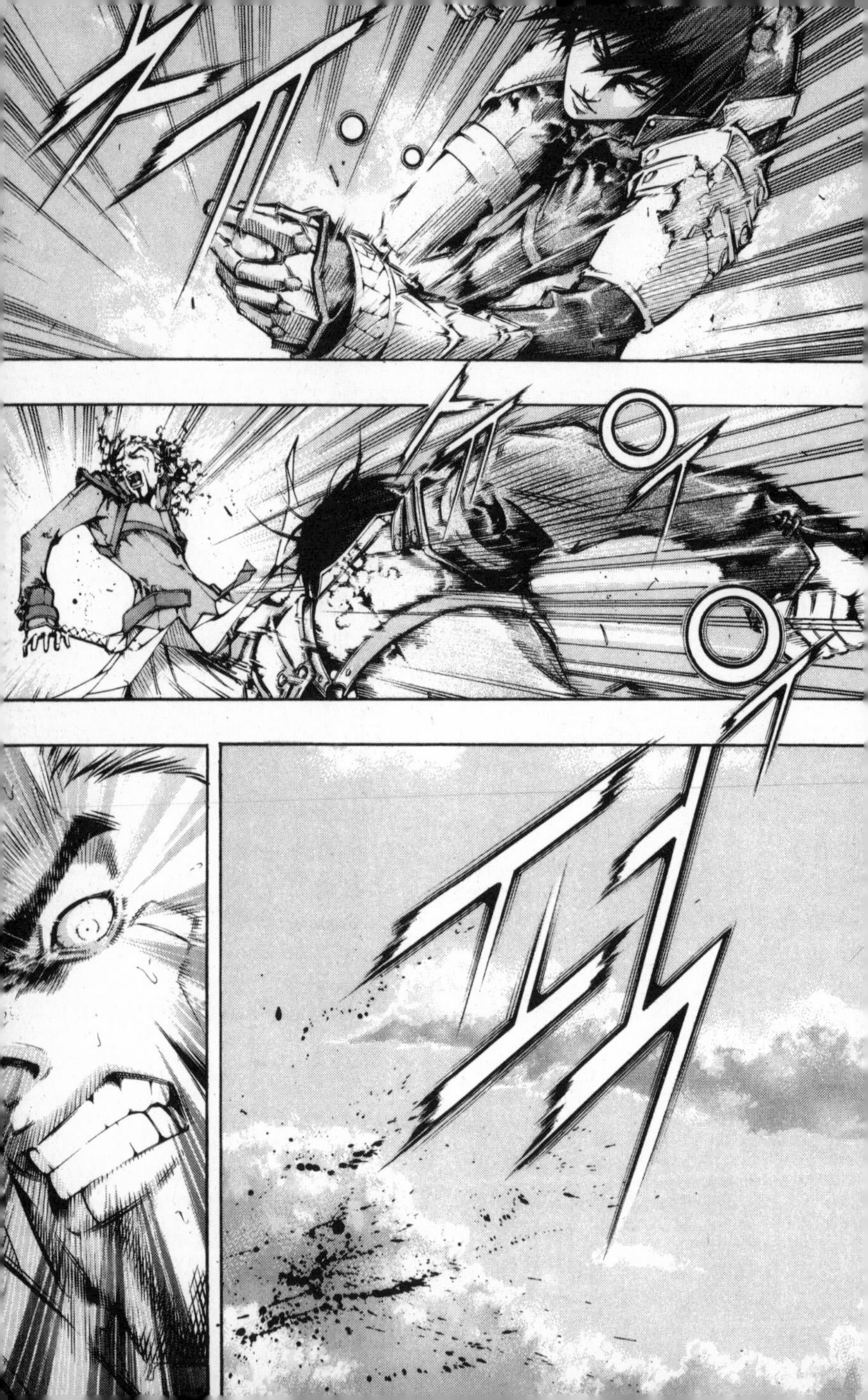

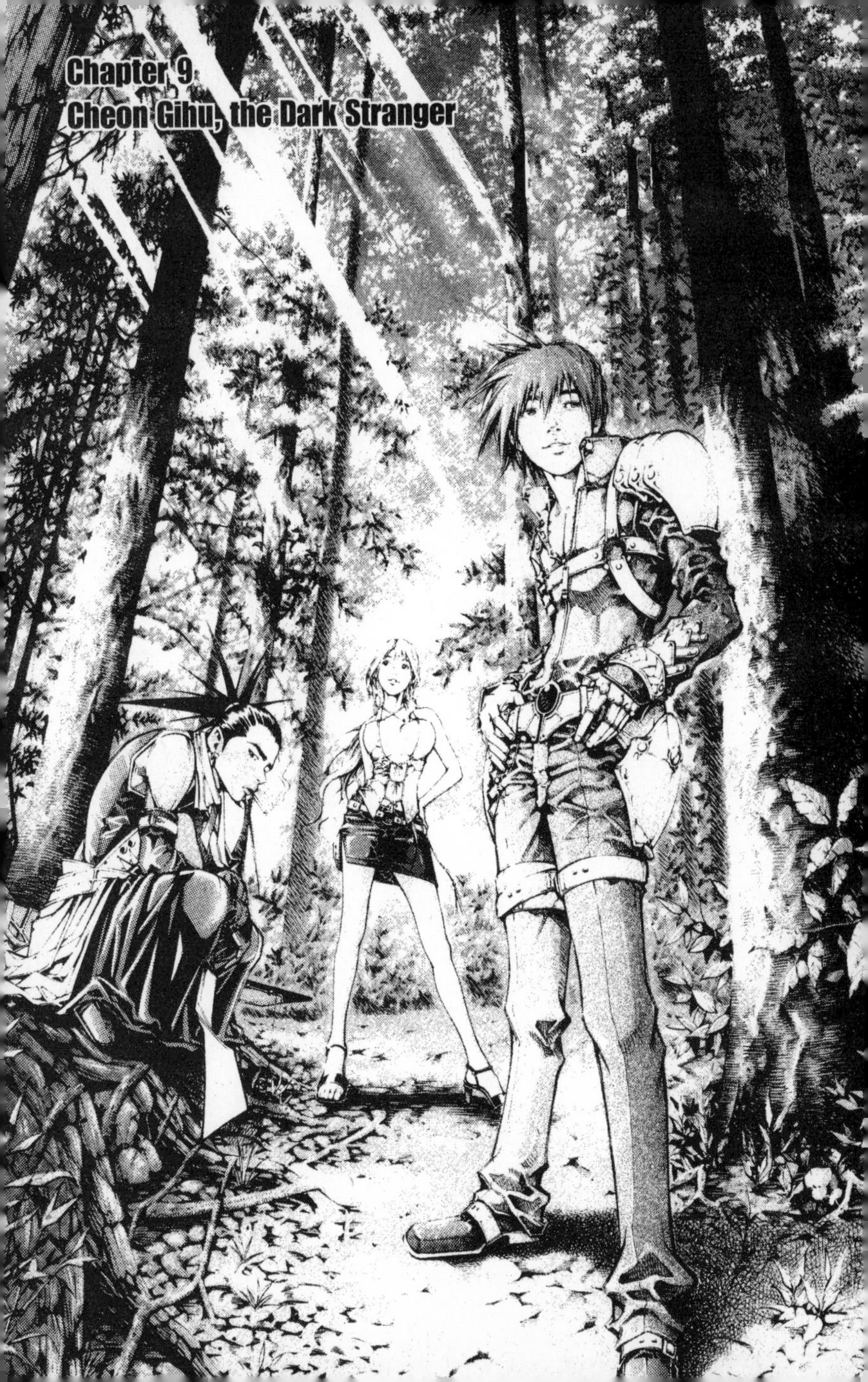
Chapter 9
Cheon Gihu, the Dark Stranger

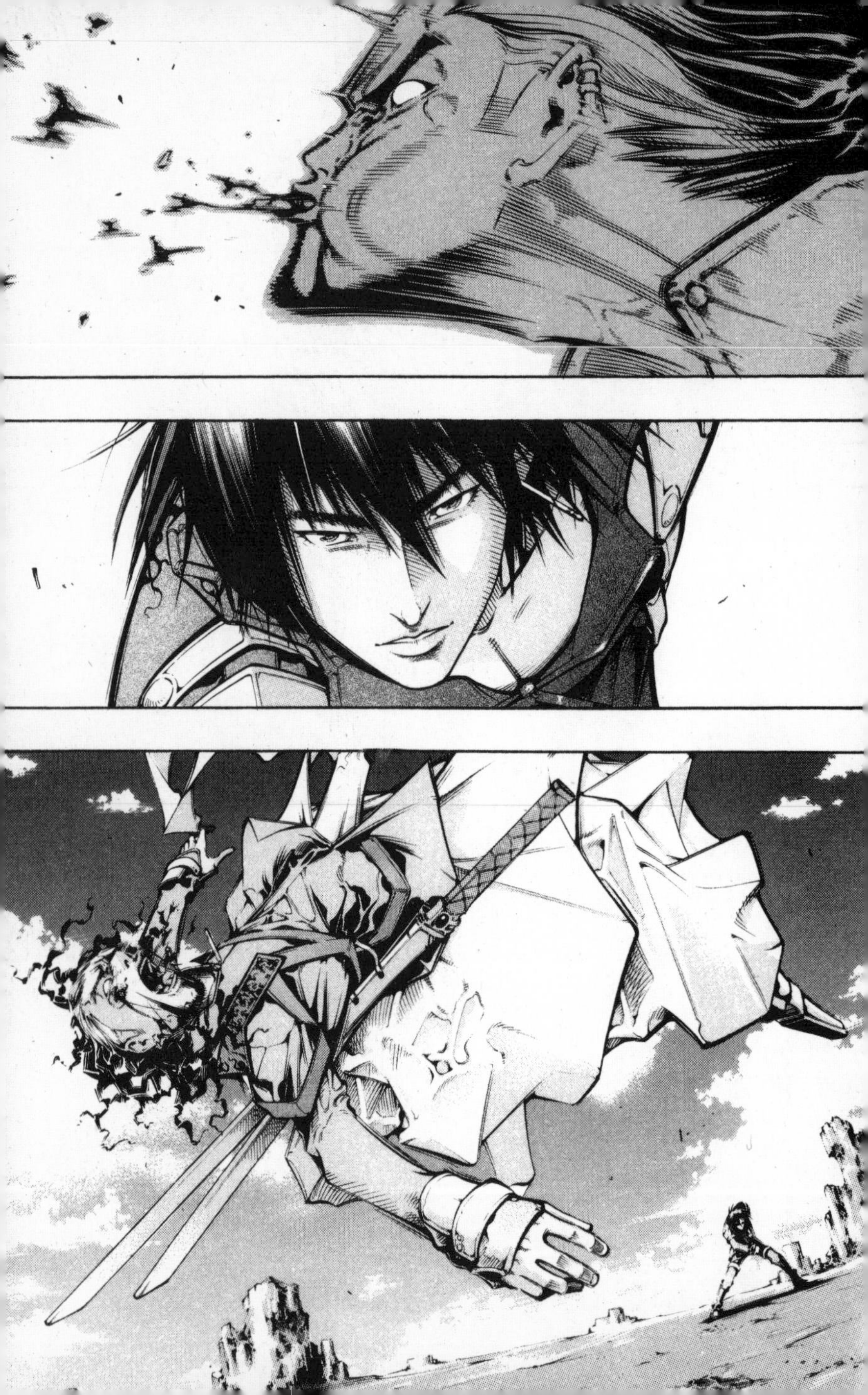

GET UP! I'M NOT DONE WITH YOU YET!

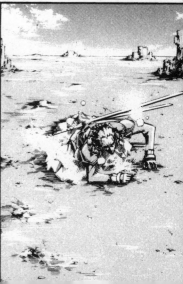

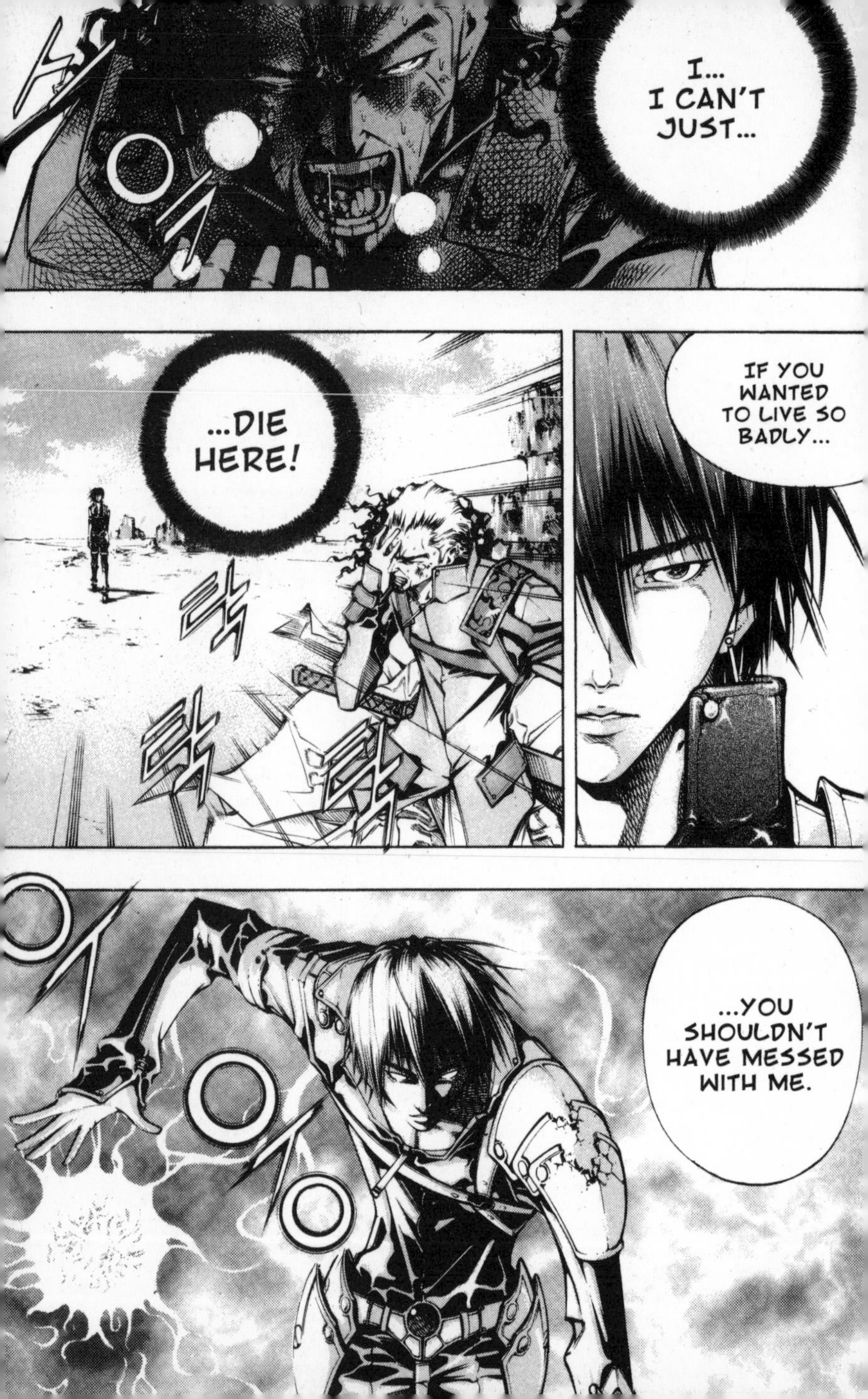
I... I CAN'T JUST...
...DIE HERE!
IF YOU WANTED TO LIVE SO BADLY...
...YOU SHOULDN'T HAVE MESSED WITH ME.

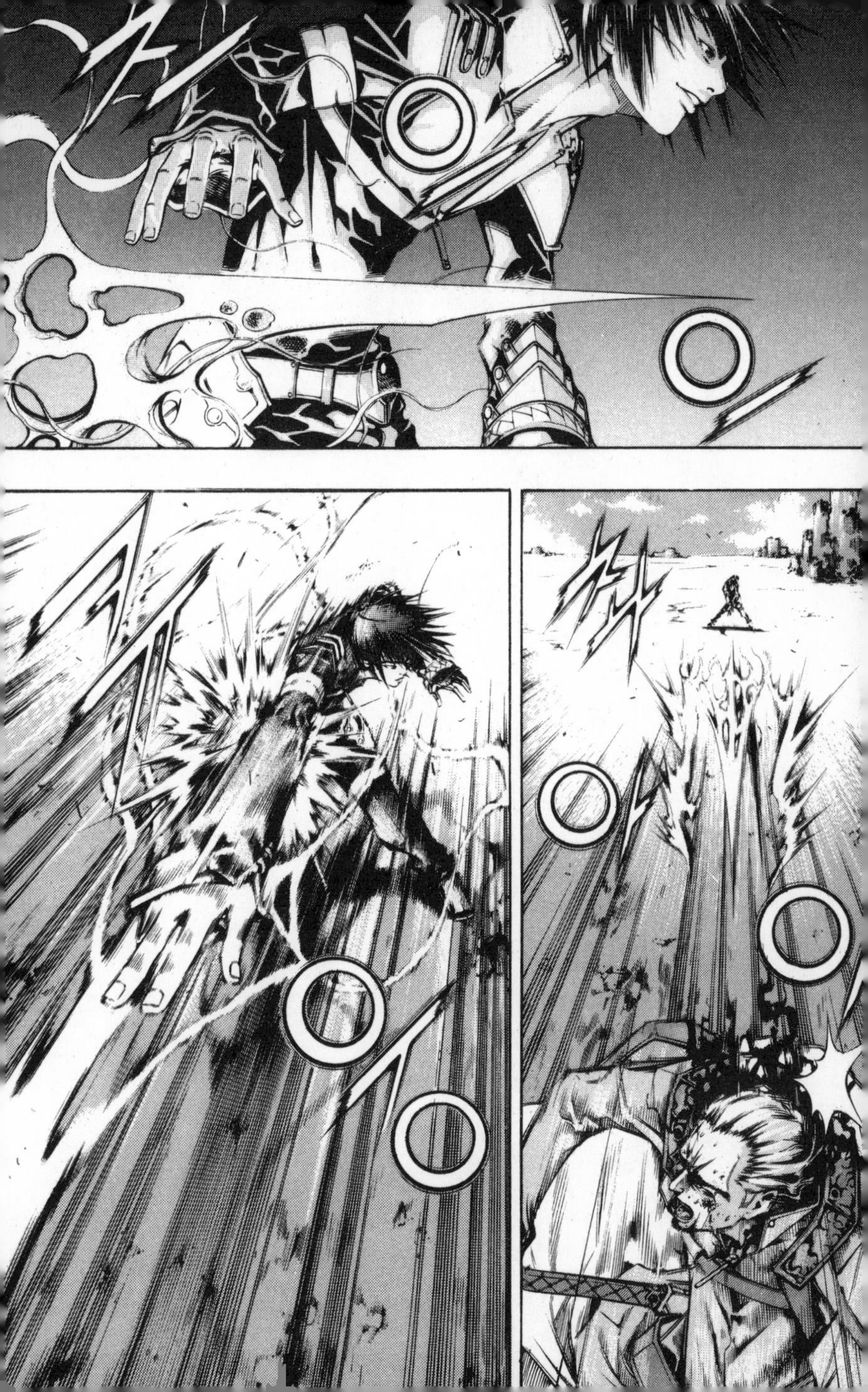

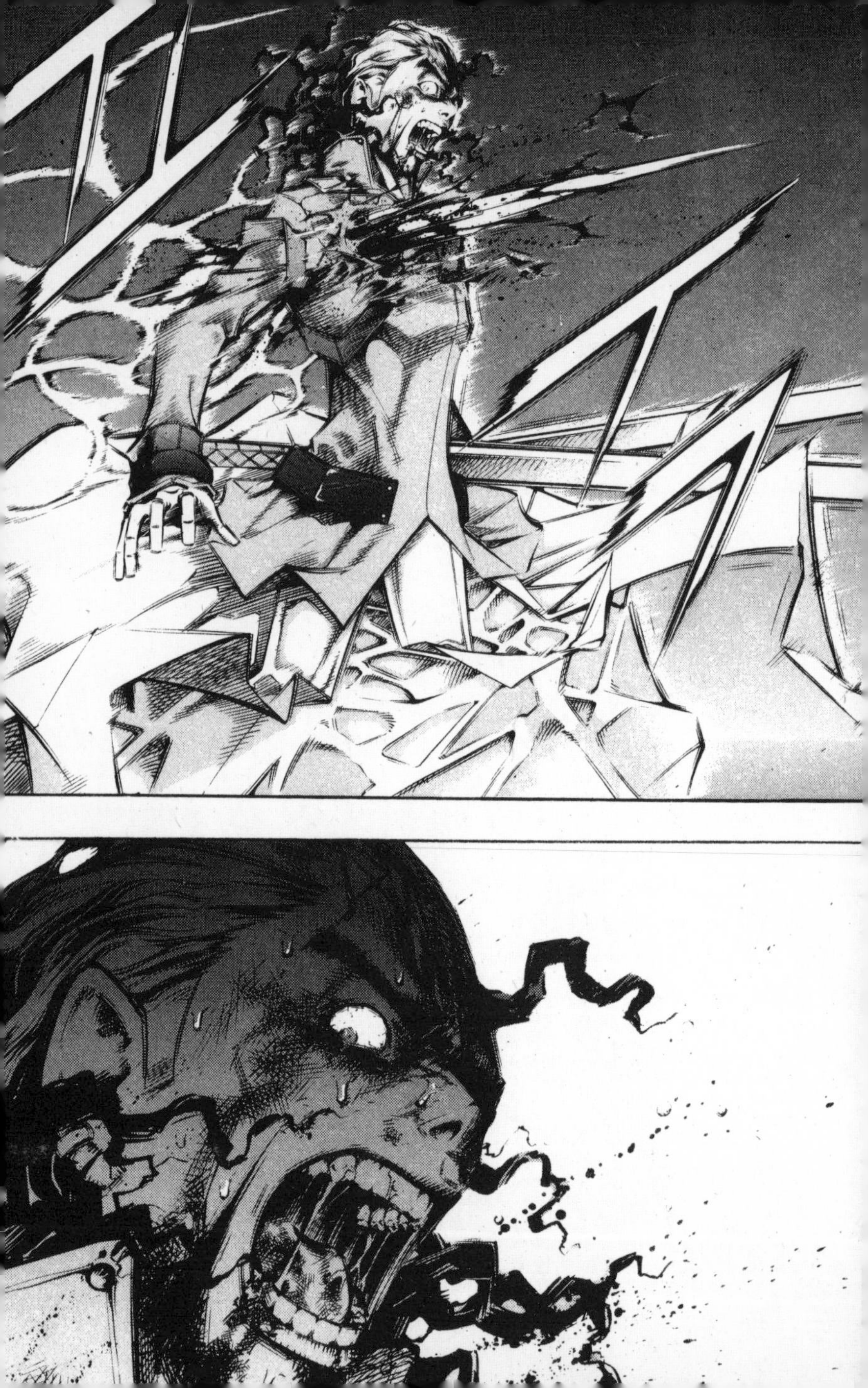

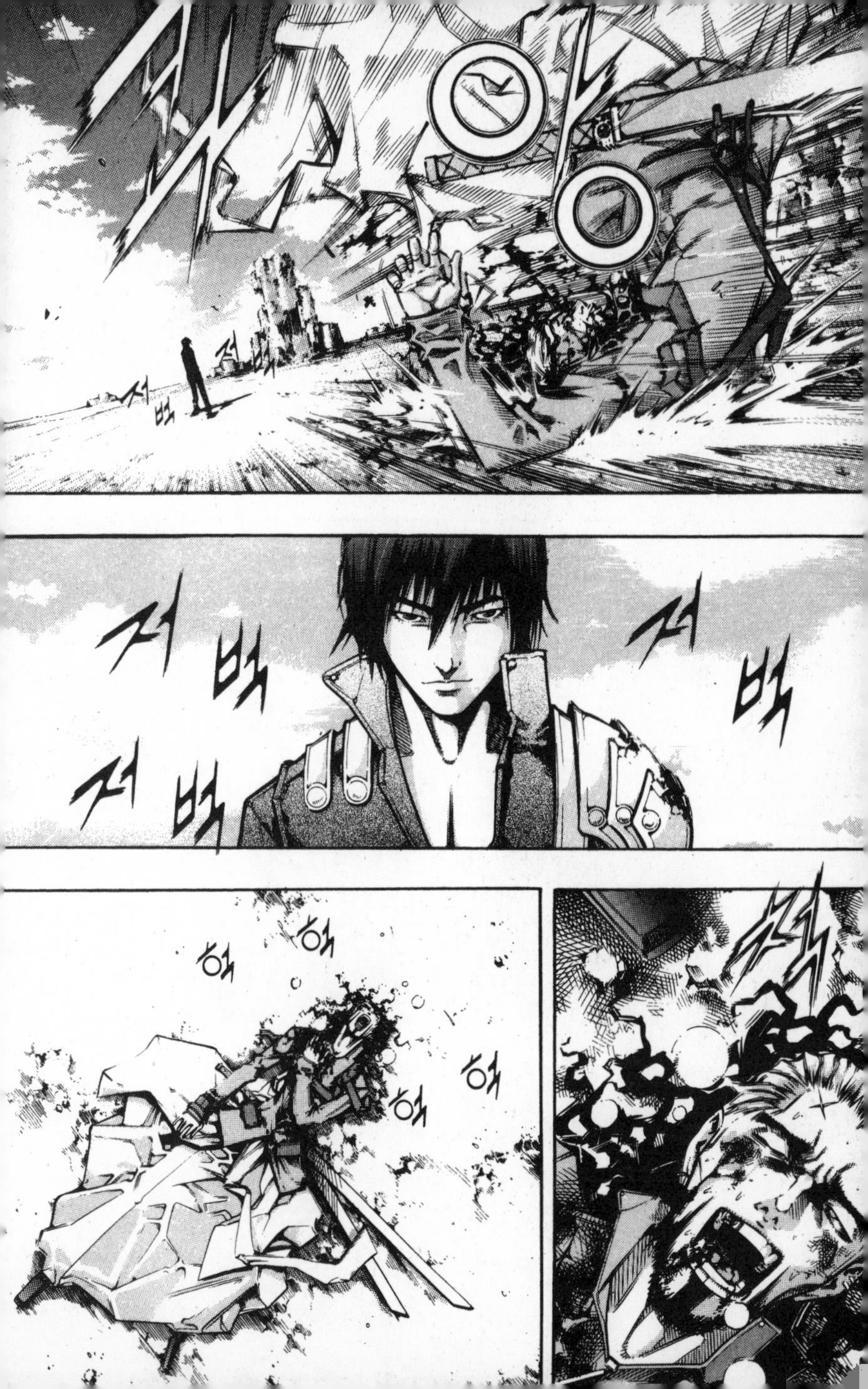

저벅
저벅
저벅
저벅
저벅
헉
헉
헉
헉

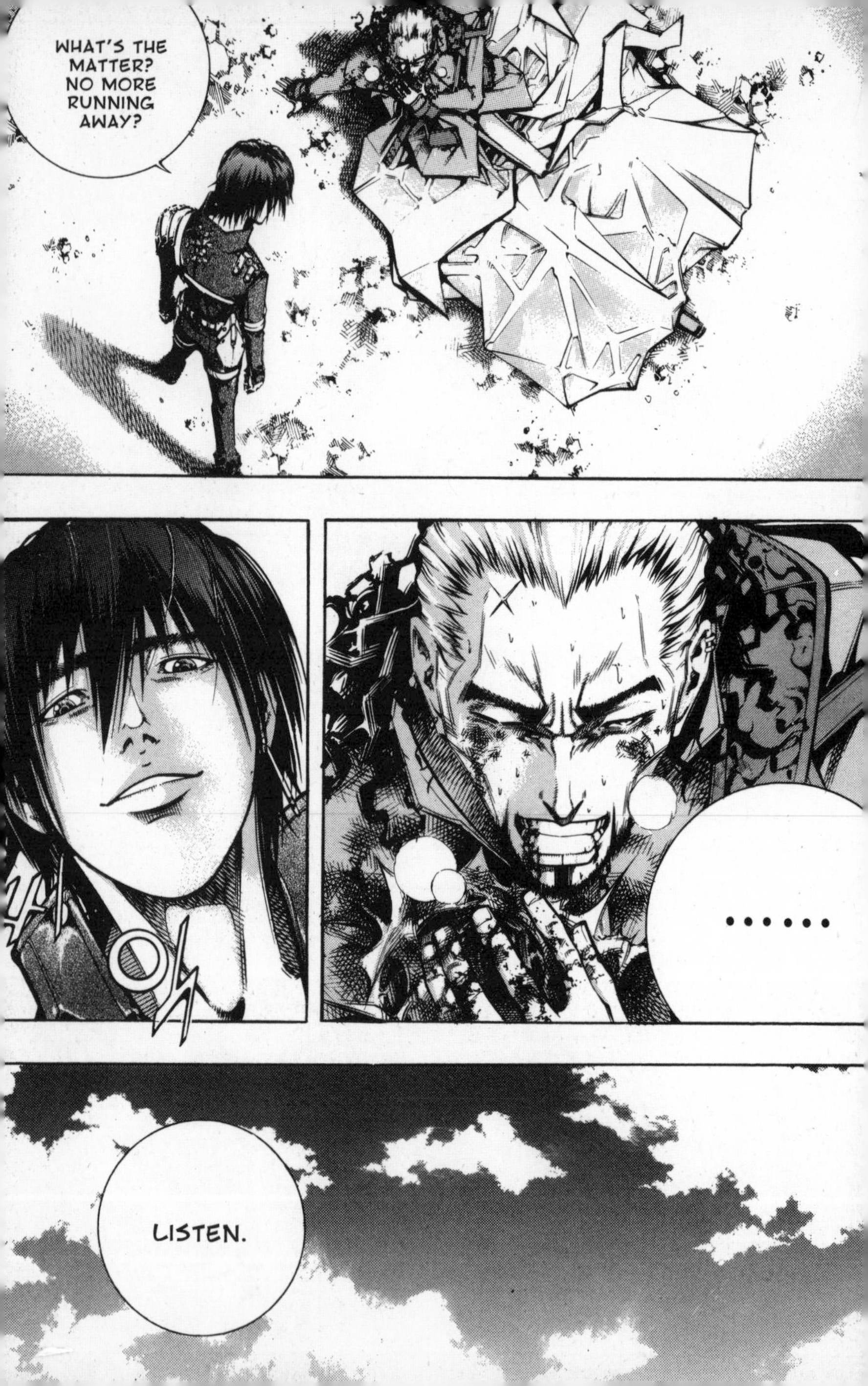
WHAT'S THE MATTER? NO MORE RUNNING AWAY?
......
LISTEN.

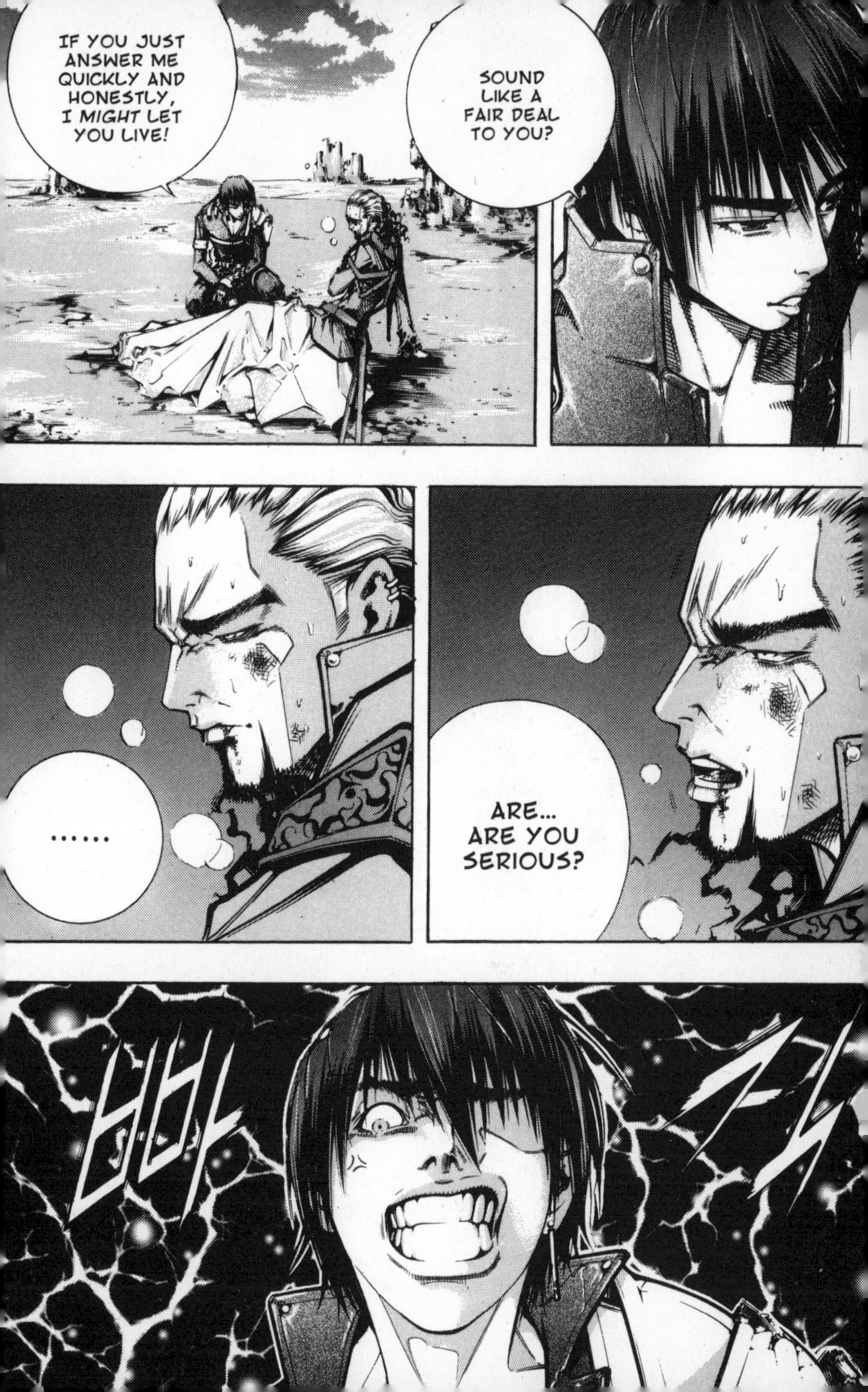
IF YOU JUST ANSWER ME QUICKLY AND HONESTLY, I MIGHT LET YOU LIVE!
SOUND LIKE A FAIR DEAL TO YOU?
......
ARE... ARE YOU SERIOUS?

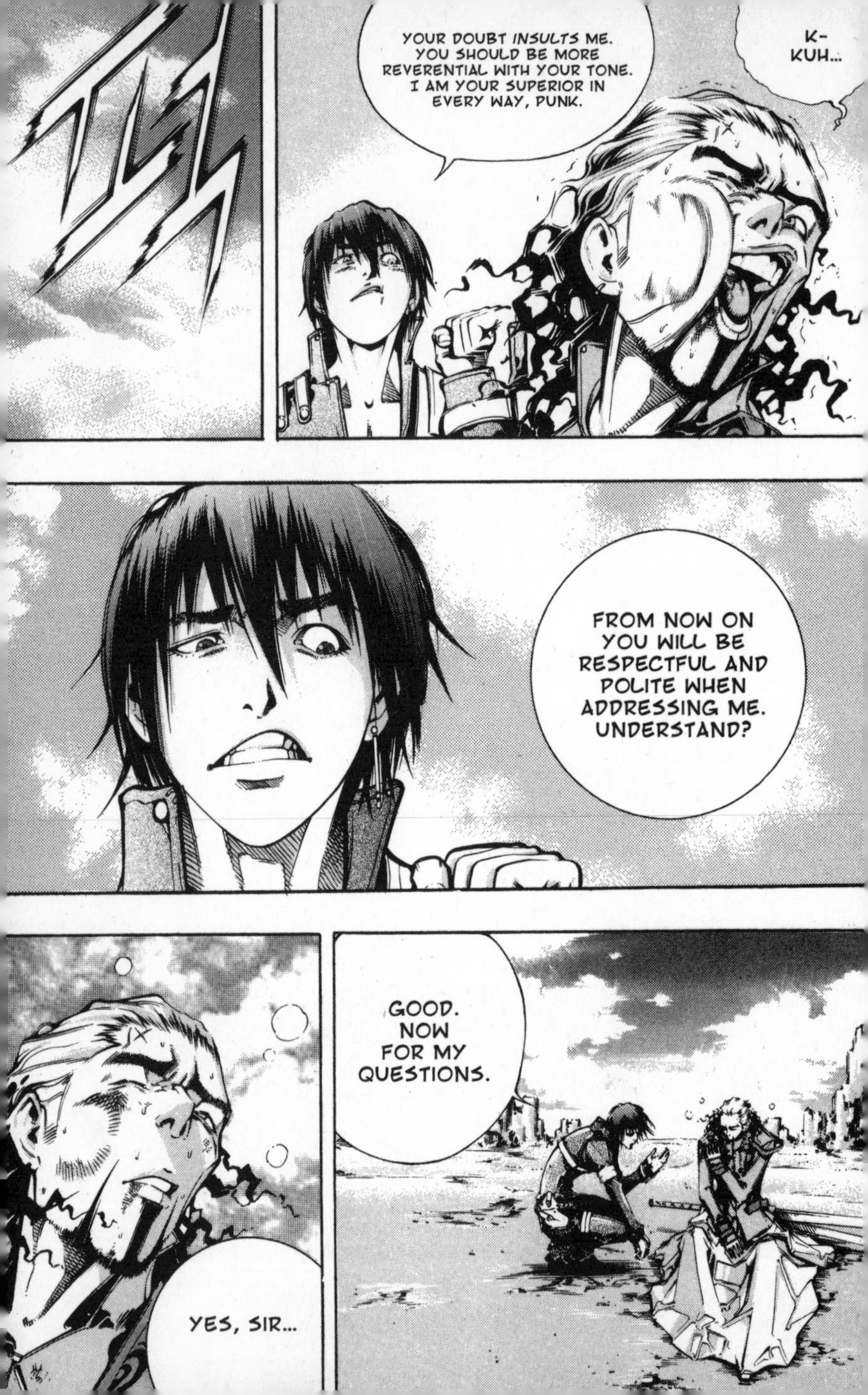

YOUR DOUBT INSULTS ME. YOU SHOULD BE MORE REVERENTIAL WITH YOUR TONE. I AM YOUR SUPERIOR IN EVERY WAY, PUNK.
K-KUH...
FROM NOW ON YOU WILL BE RESPECTFUL AND POLITE WHEN ADDRESSING ME. UNDERSTAND?
YES, SIR...
GOOD. NOW FOR MY QUESTIONS.

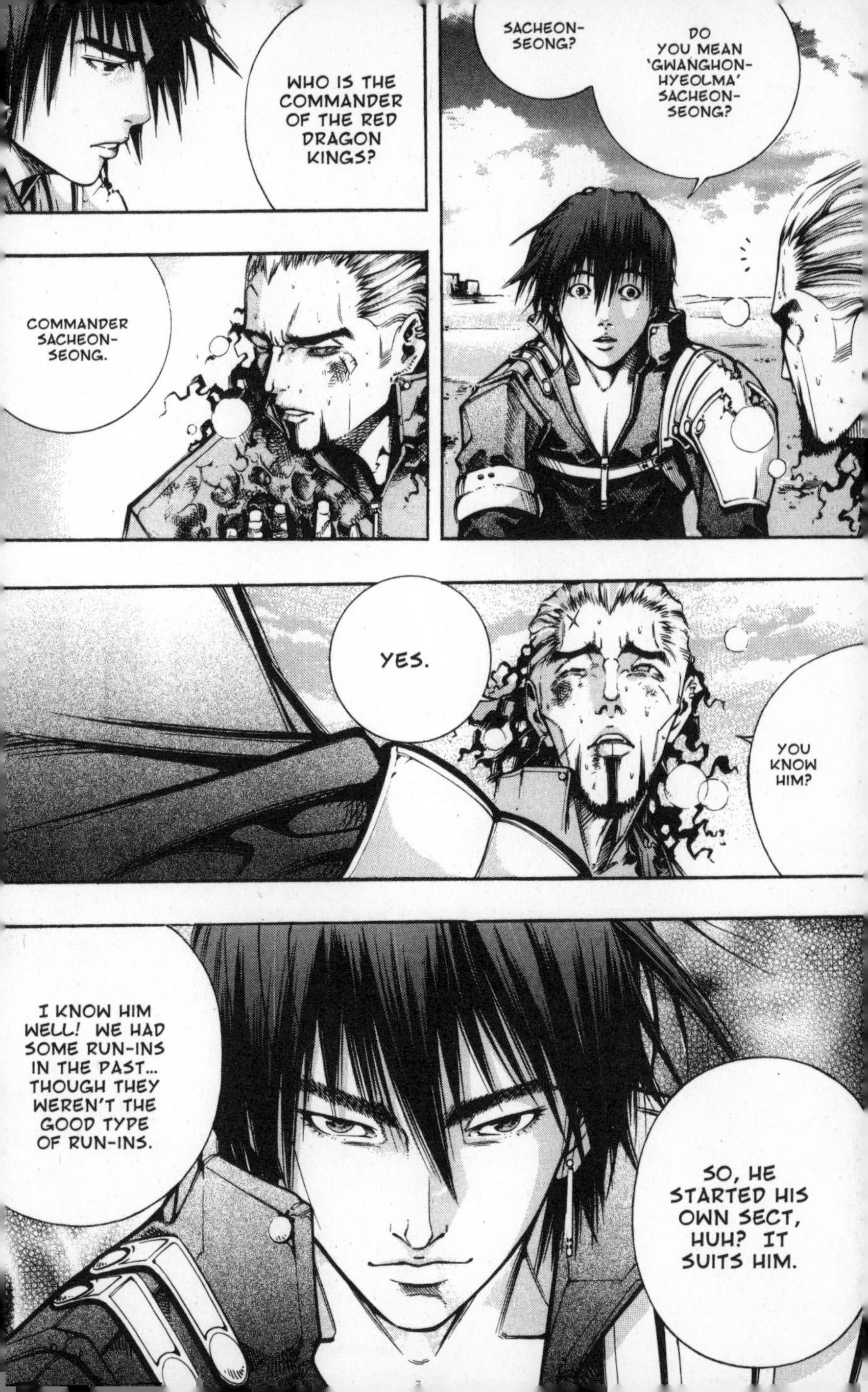

WHO IS THE COMMANDER OF THE RED DRAGON KINGS?
SACHEON-SEONG?
DO YOU MEAN 'GWANGHON-HYEOLMA' SACHEON-SEONG?
COMMANDER SACHEON-SEONG.
YES.
YOU KNOW HIM?
I KNOW HIM WELL! WE HAD SOME RUN-INS IN THE PAST... THOUGH THEY WEREN'T THE GOOD TYPE OF RUN-INS.
SO, HE STARTED HIS OWN SECT, HUH? IT SUITS HIM.

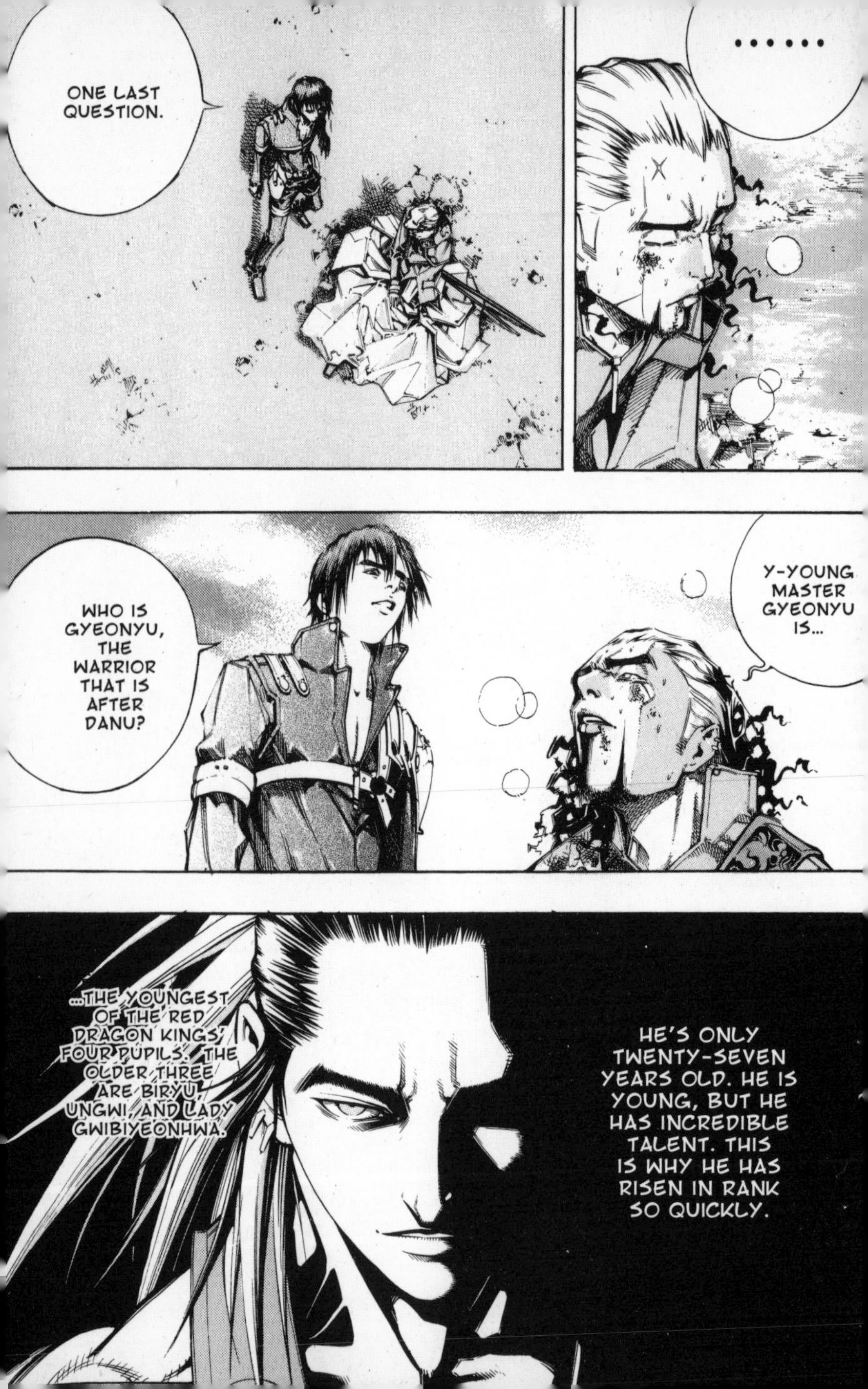

ONE LAST QUESTION.
......
WHO IS GYEONYU, THE WARRIOR THAT IS AFTER DANU?
Y-YOUNG MASTER GYEONYU IS...
...THE YOUNGEST OF THE RED DRAGON KINGS' FOUR PUPILS. THE OLDER THREE ARE BIRYU, UNGWI, AND LADY GWIBIYEONHWA.
HE'S ONLY TWENTY-SEVEN YEARS OLD. HE IS YOUNG, BUT HE HAS INCREDIBLE TALENT. THIS IS WHY HE HAS RISEN IN RANK SO QUICKLY.

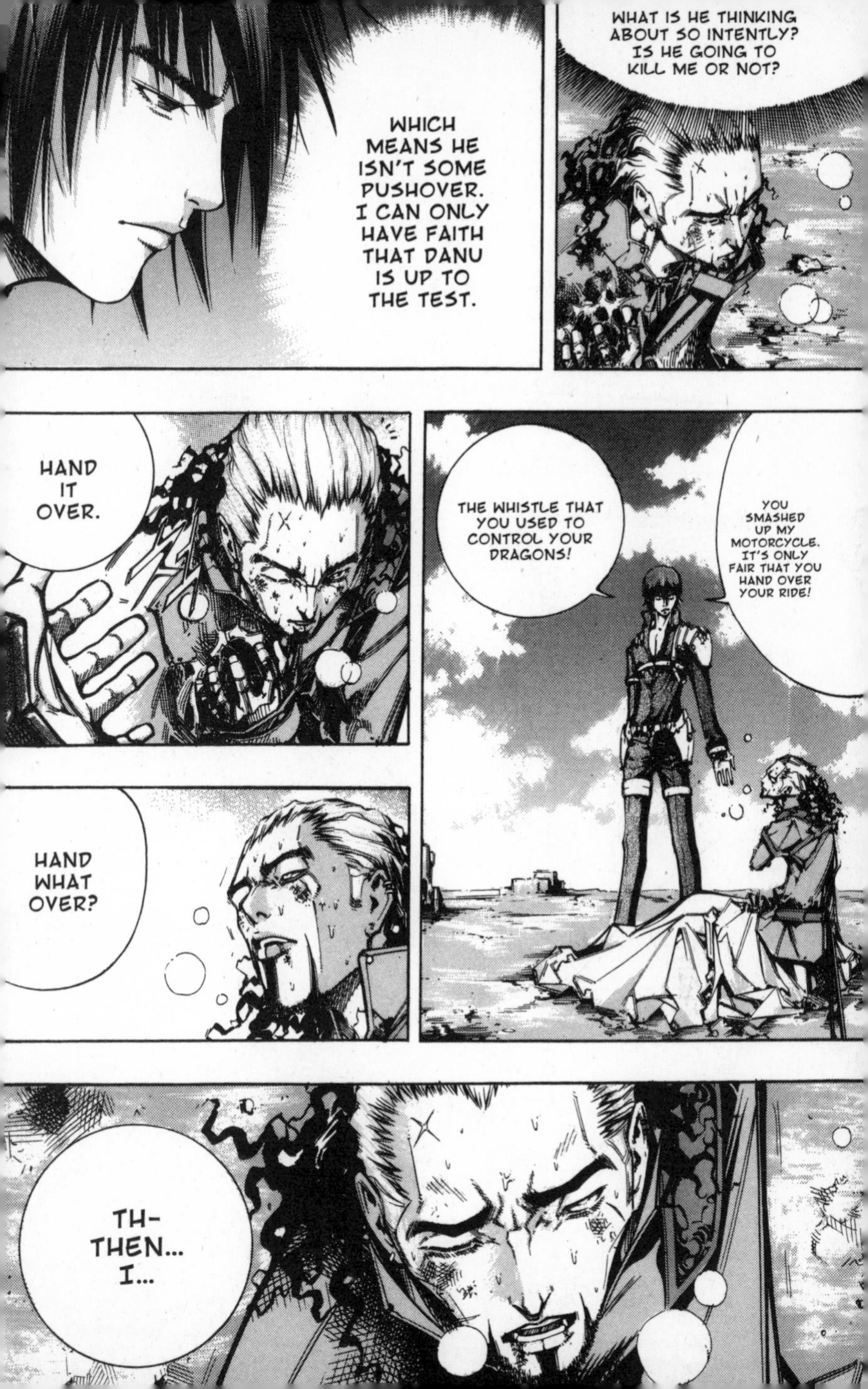
WHICH MEANS HE ISN'T SOME PUSHOVER. I CAN ONLY HAVE FAITH THAT DANU IS UP TO THE TEST.
WHAT IS HE THINKING ABOUT SO INTENTLY? IS HE GOING TO KILL ME OR NOT?
YOU SMASHED UP MY MOTORCYCLE. IT'S ONLY FAIR THAT YOU HAND OVER YOUR RIDE!
THE WHISTLE THAT YOU USED TO CONTROL YOUR DRAGONS!
HAND IT OVER.
HAND WHAT OVER?
TH-THEN... I...

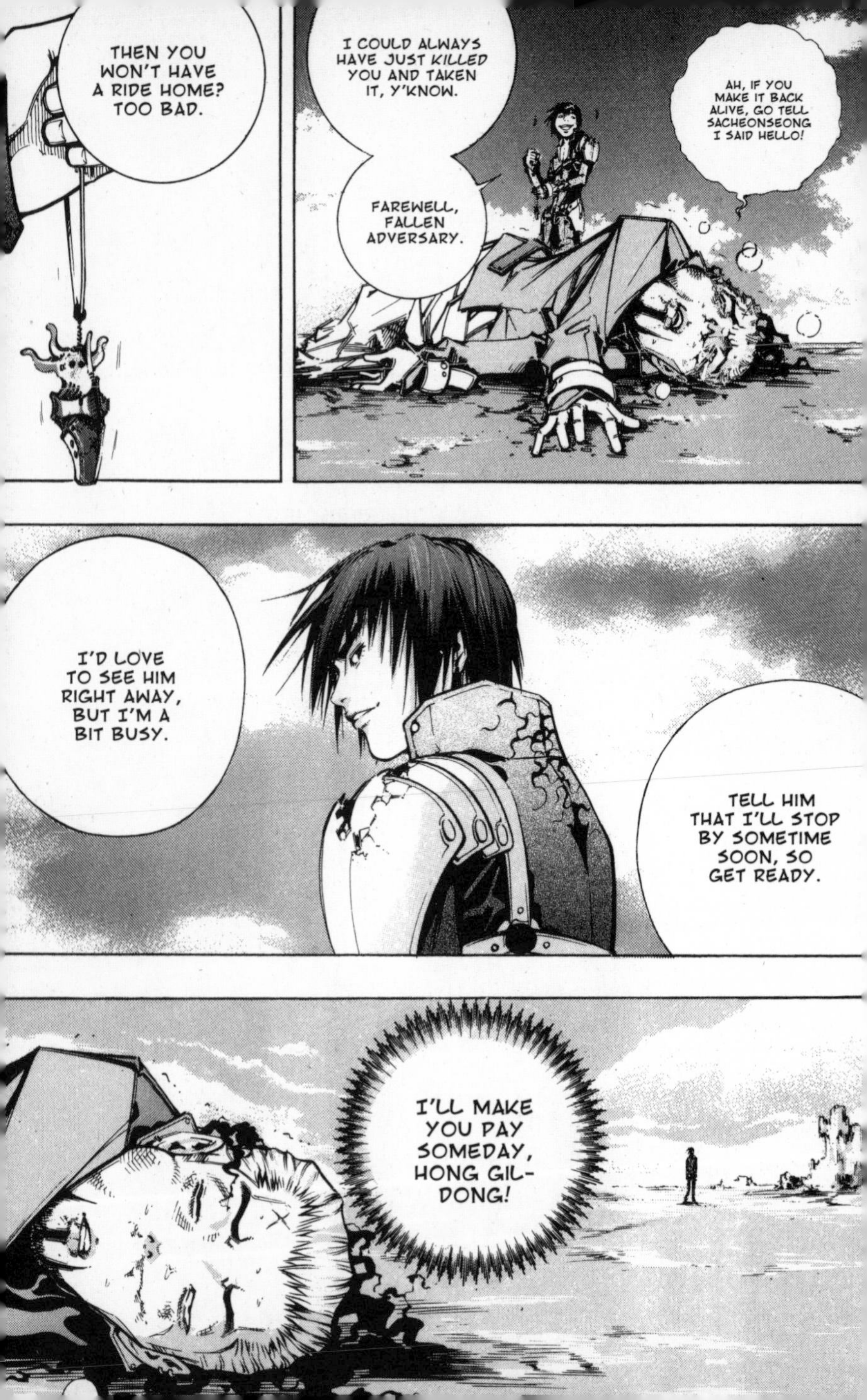
THEN YOU WON'T HAVE A RIDE HOME? TOO BAD.
I COULD ALWAYS HAVE JUST KILLED YOU AND TAKEN IT, Y'KNOW.
FAREWELL, FALLEN ADVERSARY.
AH, IF YOU MAKE IT BACK ALIVE, GO TELL SACHEONSEONG I SAID HELLO!
I'D LOVE TO SEE HIM RIGHT AWAY, BUT I'M A BIT BUSY.
TELL HIM THAT I'LL STOP BY SOMETIME SOON, SO GET READY.
I'LL MAKE YOU PAY SOMEDAY, HONG GIL-DONG!

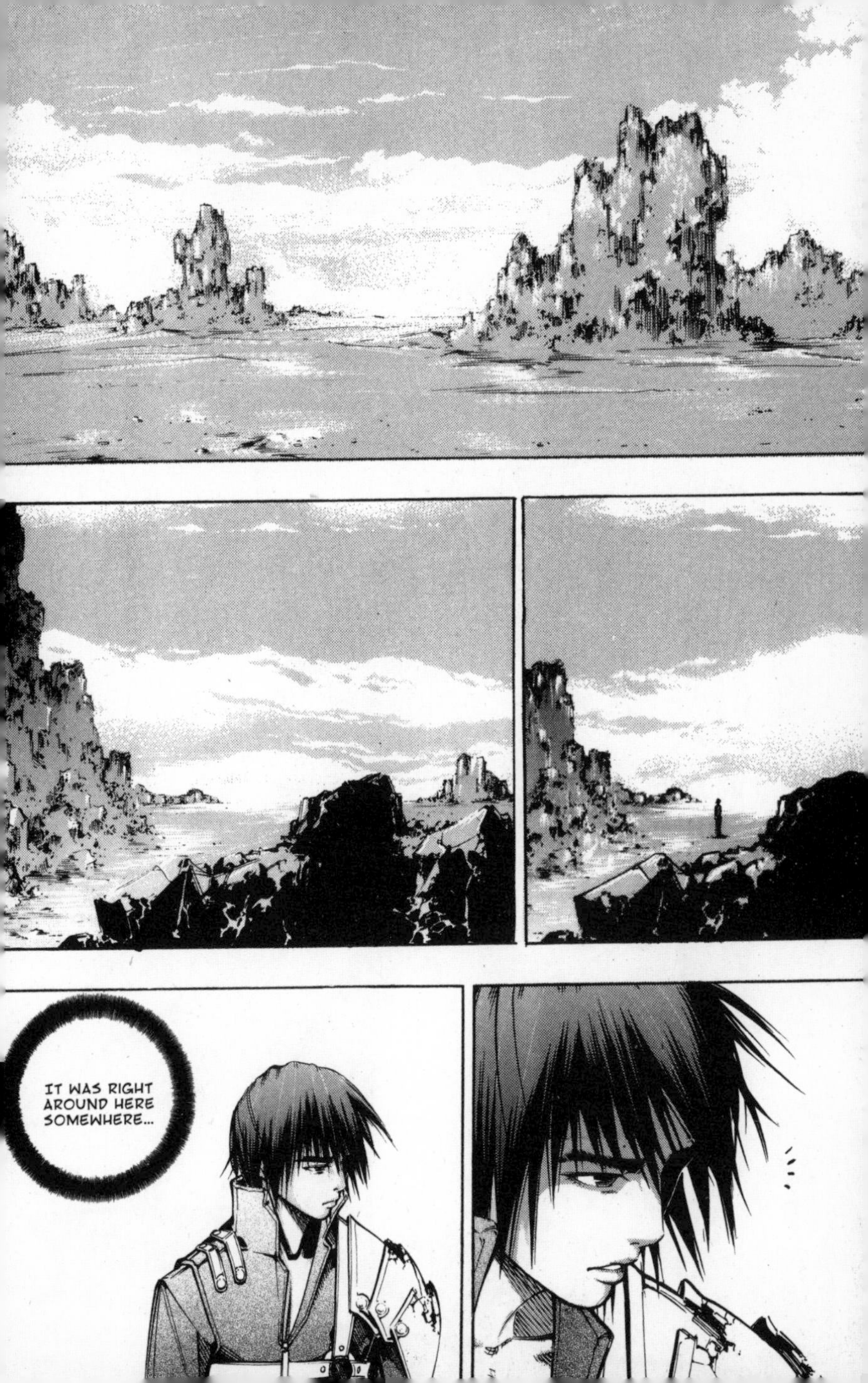
IT WAS RIGHT AROUND HERE SOMEWHERE...

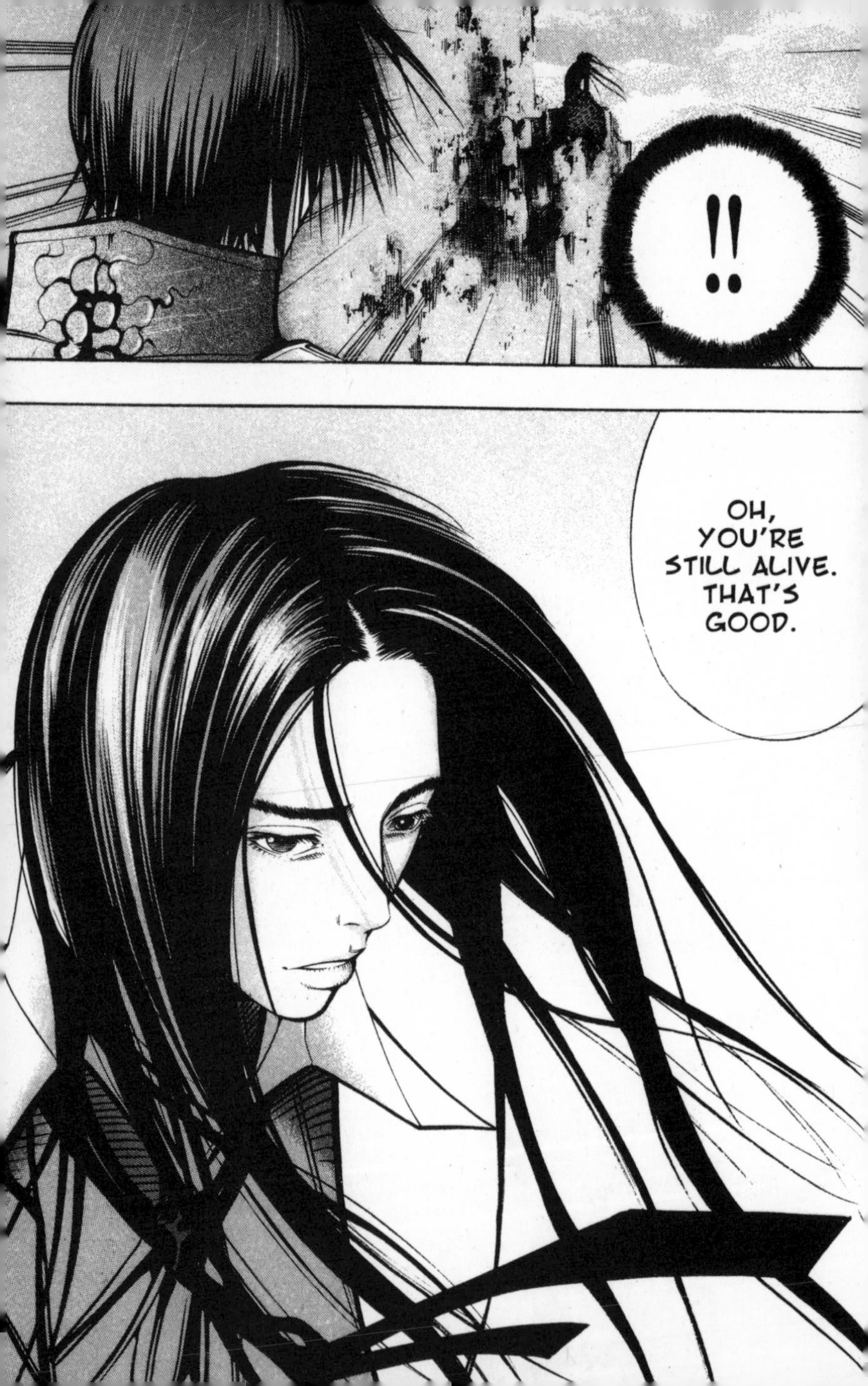
!!
OH, YOU'RE STILL ALIVE. THAT'S GOOD.

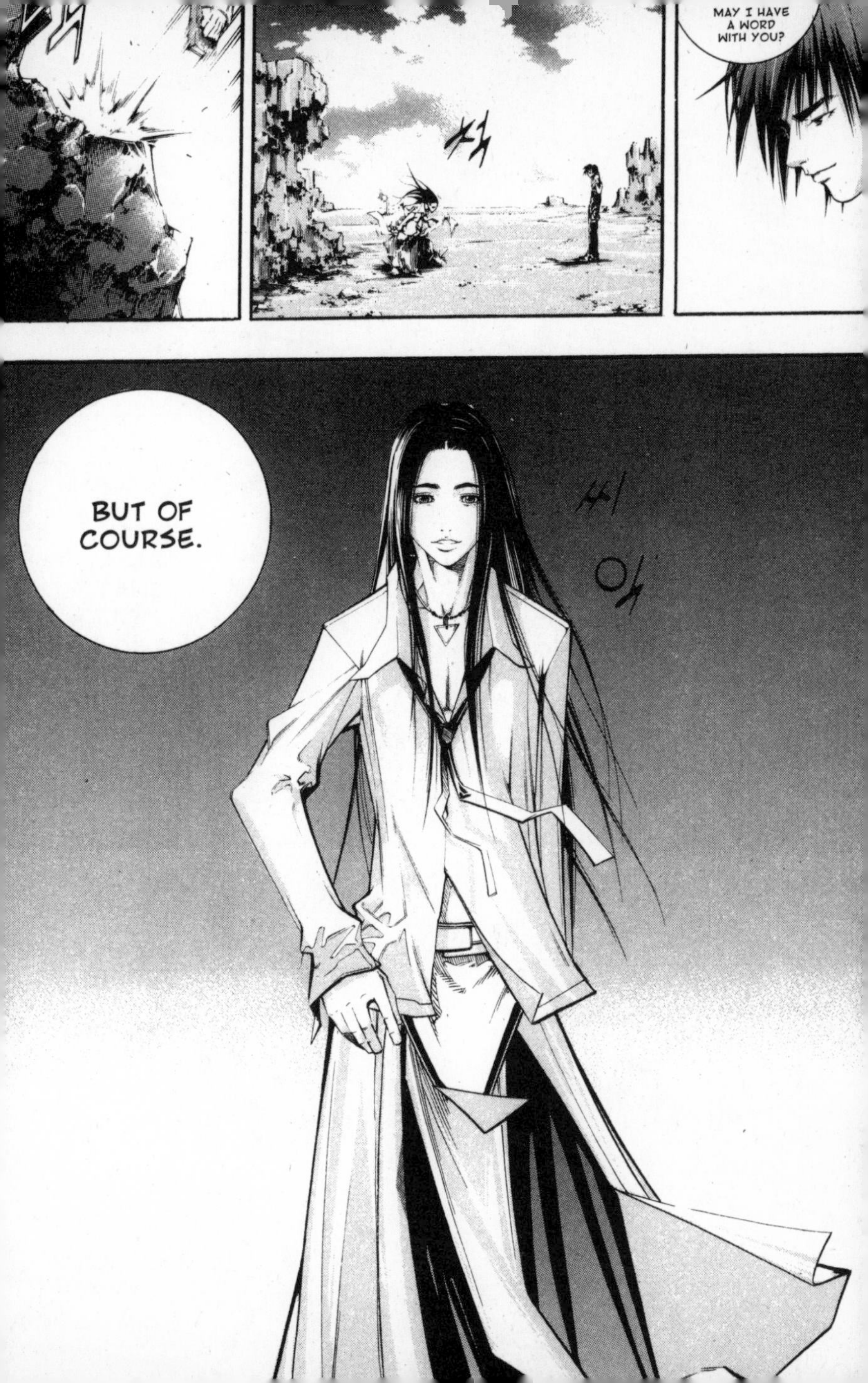
MAY I HAVE A WORD WITH YOU?
BUT OF COURSE.

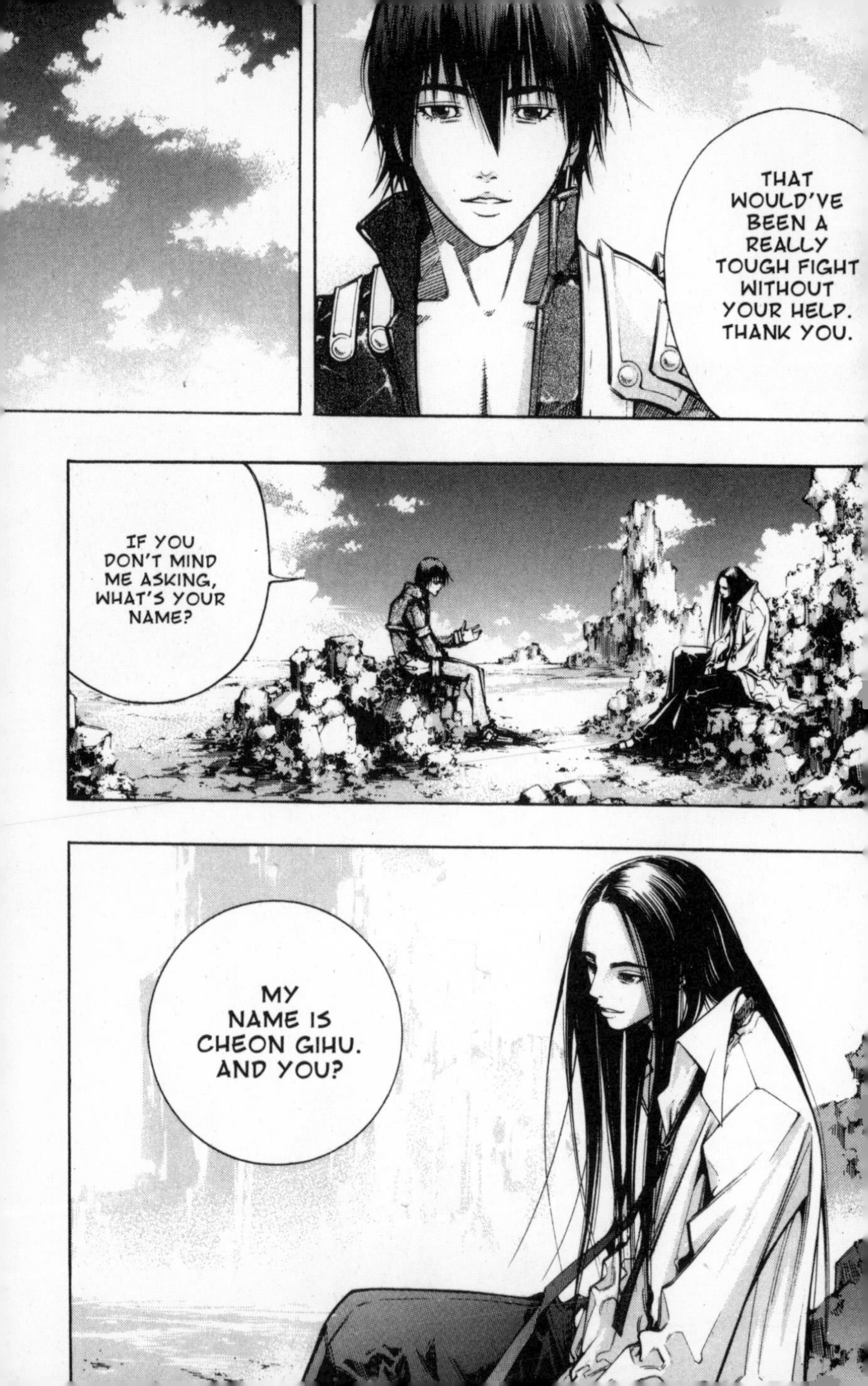
THAT WOULD'VE BEEN A REALLY TOUGH FIGHT WITHOUT YOUR HELP. THANK YOU.
IF YOU DON'T MIND ME ASKING, WHAT'S YOUR NAME?
MY NAME IS CHEON GIHU. AND YOU?

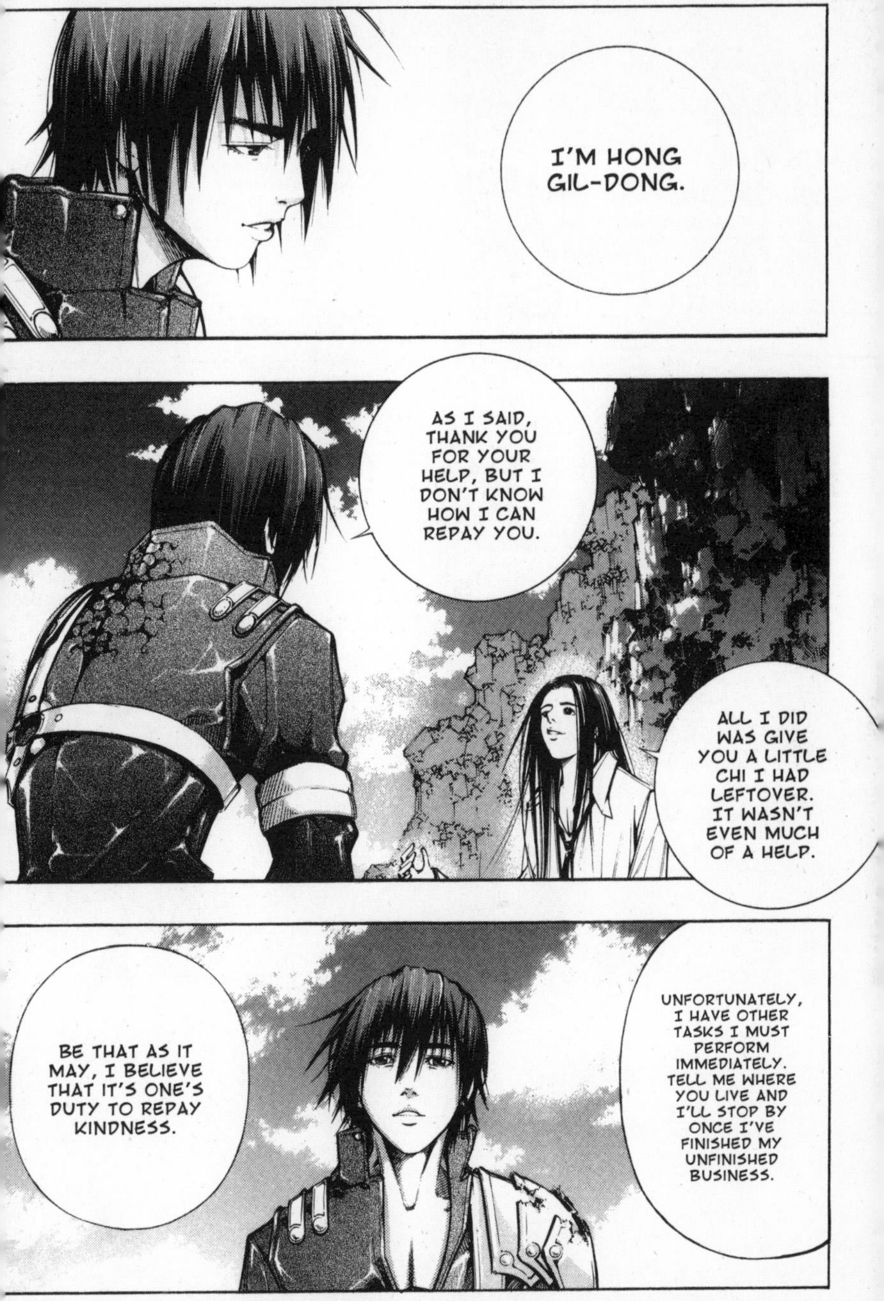
I'M HONG GIL-DONG.
AS I SAID, THANK YOU FOR YOUR HELP, BUT I DON'T KNOW HOW I CAN REPAY YOU.
ALL I DID WAS GIVE YOU A LITTLE CHI I HAD LEFTOVER. IT WASN'T EVEN MUCH OF A HELP.
UNFORTUNATELY, I HAVE OTHER TASKS I MUST PERFORM IMMEDIATELY. TELL ME WHERE YOU LIVE AND I'LL STOP BY ONCE I'VE FINISHED MY UNFINISHED BUSINESS.
BE THAT AS IT MAY, I BELIEVE THAT IT'S ONE'S DUTY TO REPAY KINDNESS.

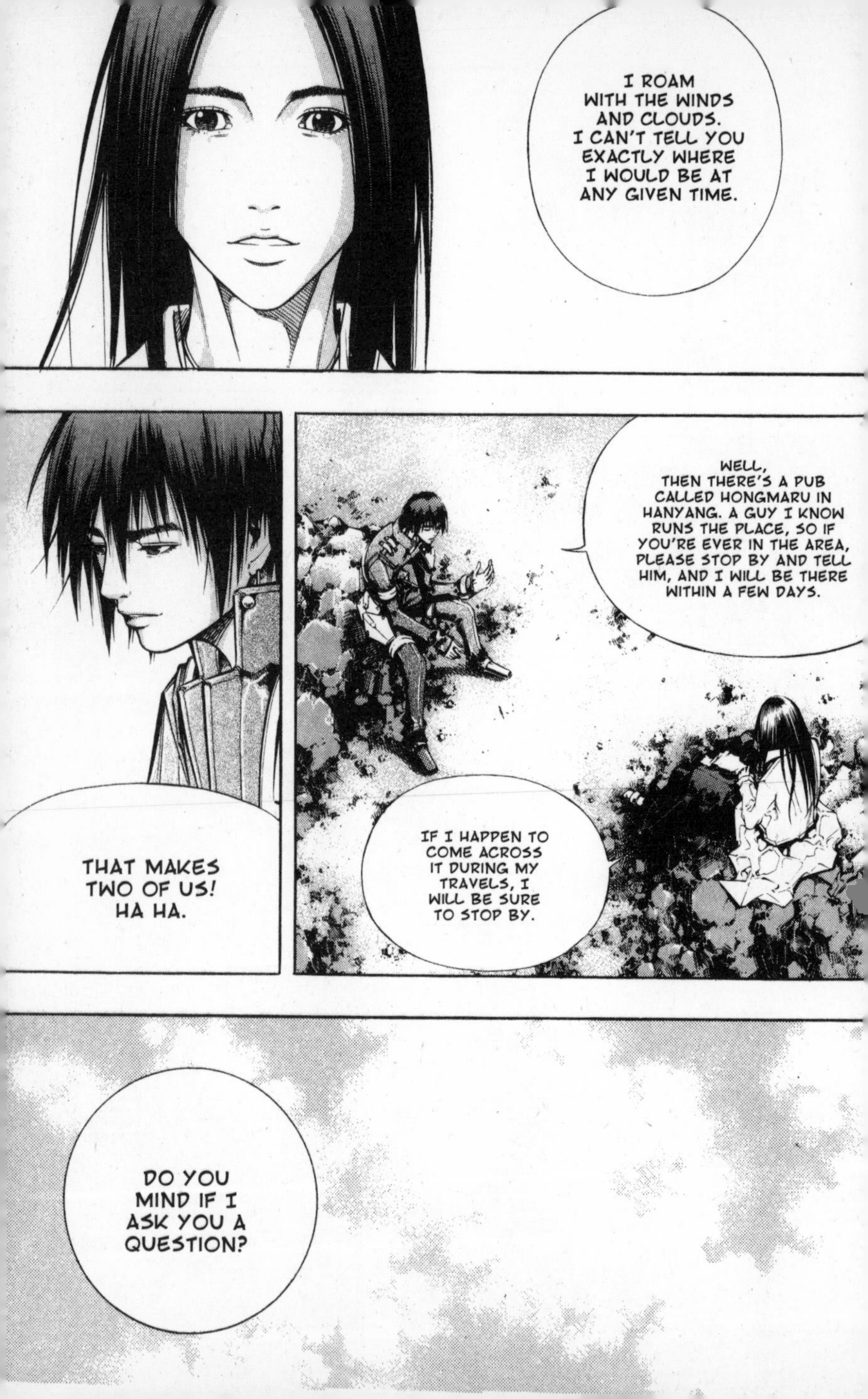
I ROAM WITH THE WINDS AND CLOUDS. I CAN'T TELL YOU EXACTLY WHERE I WOULD BE AT ANY GIVEN TIME.
WELL, THEN THERE'S A PUB CALLED HONGMARU IN HANYANG. A GUY I KNOW RUNS THE PLACE, SO IF YOU'RE EVER IN THE AREA, PLEASE STOP BY AND TELL HIM, AND I WILL BE THERE WITHIN A FEW DAYS.
THAT MAKES TWO OF US! HA HA.
IF I HAPPEN TO COME ACROSS IT DURING MY TRAVELS, I WILL BE SURE TO STOP BY.
DO YOU MIND IF I ASK YOU A QUESTION?

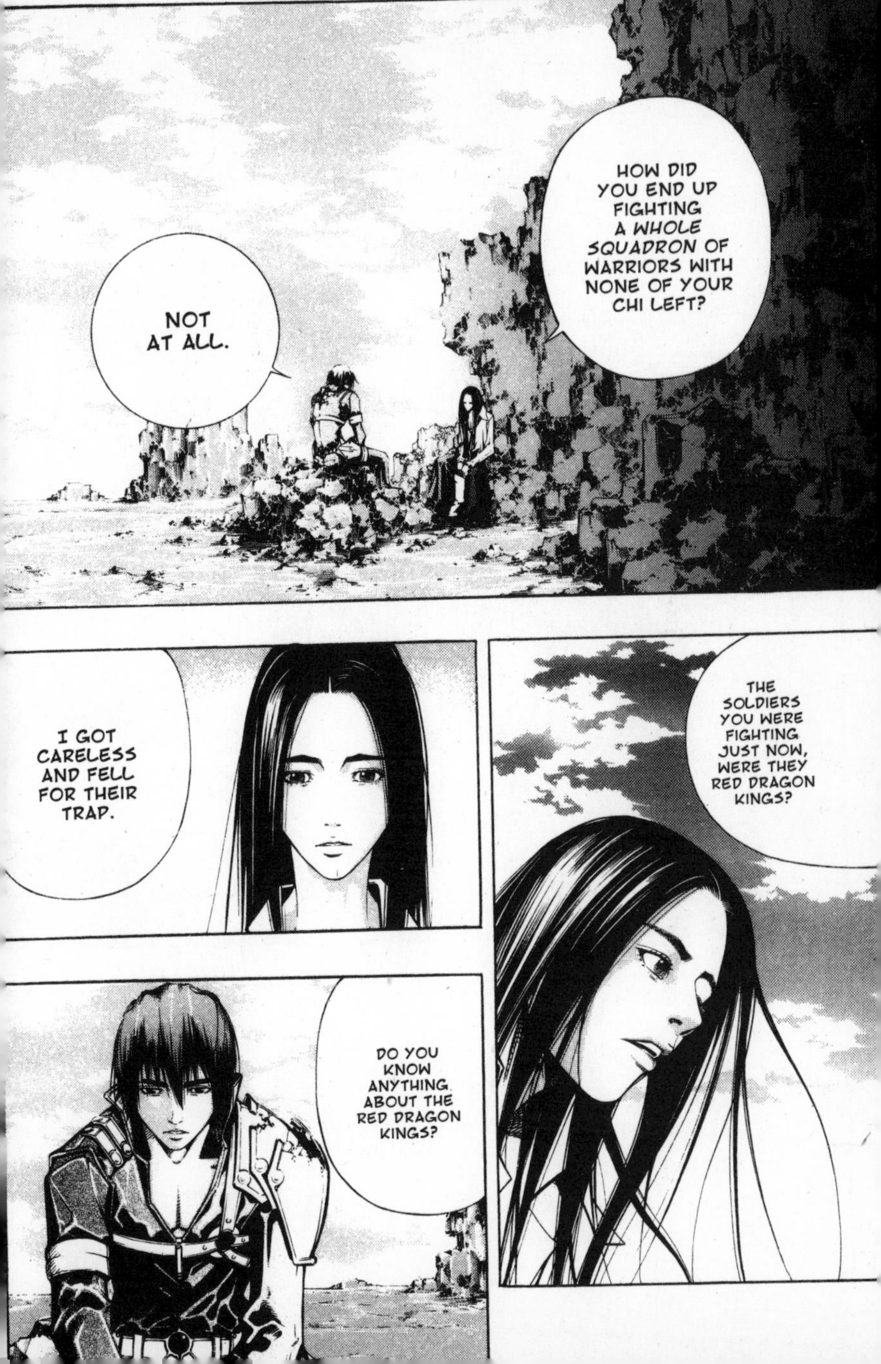
HOW DID YOU END UP FIGHTING A *WHOLE* SQUADRON OF WARRIORS WITH NONE OF YOUR CHI LEFT?
NOT AT ALL.
THE SOLDIERS YOU WERE FIGHTING JUST NOW, WERE THEY RED DRAGON KINGS?
I GOT CARELESS AND FELL FOR THEIR TRAP.
DO YOU KNOW ANYTHING ABOUT THE RED DRAGON KINGS?

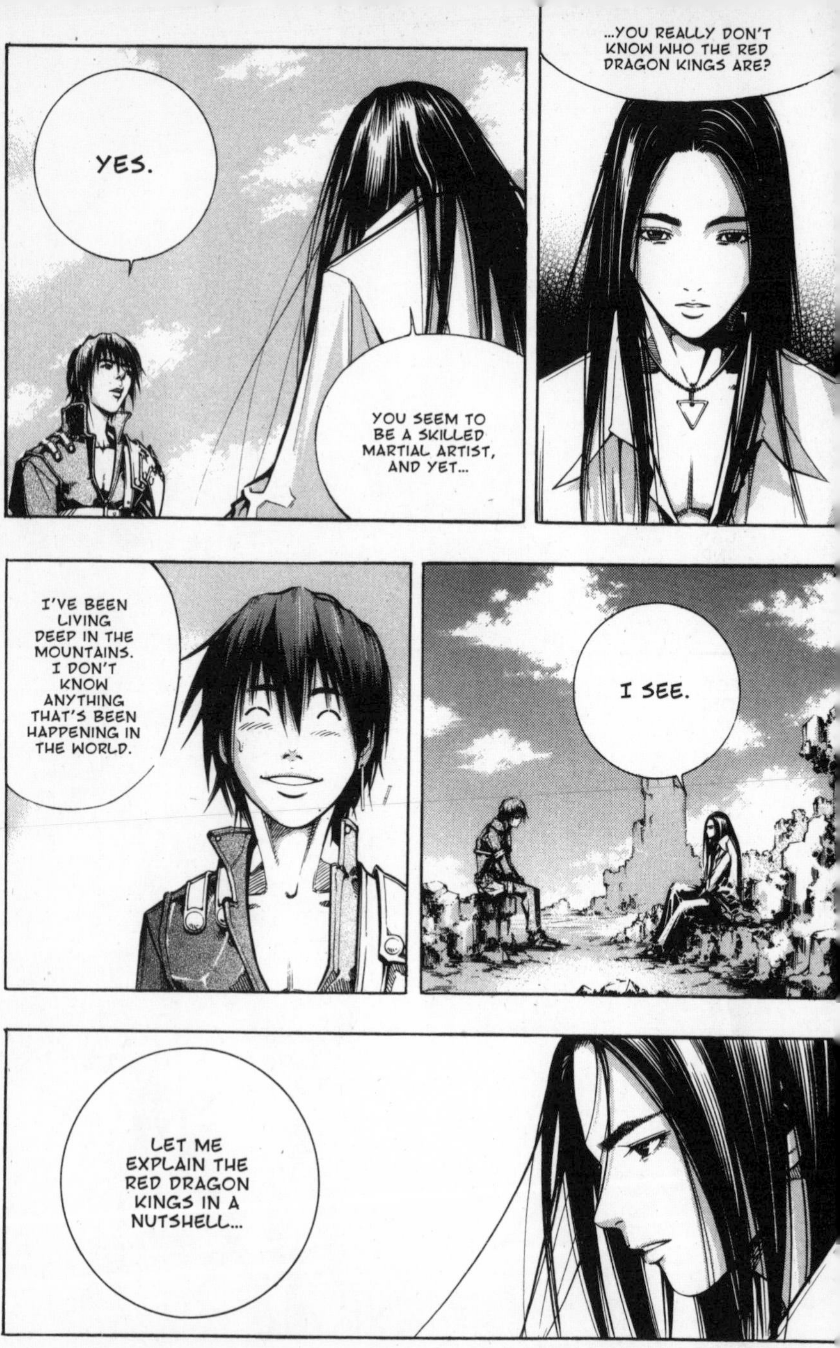
YES.
YOU SEEM TO BE A SKILLED MARTIAL ARTIST, AND YET...
...YOU REALLY DON'T KNOW WHO THE RED DRAGON KINGS ARE?
I'VE BEEN LIVING DEEP IN THE MOUNTAINS. I DON'T KNOW ANYTHING THAT'S BEEN HAPPENING IN THE WORLD.
I SEE.
LET ME EXPLAIN THE RED DRAGON KINGS IN A NUTSHELL...

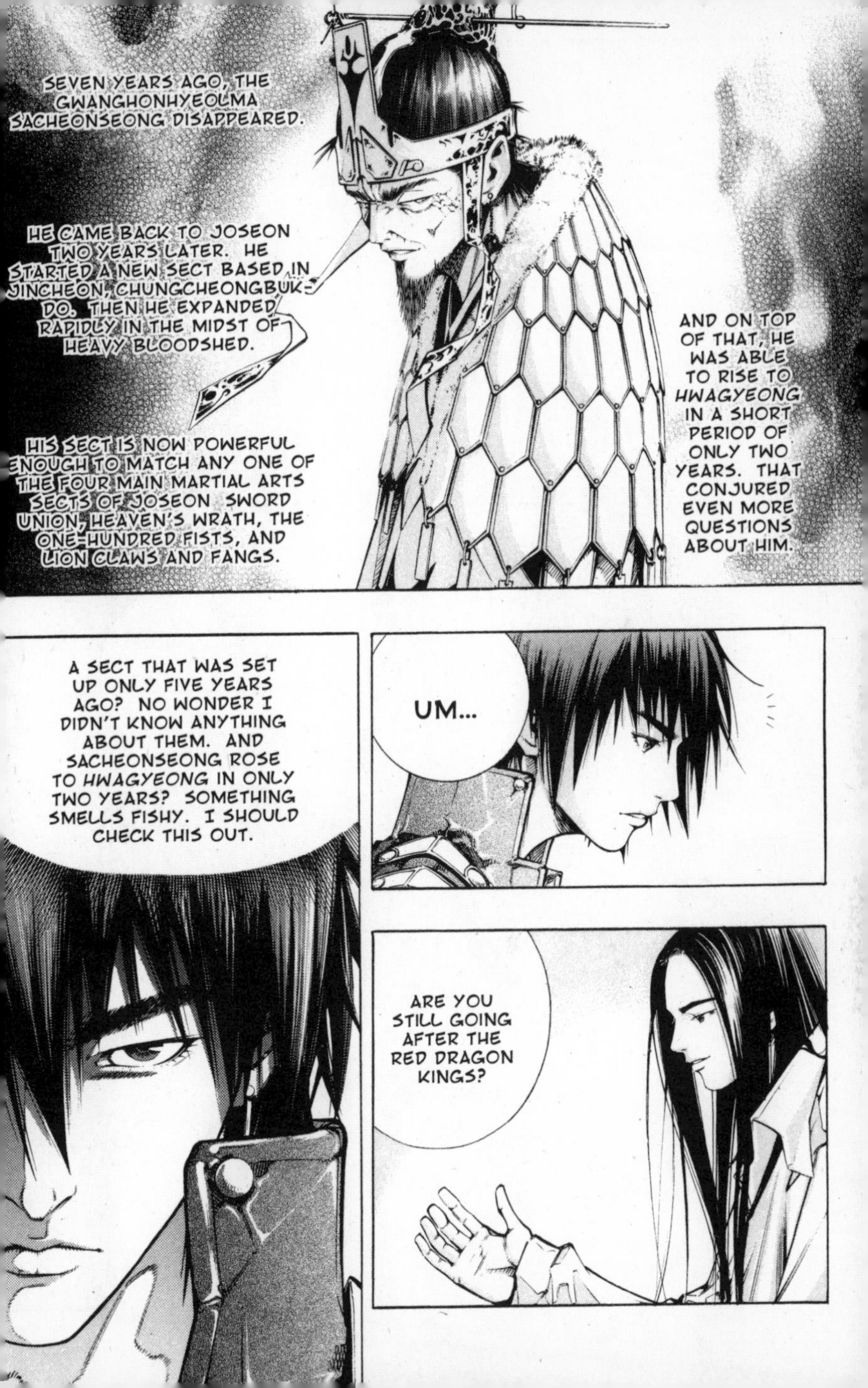
SEVEN YEARS AGO, THE GWANGHONHYEOLMA SACHEONSEONG DISAPPEARED.
HE CAME BACK TO JOSEON TWO YEARS LATER. HE STARTED A NEW SECT BASED IN JINCHEON, CHUNGCHEONGBUK-DO. THEN HE EXPANDED RAPIDLY IN THE MIDST OF HEAVY BLOODSHED.
HIS SECT IS NOW POWERFUL ENOUGH TO MATCH ANY ONE OF THE FOUR MAIN MARTIAL ARTS SECTS OF JOSEON SWORD UNION, HEAVEN'S WRATH, THE ONE-HUNDRED FISTS, AND LION CLAWS AND FANGS.
AND ON TOP OF THAT, HE WAS ABLE TO RISE TO HWAGYEONG IN A SHORT PERIOD OF ONLY TWO YEARS. THAT CONJURED EVEN MORE QUESTIONS ABOUT HIM.
A SECT THAT WAS SET UP ONLY FIVE YEARS AGO? NO WONDER I DIDN'T KNOW ANYTHING ABOUT THEM. AND SACHEONSEONG ROSE TO HWAGYEONG IN ONLY TWO YEARS? SOMETHING SMELLS FISHY. I SHOULD CHECK THIS OUT.
UM...
ARE YOU STILL GOING AFTER THE RED DRAGON KINGS?

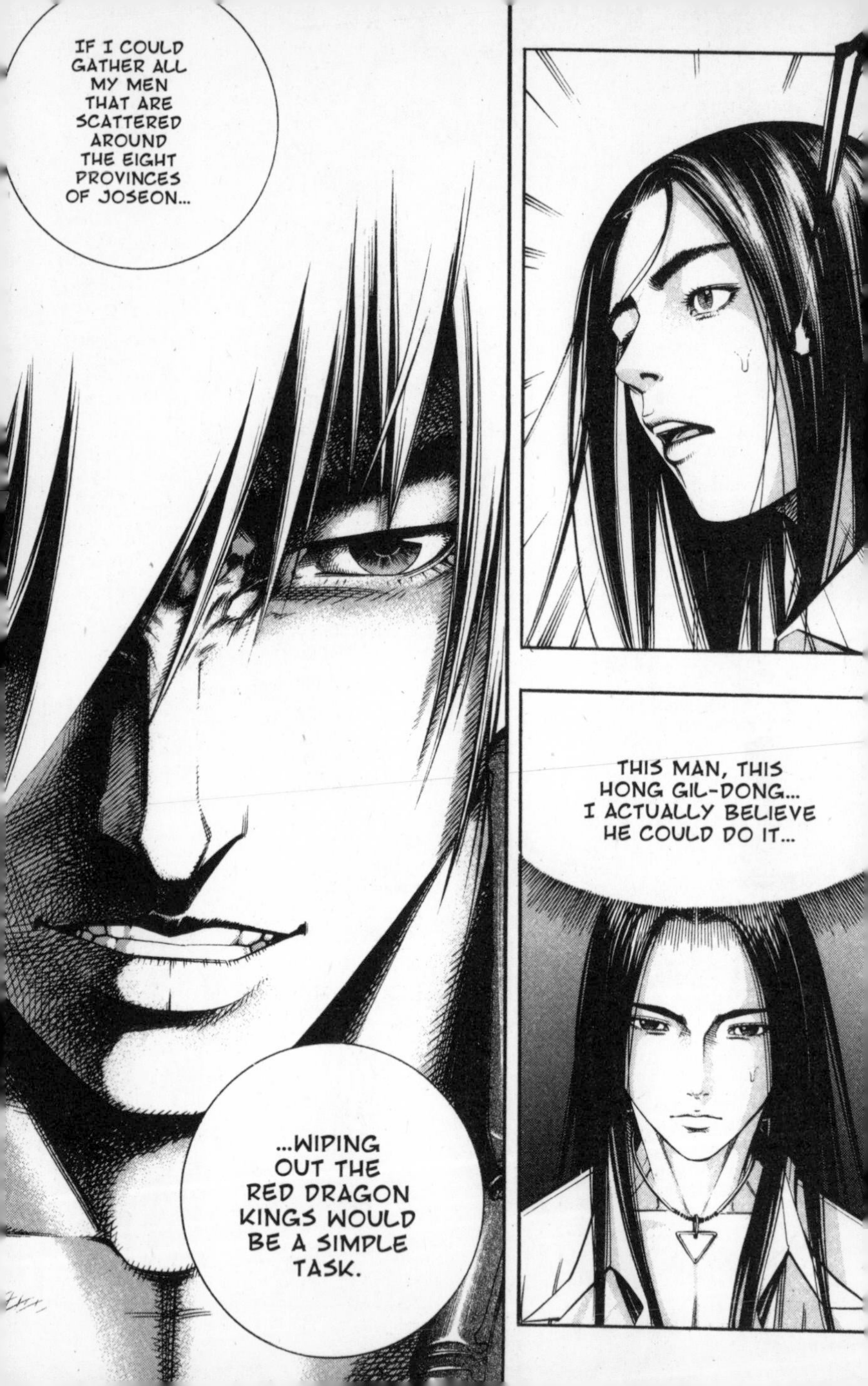
IF I COULD GATHER ALL MY MEN THAT ARE SCATTERED AROUND THE EIGHT PROVINCES OF JOSEON...
...WIPING OUT THE RED DRAGON KINGS WOULD BE A SIMPLE TASK.
THIS MAN, THIS HONG GIL-DONG... I ACTUALLY BELIEVE HE COULD DO IT...

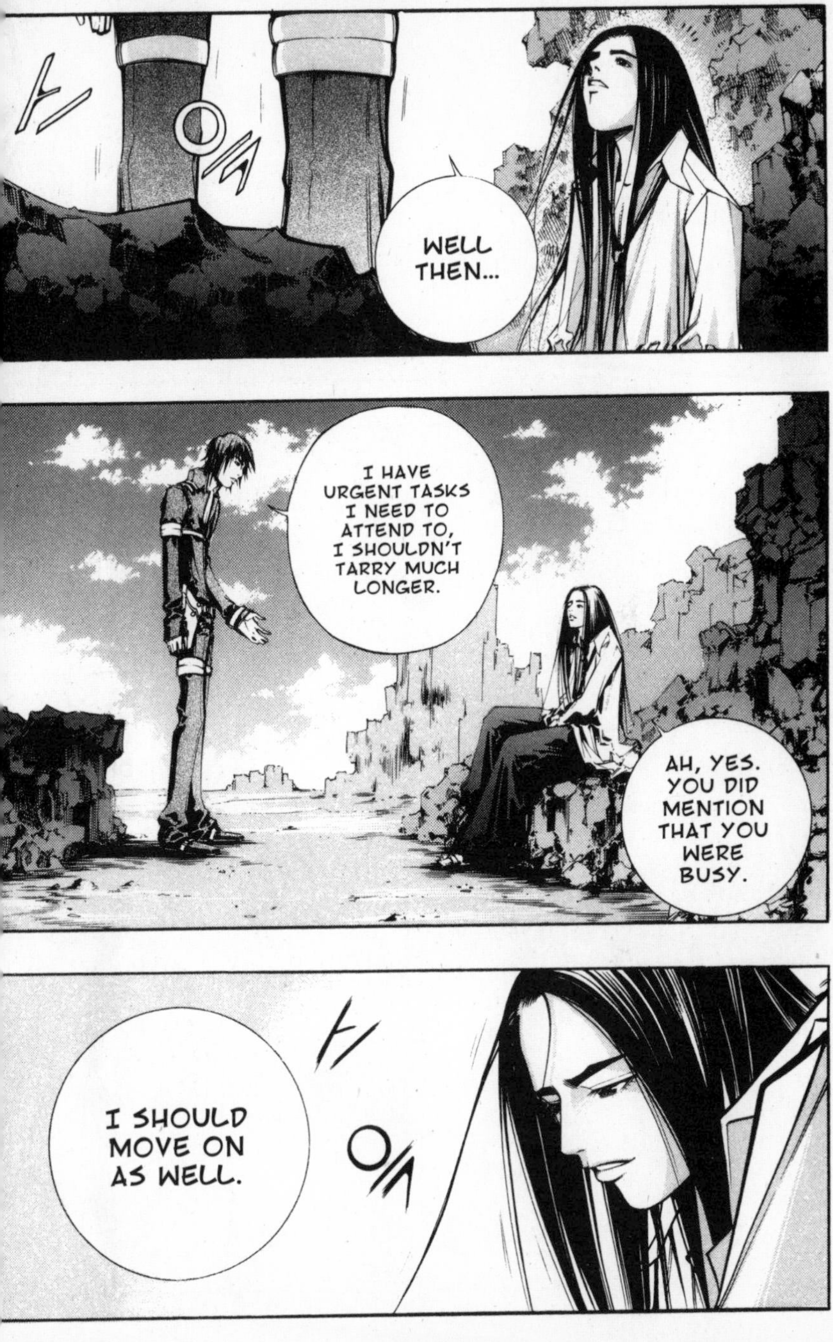
WELL THEN...
I HAVE URGENT TASKS I NEED TO ATTEND TO, I SHOULDN'T TARRY MUCH LONGER.
AH, YES. YOU DID MENTION THAT YOU WERE BUSY.
I SHOULD MOVE ON AS WELL.

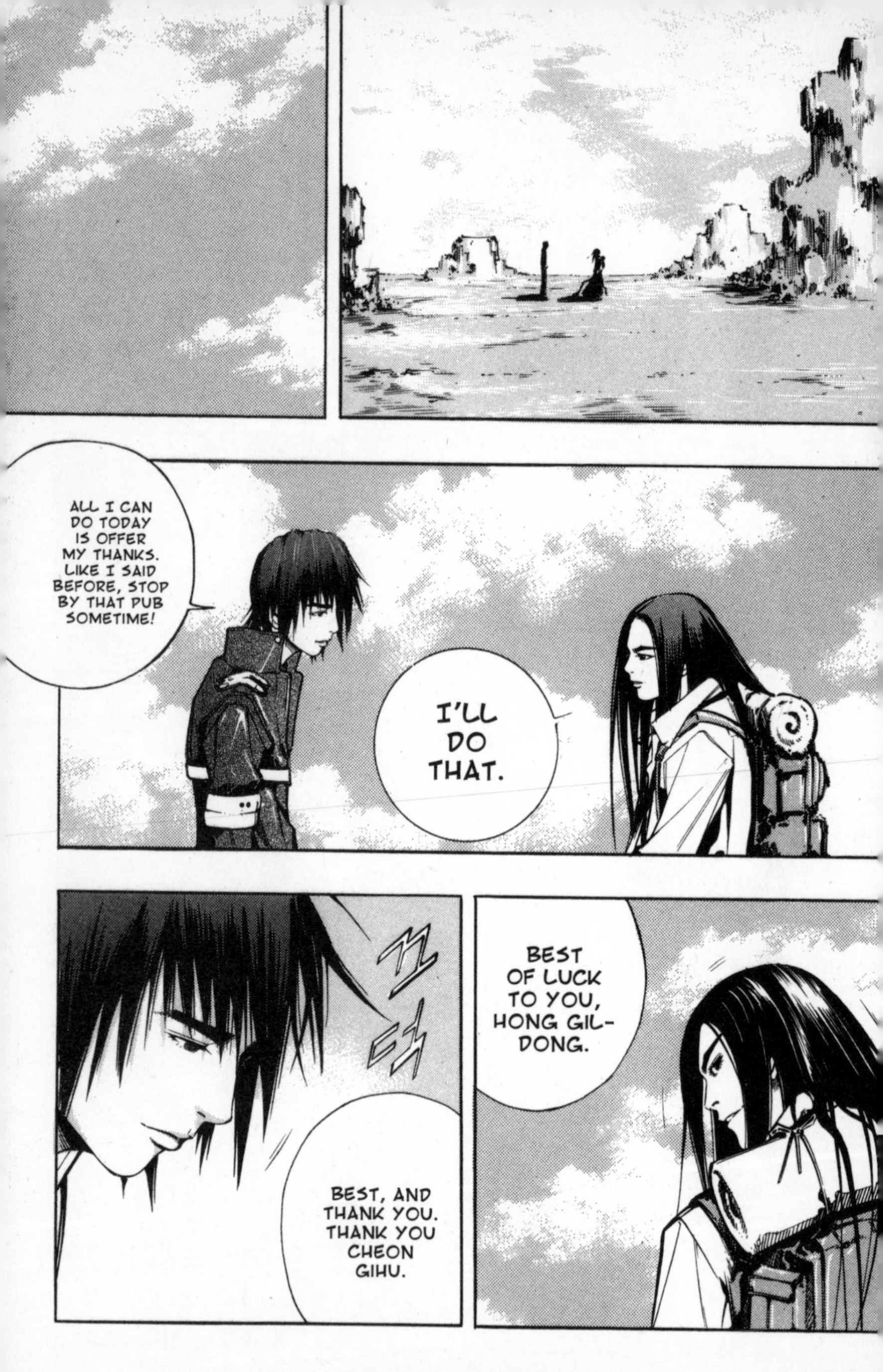
ALL I CAN DO TODAY IS OFFER MY THANKS. LIKE I SAID BEFORE, STOP BY THAT PUB SOMETIME!
I'LL DO THAT.
BEST OF LUCK TO YOU, HONG GIL-DONG.
BEST, AND THANK YOU. THANK YOU CHEON GIHU.

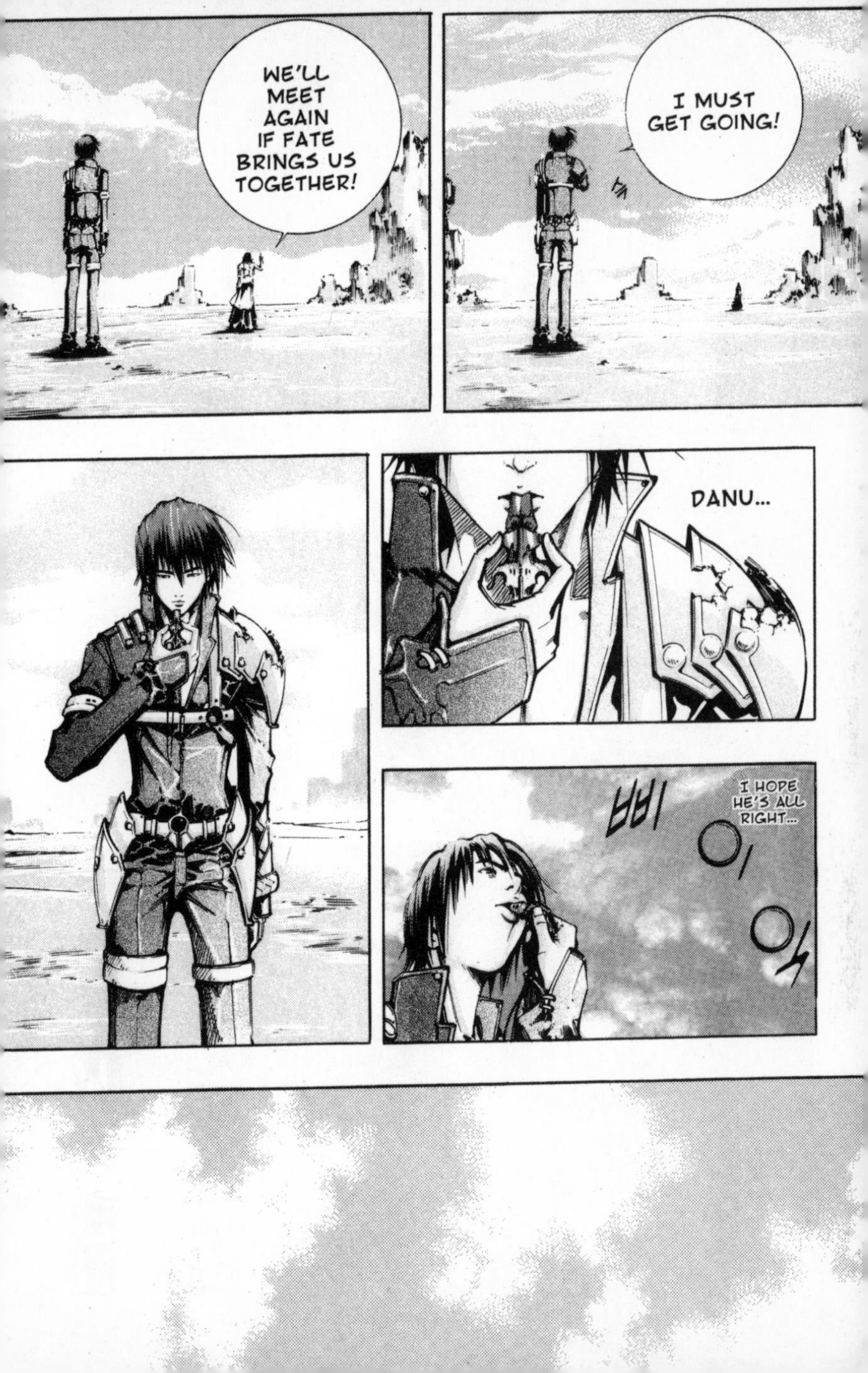
WE'LL MEET AGAIN IF FATE BRINGS US TOGETHER!
I MUST GET GOING!
DANU...
I HOPE HE'S ALL RIGHT...

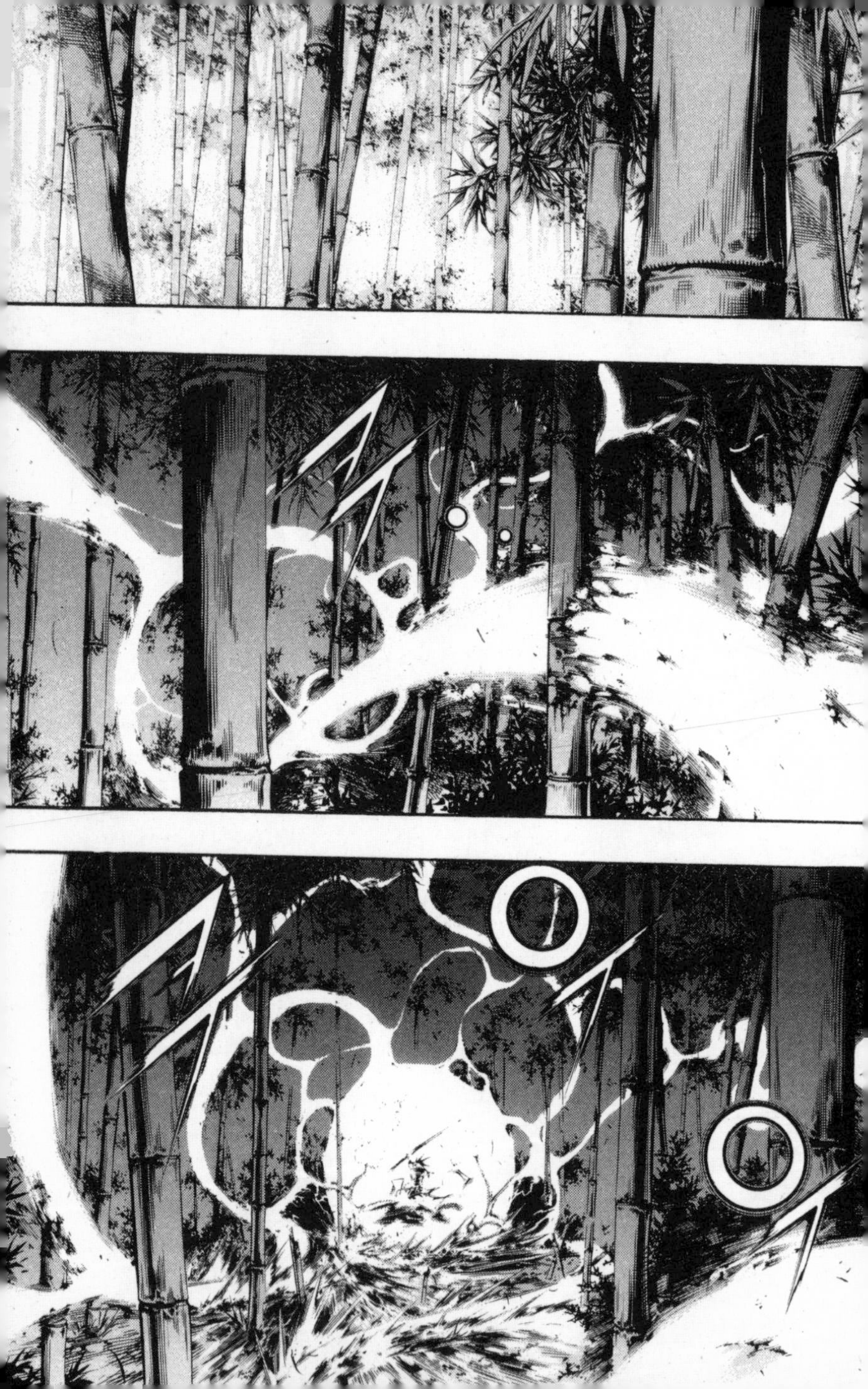

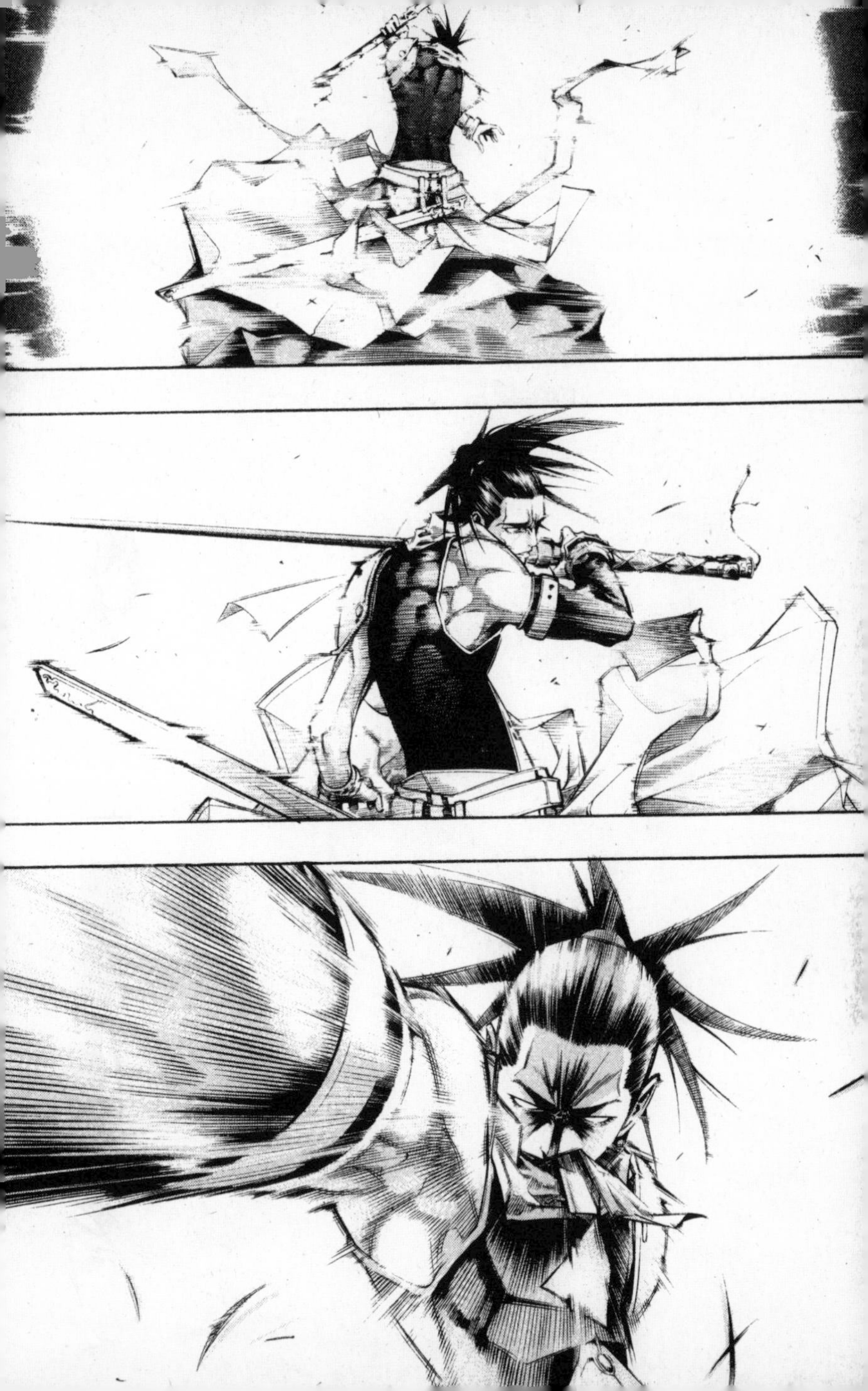

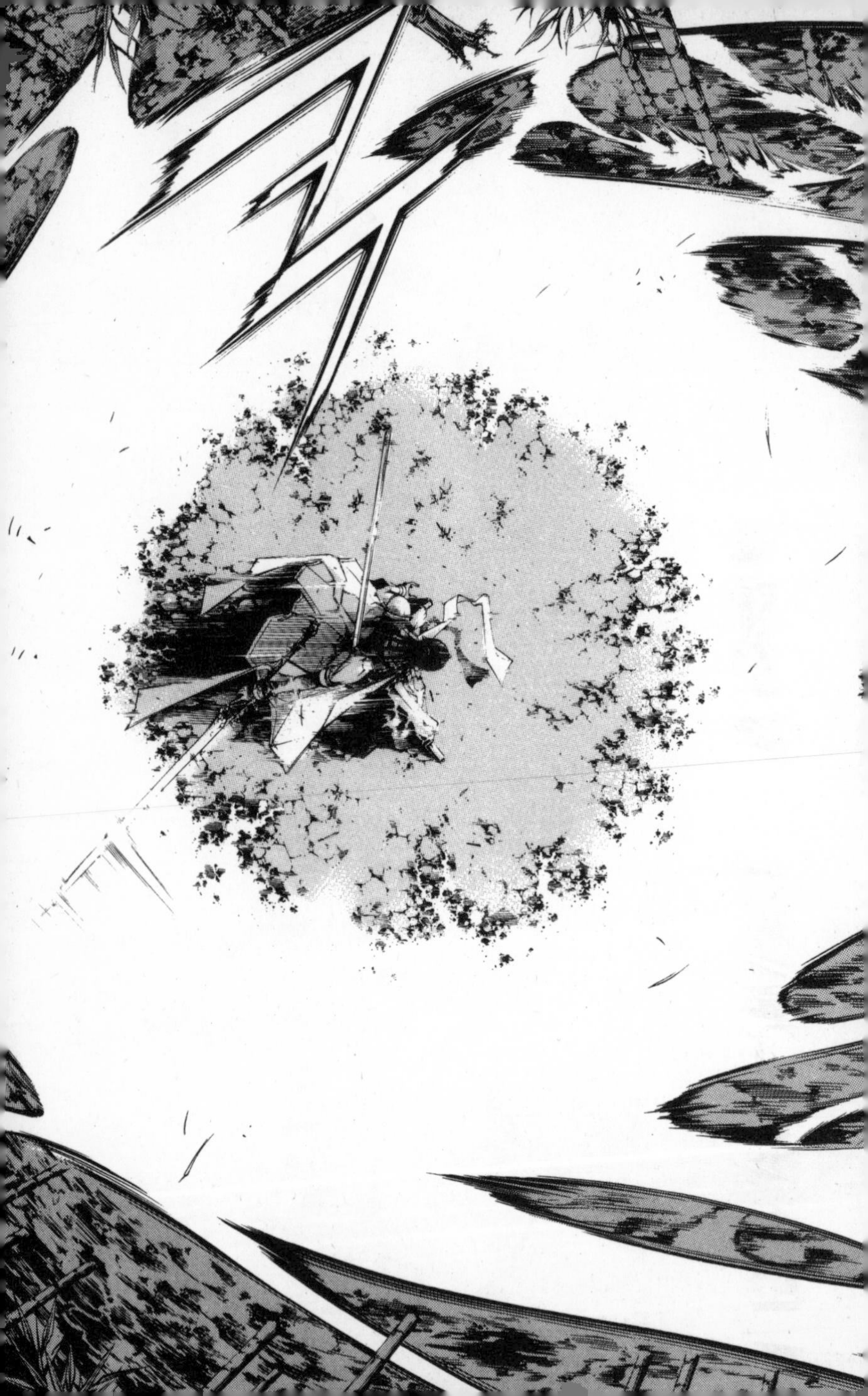

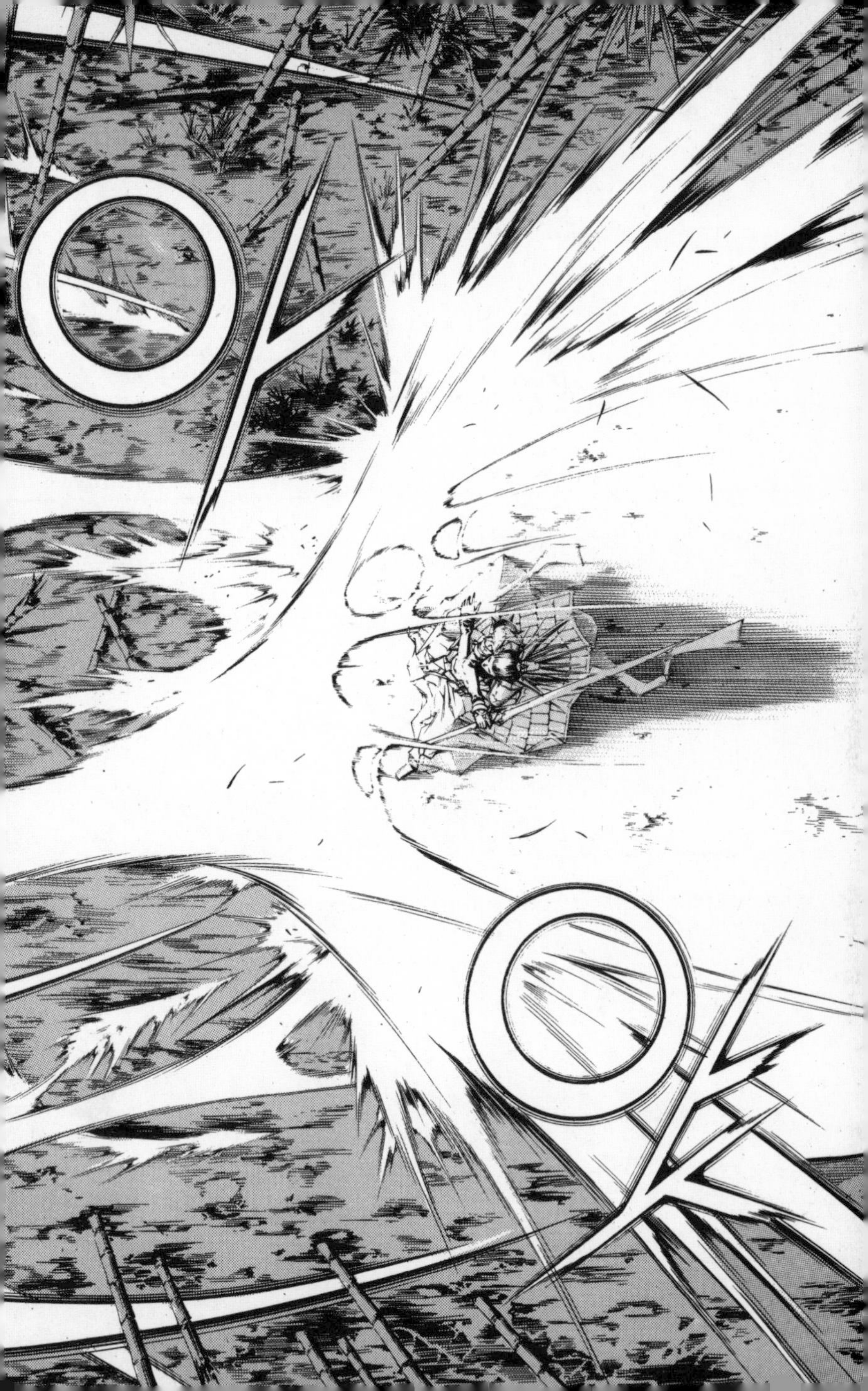

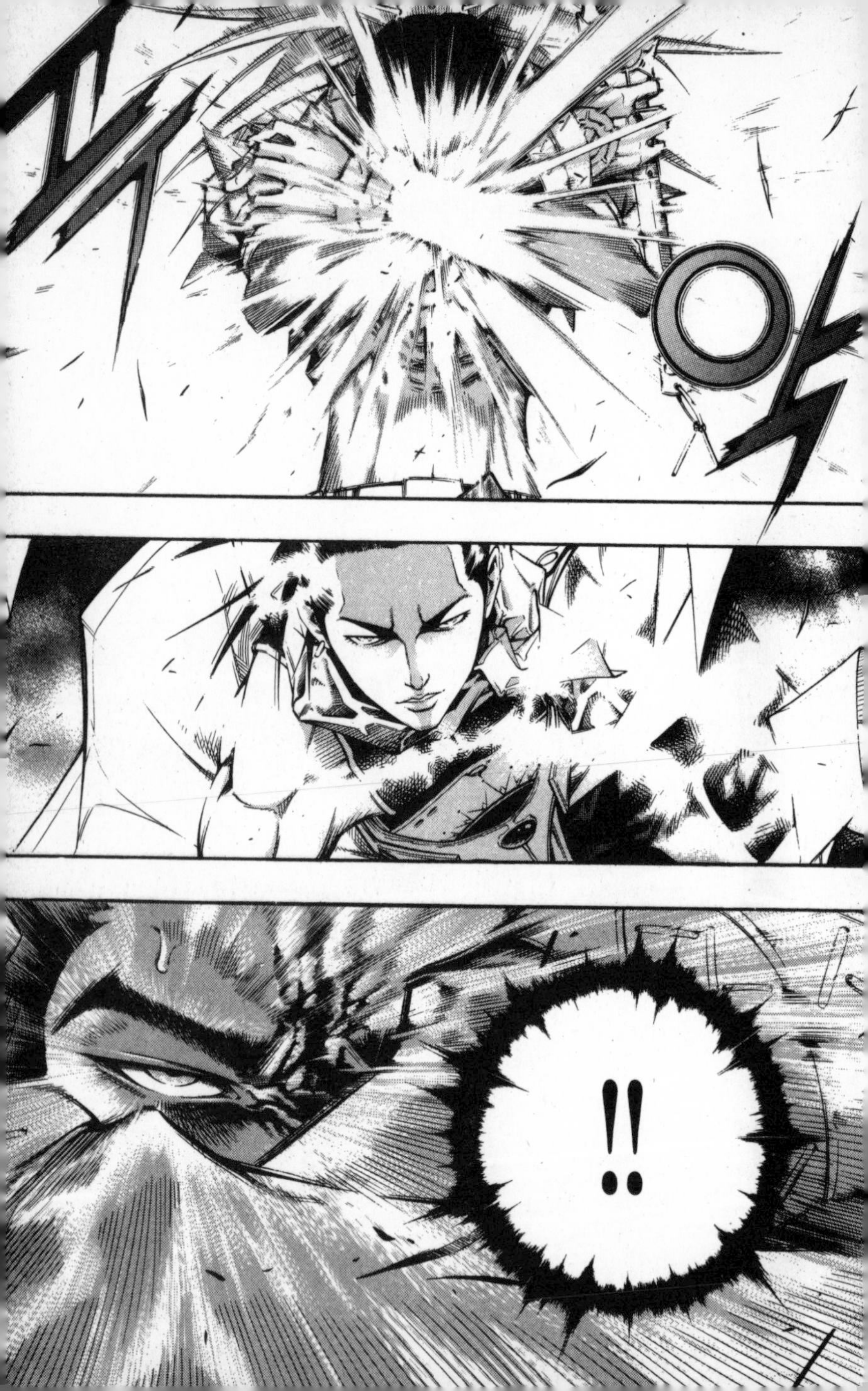
!!

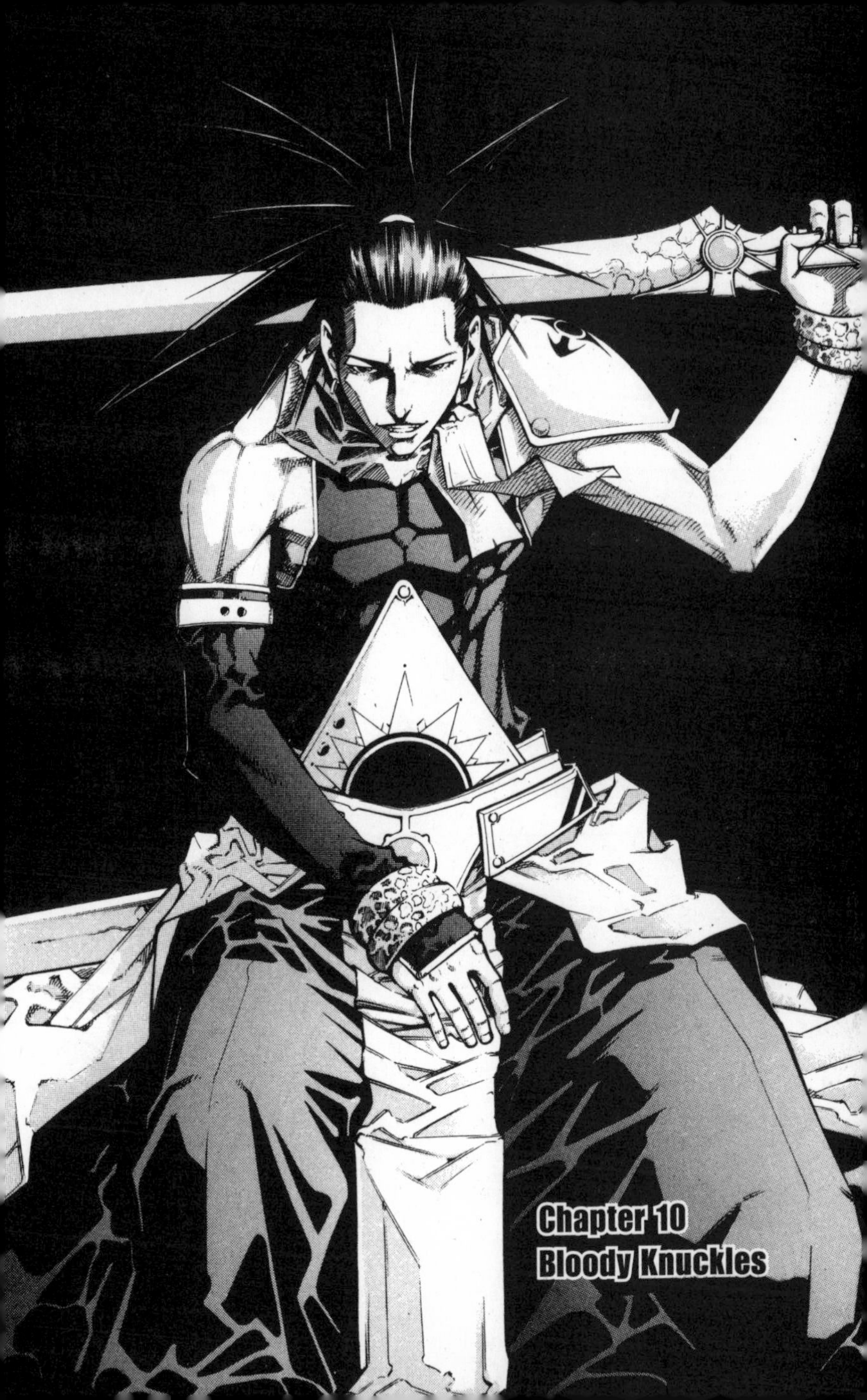
Chapter 10
Bloody Knuckles

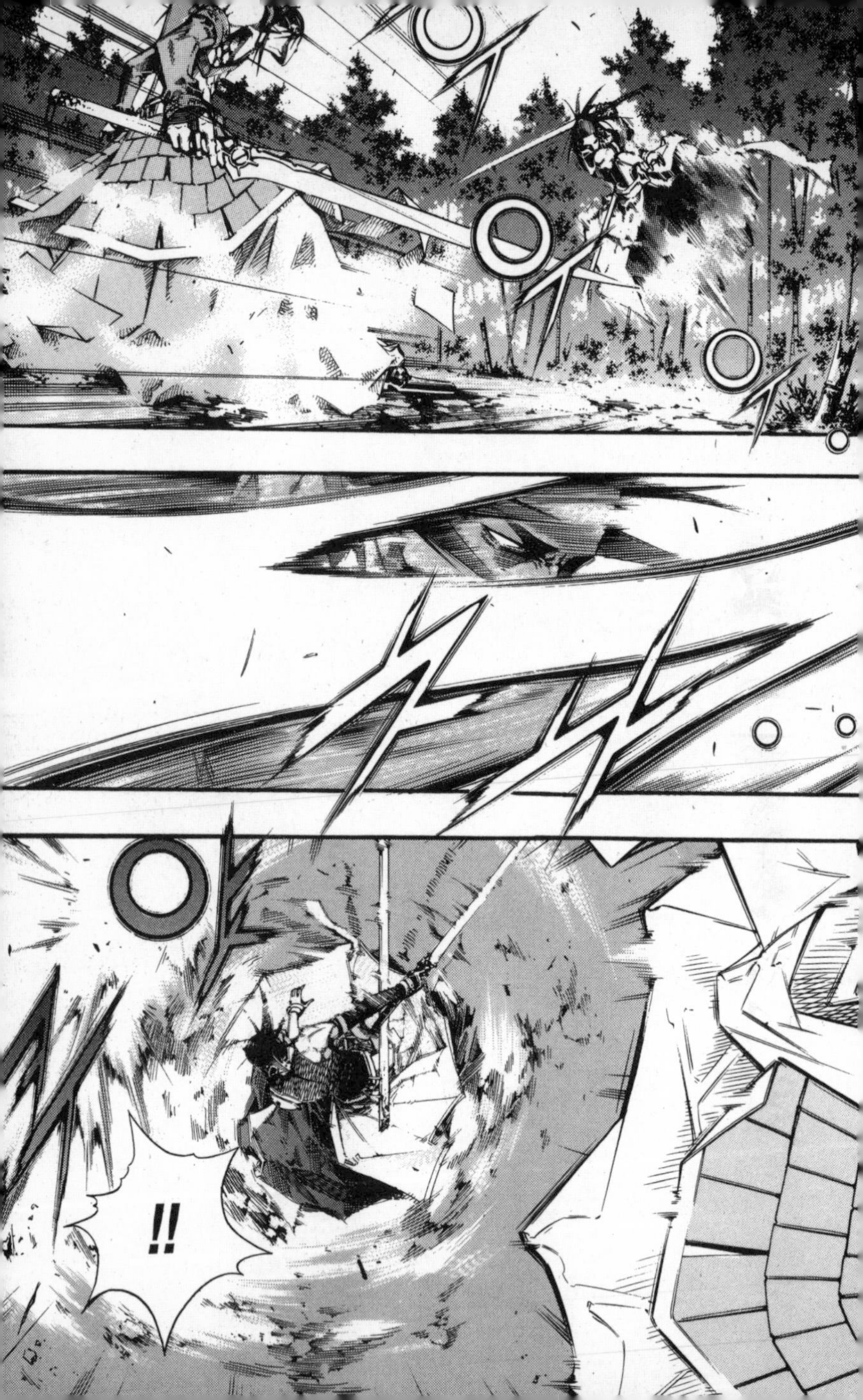
!!

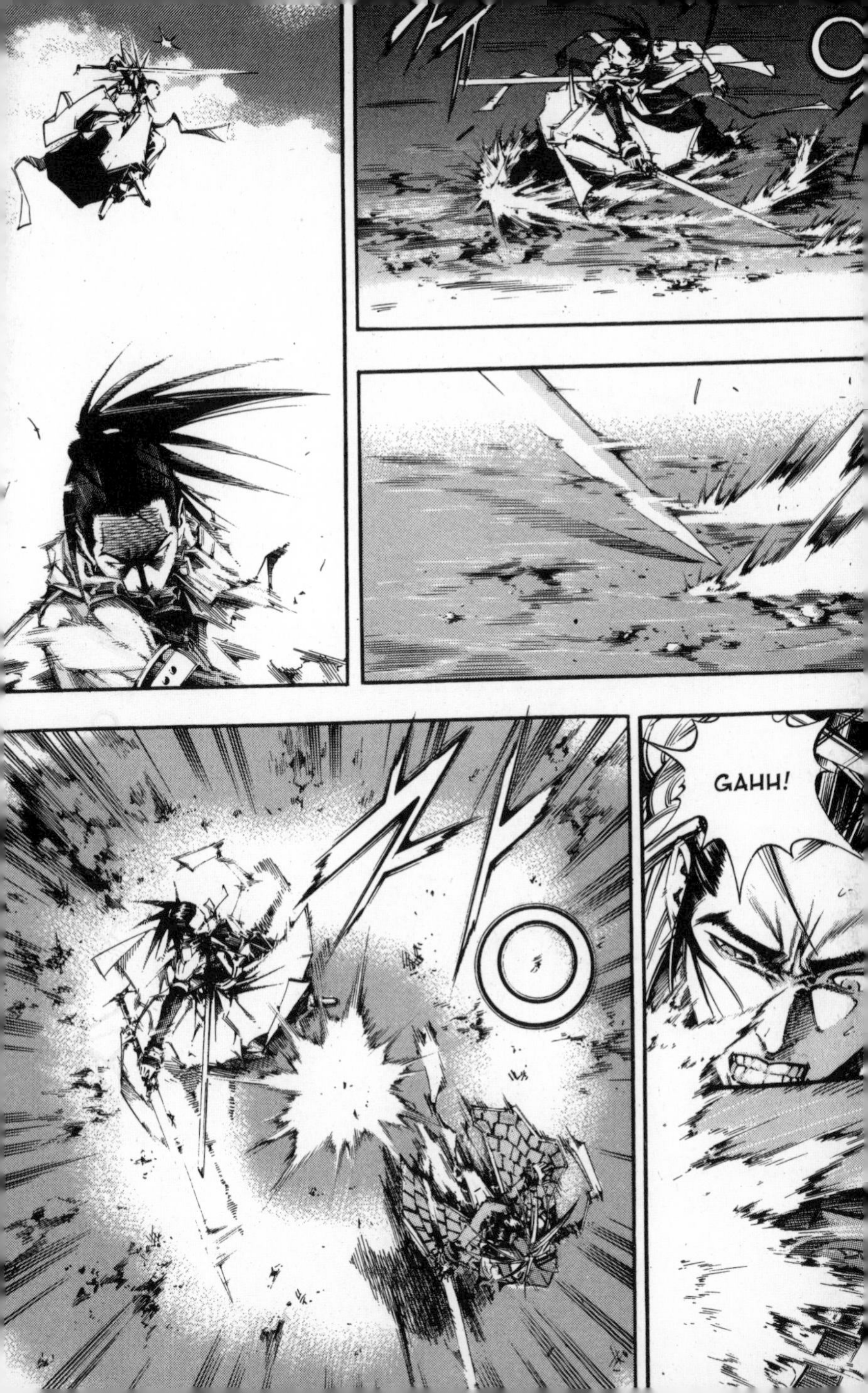
GAHH!

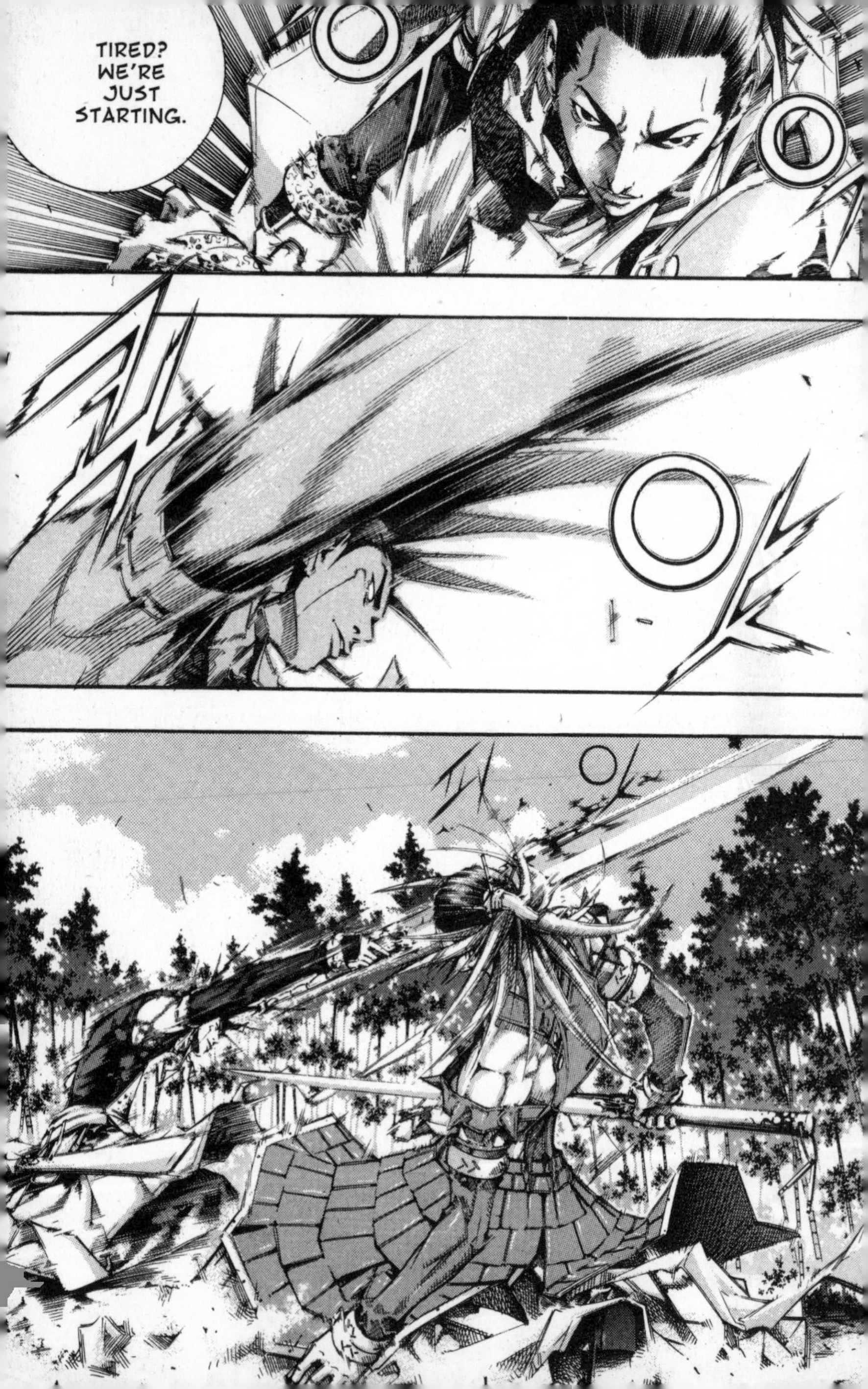
TIRED? WE'RE JUST STARTING.

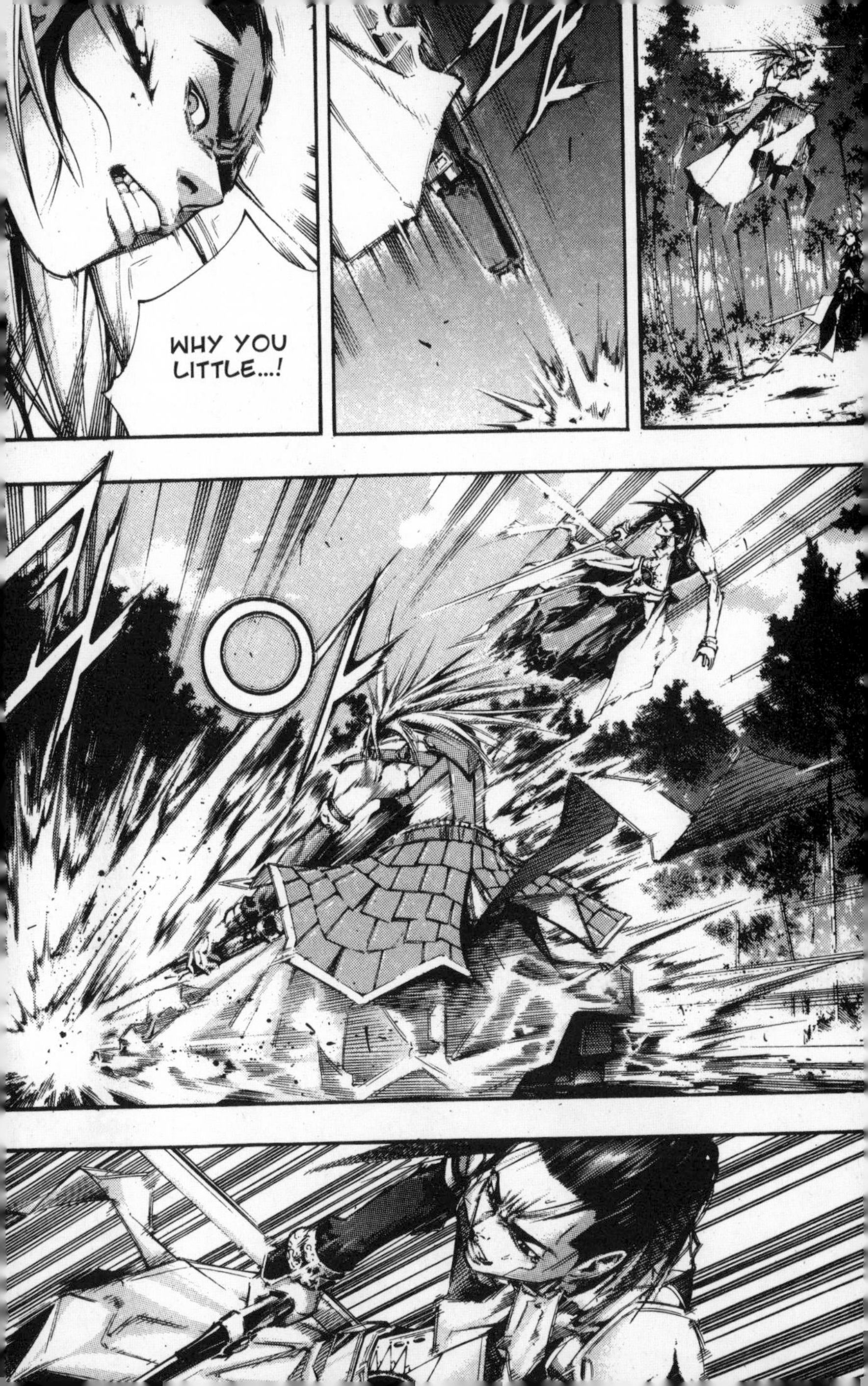
WHY YOU
LITTLE...!

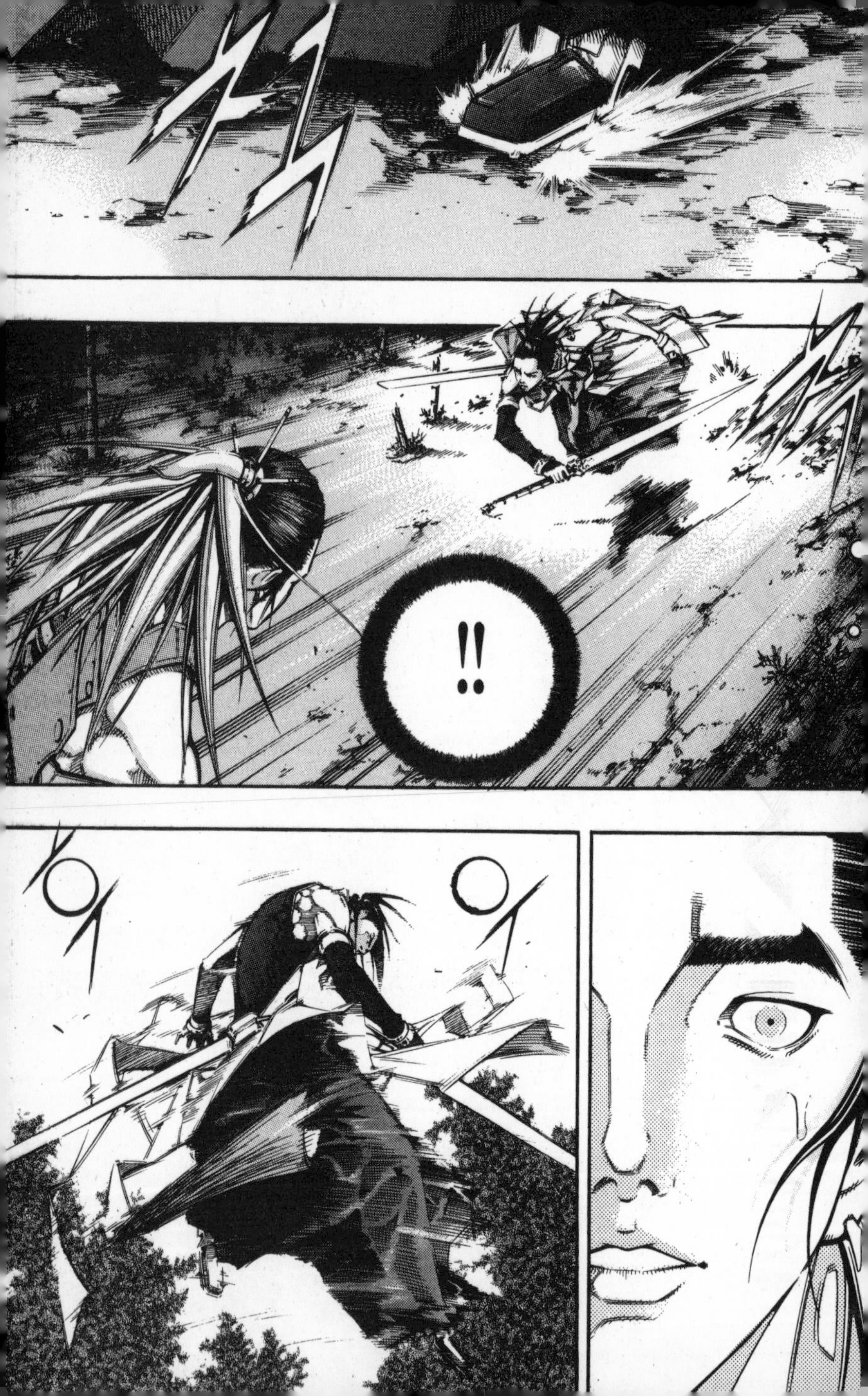
!!

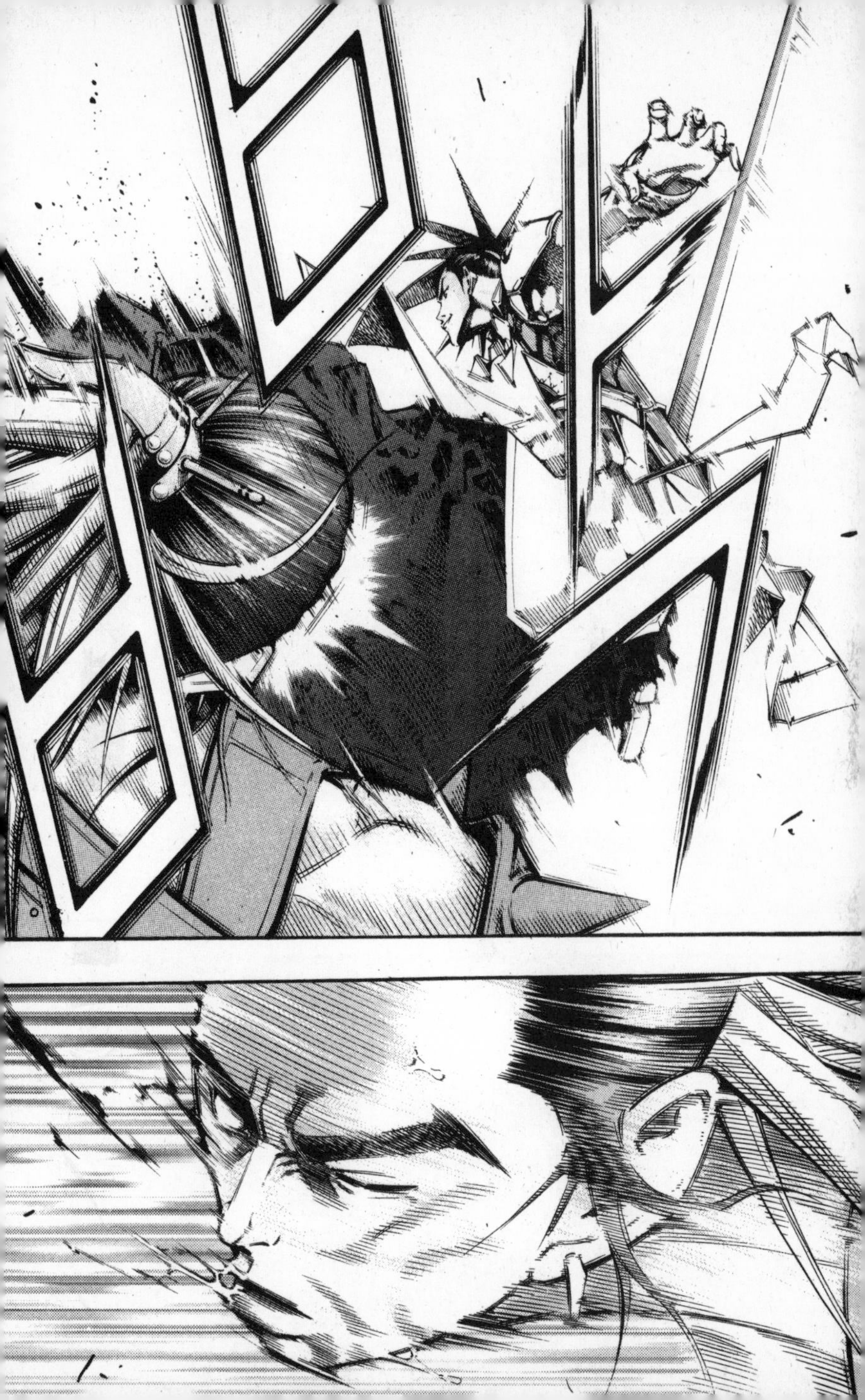

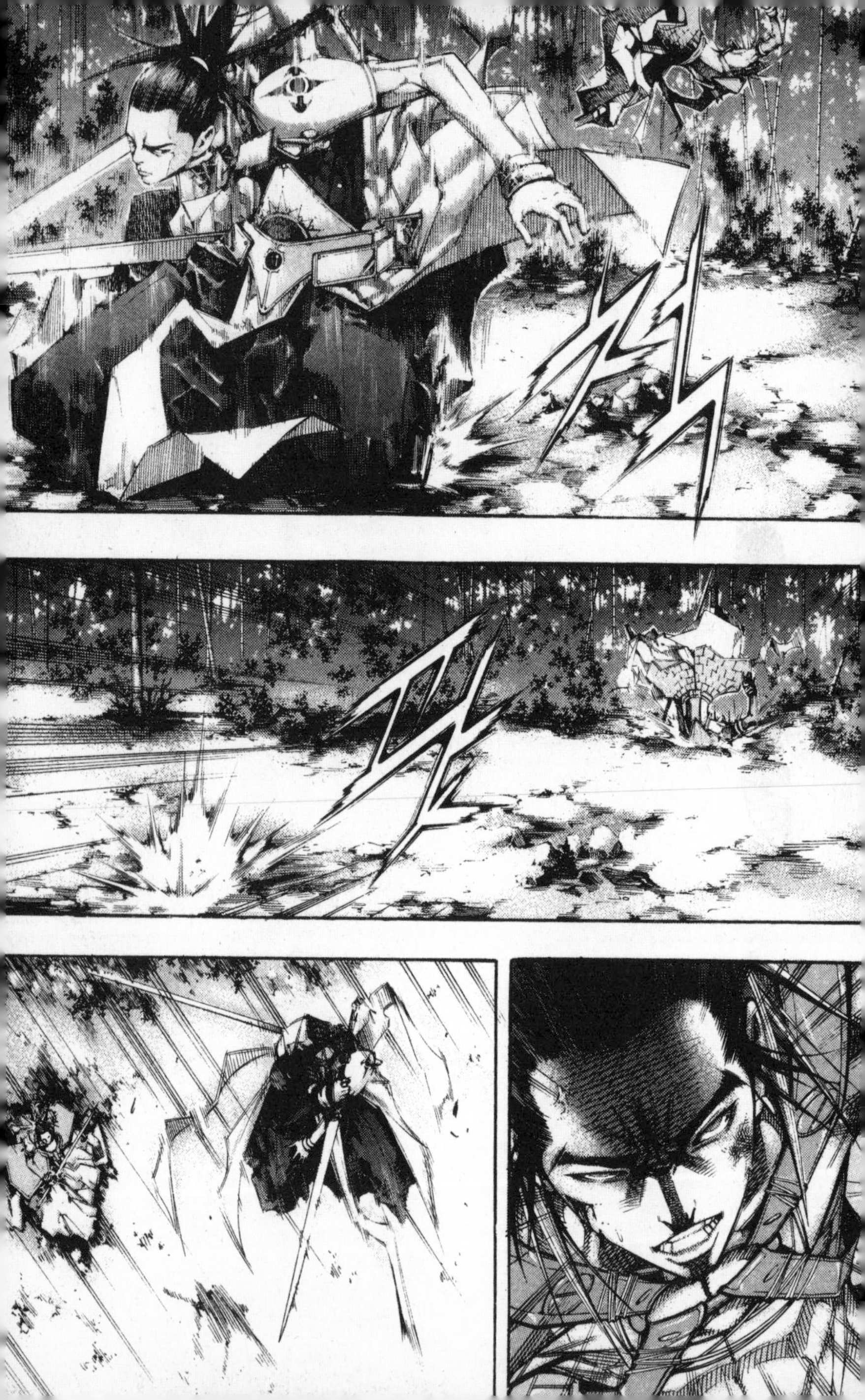

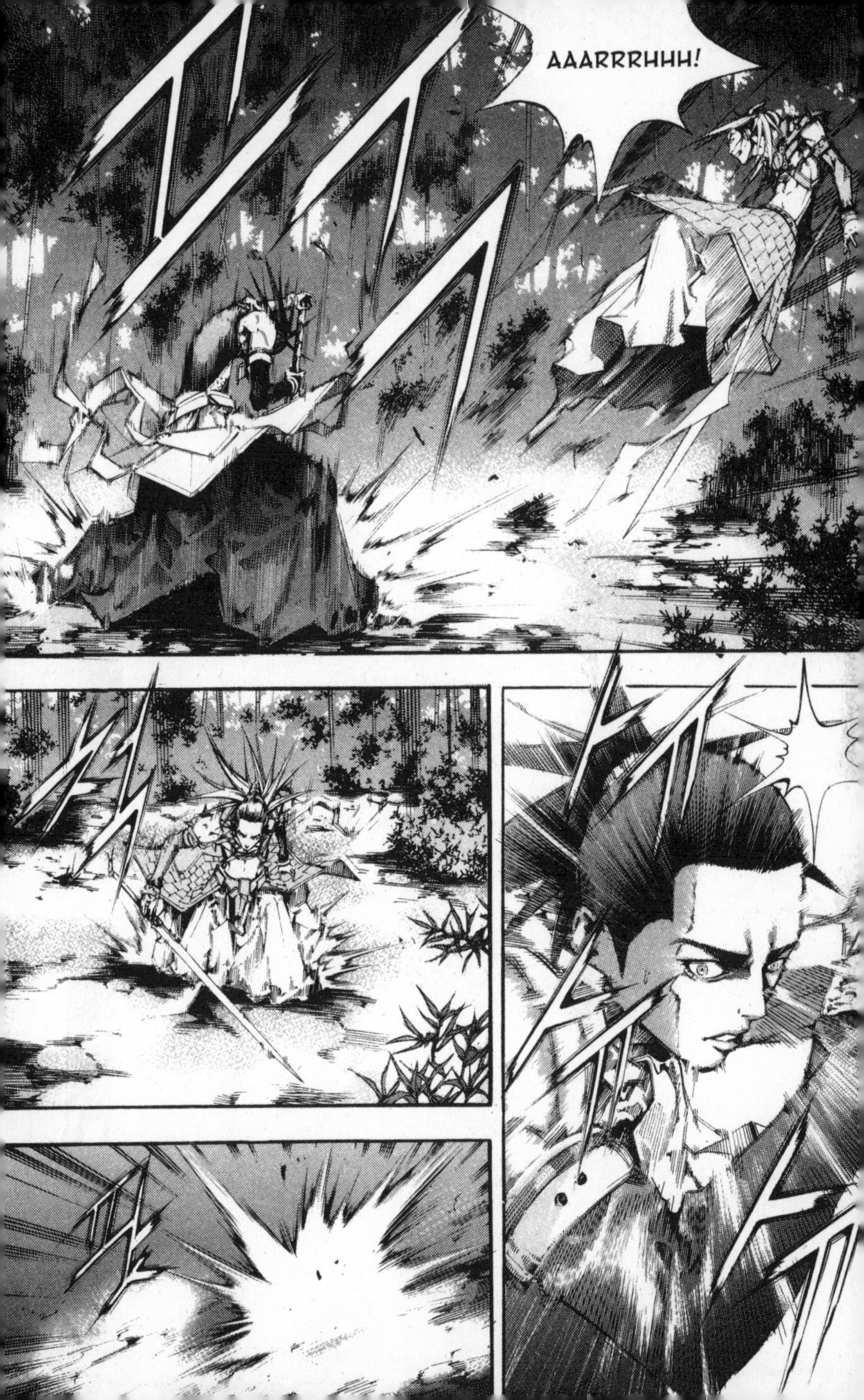
AAARRRHHH!

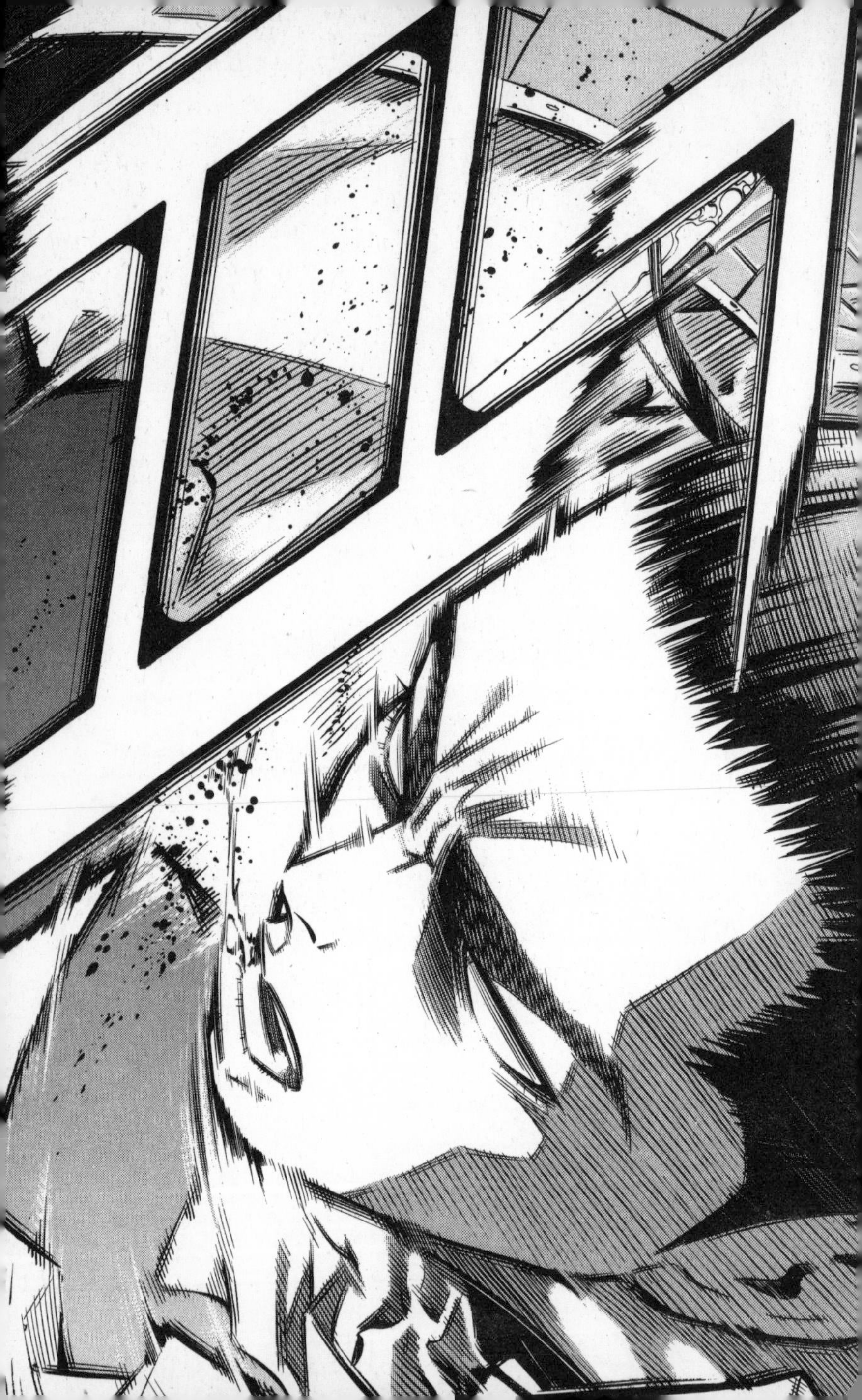

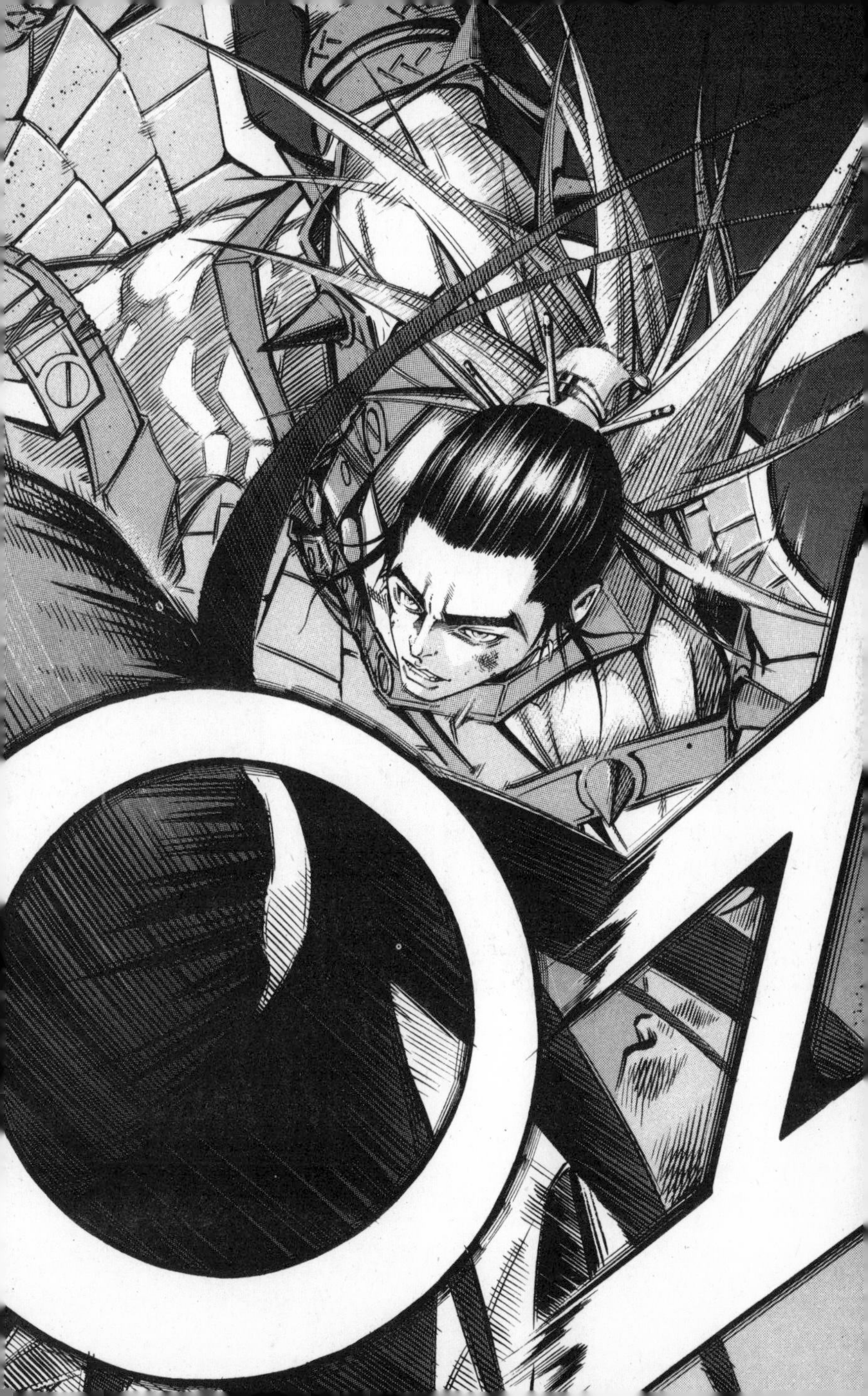

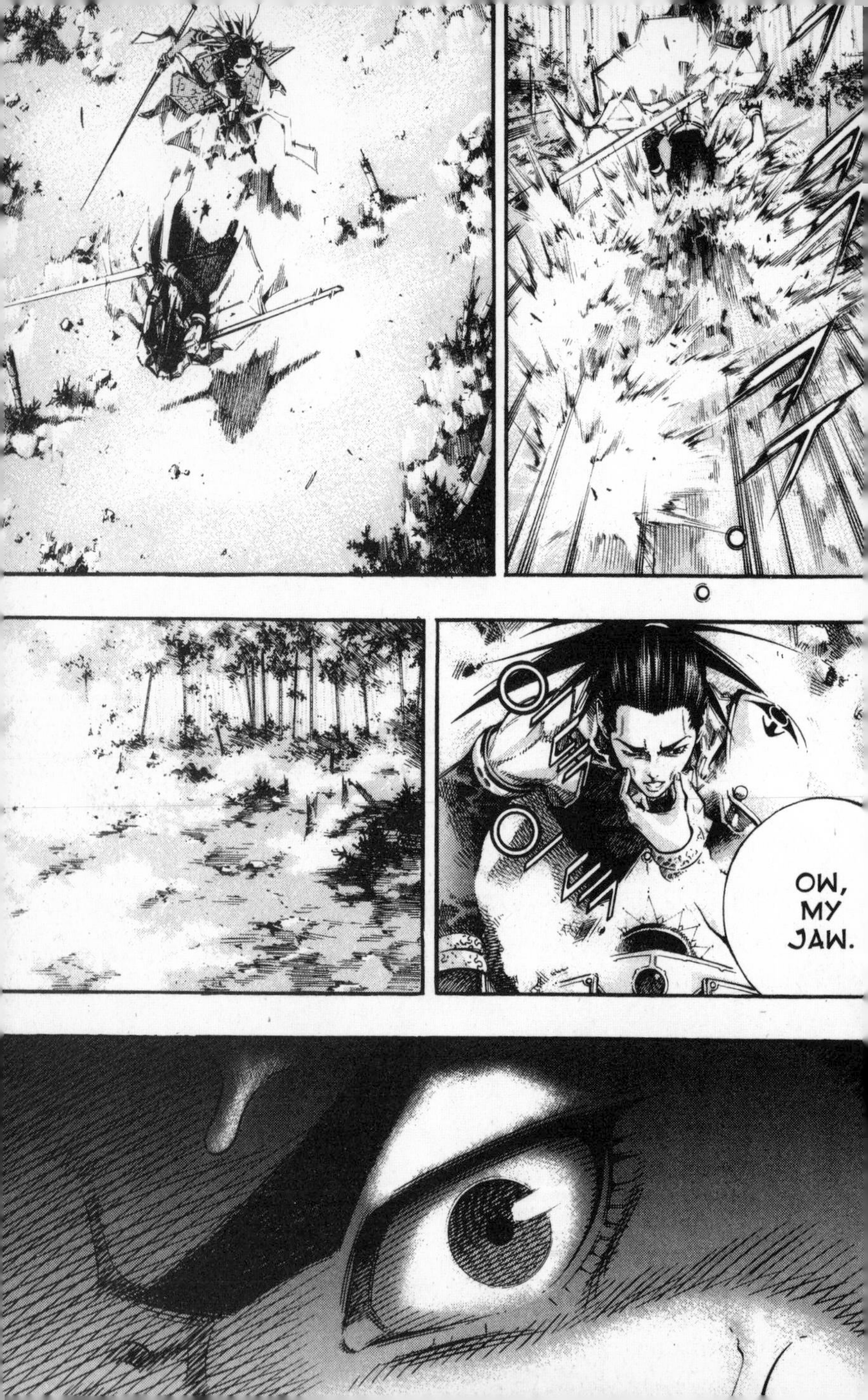
OW, MY JAW.

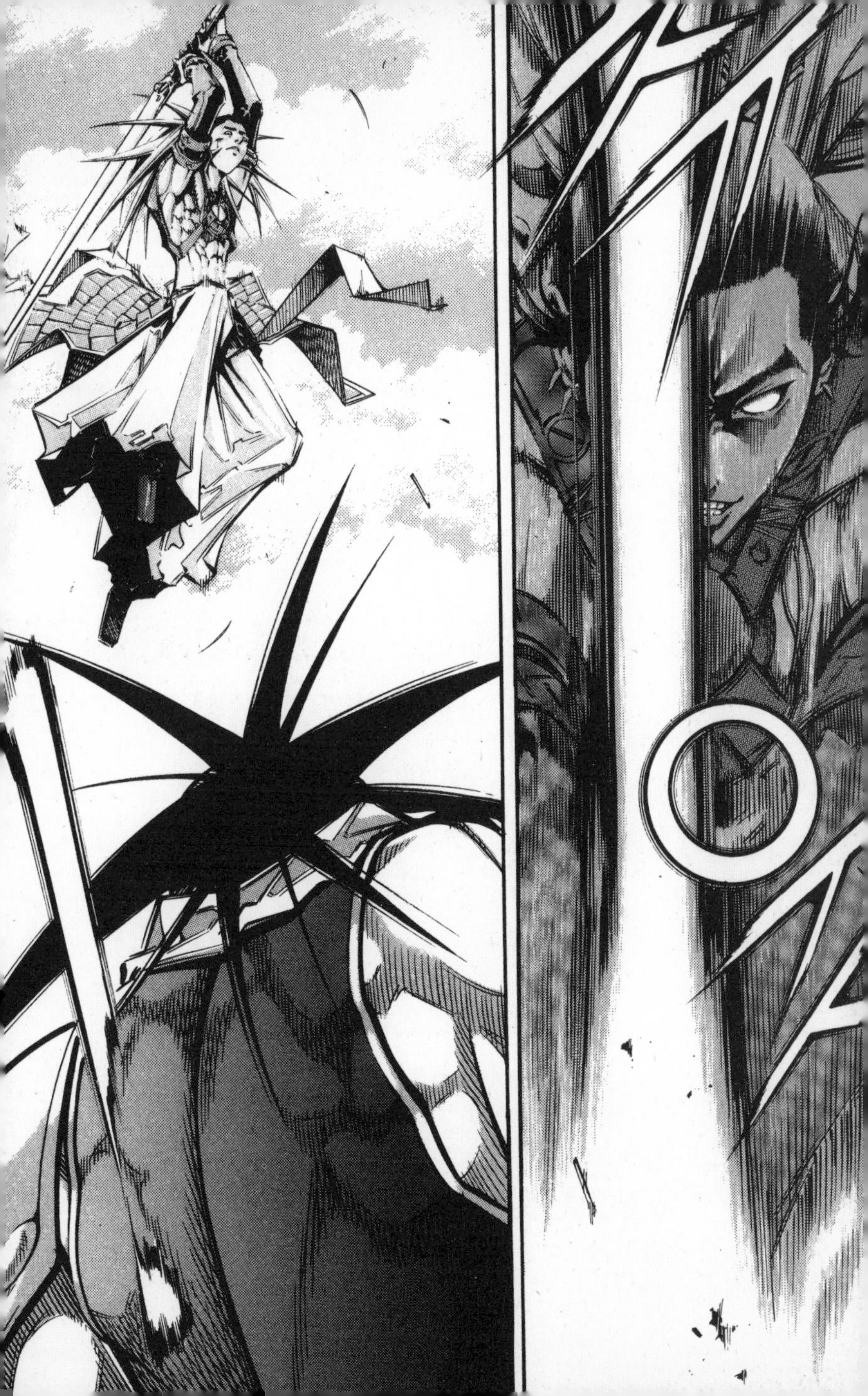

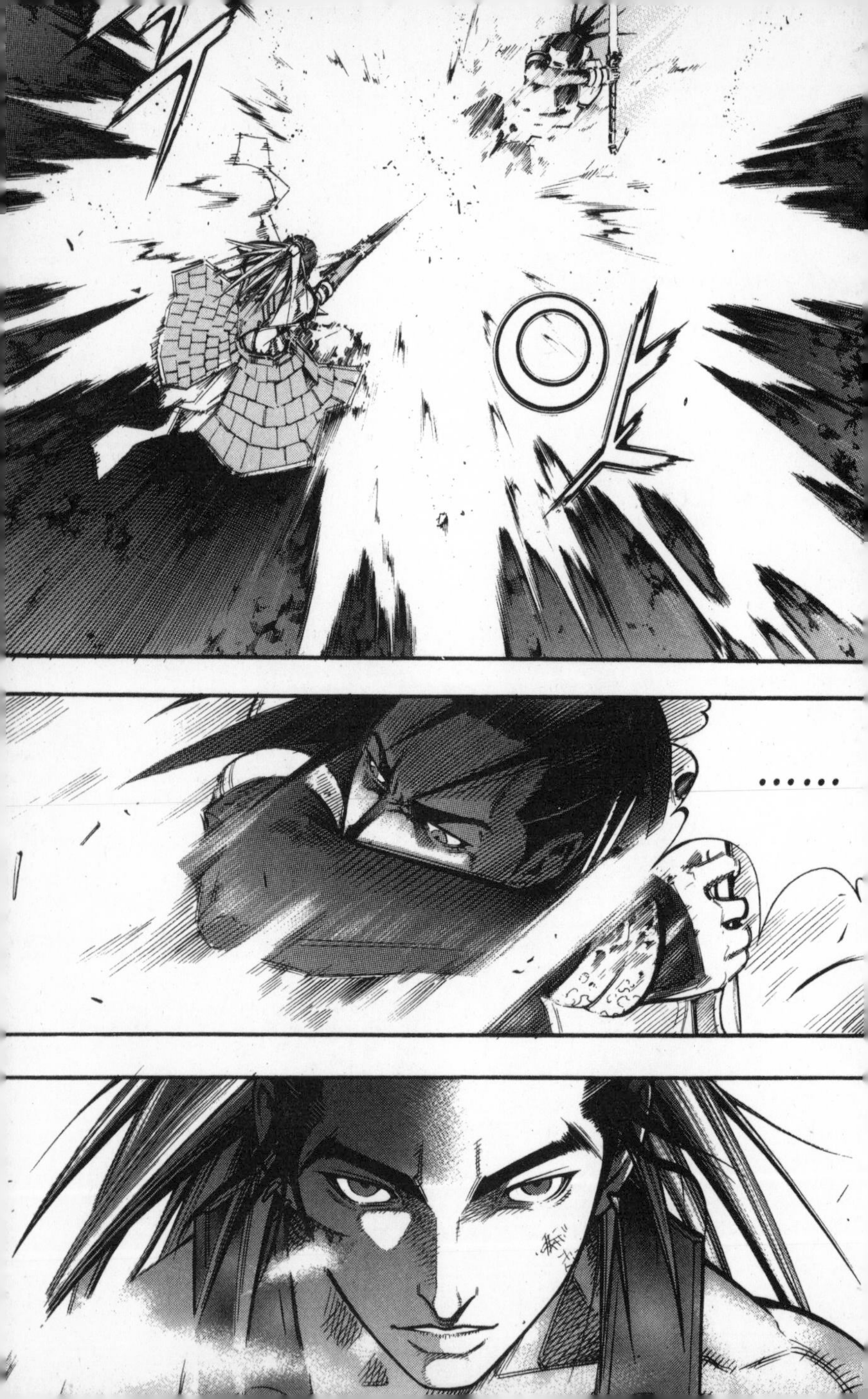
......

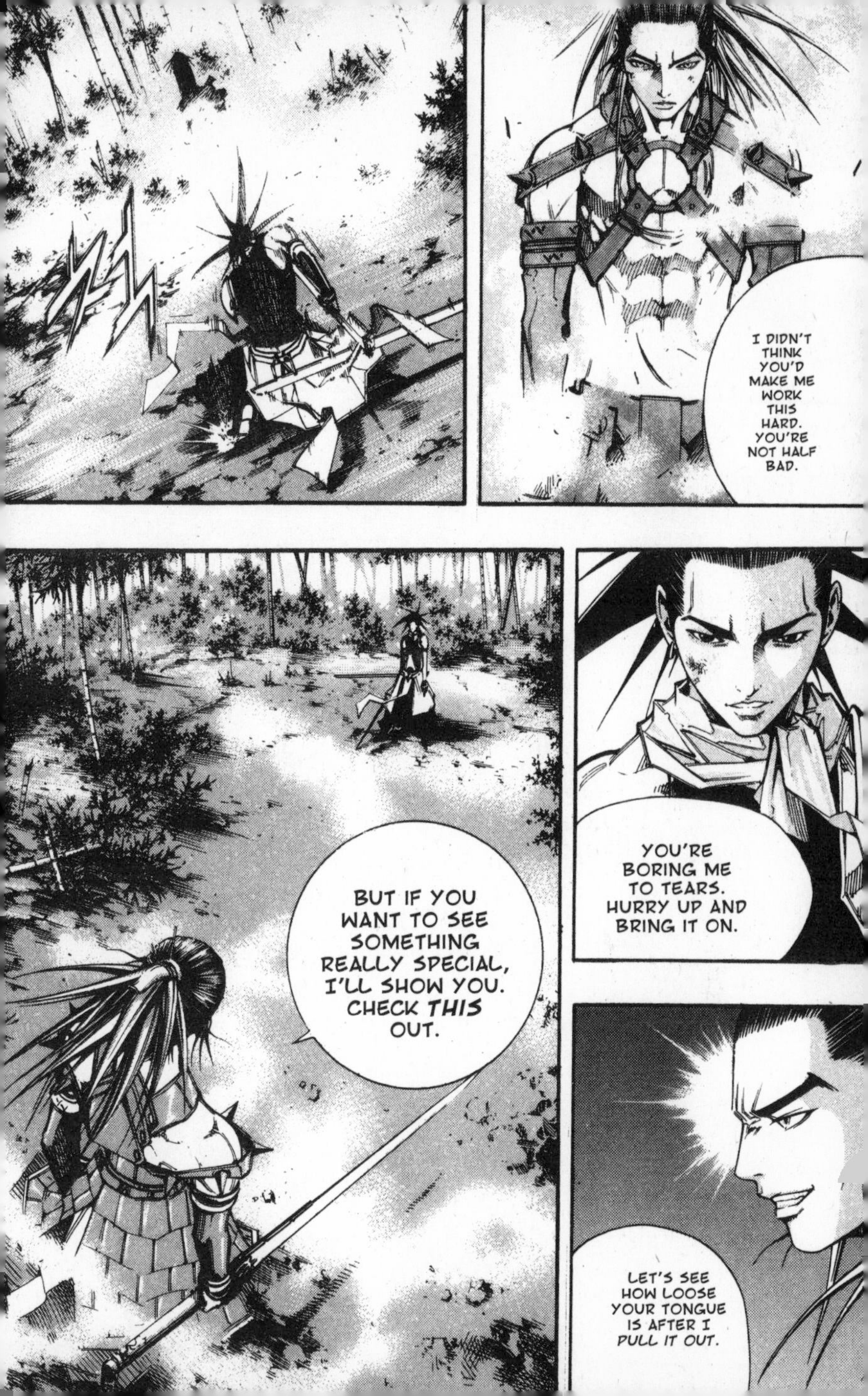
I DIDN'T THINK YOU'D MAKE ME WORK THIS HARD. YOU'RE NOT HALF BAD.
BUT IF YOU WANT TO SEE SOMETHING REALLY SPECIAL, I'LL SHOW YOU. CHECK *THIS* OUT.
YOU'RE BORING ME TO TEARS. HURRY UP AND BRING IT ON.
LET'S SEE HOW LOOSE YOUR TONGUE IS AFTER I PULL IT OUT.

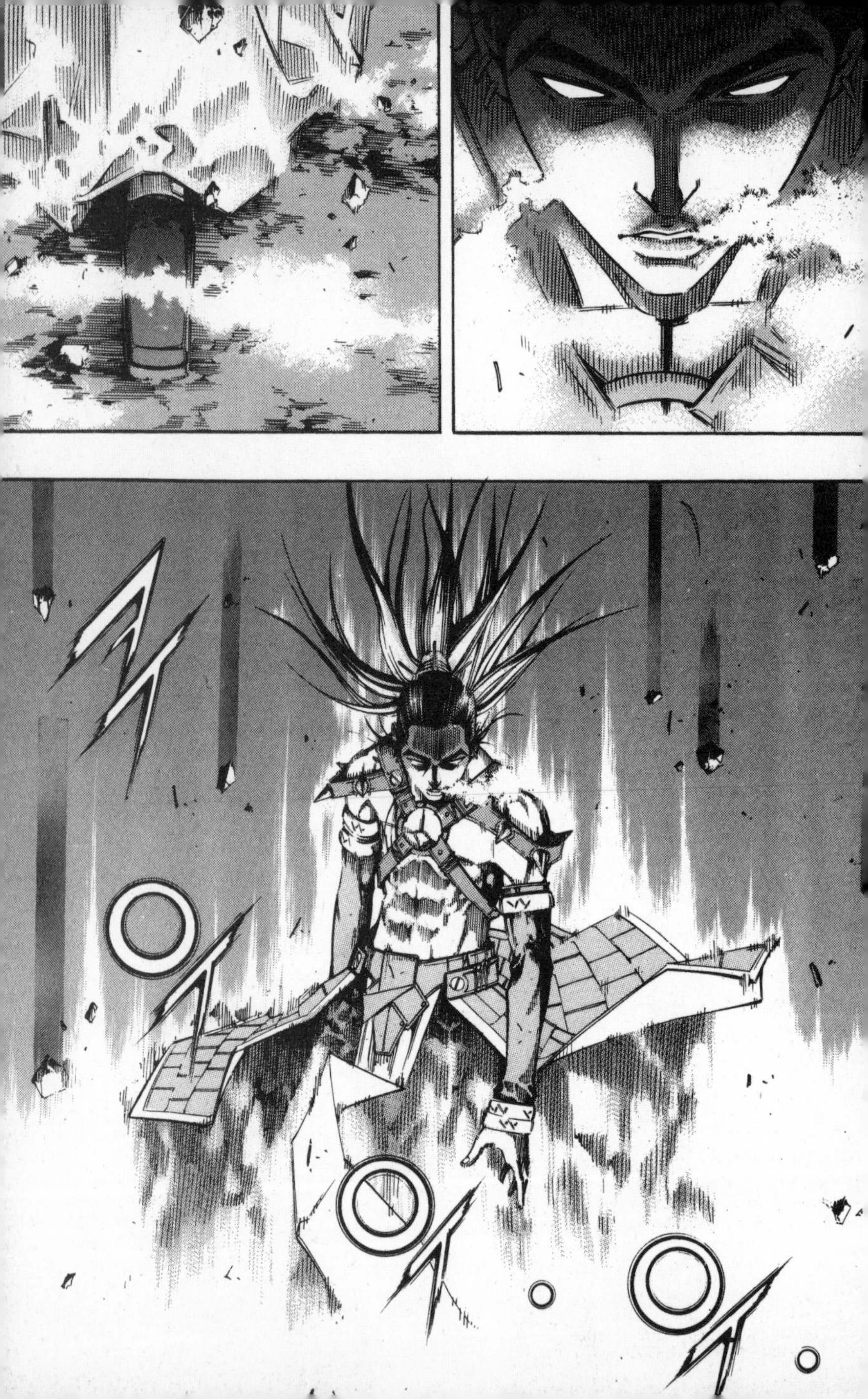

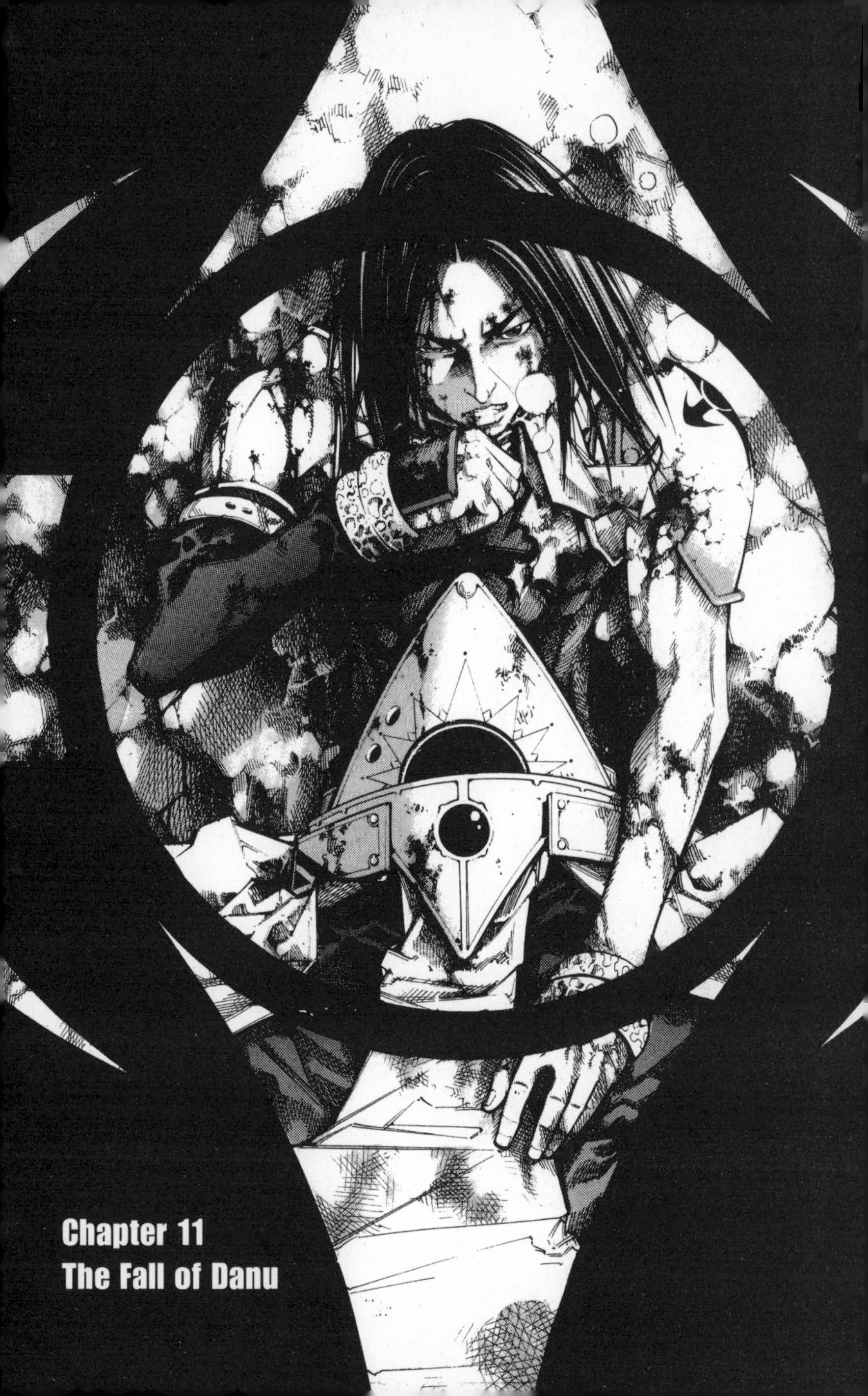

Chapter 11
The Fall of Danu

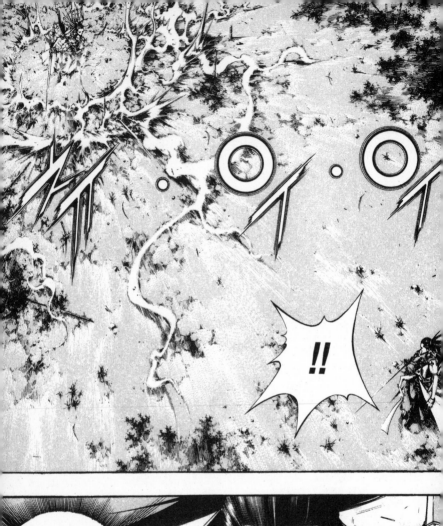

!!

I CAN FEEL
HIS MANEUVER
BUZZING IN THE
MARROW OF MY
BONES. THIS
IS NO JOKE!

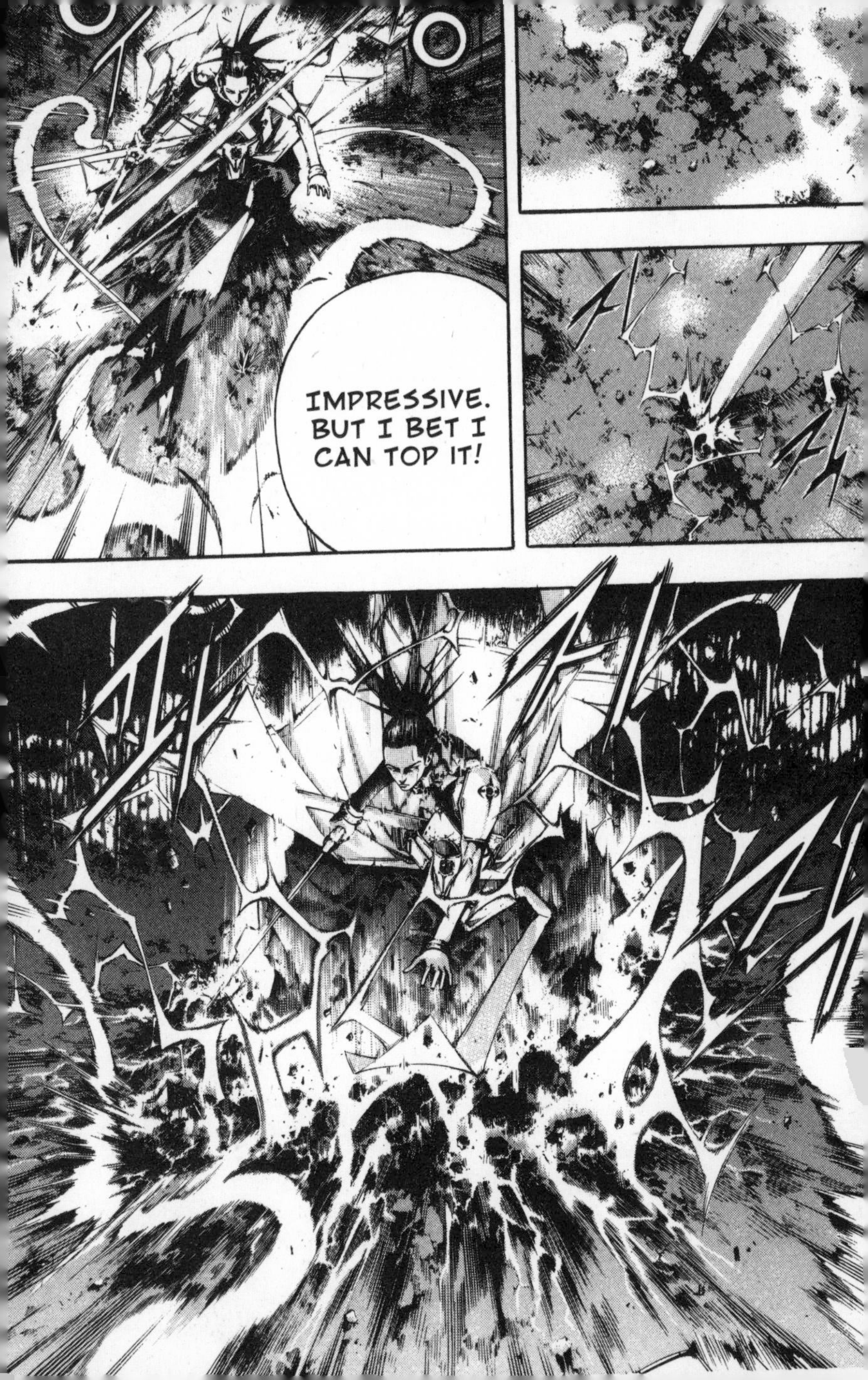
IMPRESSIVE. BUT I BET I CAN TOP IT!

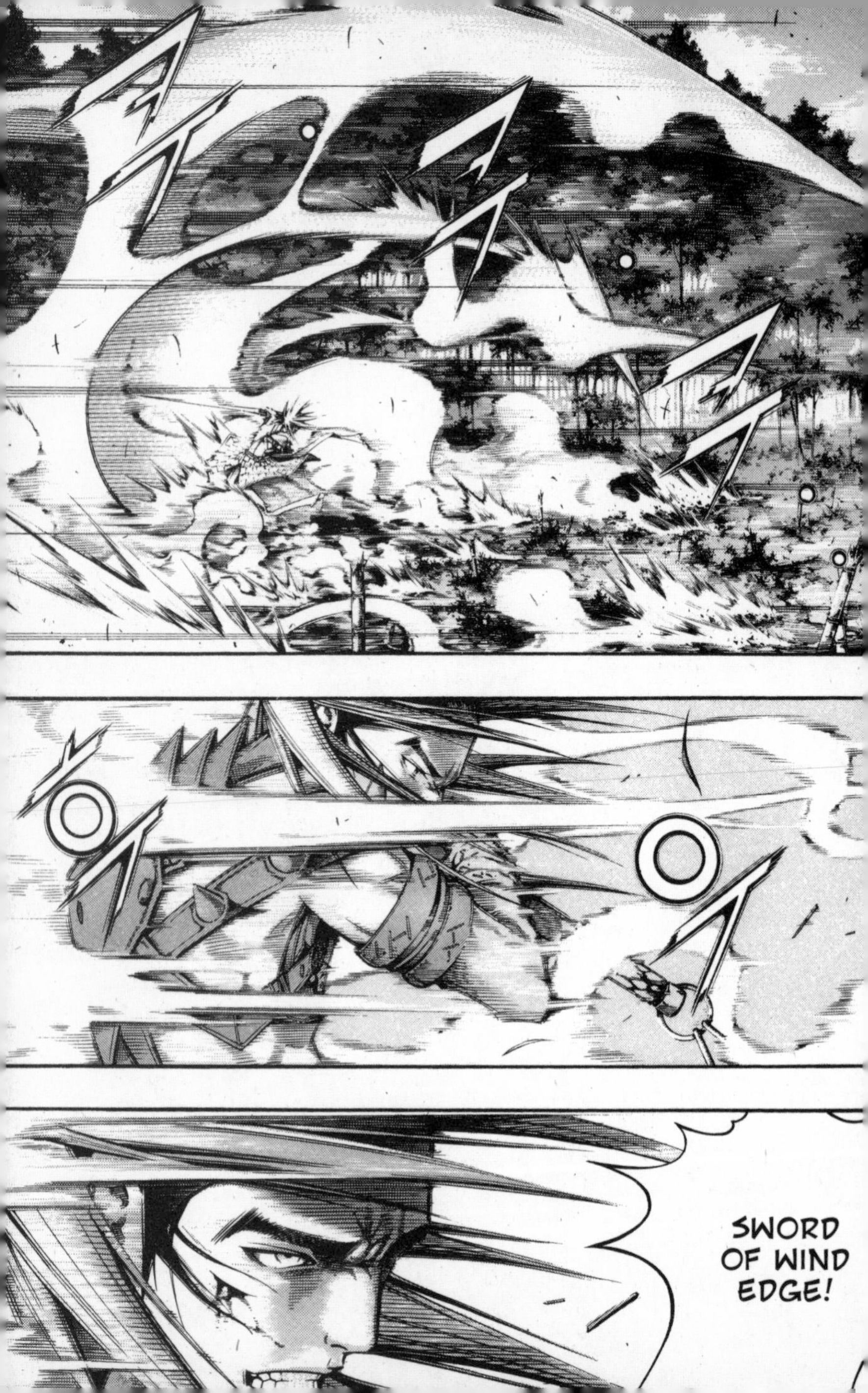
SWORD OF WIND EDGE!

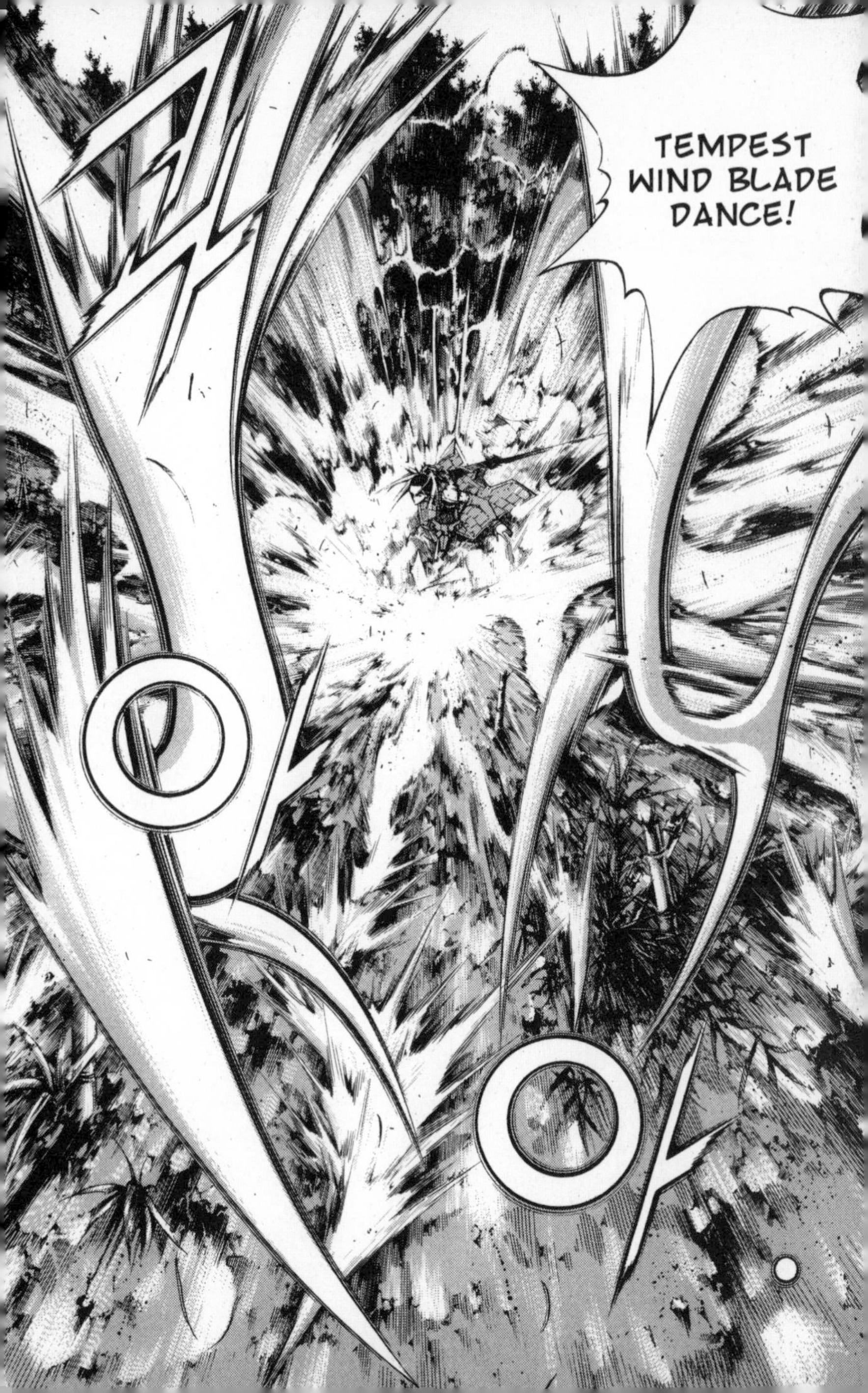
TEMPEST WIND BLADE DANCE!

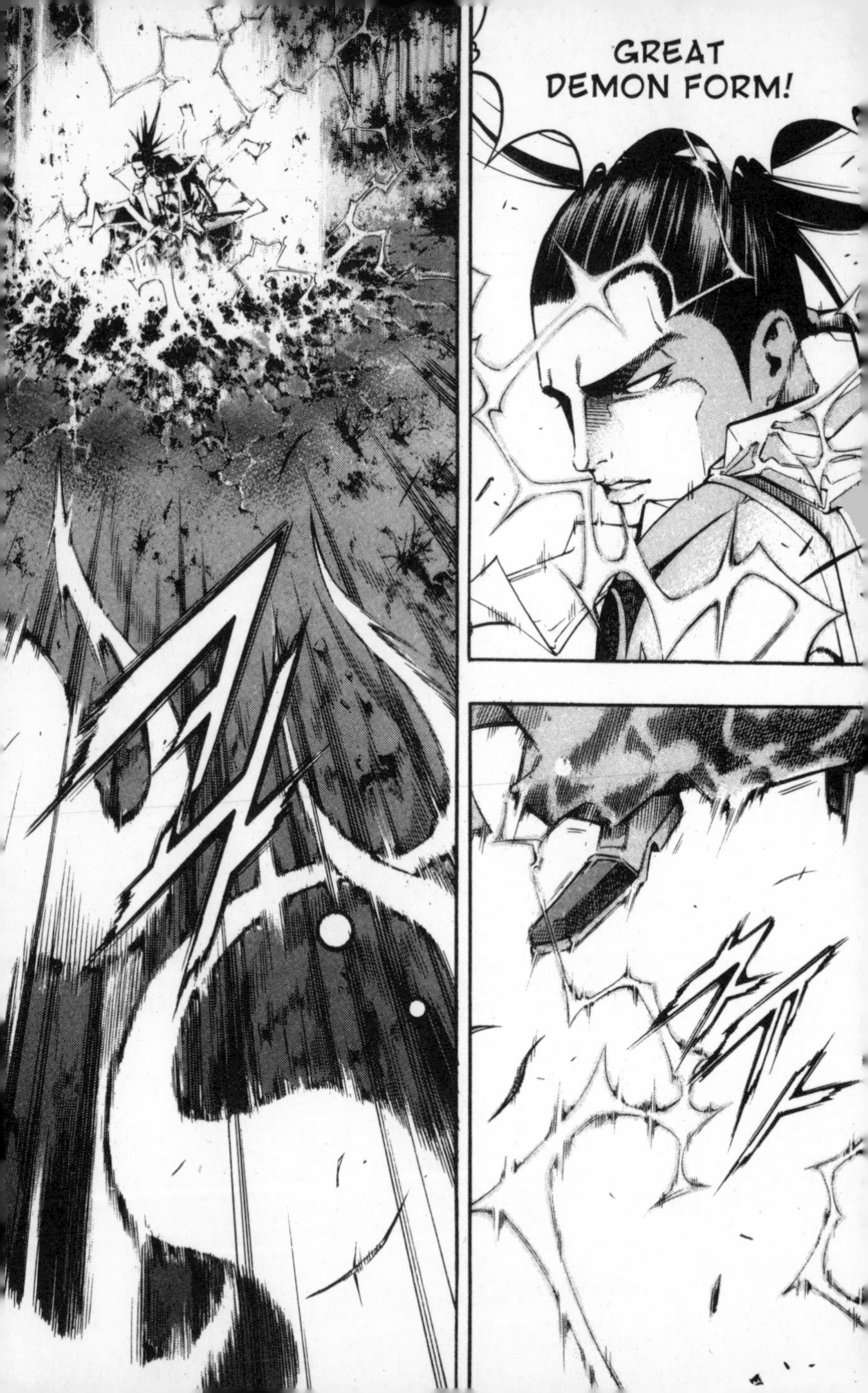
GREAT DEMON FORM!

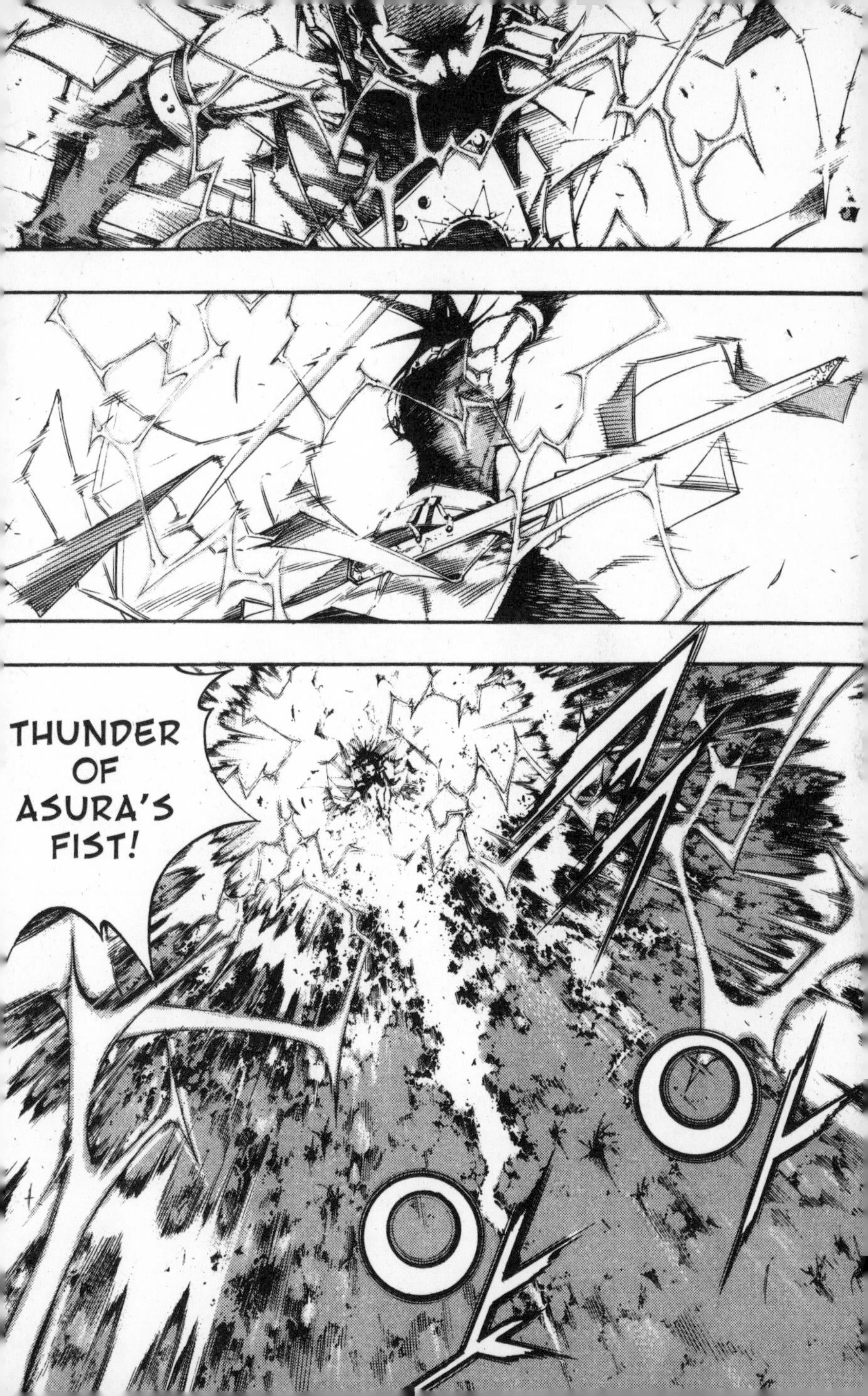
THUNDER OF ASURA'S FIST!

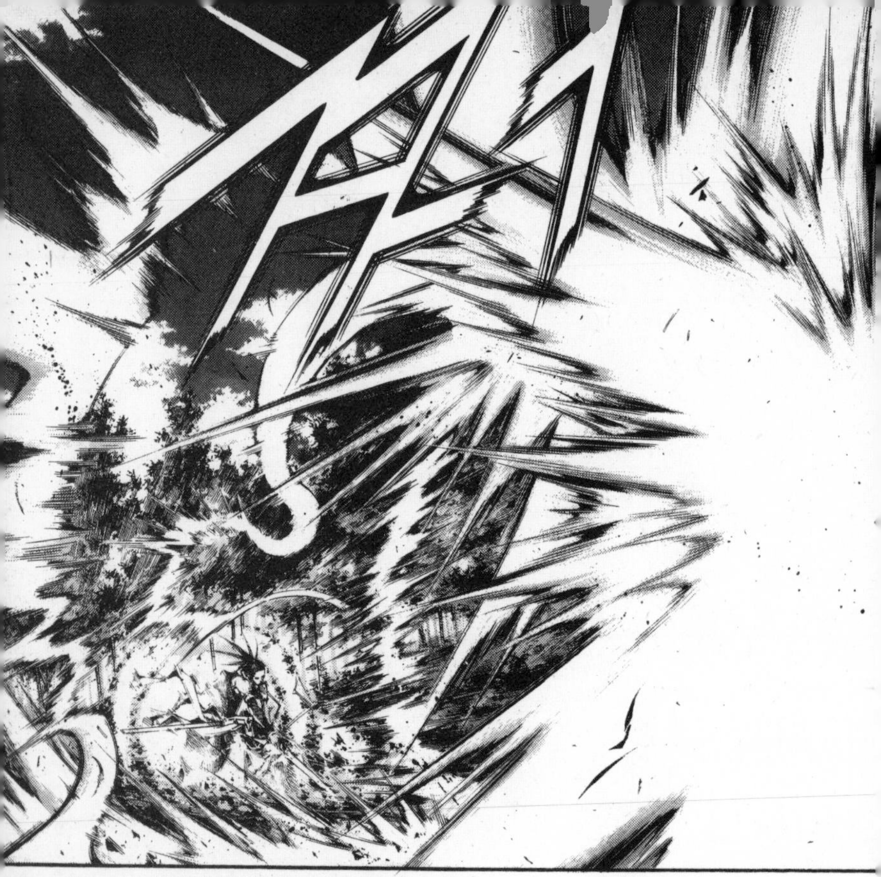

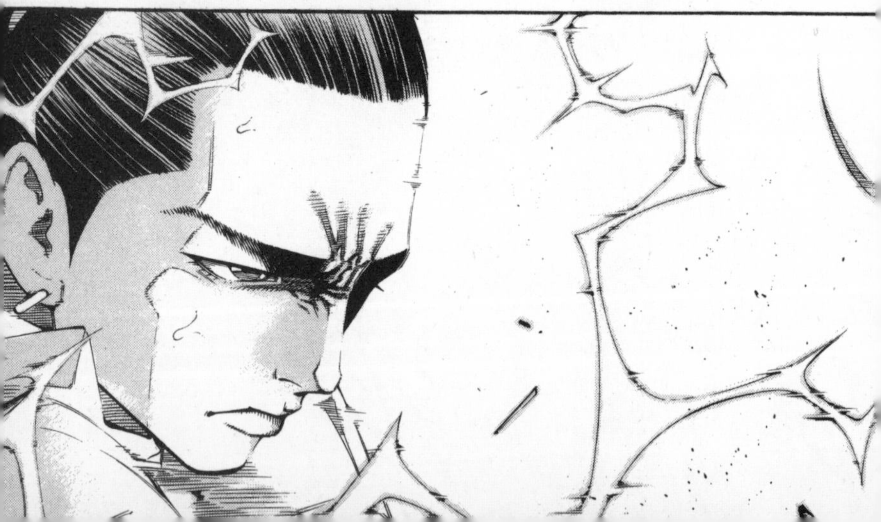

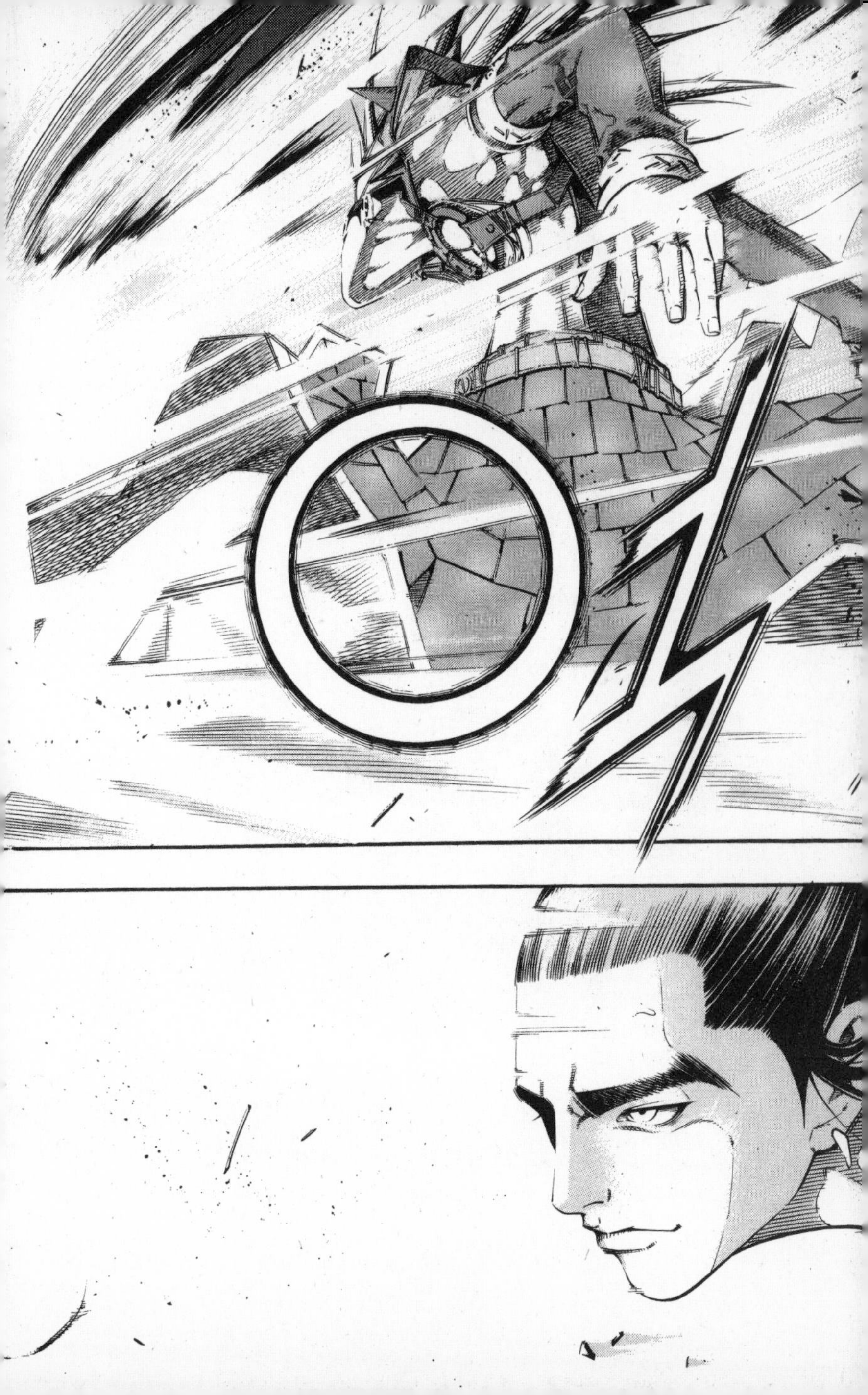

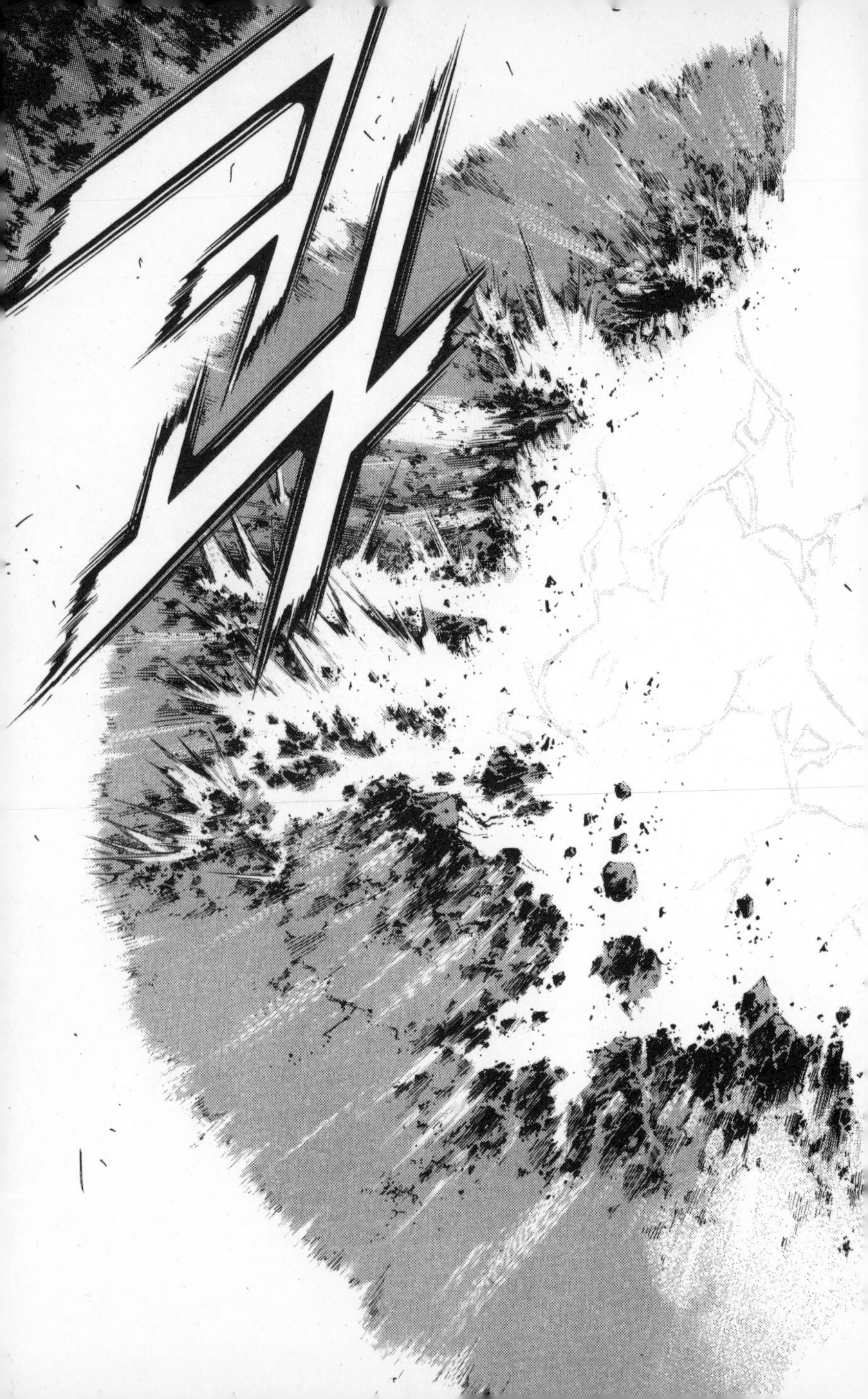

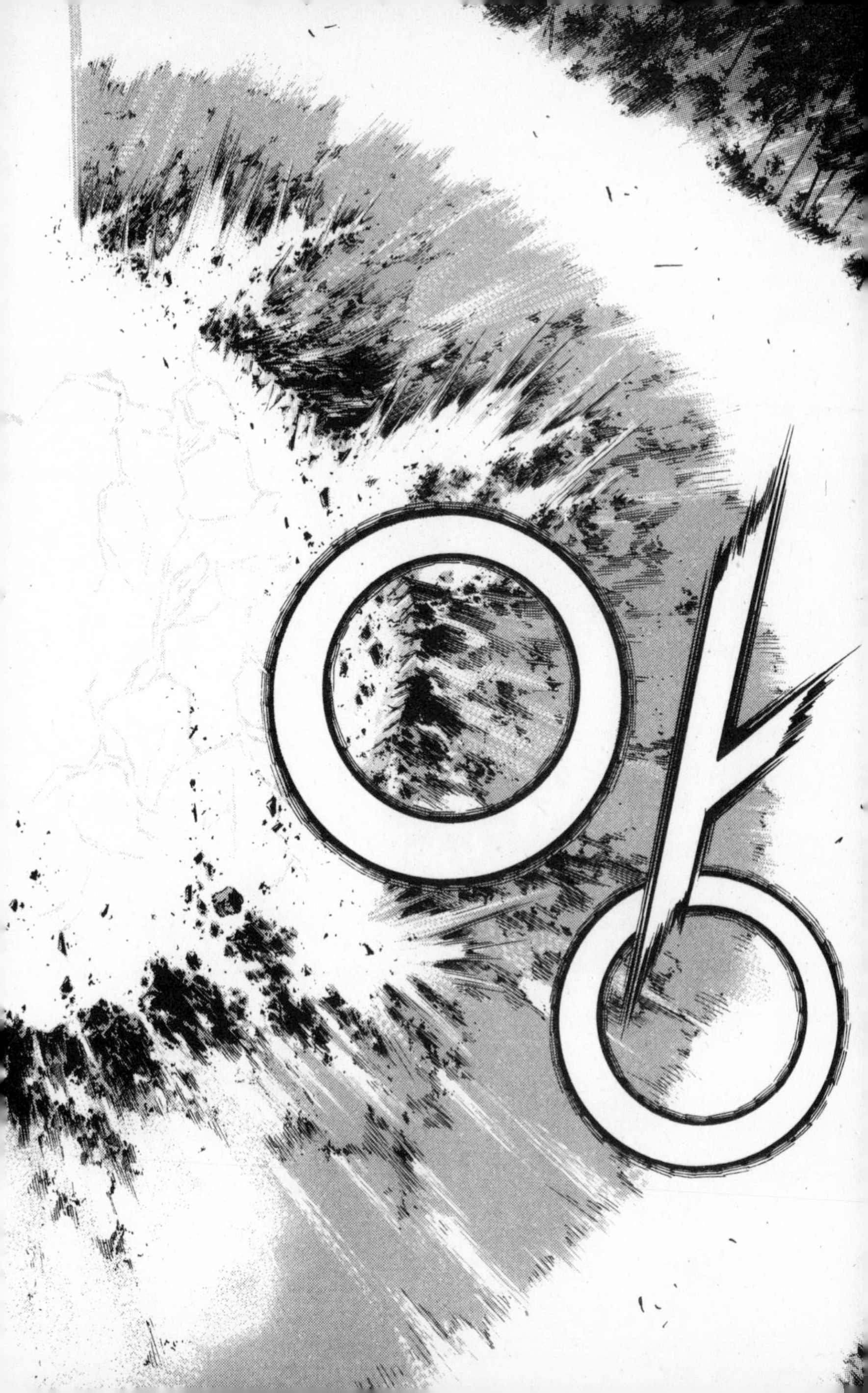

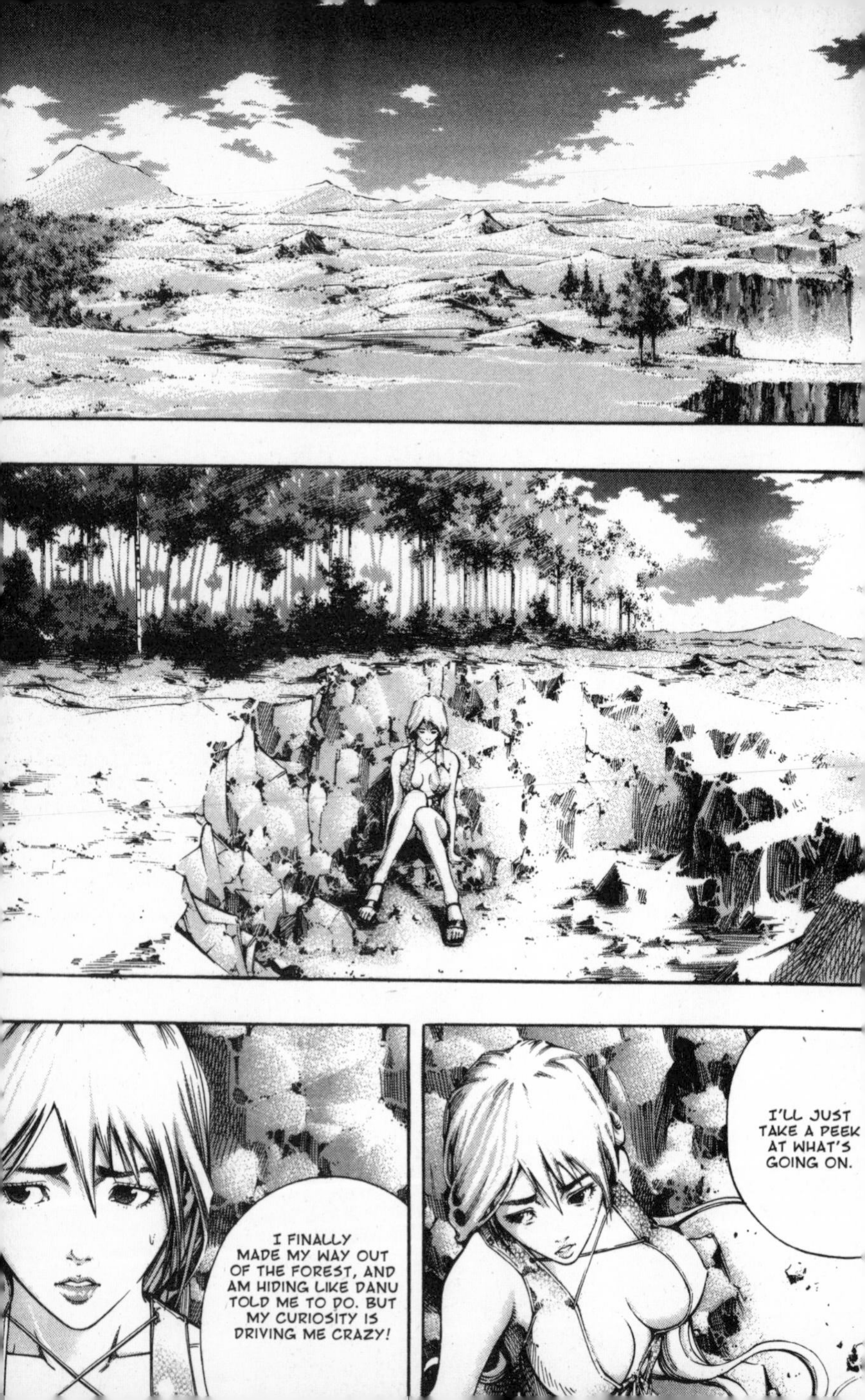
I'LL JUST TAKE A PEEK AT WHAT'S GOING ON.
I FINALLY MADE MY WAY OUT OF THE FOREST, AND AM HIDING LIKE DANU TOLD ME TO DO. BUT MY CURIOSITY IS DRIVING ME CRAZY!

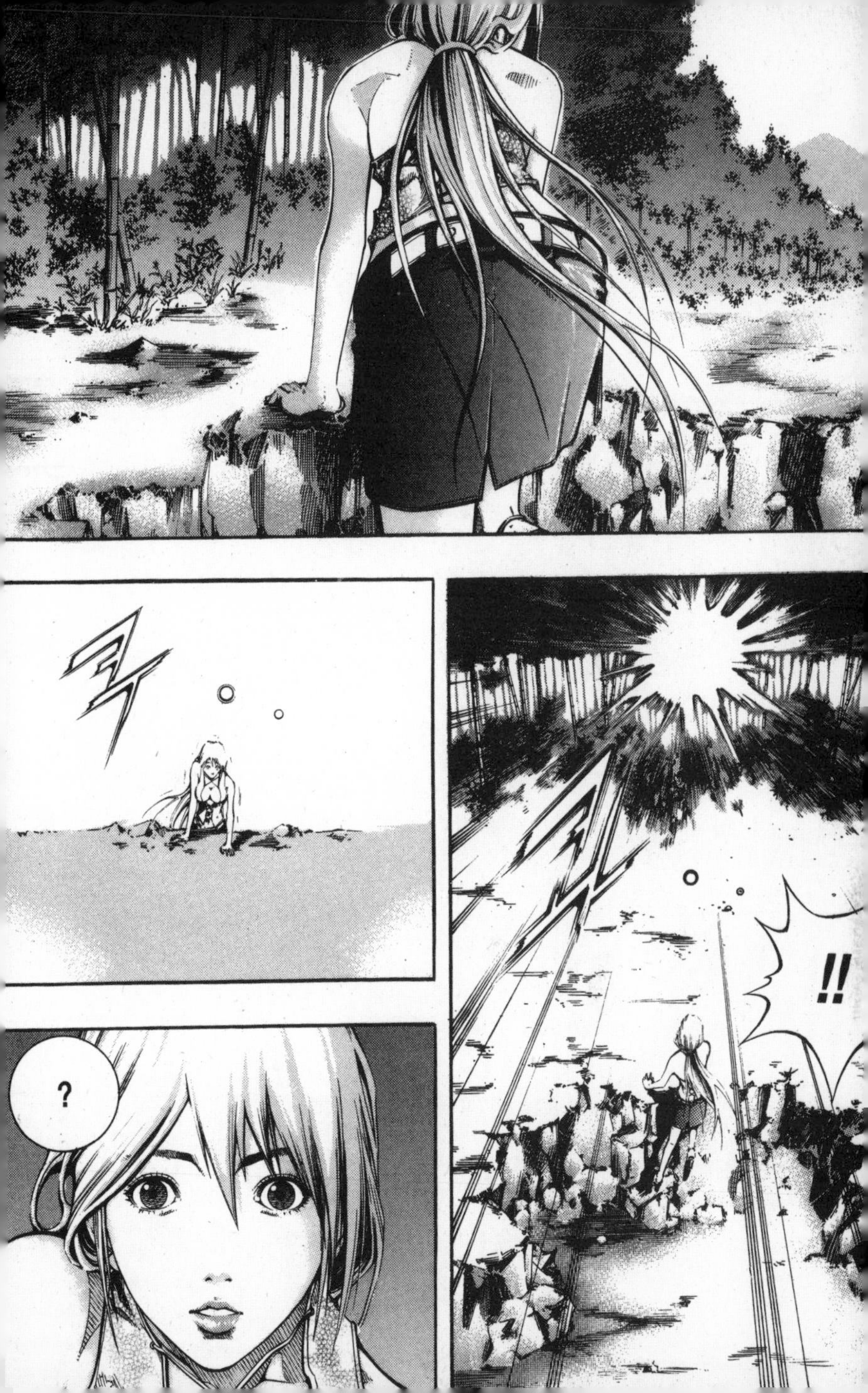
!!
?

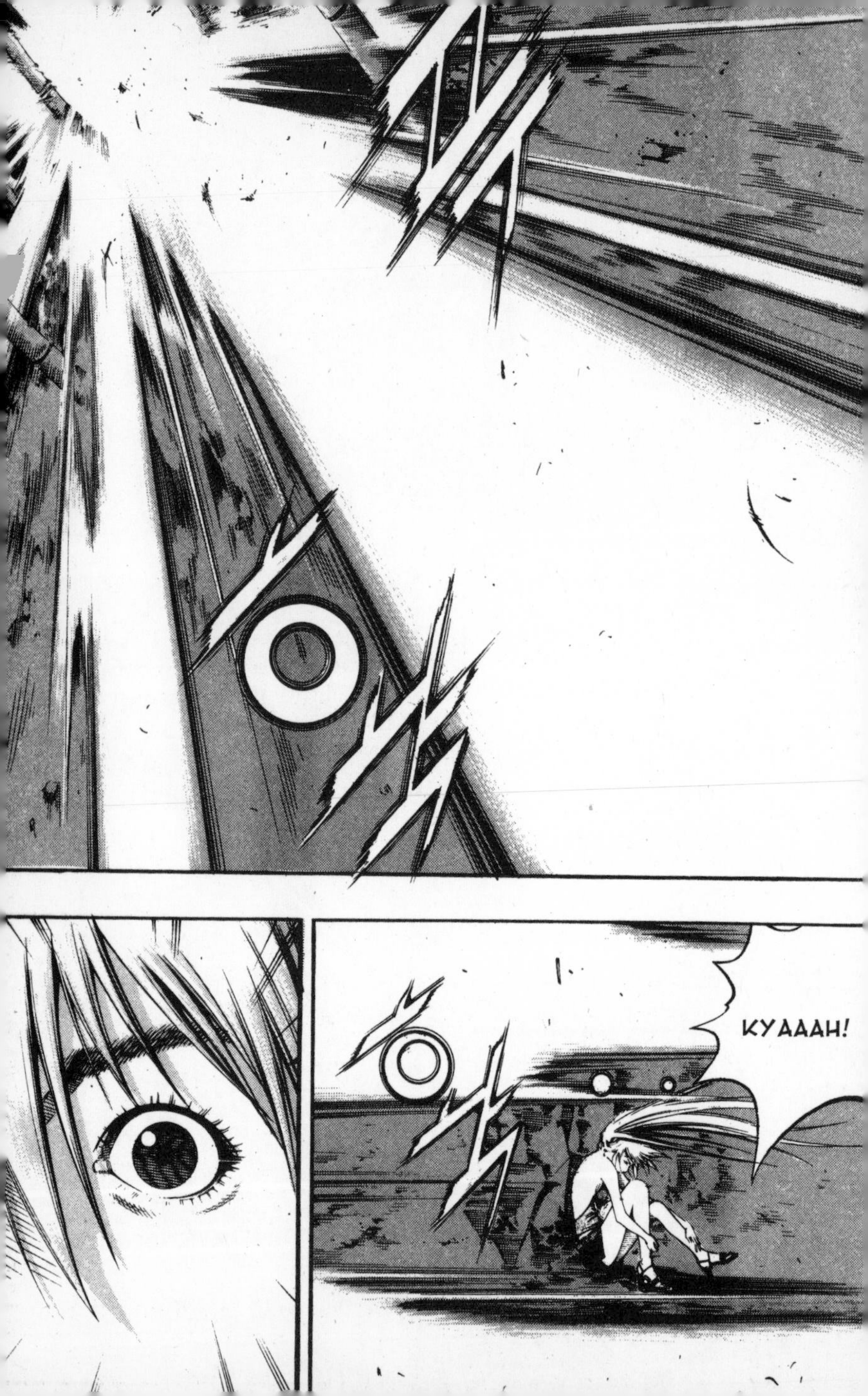
KYAAAH!

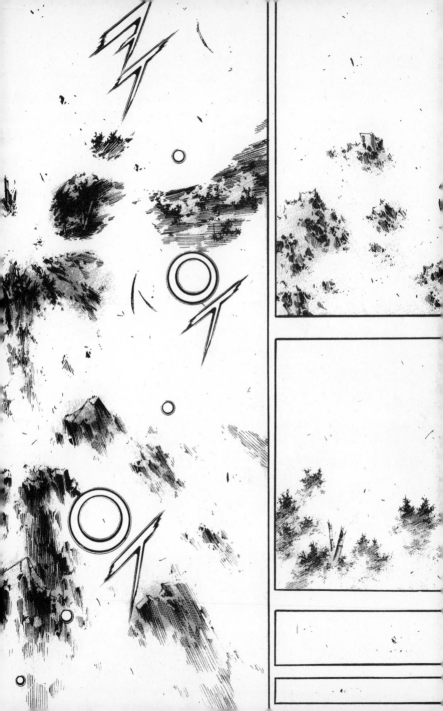

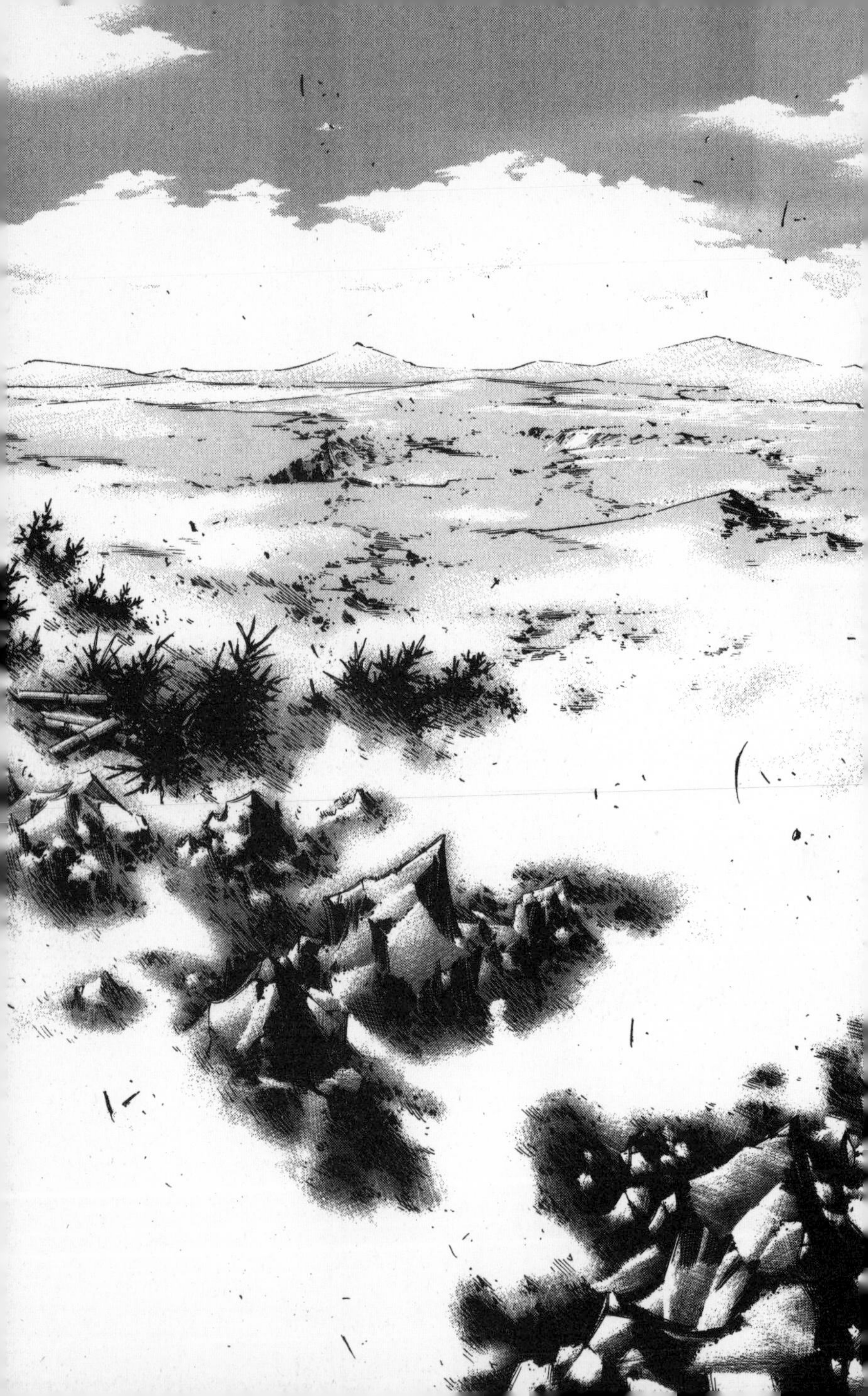

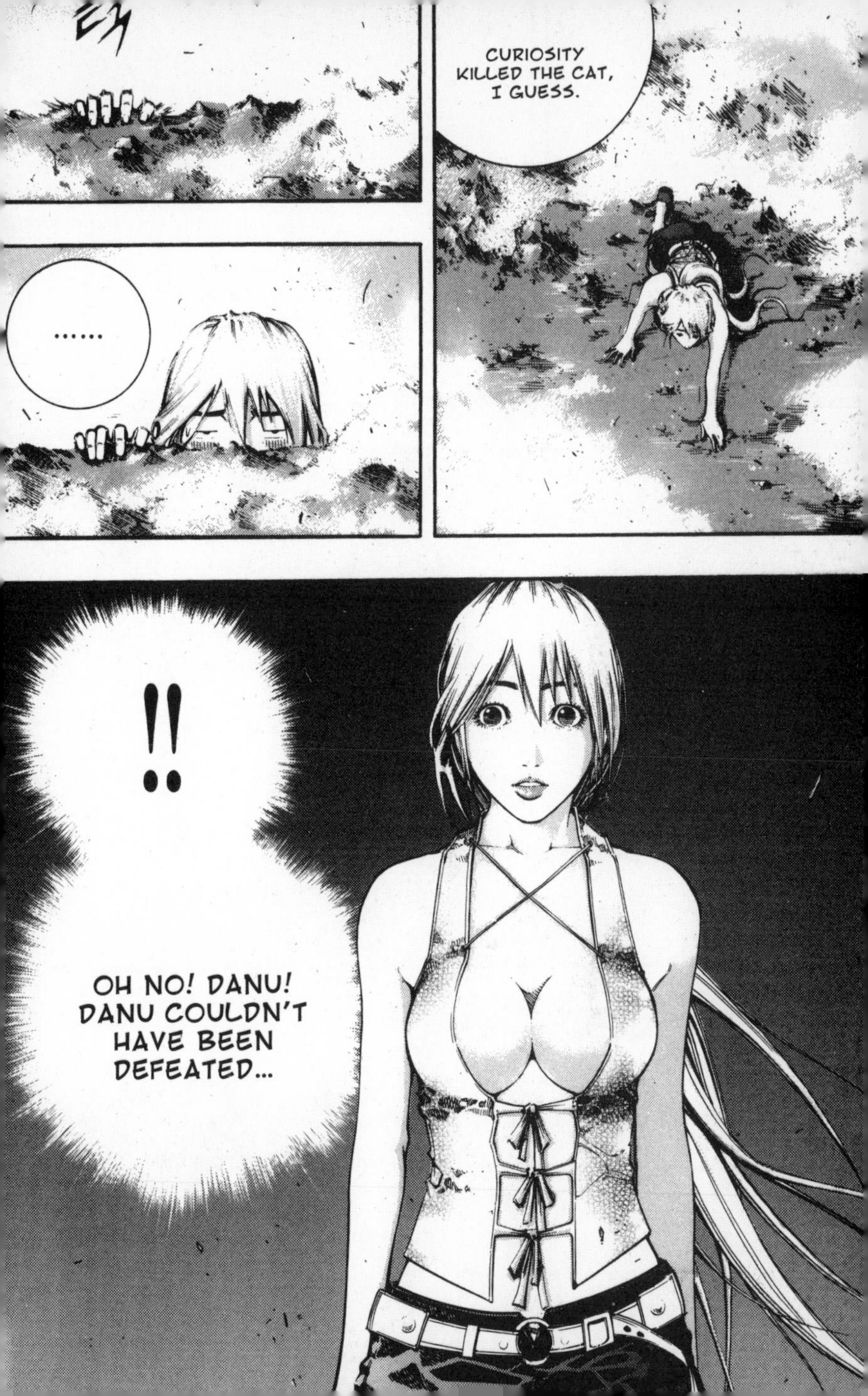

CURIOSITY KILLED THE CAT, I GUESS.
......
!!
OH NO! DANU! DANU COULDN'T HAVE BEEN DEFEATED...

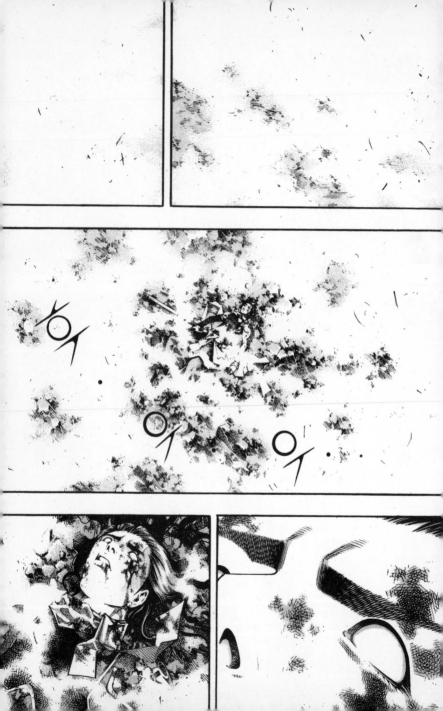

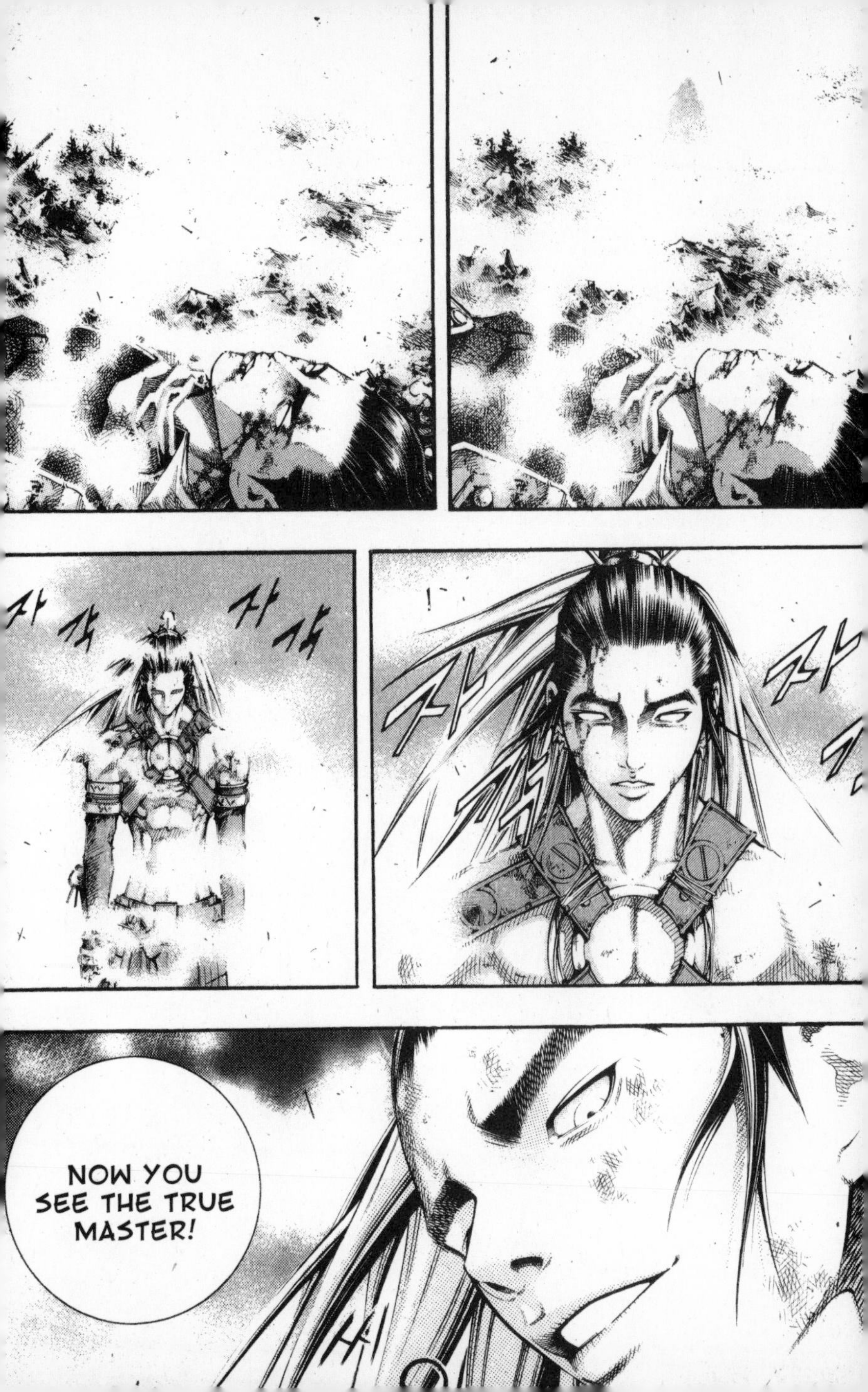
NOW YOU SEE THE TRUE MASTER!

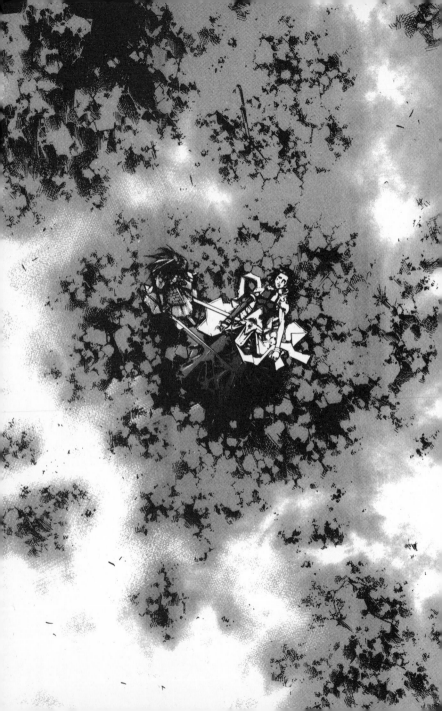

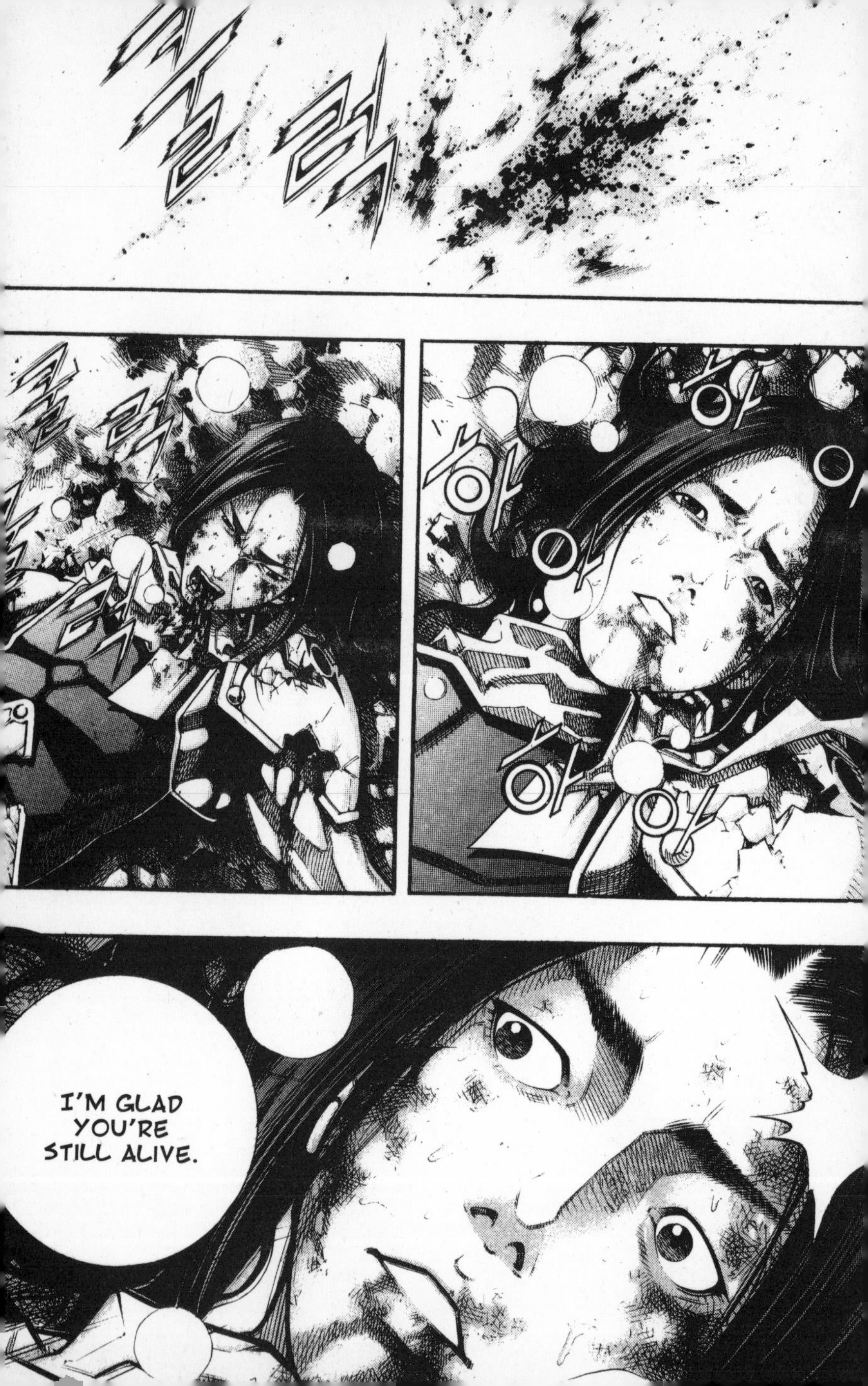
I'M GLAD YOU'RE STILL ALIVE.

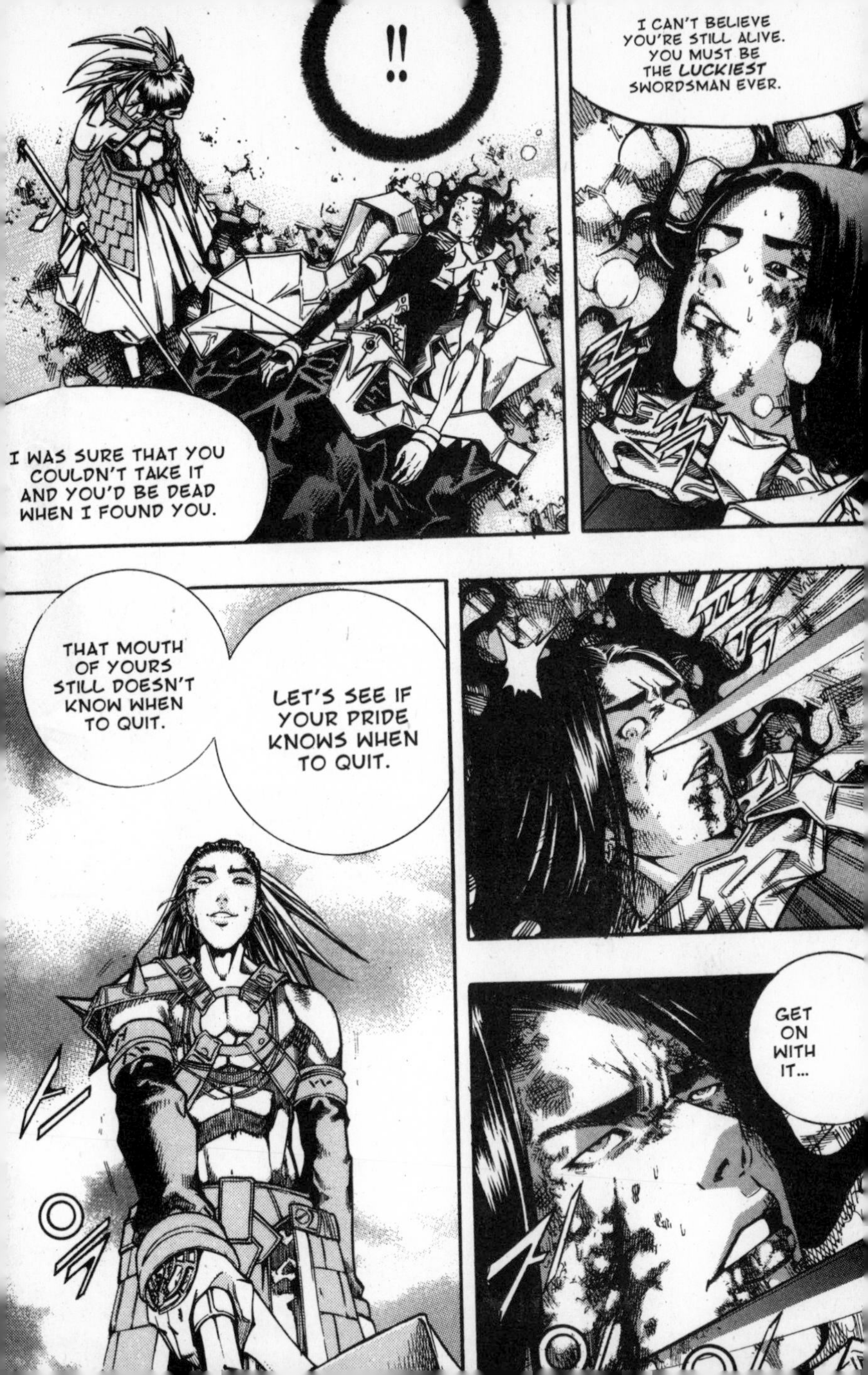
!!
I CAN'T BELIEVE YOU'RE STILL ALIVE. YOU MUST BE THE LUCKIEST SWORDSMAN EVER.
I WAS SURE THAT YOU COULDN'T TAKE IT AND YOU'D BE DEAD WHEN I FOUND YOU.
THAT MOUTH OF YOURS STILL DOESN'T KNOW WHEN TO QUIT.
LET'S SEE IF YOUR PRIDE KNOWS WHEN TO QUIT.
GET ON WITH IT...

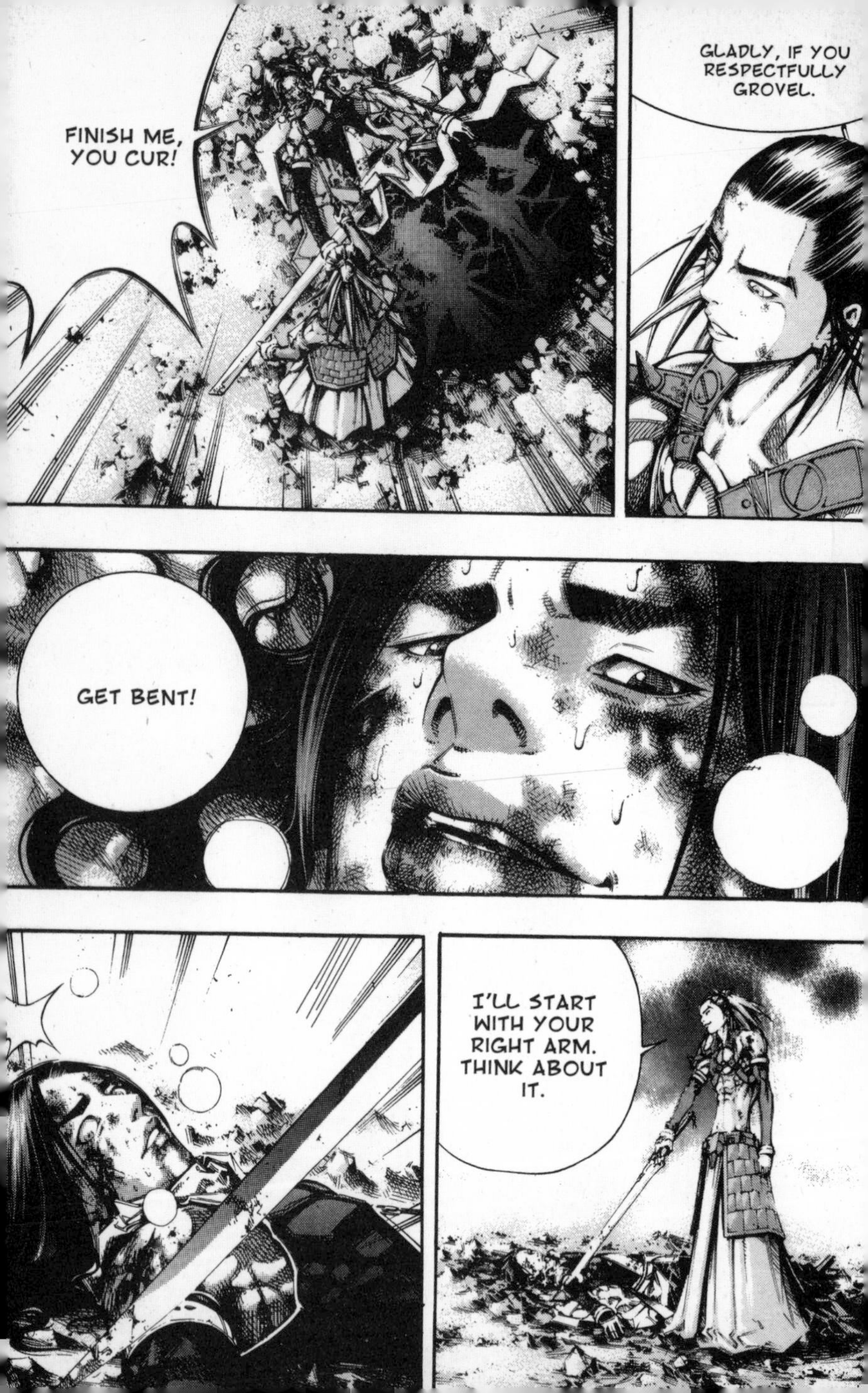
FINISH ME, YOU CUR!
GLADLY, IF YOU RESPECTFULLY GROVEL.
GET BENT!
I'LL START WITH YOUR RIGHT ARM. THINK ABOUT IT.

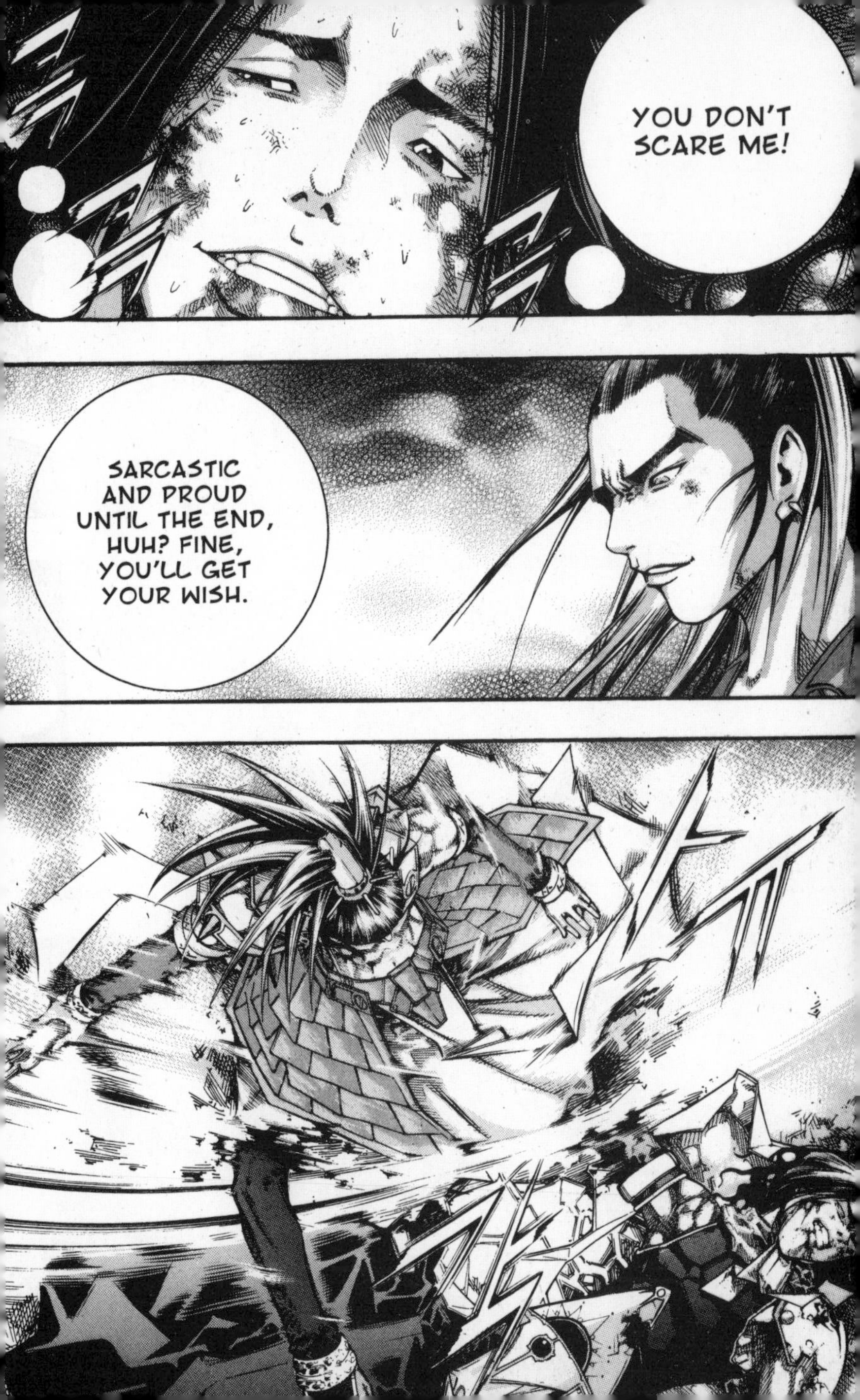
YOU DON'T SCARE ME!
SARCASTIC AND PROUD UNTIL THE END, HUH? FINE, YOU'LL GET YOUR WISH.

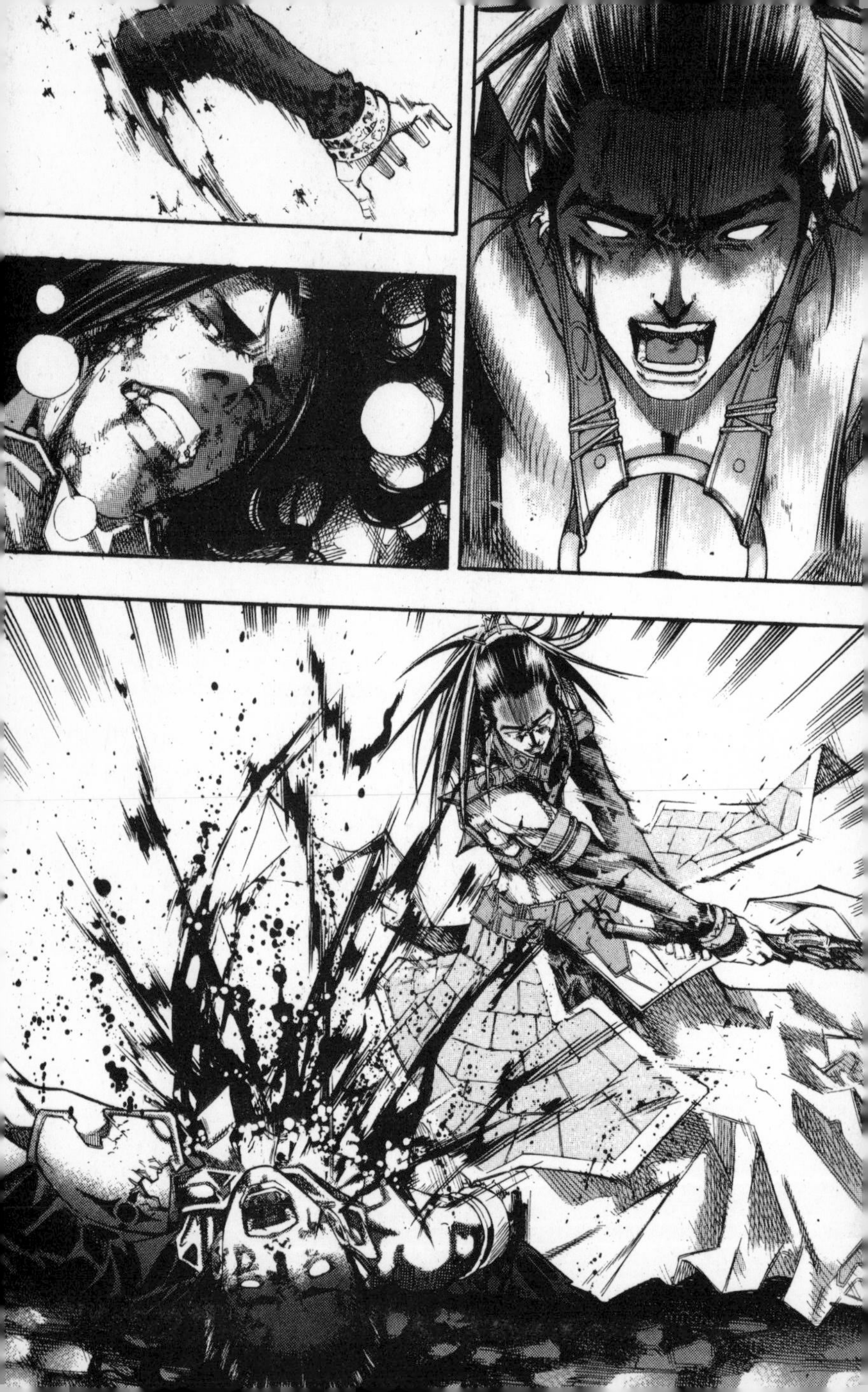

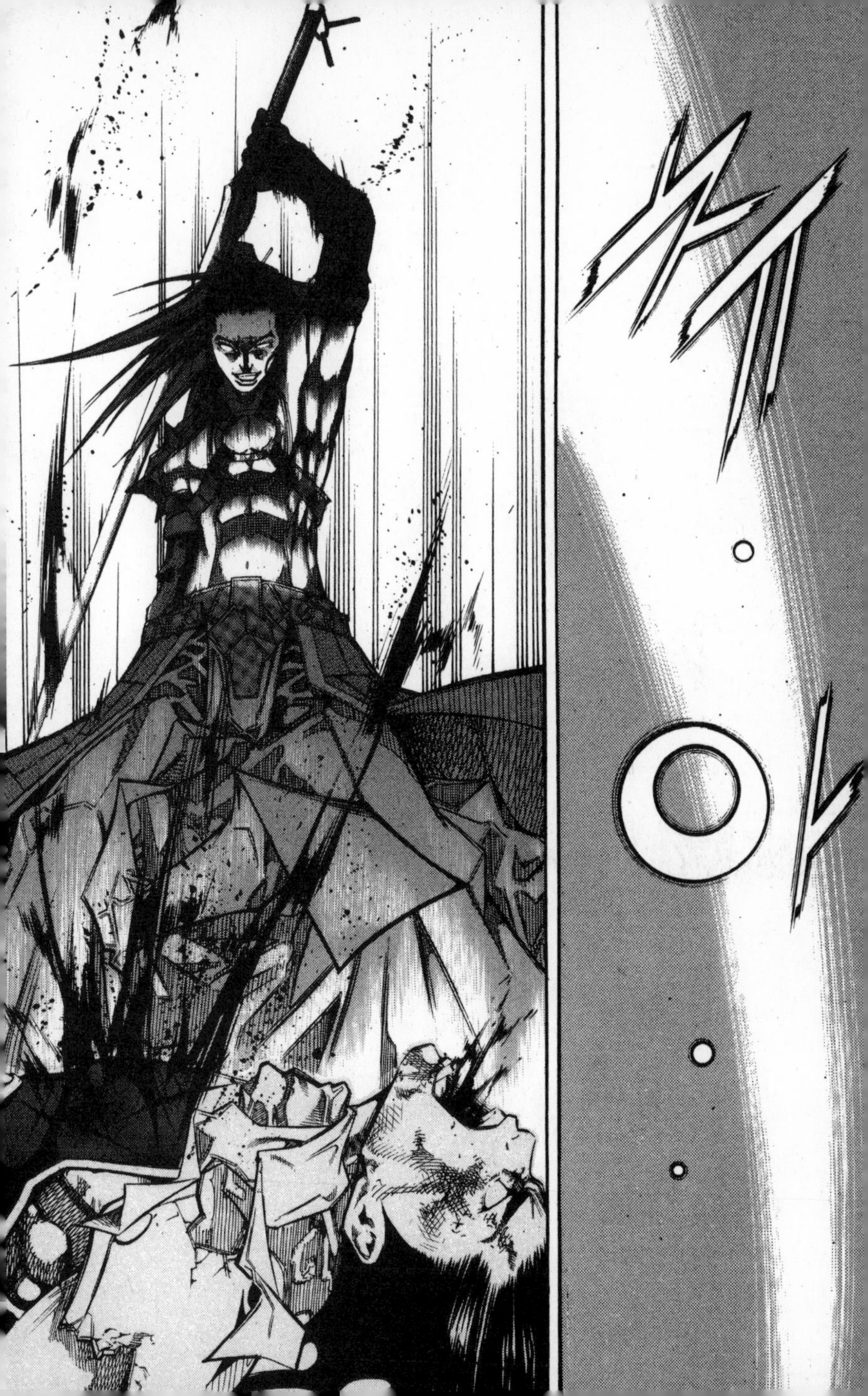

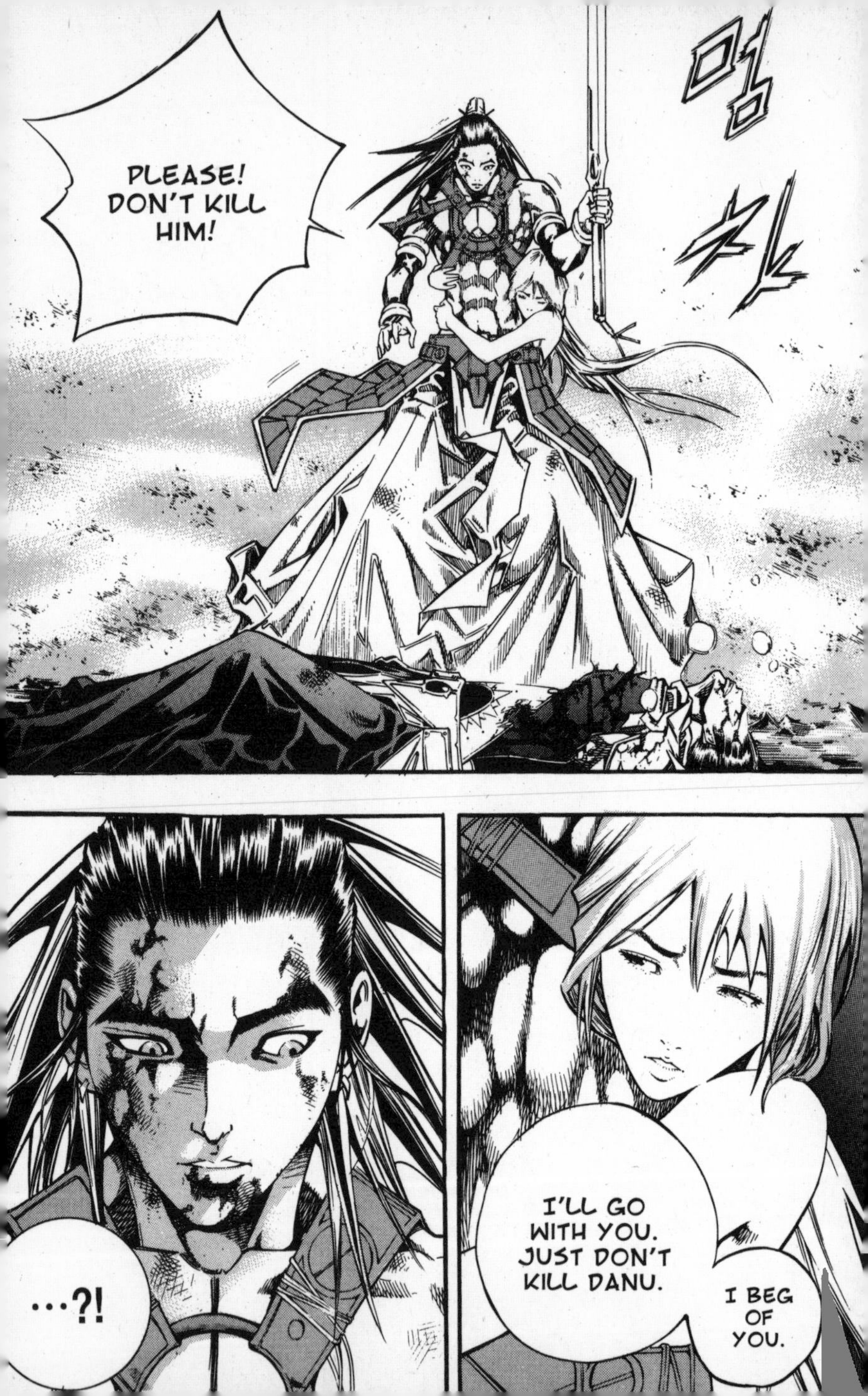
PLEASE! DON'T KILL HIM!
...?!
I'LL GO WITH YOU. JUST DON'T KILL DANU.
I BEG OF YOU.

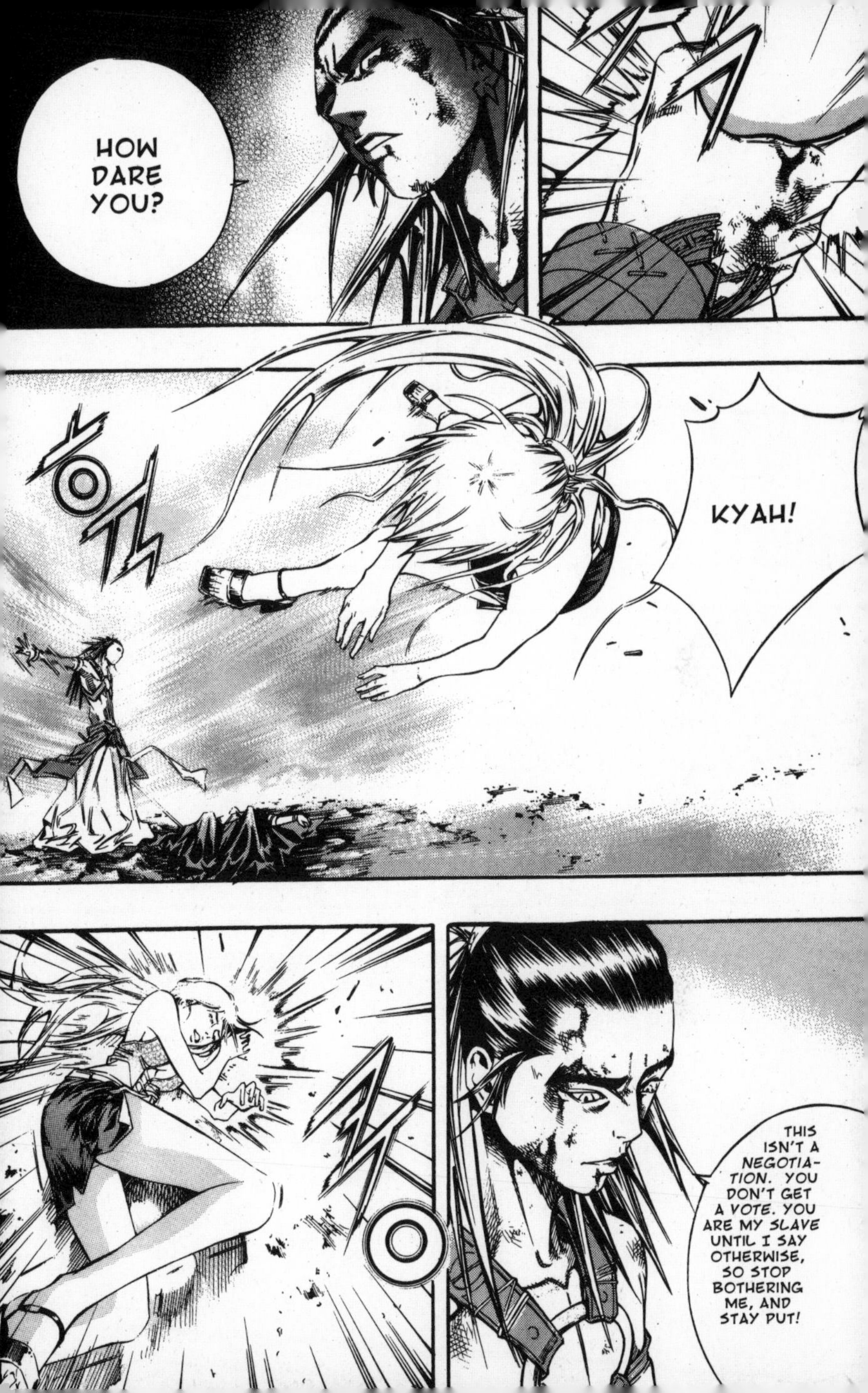
HOW DARE YOU?
KYAH!
THIS ISN'T A NEGOTIATION. YOU DON'T GET A VOTE. YOU ARE MY SLAVE UNTIL I SAY OTHERWISE, SO STOP BOTHERING ME, AND STAY PUT!

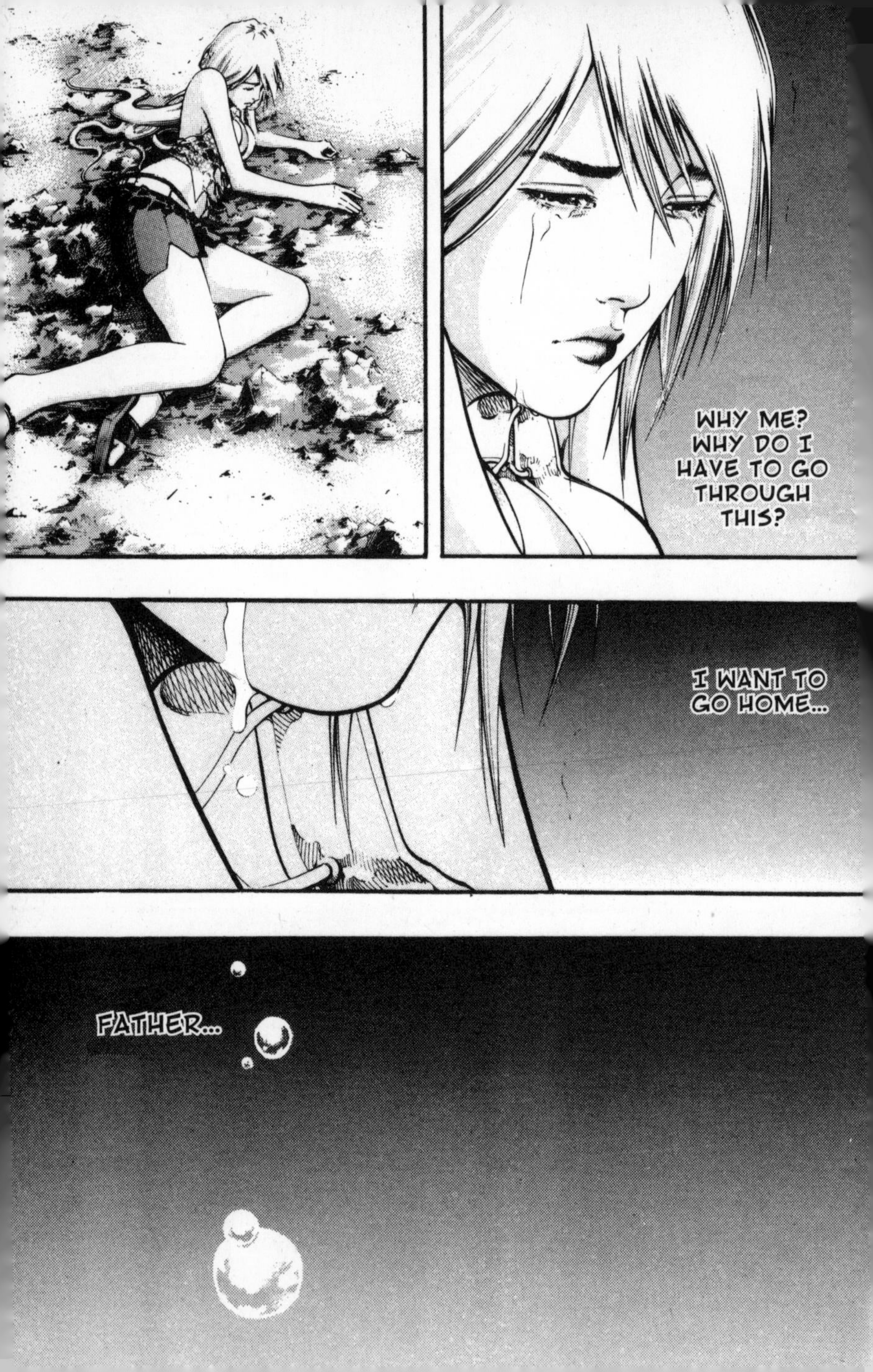
WHY ME? WHY DO I HAVE TO GO THROUGH THIS?
I WANT TO GO HOME...
FATHER...

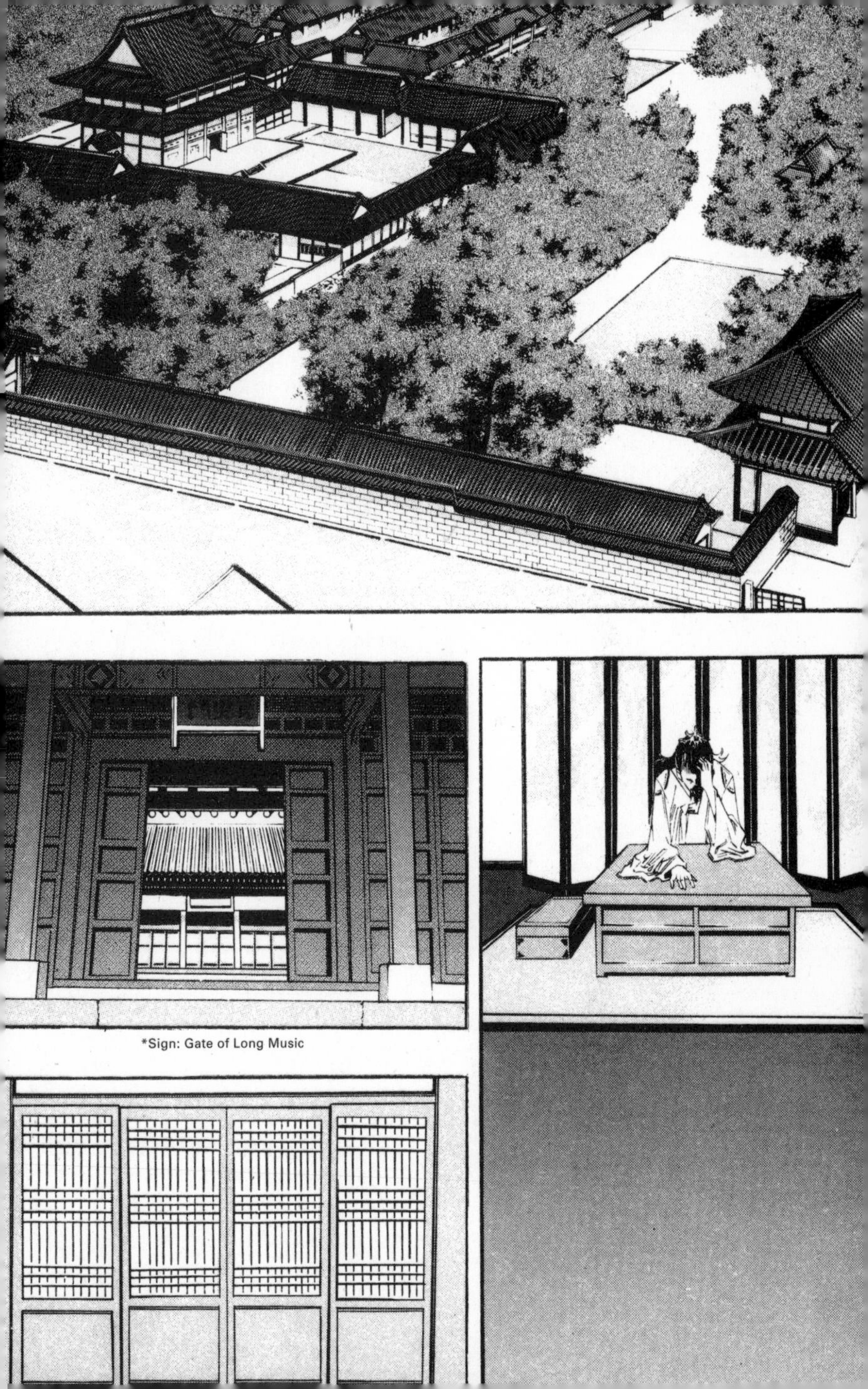
*Sign: Gate of Long Music

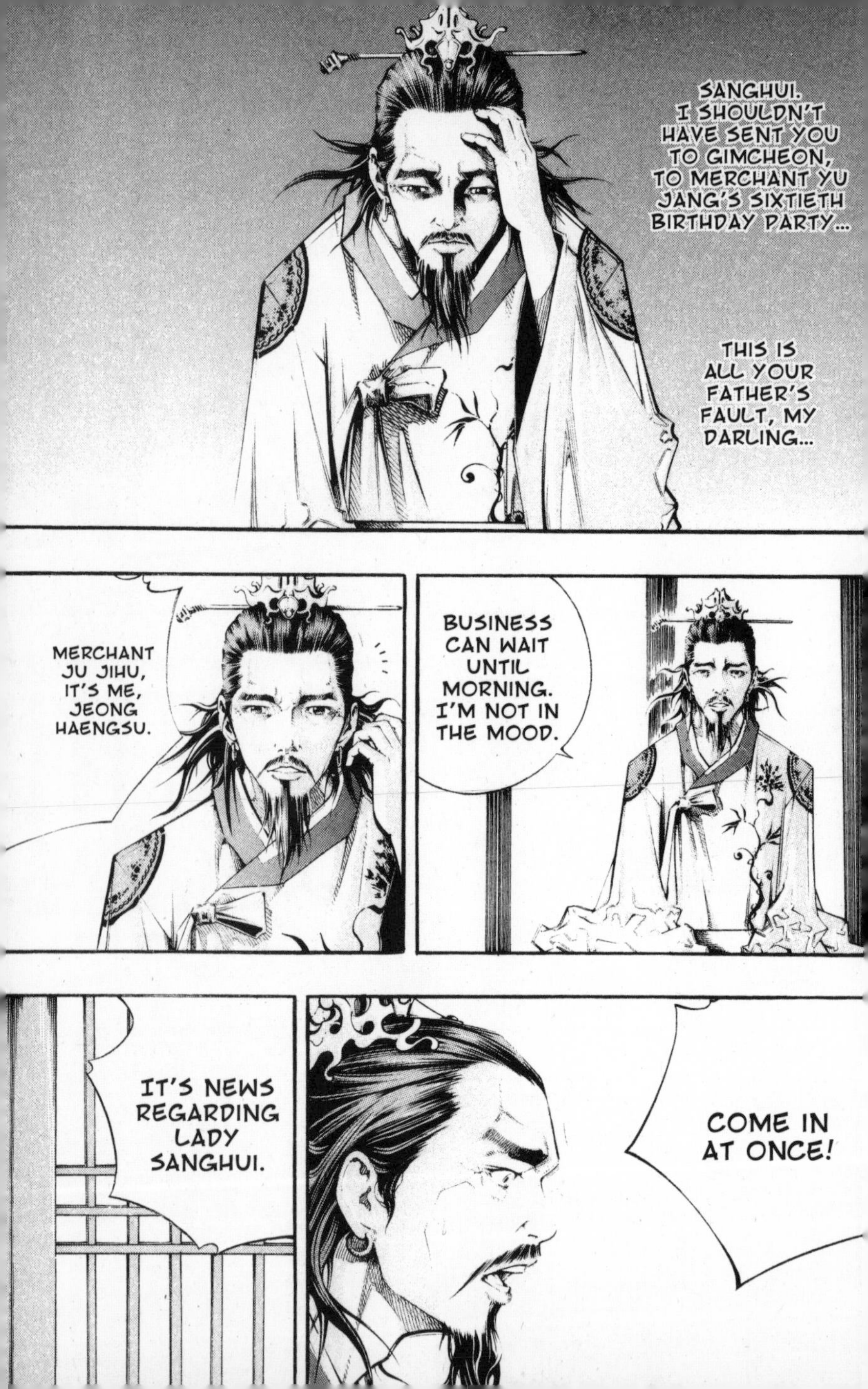
SANGHUI. I SHOULDN'T HAVE SENT YOU TO GIMCHEON, TO MERCHANT YU JANG'S SIXTIETH BIRTHDAY PARTY...
THIS IS ALL YOUR FATHER'S FAULT, MY DARLING...
MERCHANT JU JIHU, IT'S ME, JEONG HAENGSU.
BUSINESS CAN WAIT UNTIL MORNING. I'M NOT IN THE MOOD.
IT'S NEWS REGARDING LADY SANGHUI.
COME IN AT ONCE!

SO...

WHAT IS THE NEWS REGARDING SANGHUI?

LADY SANGHUI IS STILL ALIVE.

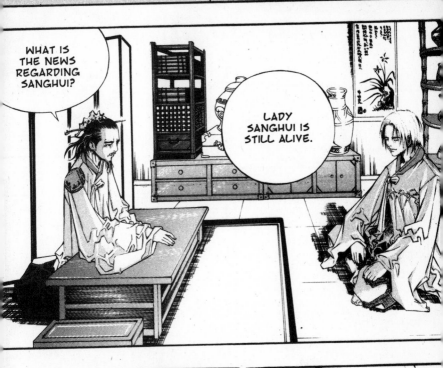

A-ALIVE?

IT'S INFORMATION I RECIEVED FROM YU SEONGJIN, COMMANDER OF HEAVEN'S WRATH, SILVER FOX DIVISION.

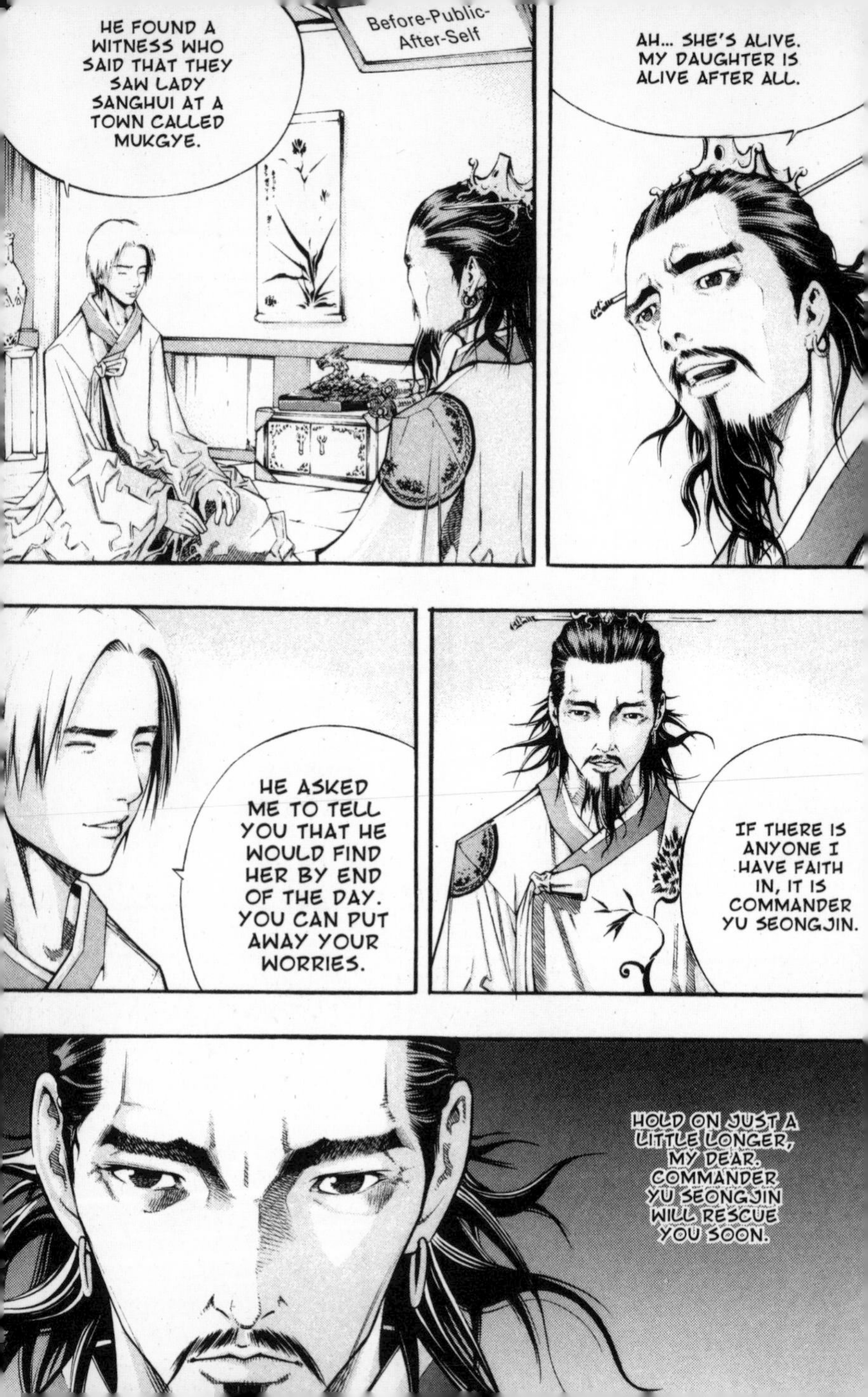
Before-Public-After-Self
HE FOUND A WITNESS WHO SAID THAT THEY SAW LADY SANGHUI AT A TOWN CALLED MUKGYE.
AH... SHE'S ALIVE. MY DAUGHTER IS ALIVE AFTER ALL.
HE ASKED ME TO TELL YOU THAT HE WOULD FIND HER BY END OF THE DAY. YOU CAN PUT AWAY YOUR WORRIES.
IF THERE IS ANYONE I HAVE FAITH IN, IT IS COMMANDER YU SEONGJIN.
HOLD ON JUST A LITTLE LONGER, MY DEAR. COMMANDER YU SEONGJIN WILL RESCUE YOU SOON.

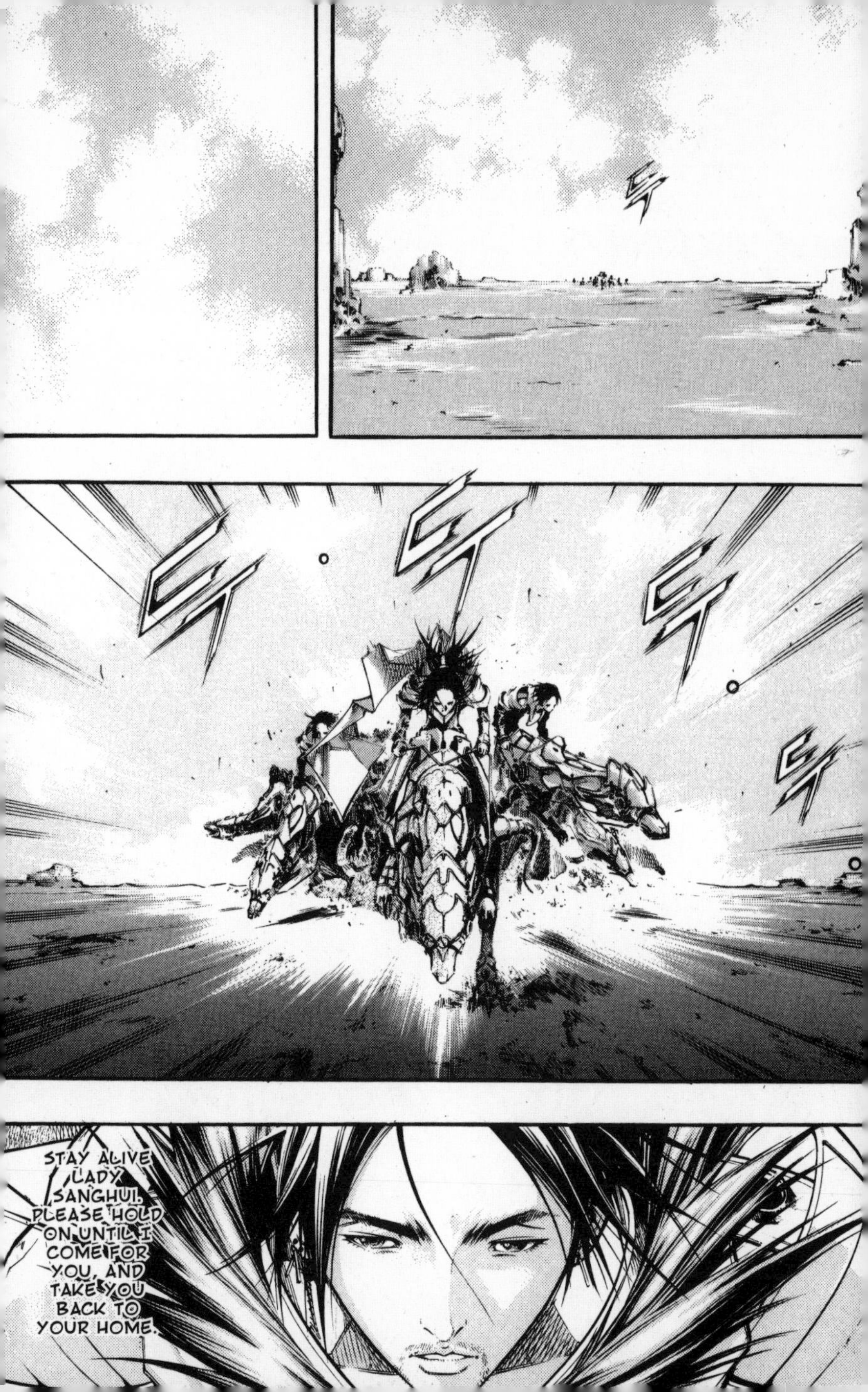
STAY ALIVE LADY SANGHUI. PLEASE HOLD ON UNTIL I COME FOR YOU, AND TAKE YOU BACK TO YOUR HOME.

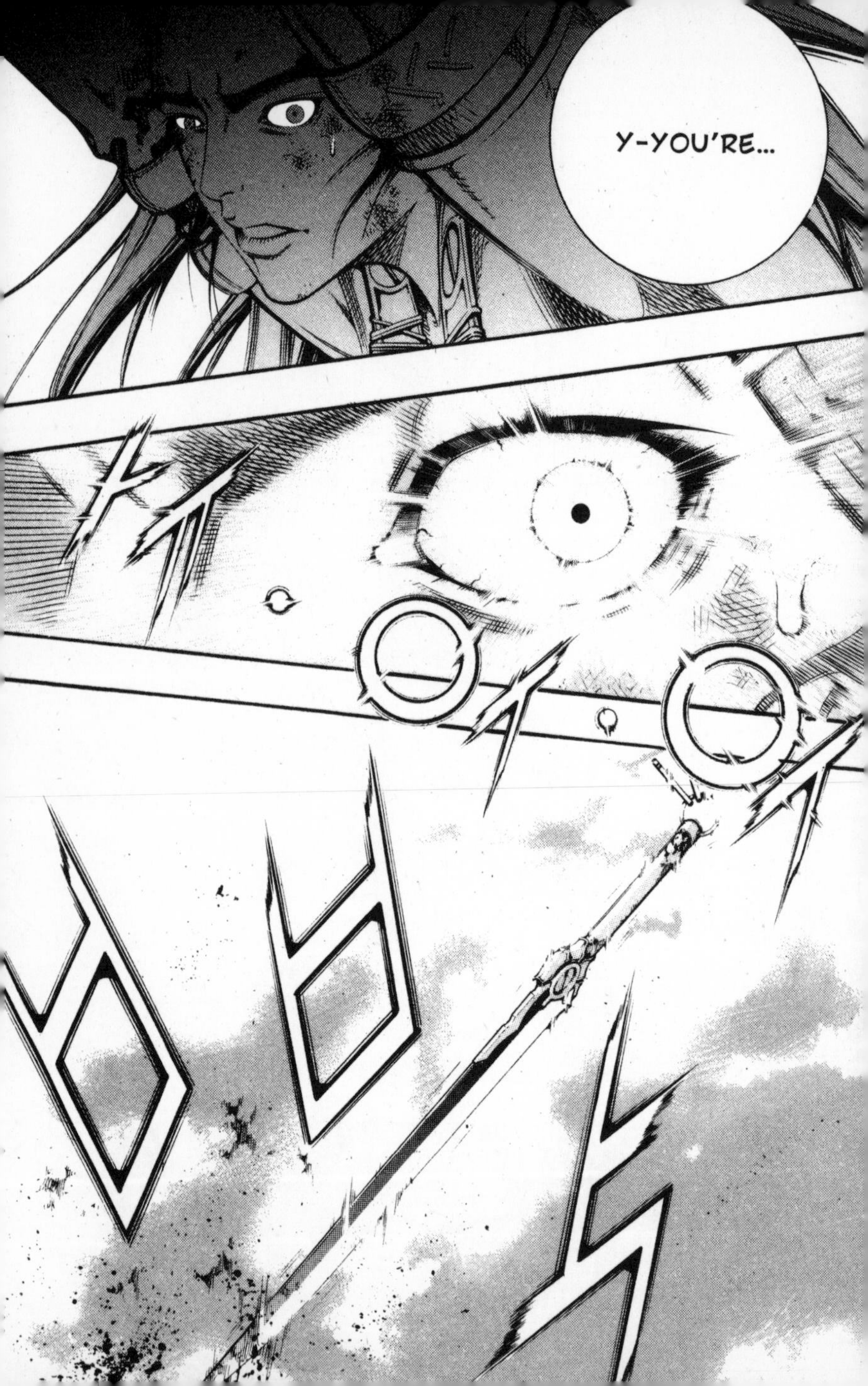
Y-YOU'RE...

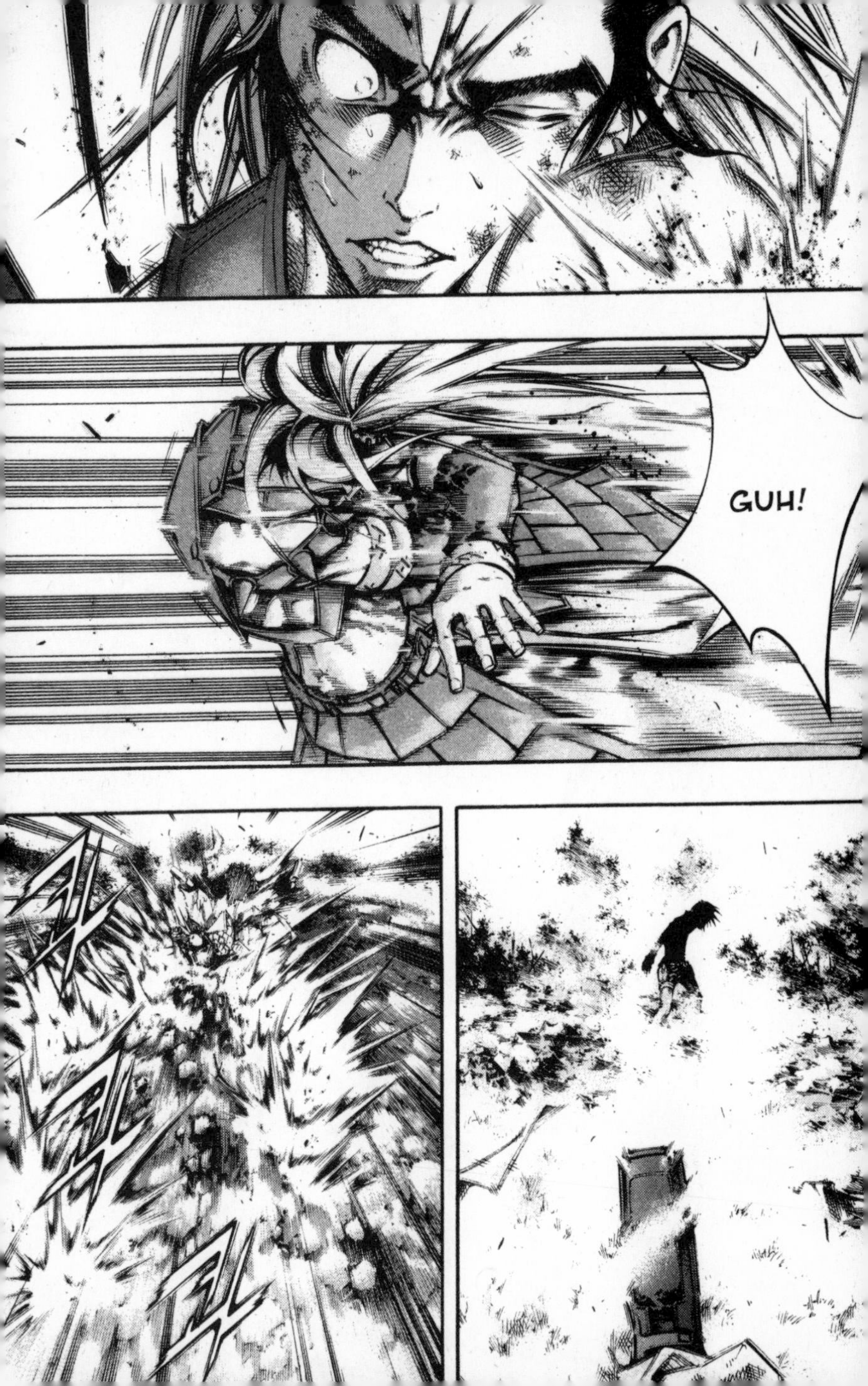
GUH!

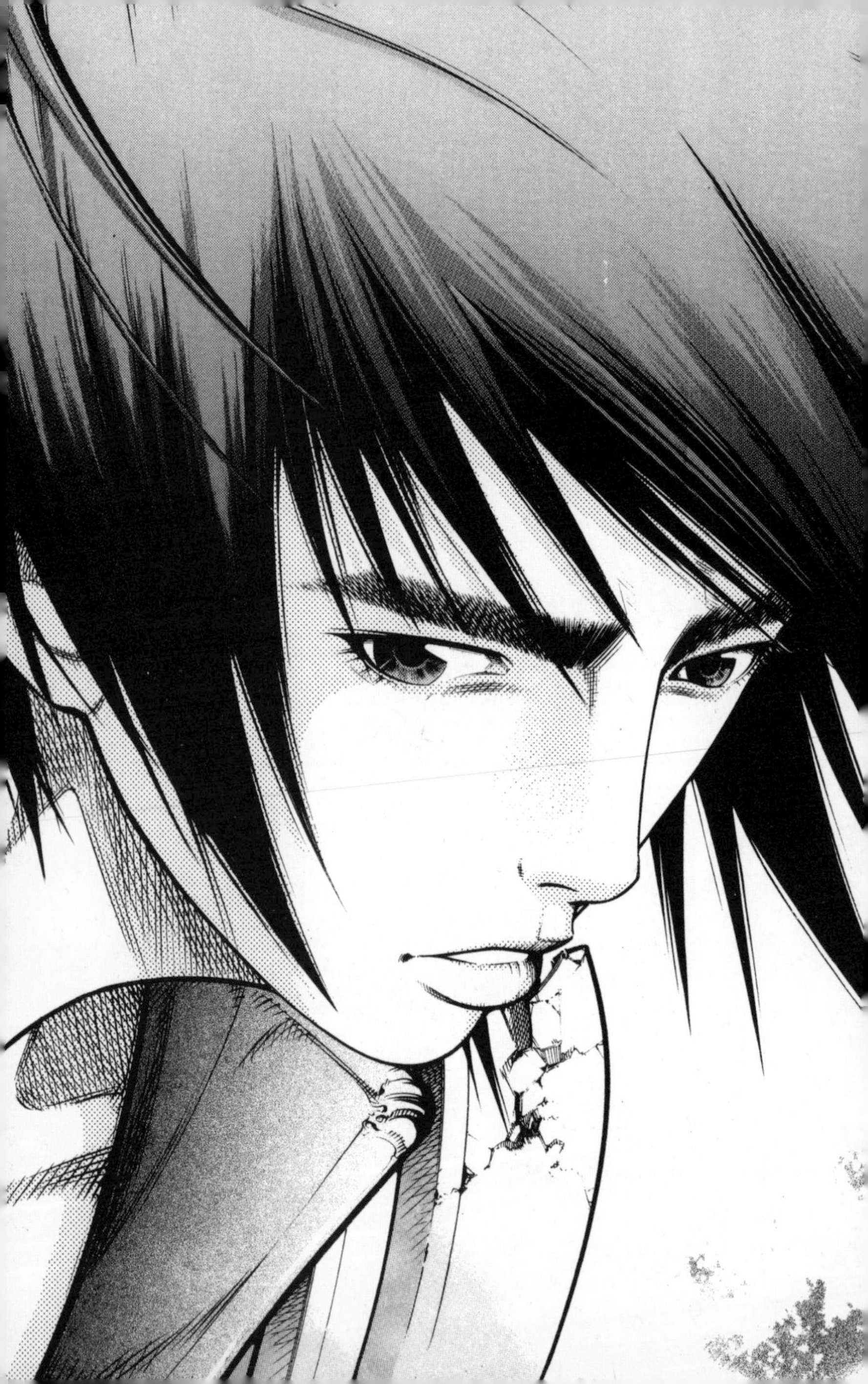

Chapter 12
Revenge!

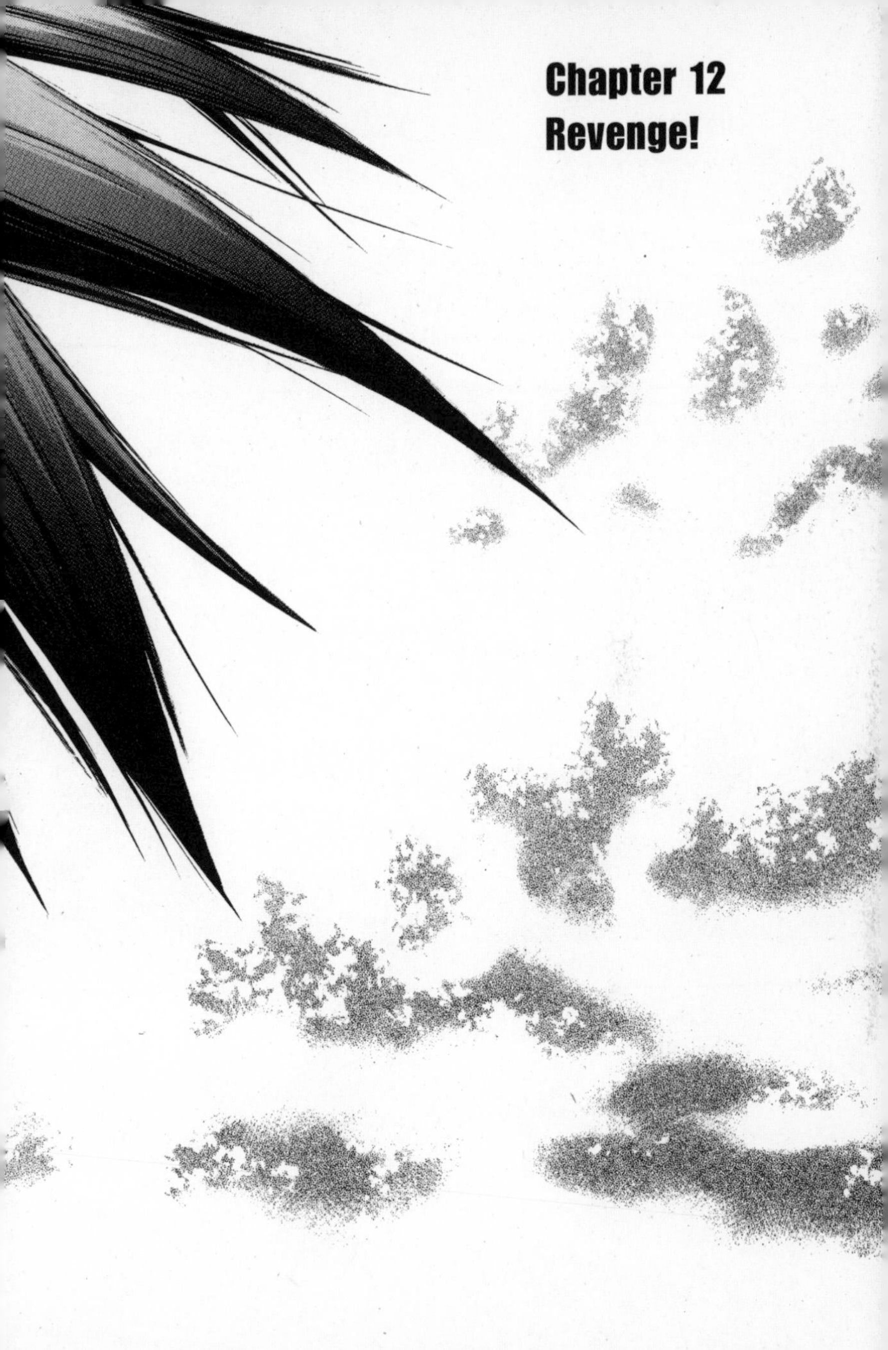

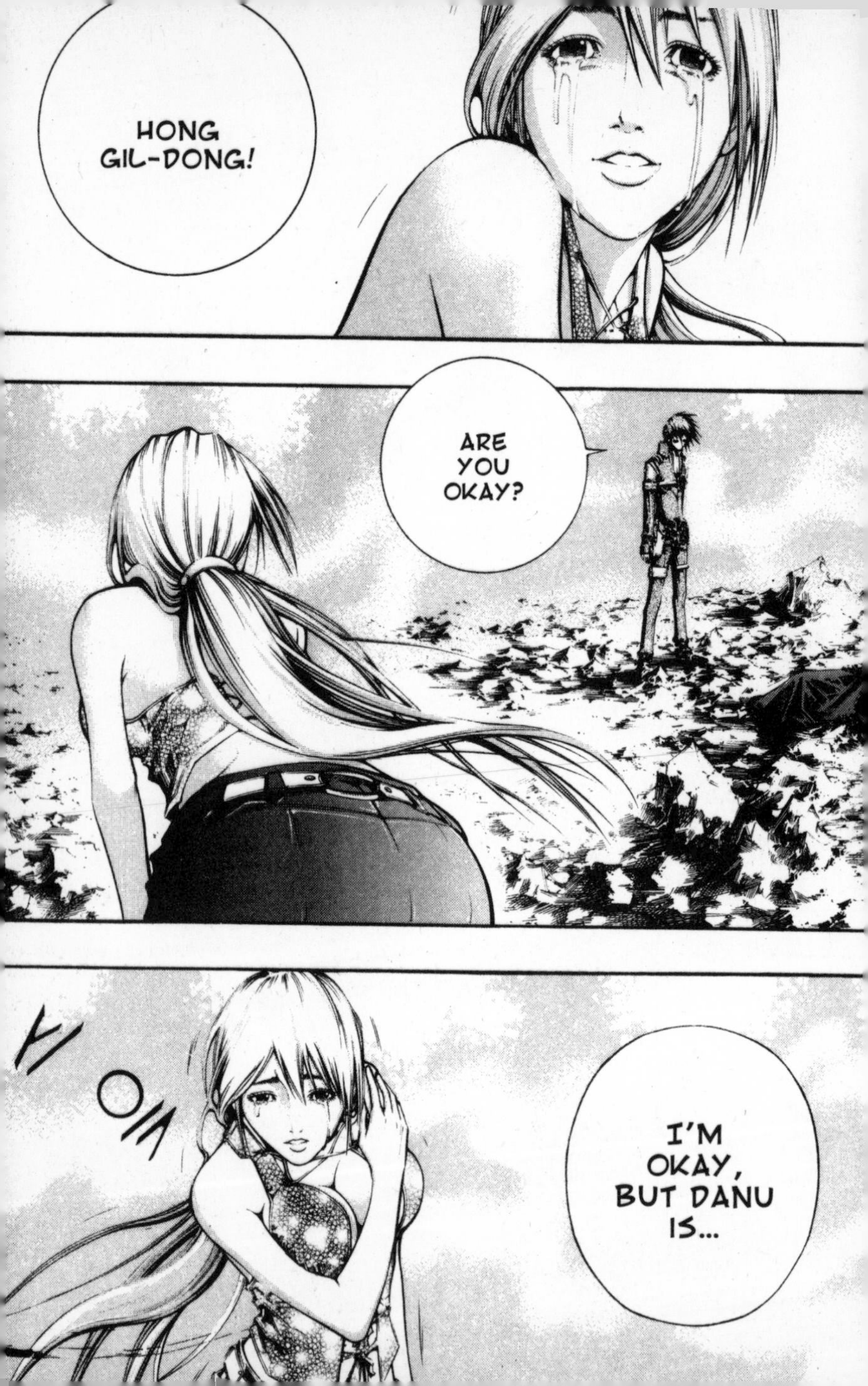
HONG GIL-DONG!
ARE YOU OKAY?
I'M OKAY, BUT DANU IS...

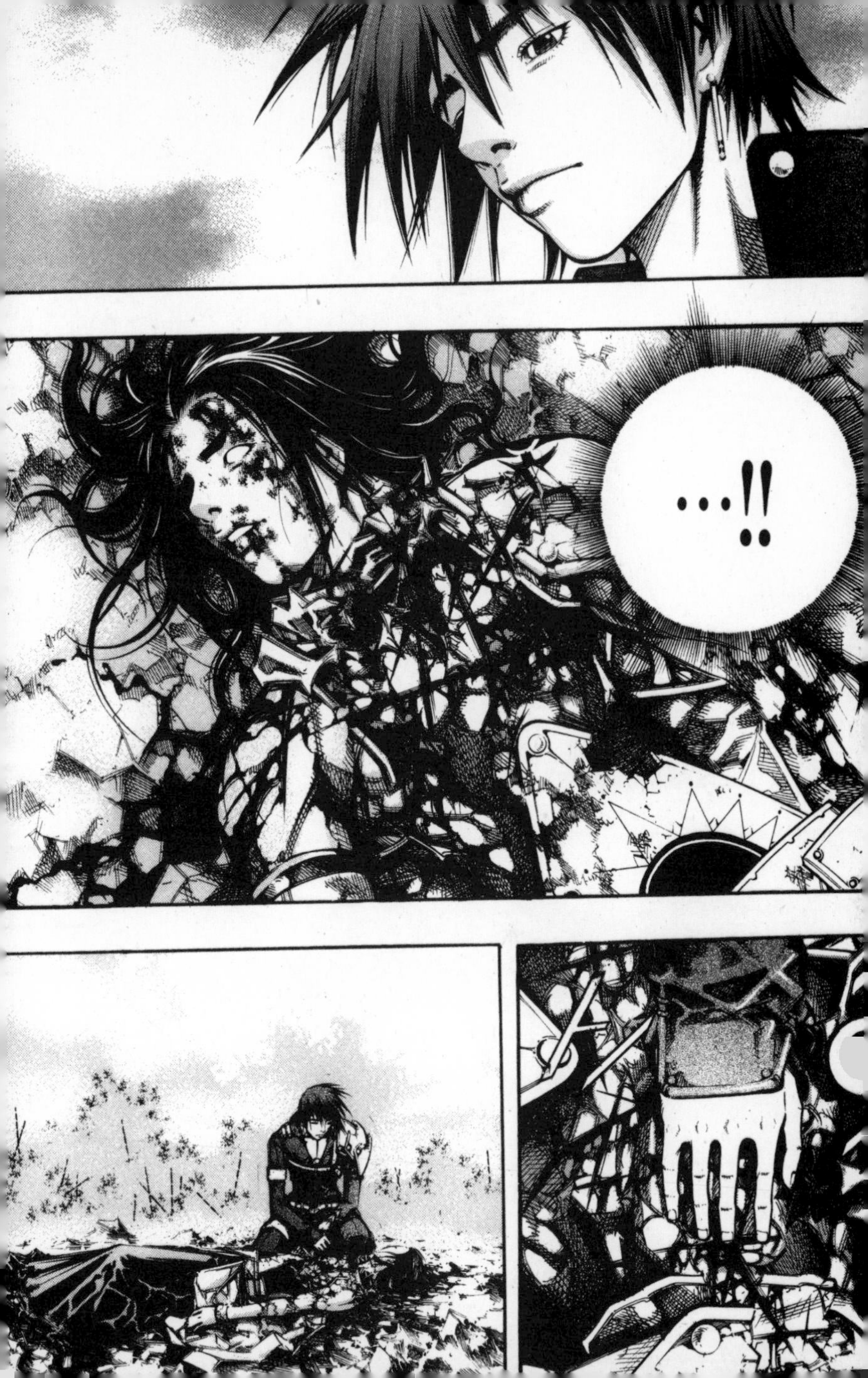
...!!

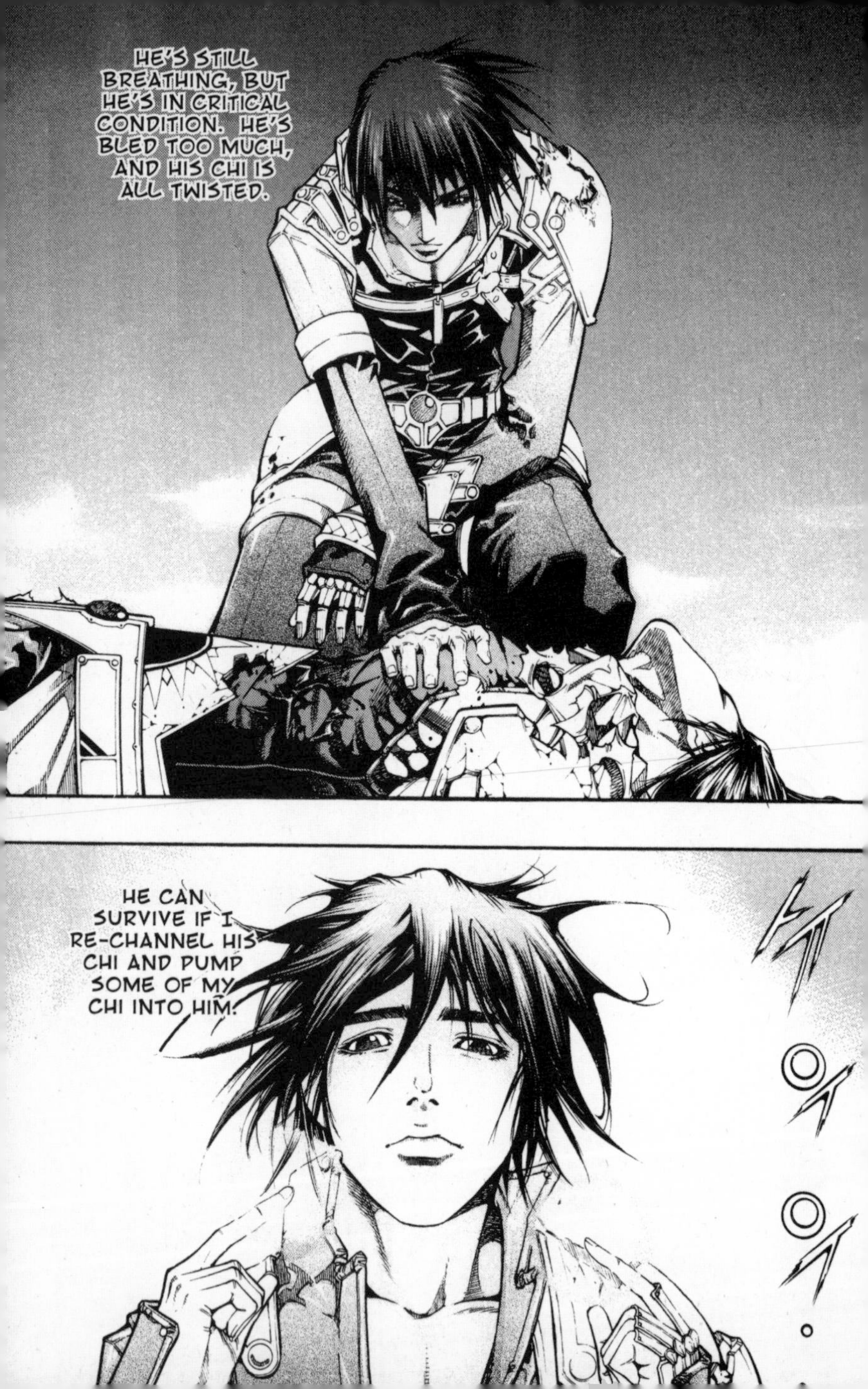
HE'S STILL BREATHING, BUT HE'S IN CRITICAL CONDITION. HE'S BLED TOO MUCH, AND HIS CHI IS ALL TWISTED.
HE CAN SURVIVE IF I RE-CHANNEL HIS CHI AND PUMP SOME OF MY CHI INTO HIM.

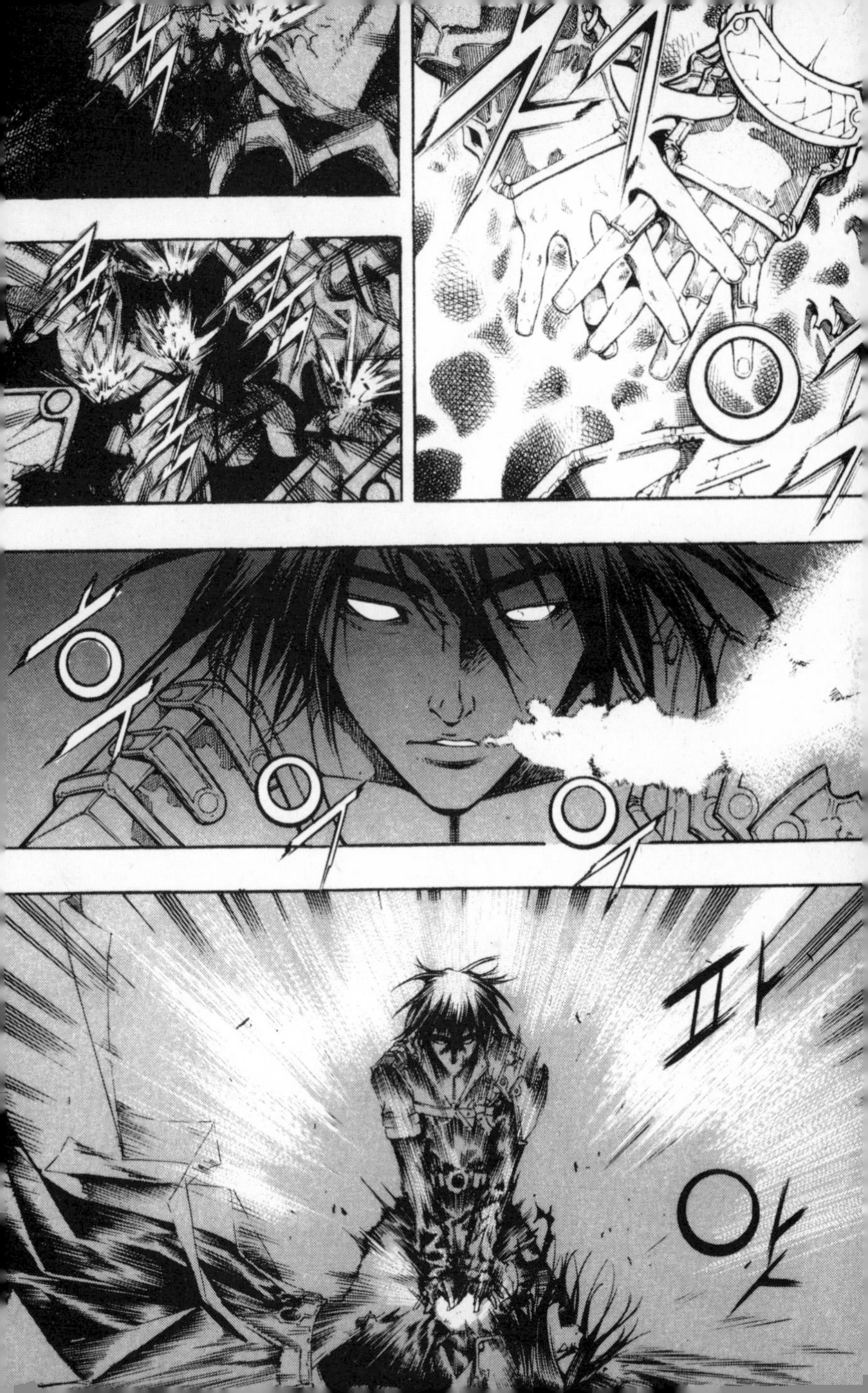

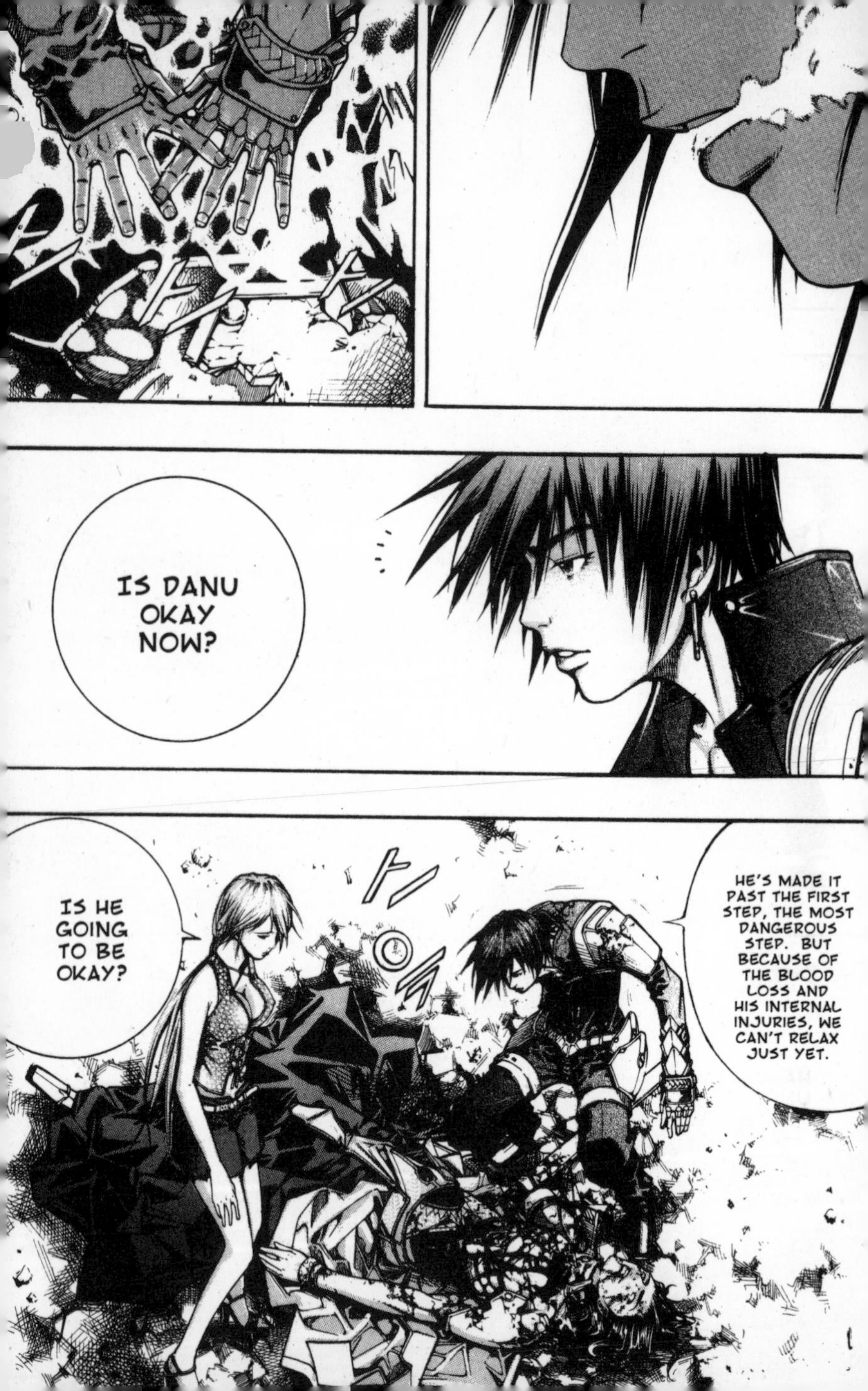
IS DANU OKAY NOW?
HE'S MADE IT PAST THE FIRST STEP, THE MOST DANGEROUS STEP. BUT BECAUSE OF THE BLOOD LOSS AND HIS INTERNAL INJURIES, WE CAN'T RELAX JUST YET.
IS HE GOING TO BE OKAY?

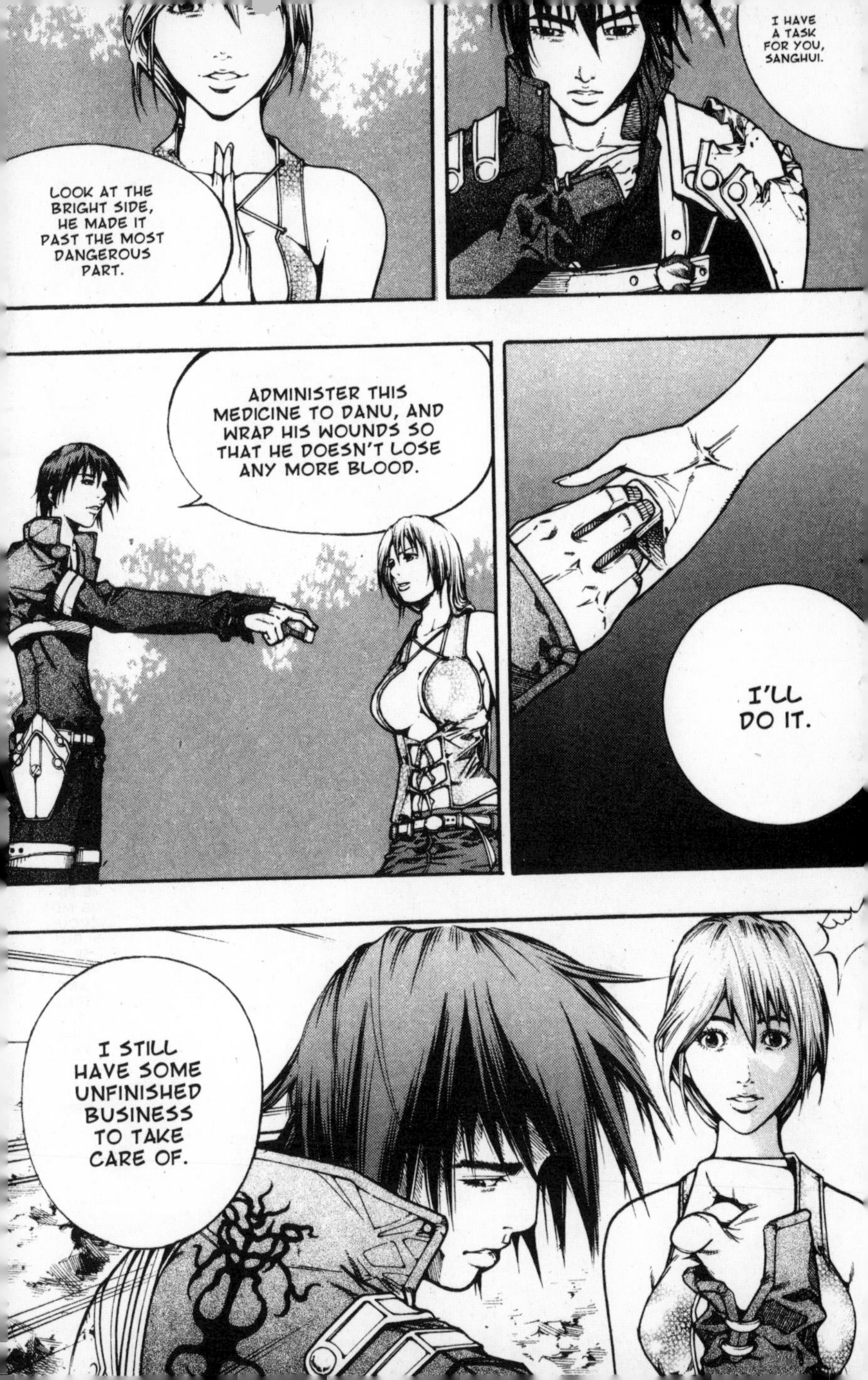
LOOK AT THE BRIGHT SIDE, HE MADE IT PAST THE MOST DANGEROUS PART.
I HAVE A TASK FOR YOU, SANGHUI.
ADMINISTER THIS MEDICINE TO DANU, AND WRAP HIS WOUNDS SO THAT HE DOESN'T LOSE ANY MORE BLOOD.
I'LL DO IT.
I STILL HAVE SOME UNFINISHED BUSINESS TO TAKE CARE OF.

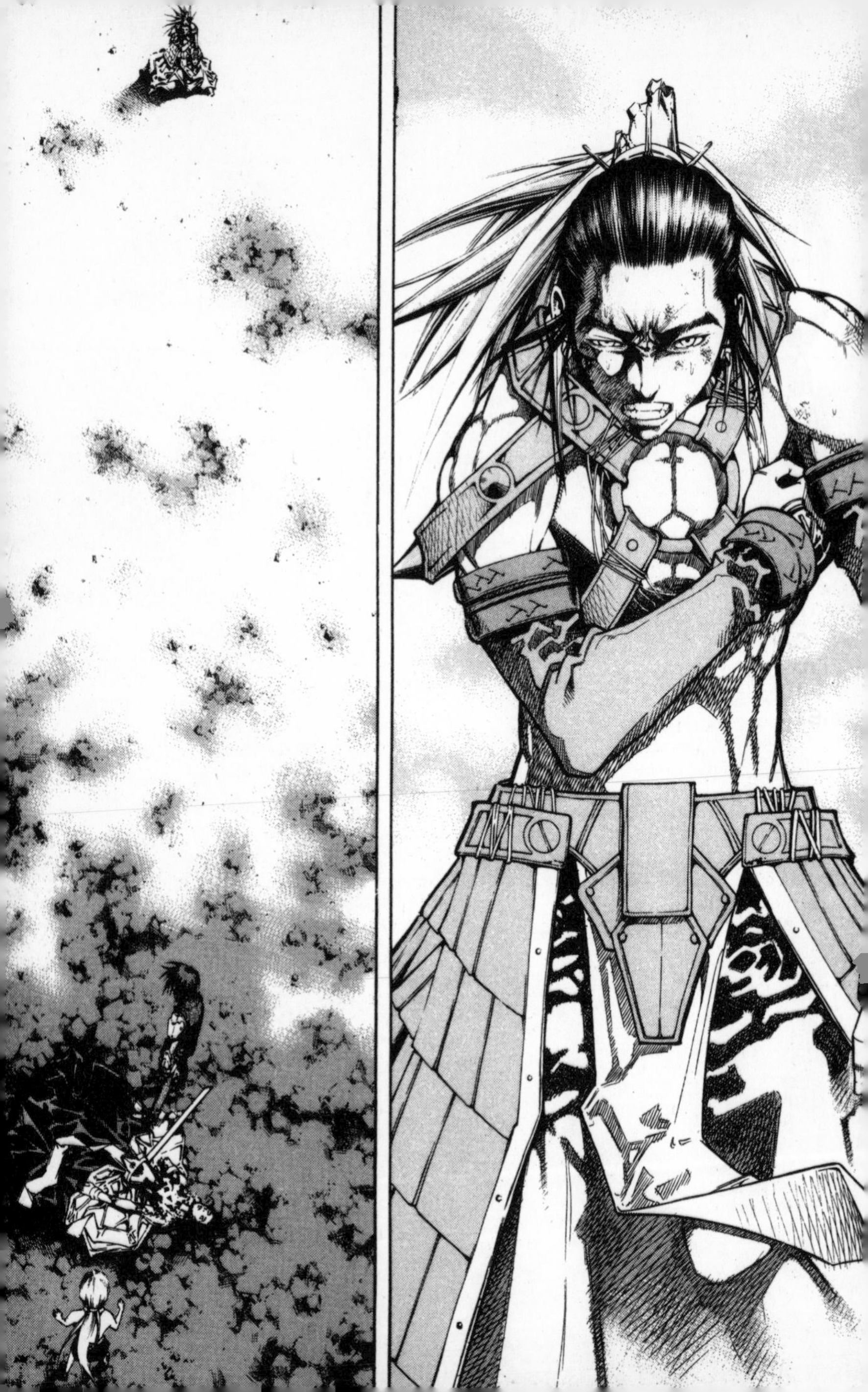

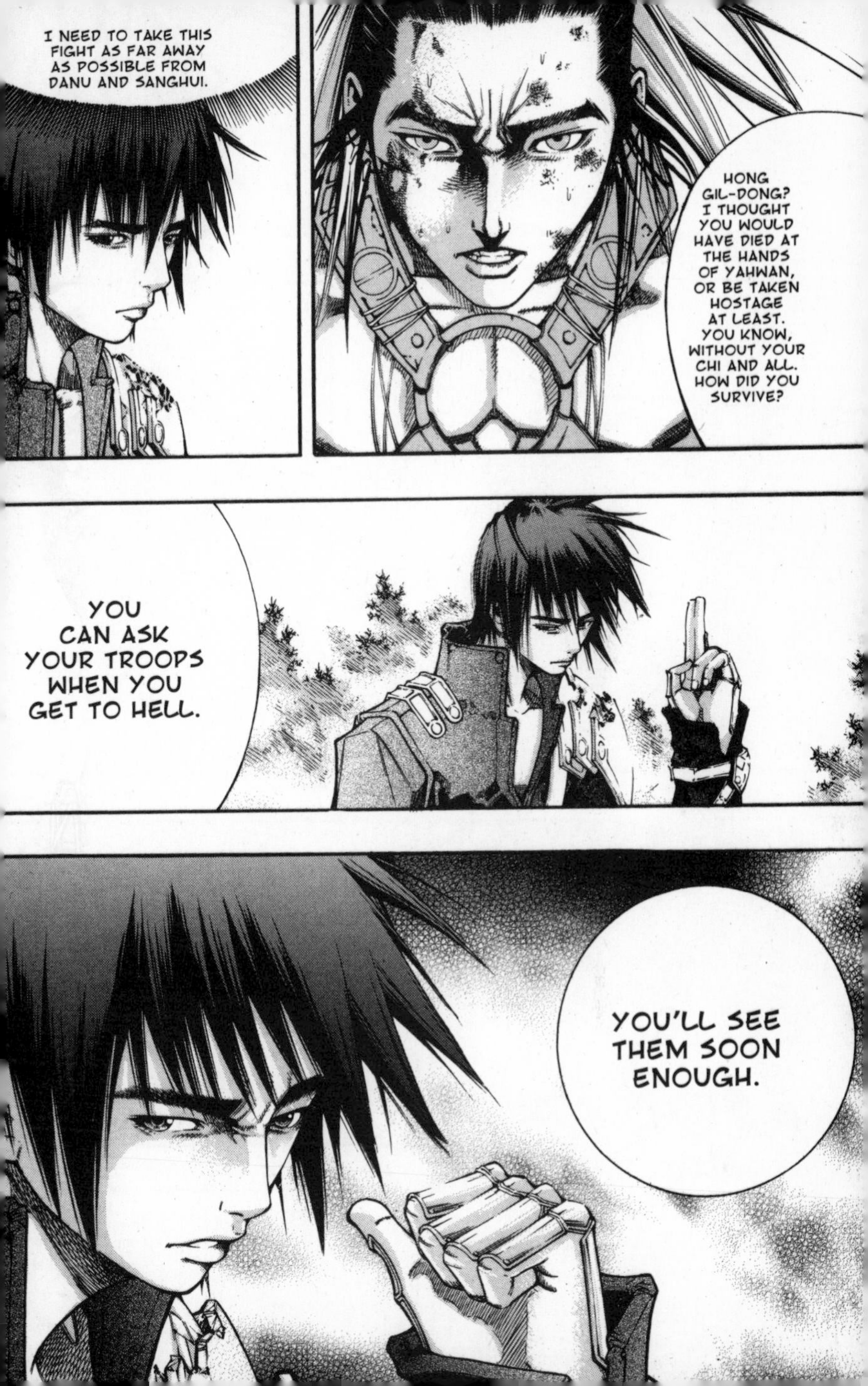
I NEED TO TAKE THIS FIGHT AS FAR AWAY AS POSSIBLE FROM DANU AND SANGHUI.
HONG GIL-DONG? I THOUGHT YOU WOULD HAVE DIED AT THE HANDS OF YAHWAN, OR BE TAKEN HOSTAGE AT LEAST. YOU KNOW, WITHOUT YOUR CHI AND ALL. HOW DID YOU SURVIVE?
YOU CAN ASK YOUR TROOPS WHEN YOU GET TO HELL.
YOU'LL SEE THEM SOON ENOUGH.

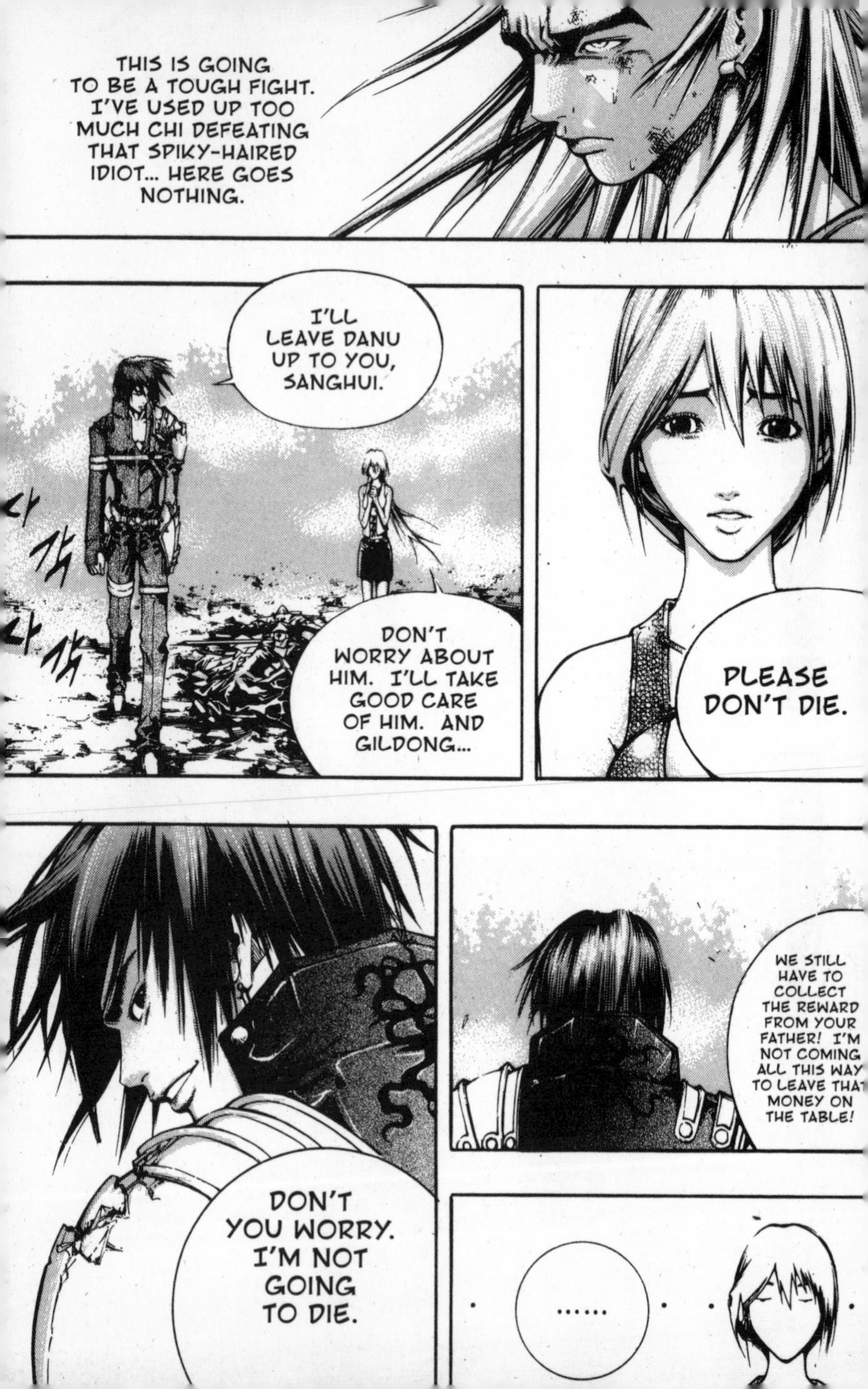
THIS IS GOING TO BE A TOUGH FIGHT. I'VE USED UP TOO MUCH CHI DEFEATING THAT SPIKY-HAIRED IDIOT... HERE GOES NOTHING.
I'LL LEAVE DANU UP TO YOU, SANGHUI.
DON'T WORRY ABOUT HIM. I'LL TAKE GOOD CARE OF HIM. AND GILDONG...
PLEASE DON'T DIE.
DON'T YOU WORRY. I'M NOT GOING TO DIE.
WE STILL HAVE TO COLLECT THE REWARD FROM YOUR FATHER! I'M NOT COMING ALL THIS WAY TO LEAVE THAT MONEY ON THE TABLE!
......

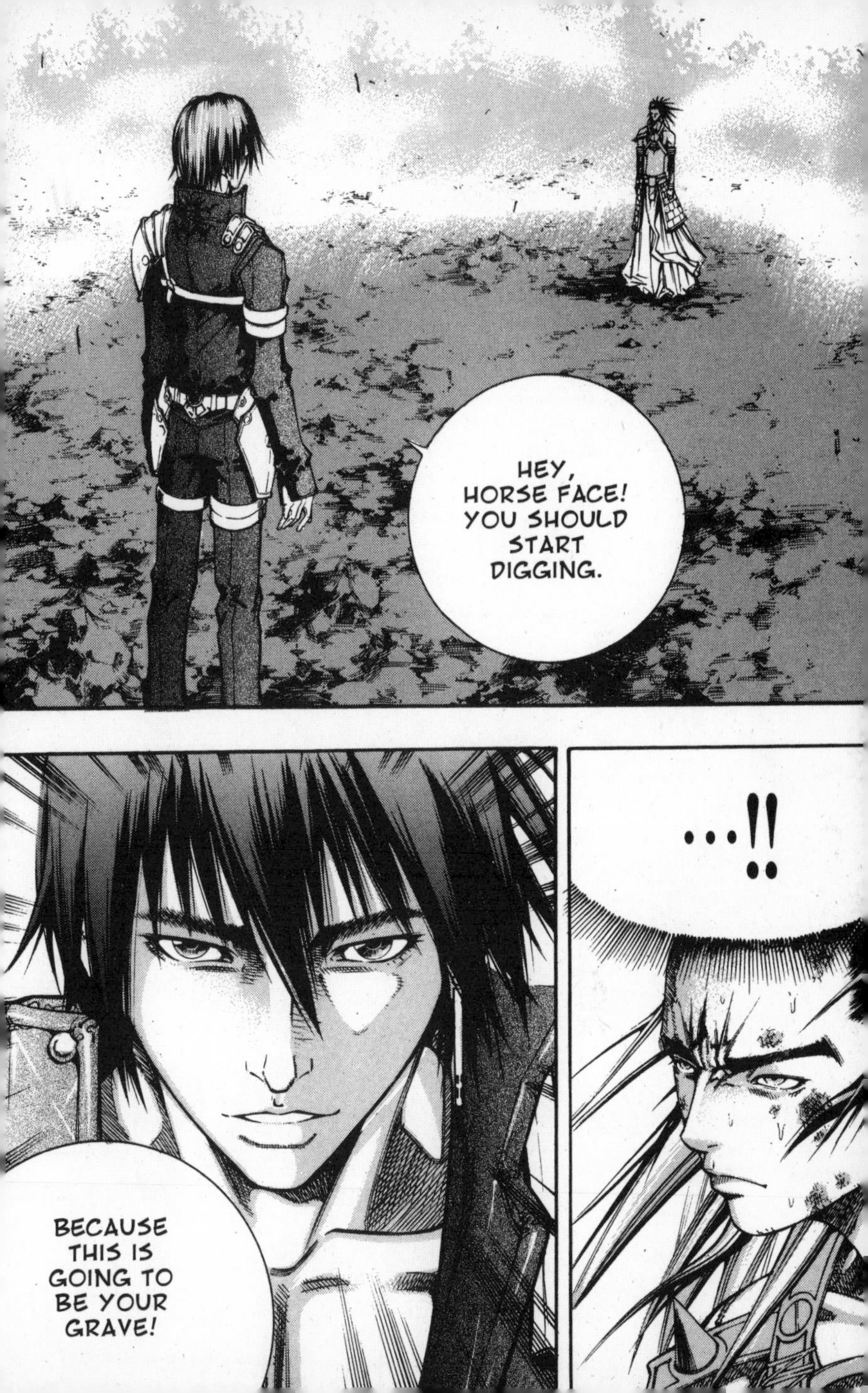
HEY, HORSE FACE! YOU SHOULD START DIGGING.
...!!
BECAUSE THIS IS GOING TO BE YOUR GRAVE!

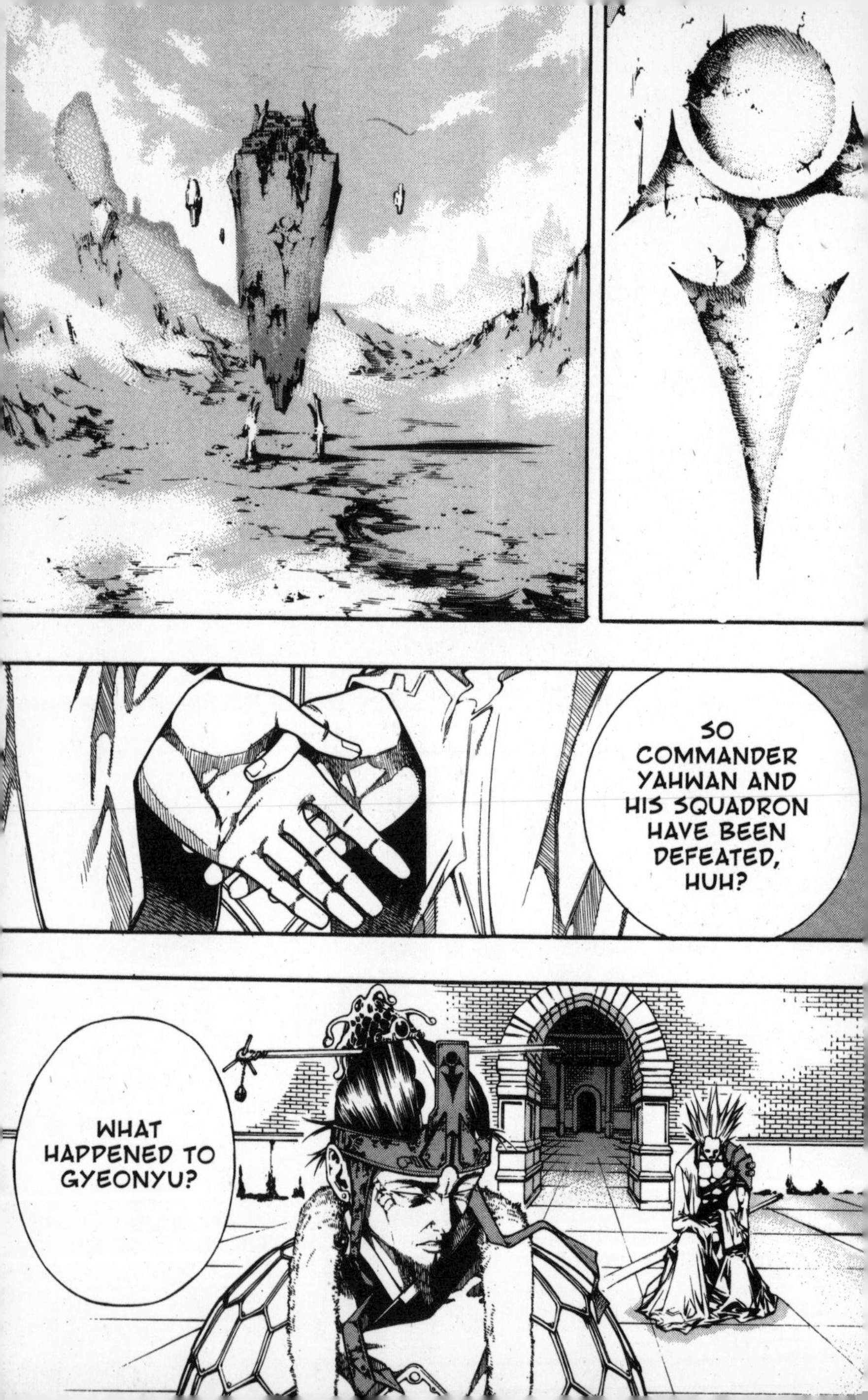
SO COMMANDER YAHWAN AND HIS SQUADRON HAVE BEEN DEFEATED, HUH?
WHAT HAPPENED TO GYEONYU?

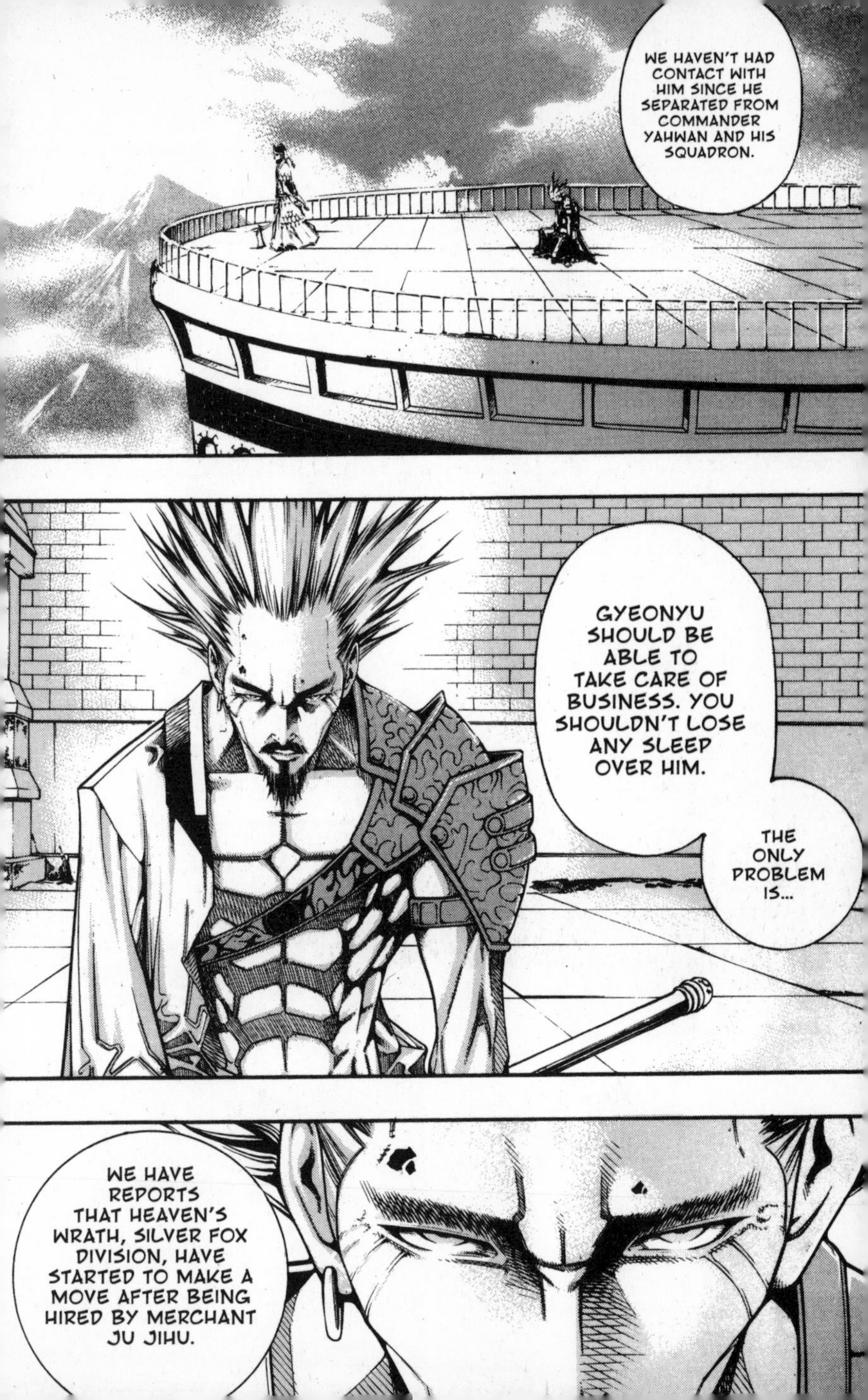
WE HAVEN'T HAD CONTACT WITH HIM SINCE HE SEPARATED FROM COMMANDER YAHWAN AND HIS SQUADRON.
GYEONYU SHOULD BE ABLE TO TAKE CARE OF BUSINESS. YOU SHOULDN'T LOSE ANY SLEEP OVER HIM.
THE ONLY PROBLEM IS...
WE HAVE REPORTS THAT HEAVEN'S WRATH, SILVER FOX DIVISION, HAVE STARTED TO MAKE A MOVE AFTER BEING HIRED BY MERCHANT JU JIHU.

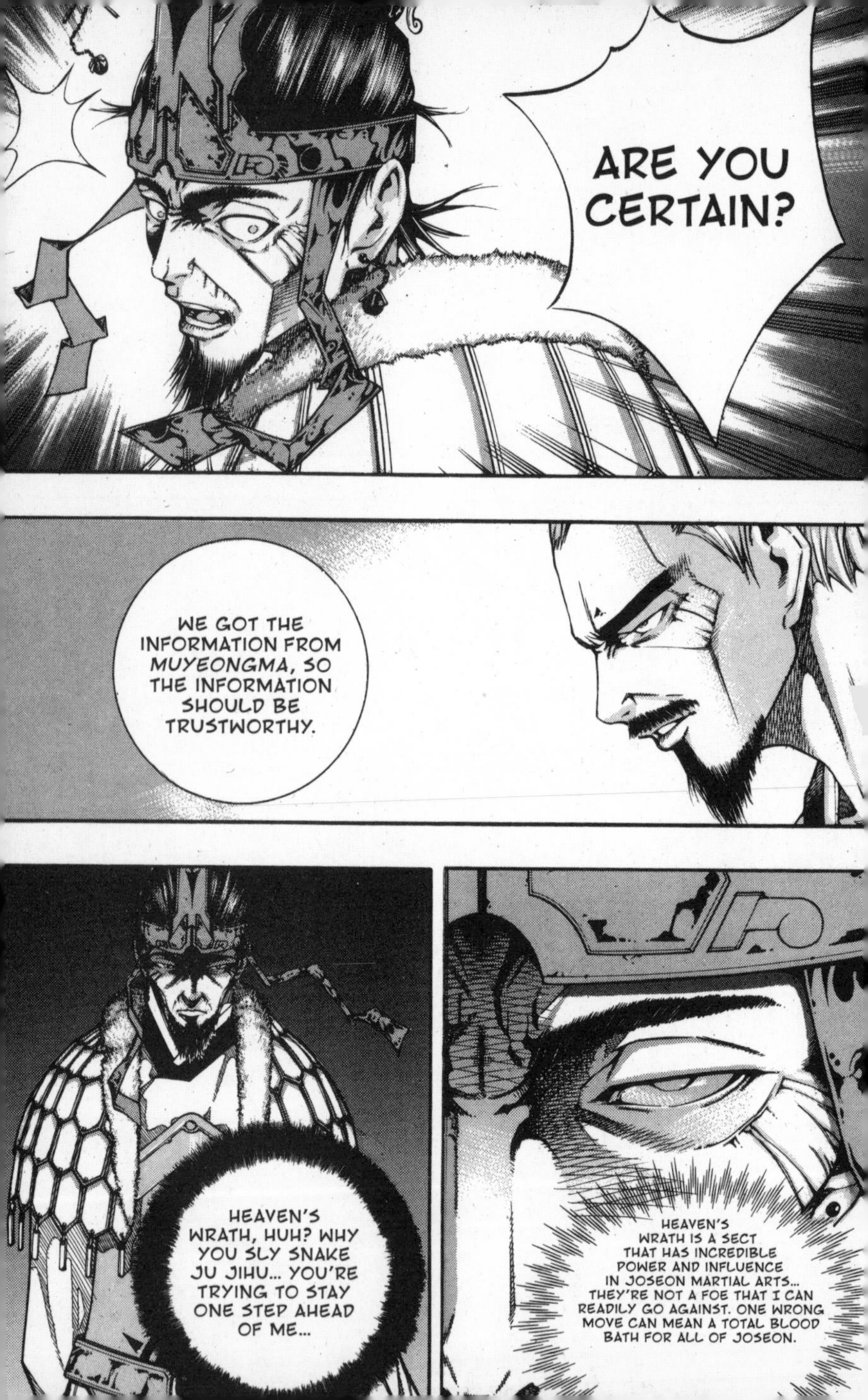
ARE YOU CERTAIN?
WE GOT THE INFORMATION FROM MUYEONGMA, SO THE INFORMATION SHOULD BE TRUSTWORTHY.
HEAVEN'S WRATH, HUH? WHY YOU SLY SNAKE JU JIHU... YOU'RE TRYING TO STAY ONE STEP AHEAD OF ME...
HEAVEN'S WRATH IS A SECT THAT HAS INCREDIBLE POWER AND INFLUENCE IN JOSEON MARTIAL ARTS... THEY'RE NOT A FOE THAT I CAN READILY GO AGAINST. ONE WRONG MOVE CAN MEAN A TOTAL BLOOD BATH FOR ALL OF JOSEON.

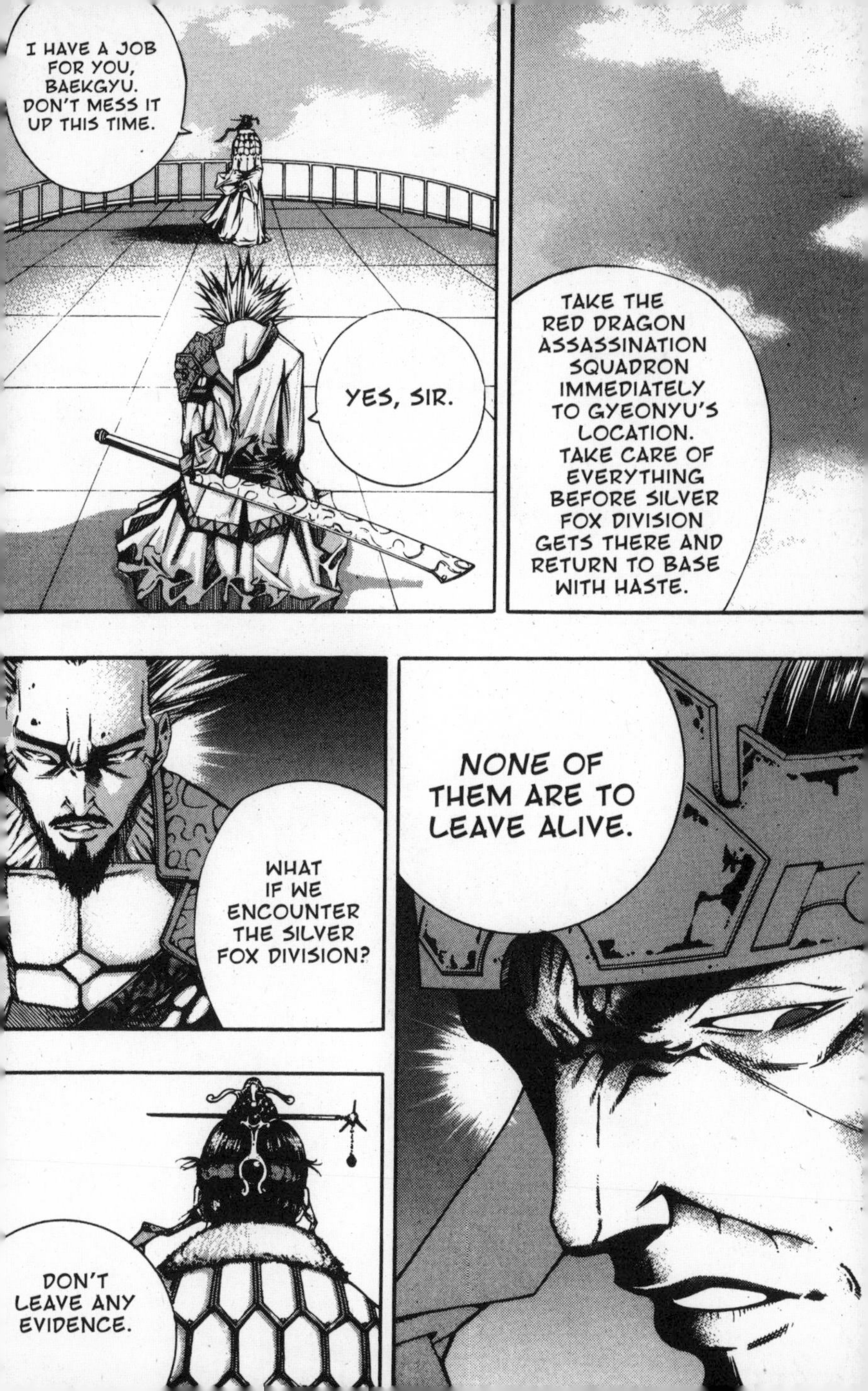
I HAVE A JOB FOR YOU, BAEKGYU. DON'T MESS IT UP THIS TIME.
YES, SIR.
TAKE THE RED DRAGON ASSASSINATION SQUADRON IMMEDIATELY TO GYEONYU'S LOCATION. TAKE CARE OF EVERYTHING BEFORE SILVER FOX DIVISION GETS THERE AND RETURN TO BASE WITH HASTE.
WHAT IF WE ENCOUNTER THE SILVER FOX DIVISION?
NONE OF THEM ARE TO LEAVE ALIVE.
DON'T LEAVE ANY EVIDENCE.

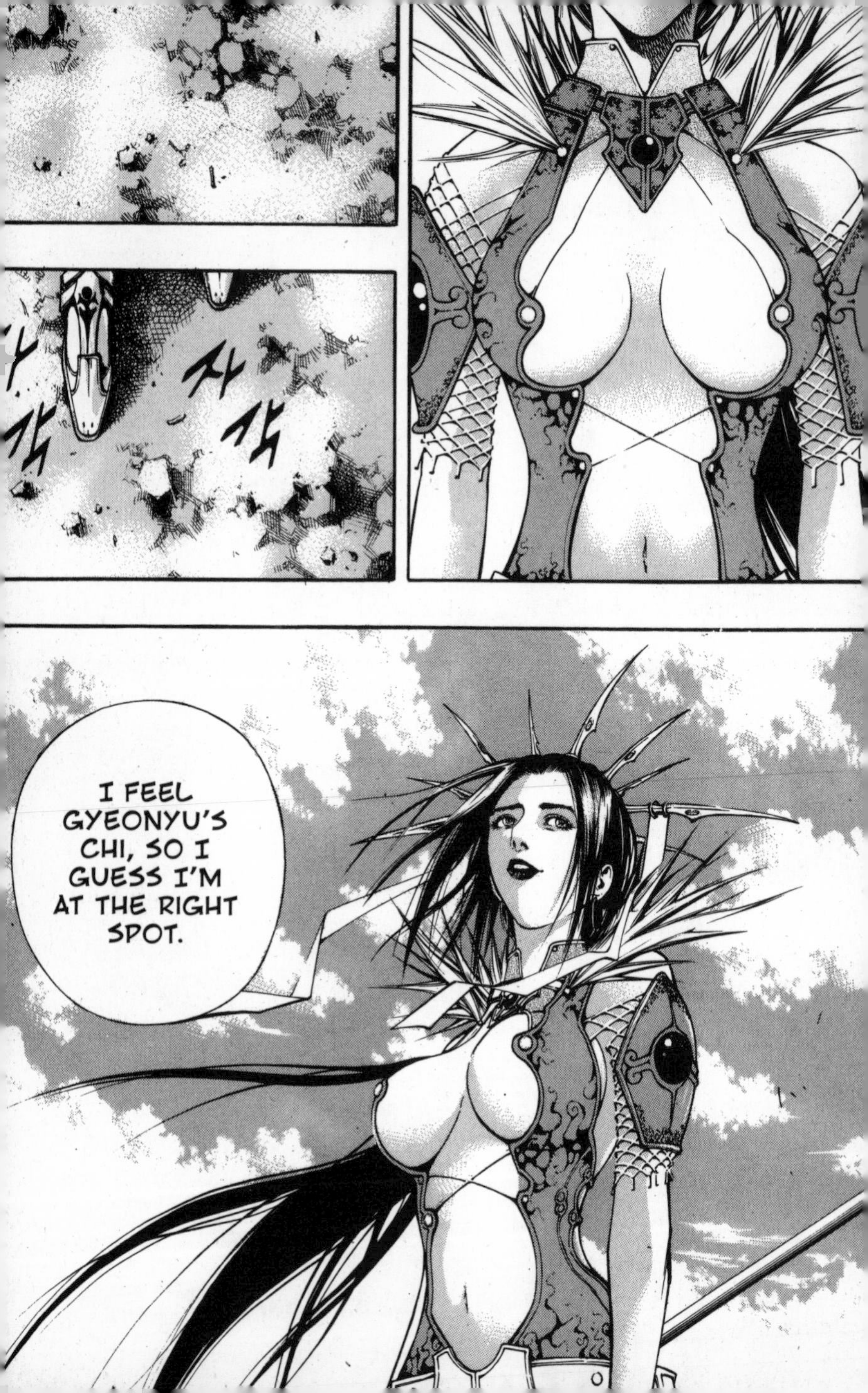
I FEEL GYEONYU'S CHI, SO I GUESS I'M AT THE RIGHT SPOT.

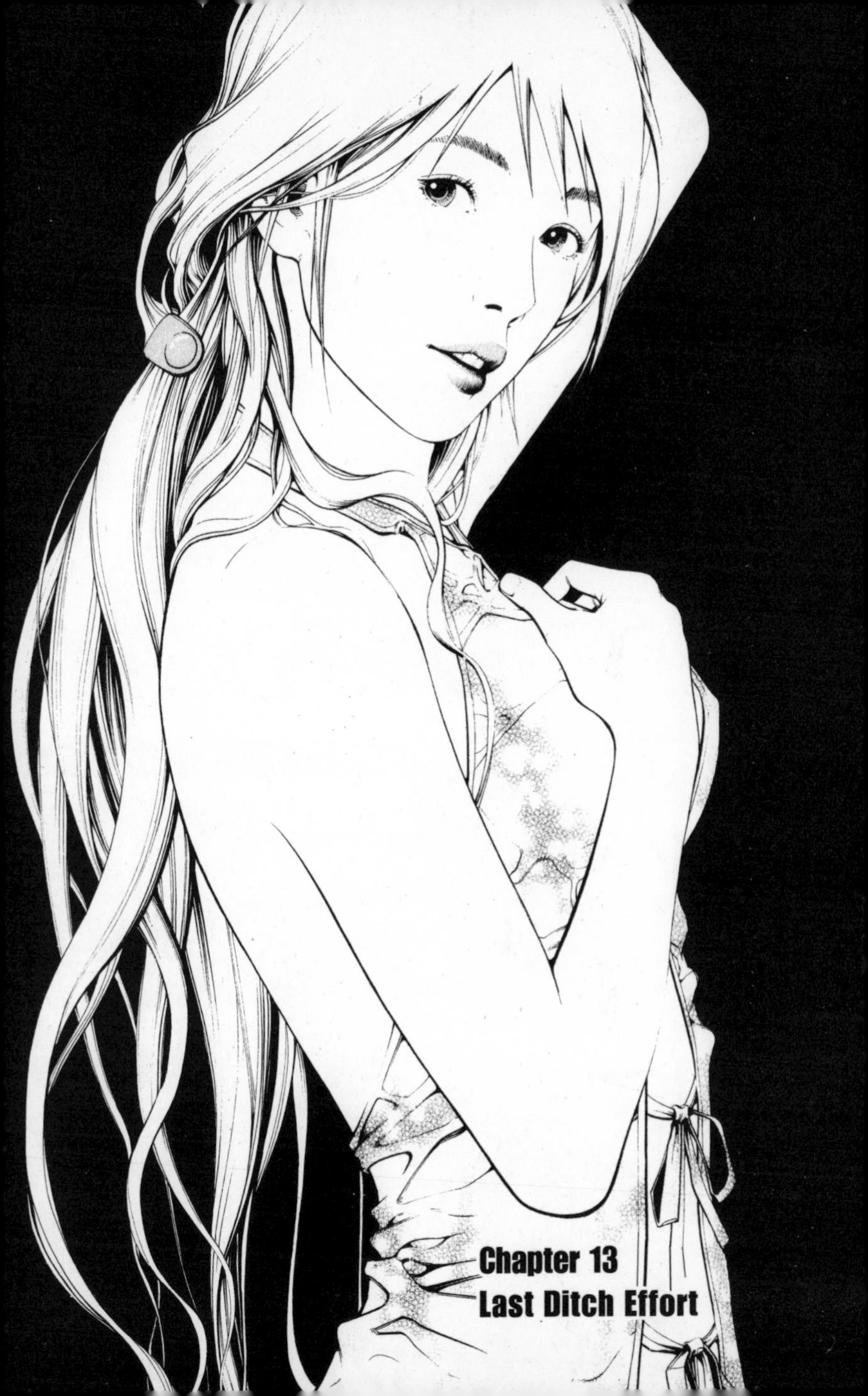
Chapter 13
Last Ditch Effort

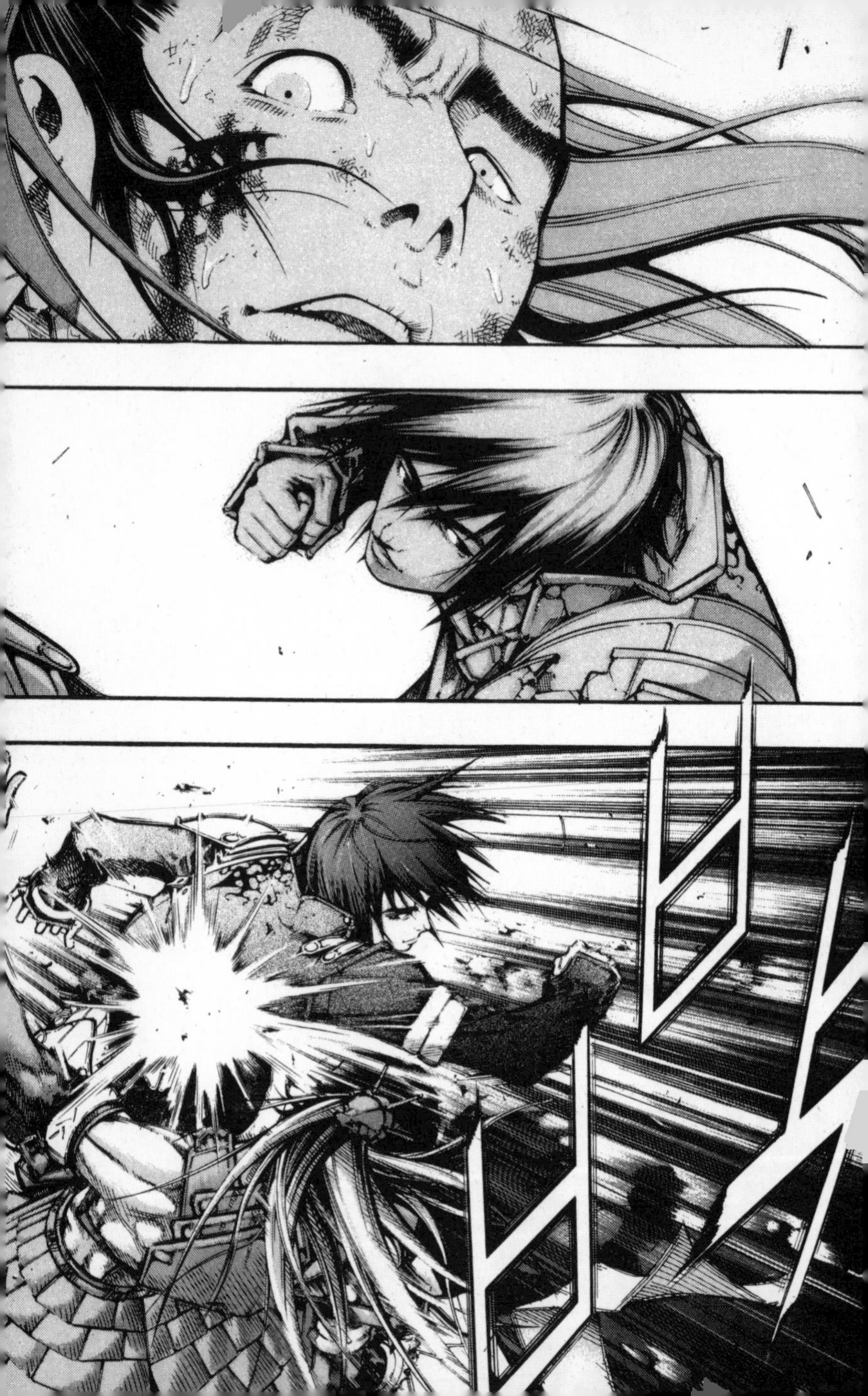

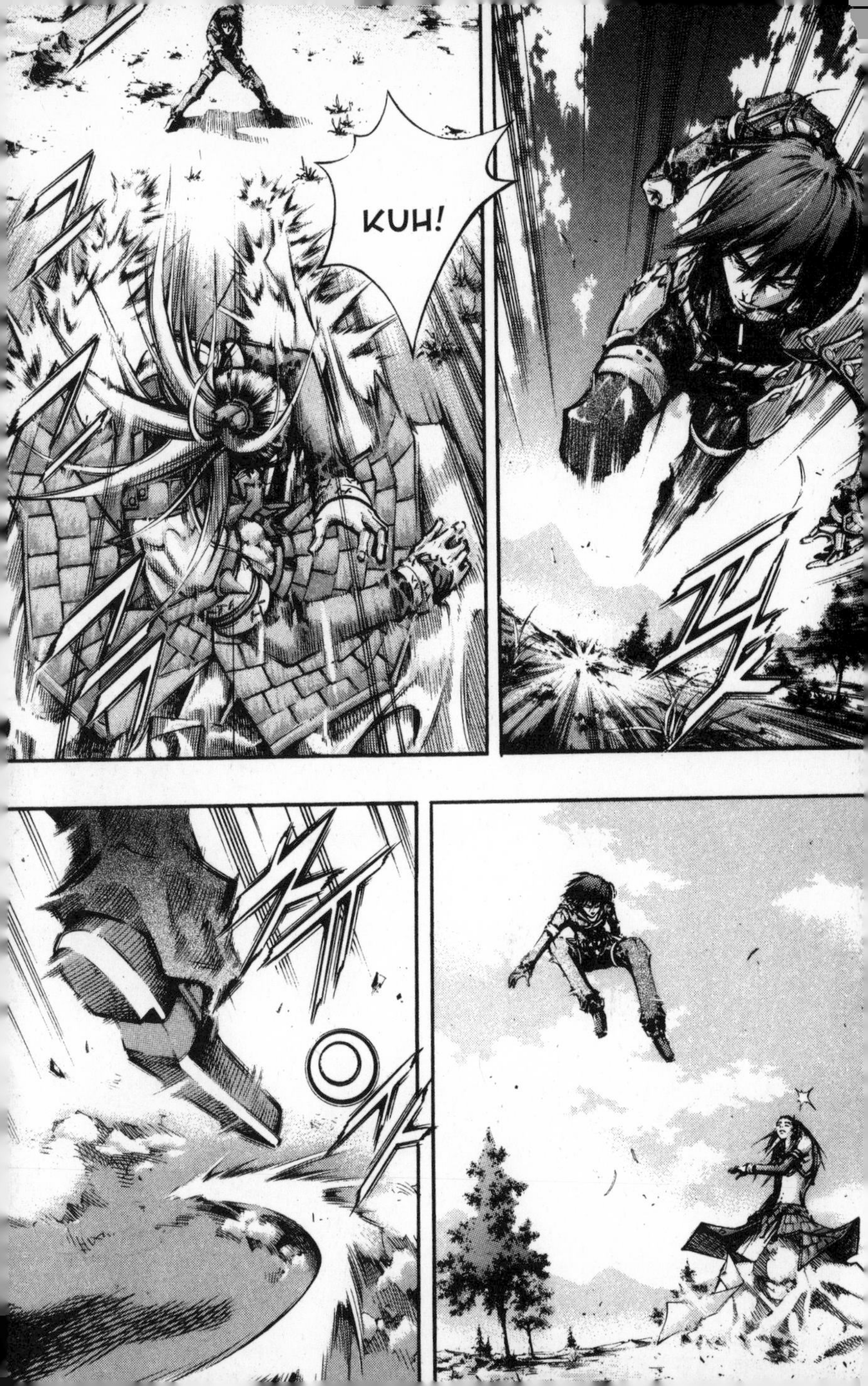
KUH!

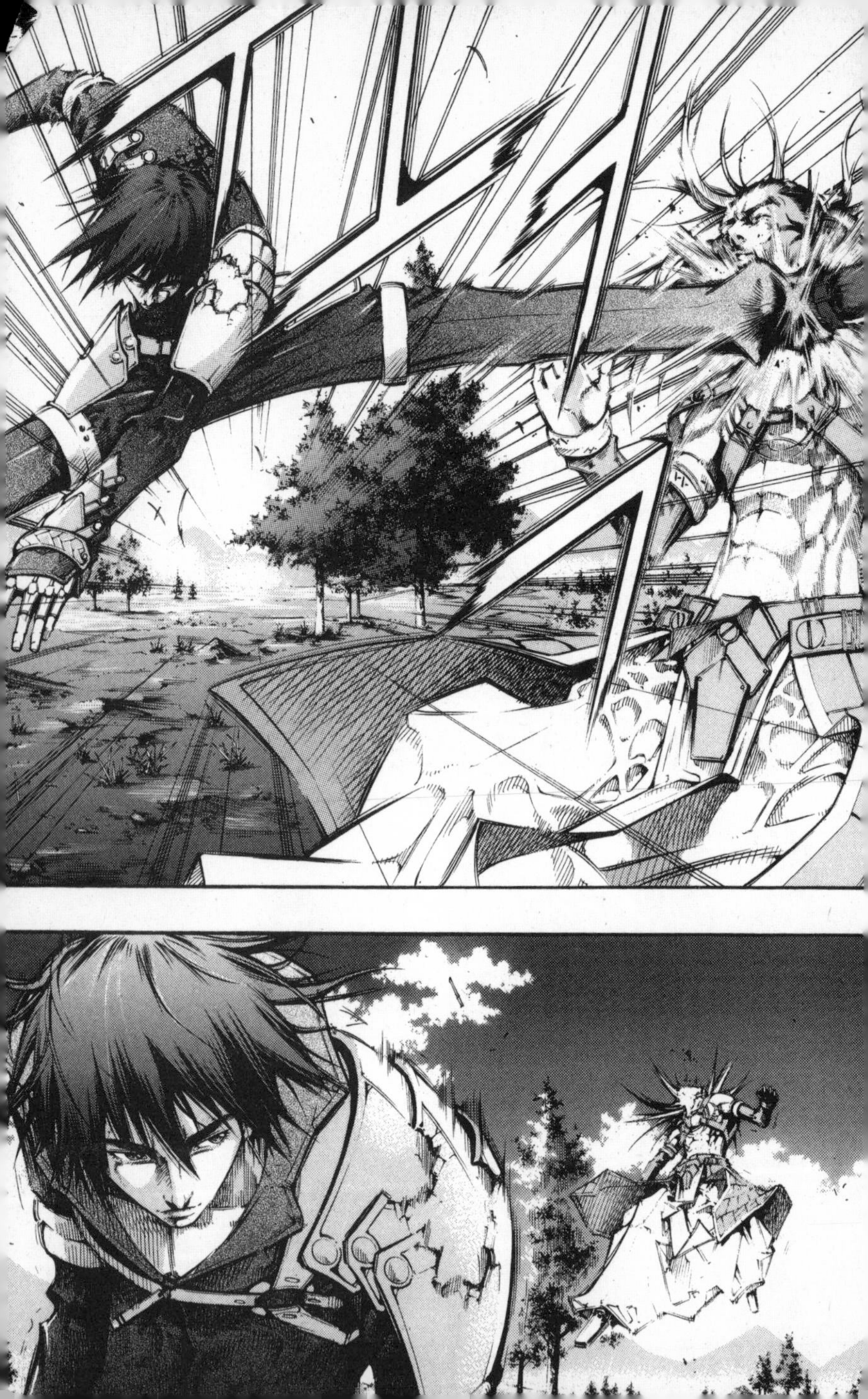

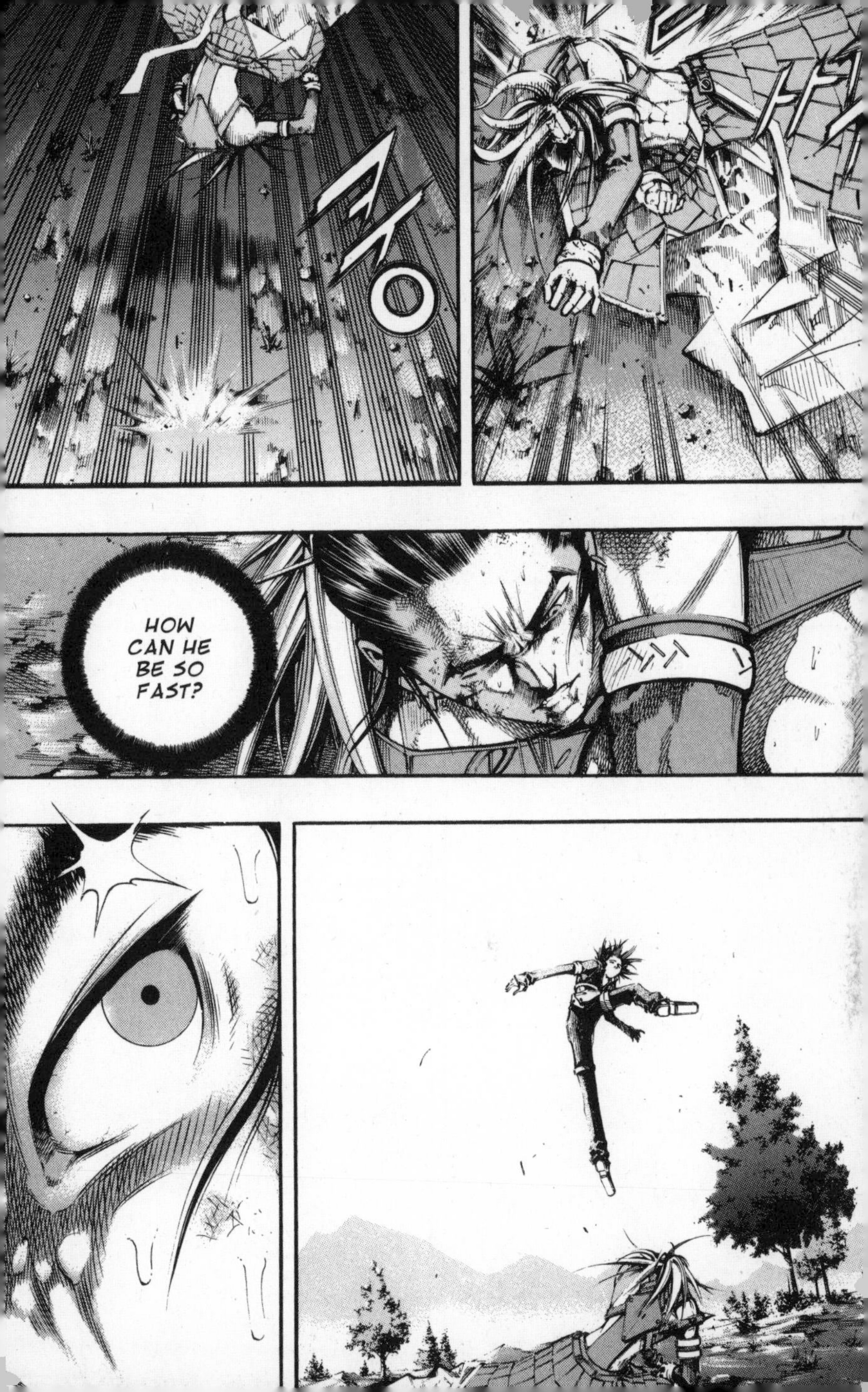
HOW CAN HE BE SO FAST?

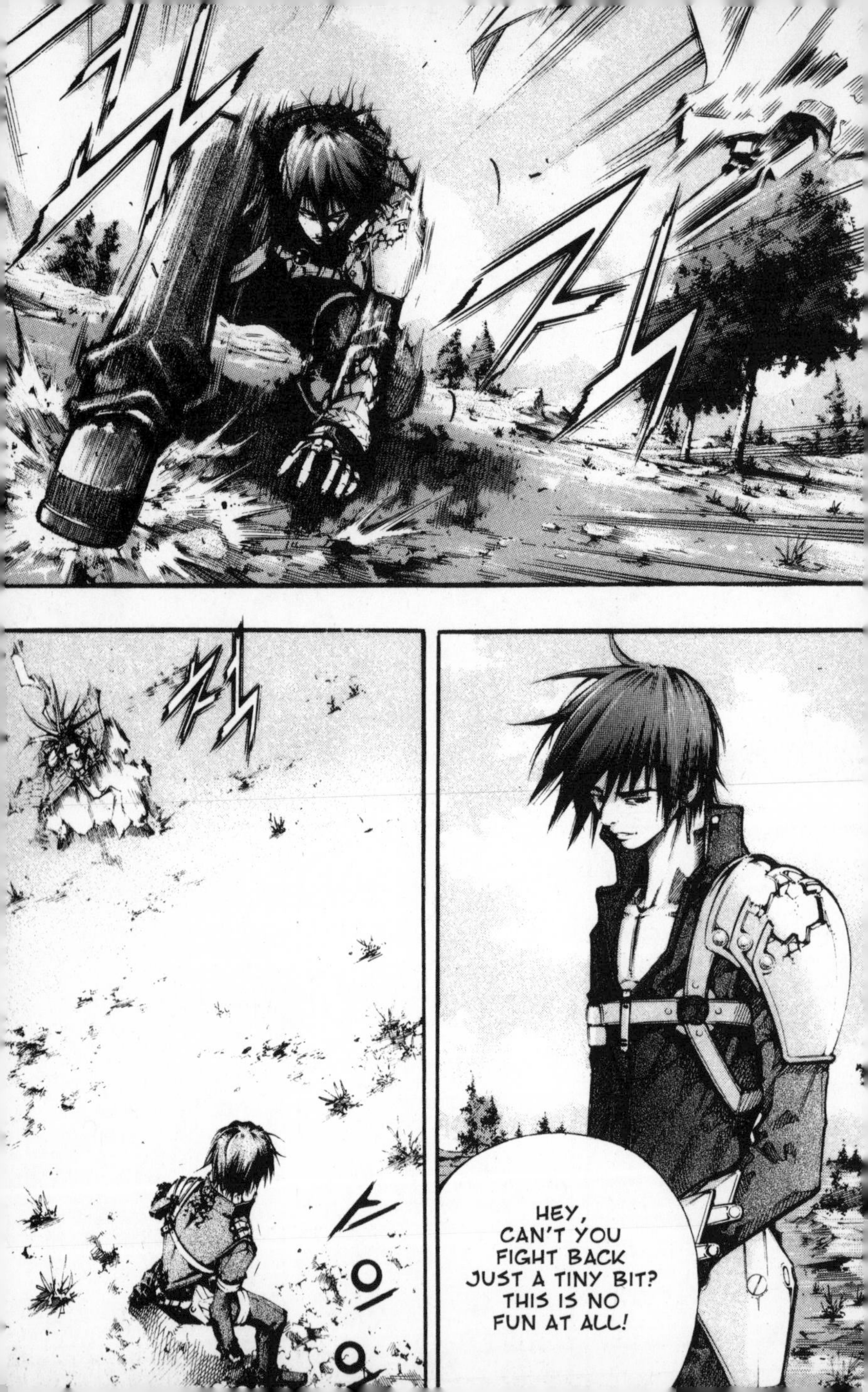
HEY, CAN'T YOU FIGHT BACK JUST A TINY BIT? THIS IS NO FUN AT ALL!

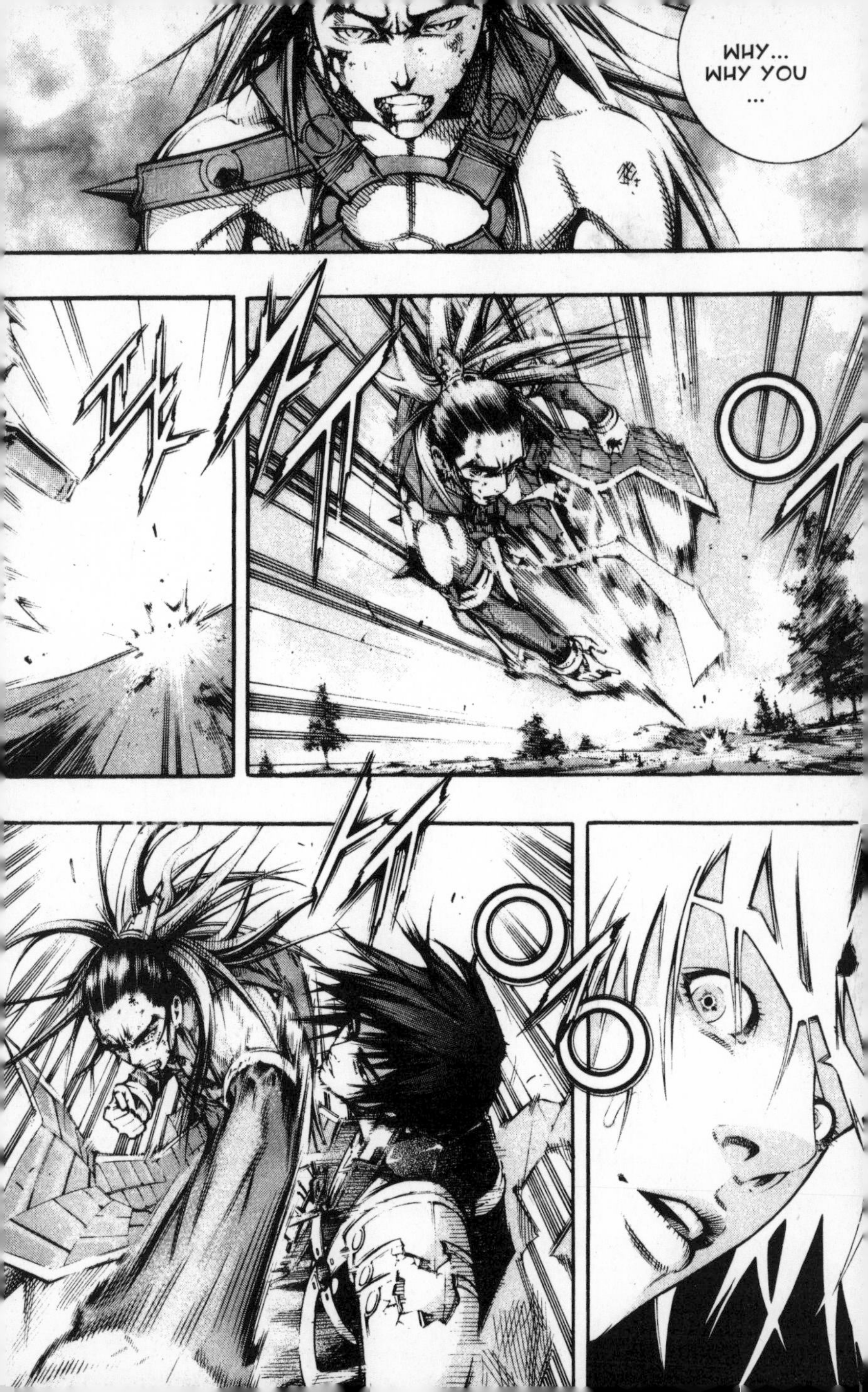
WHY...
WHY YOU
...

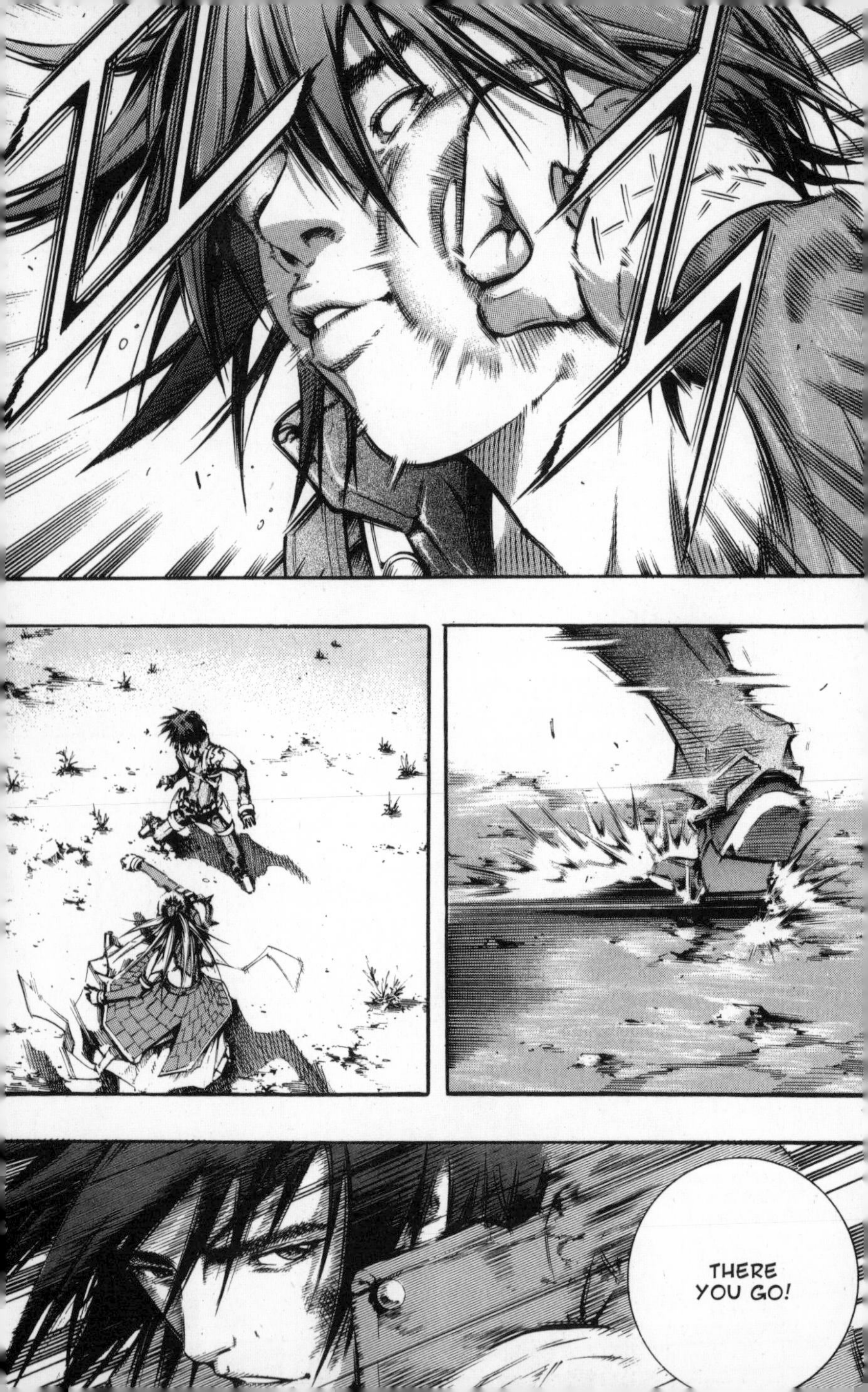
THERE YOU GO!

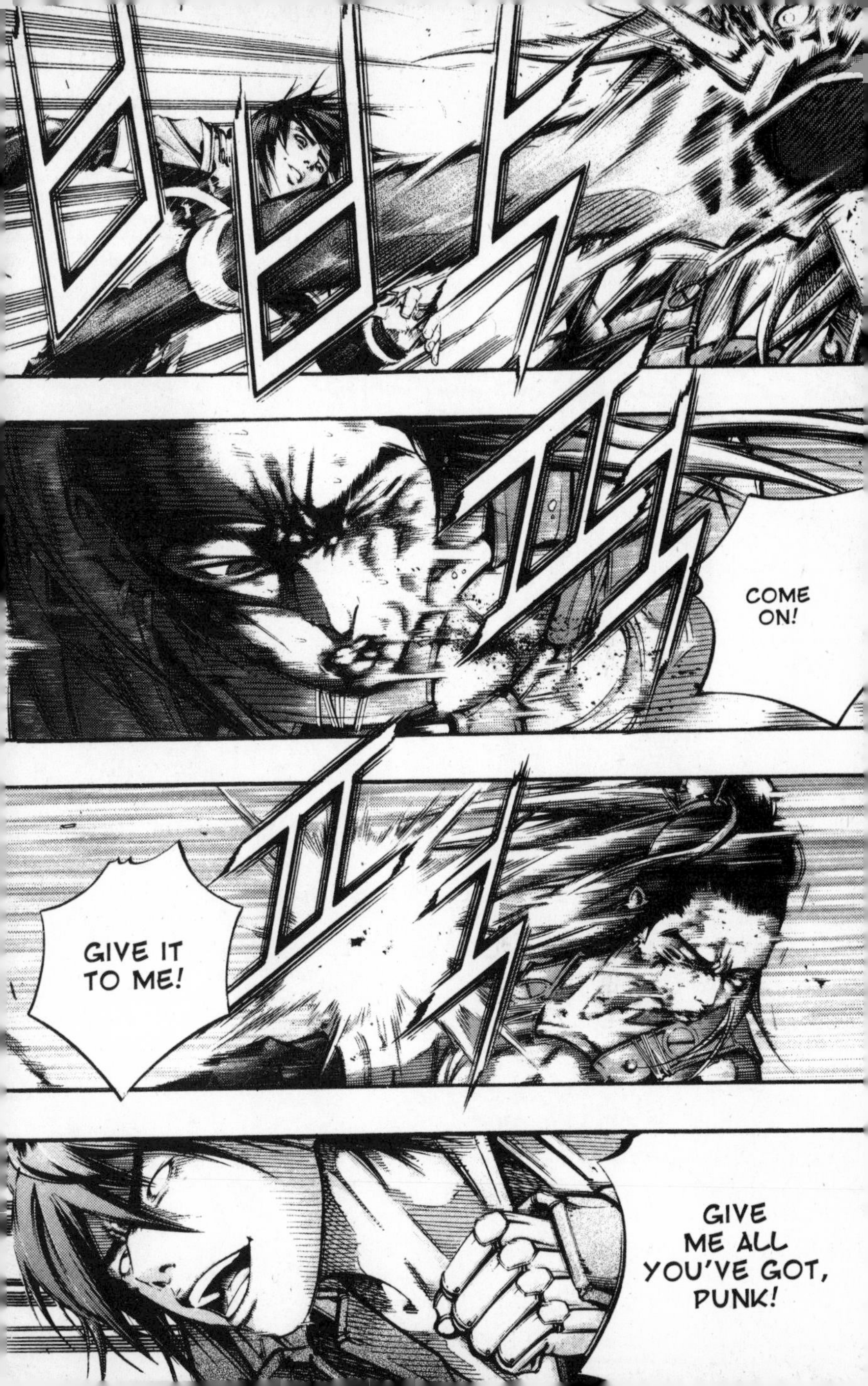
COME ON!
GIVE IT TO ME!
GIVE ME ALL YOU'VE GOT, PUNK!

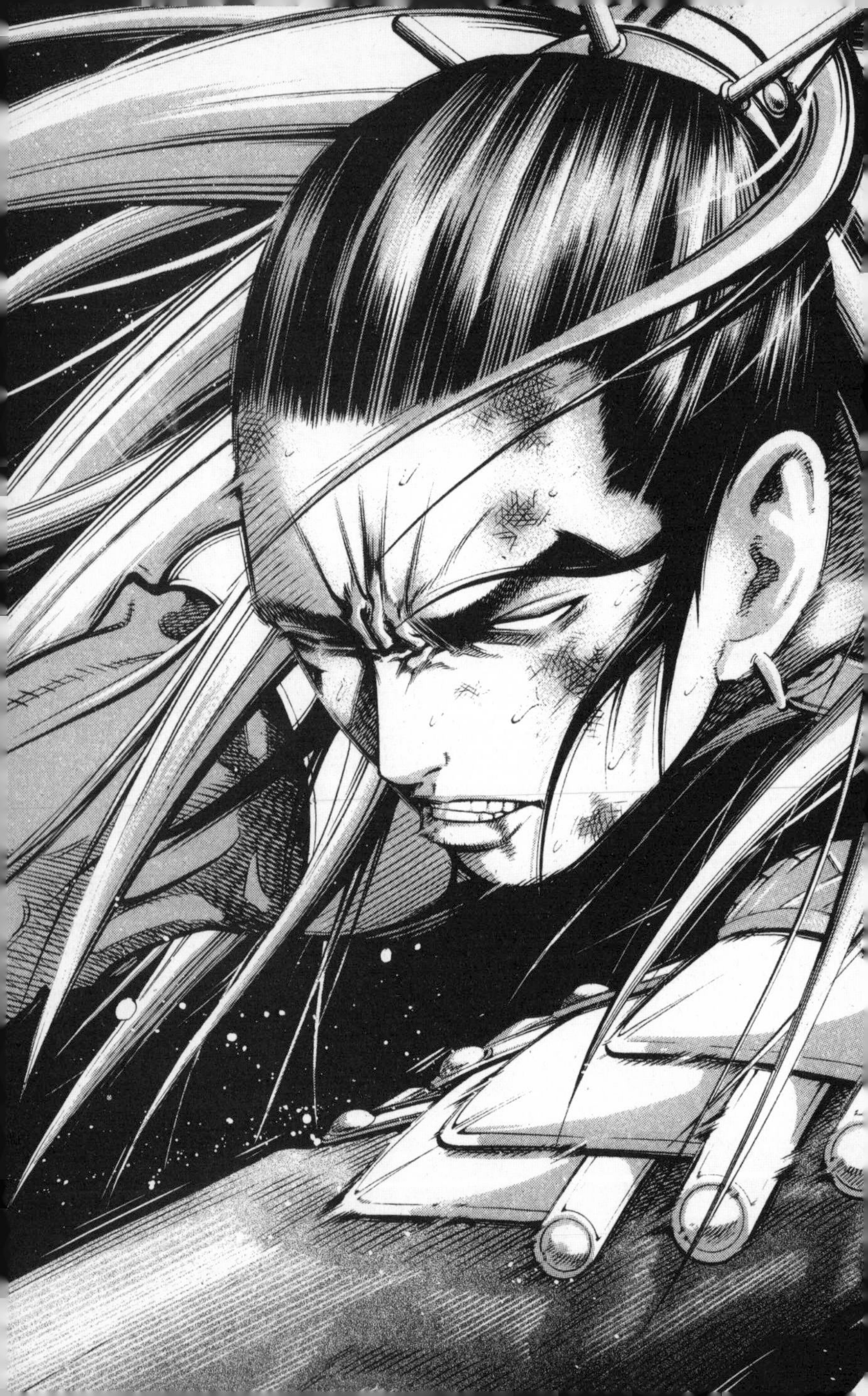

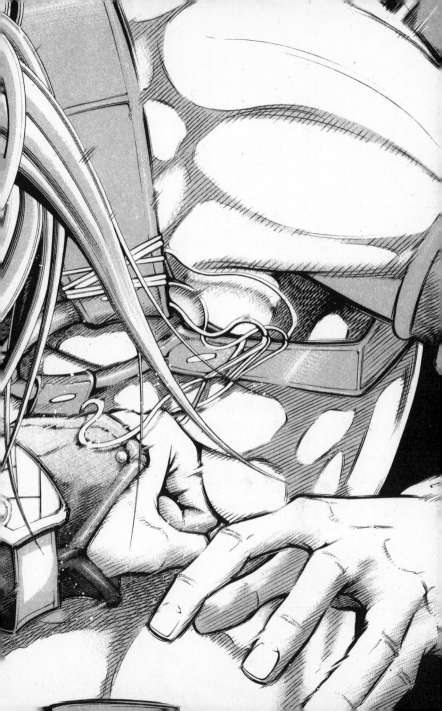

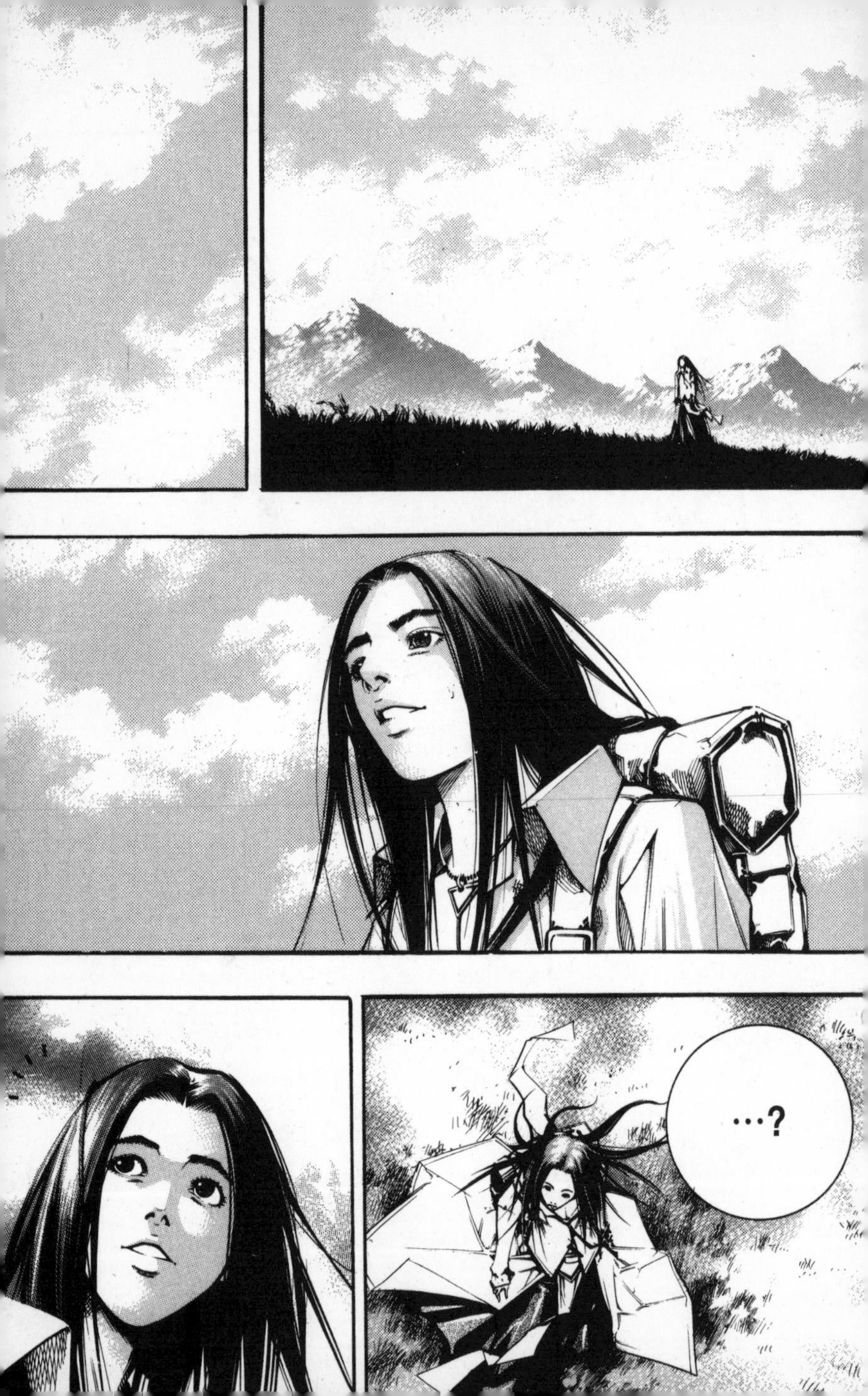
…?

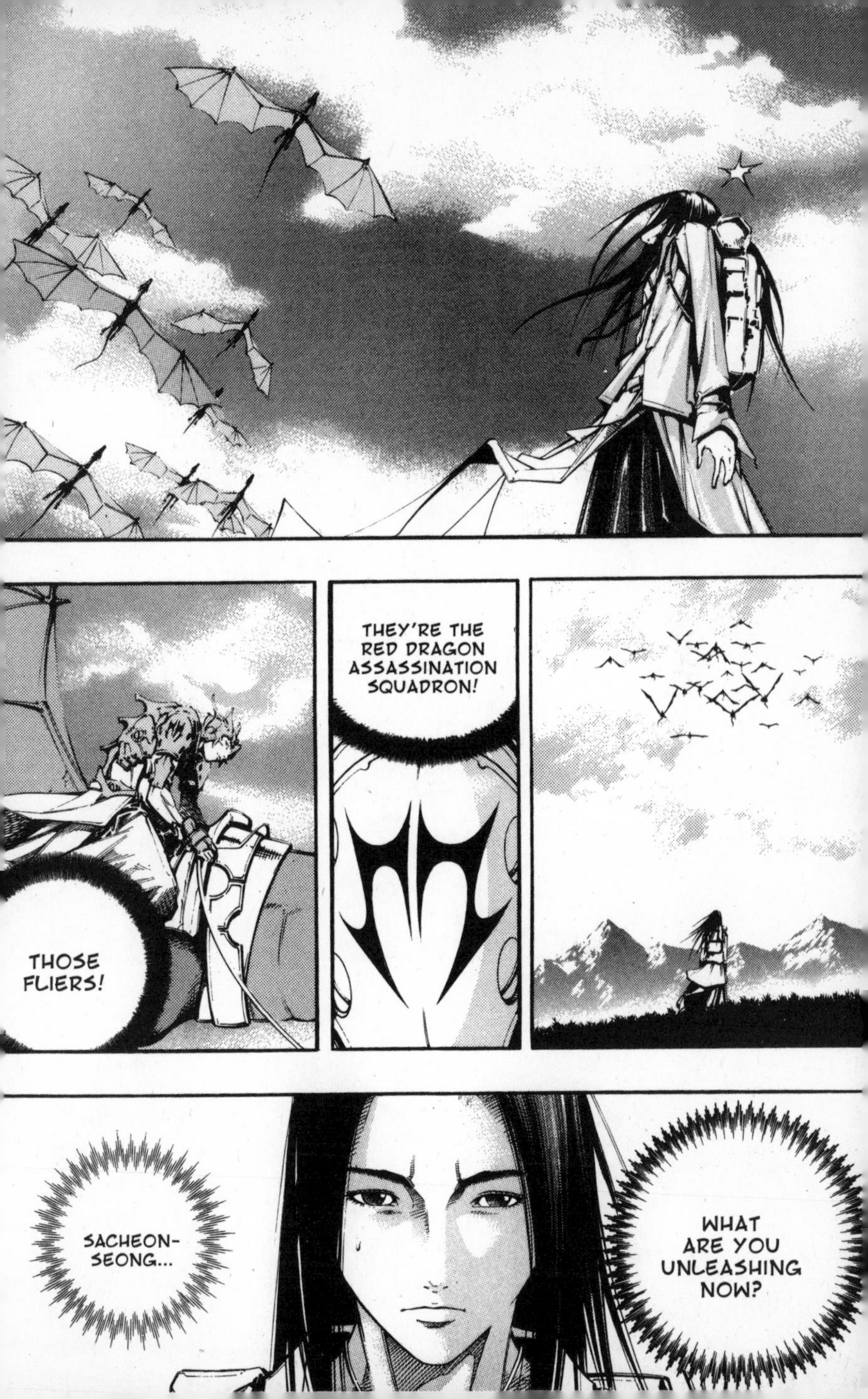
THOSE FLIERS!
THEY'RE THE RED DRAGON ASSASSINATION SQUADRON!
SACHEON-SEONG...
WHAT ARE YOU UNLEASHING NOW?

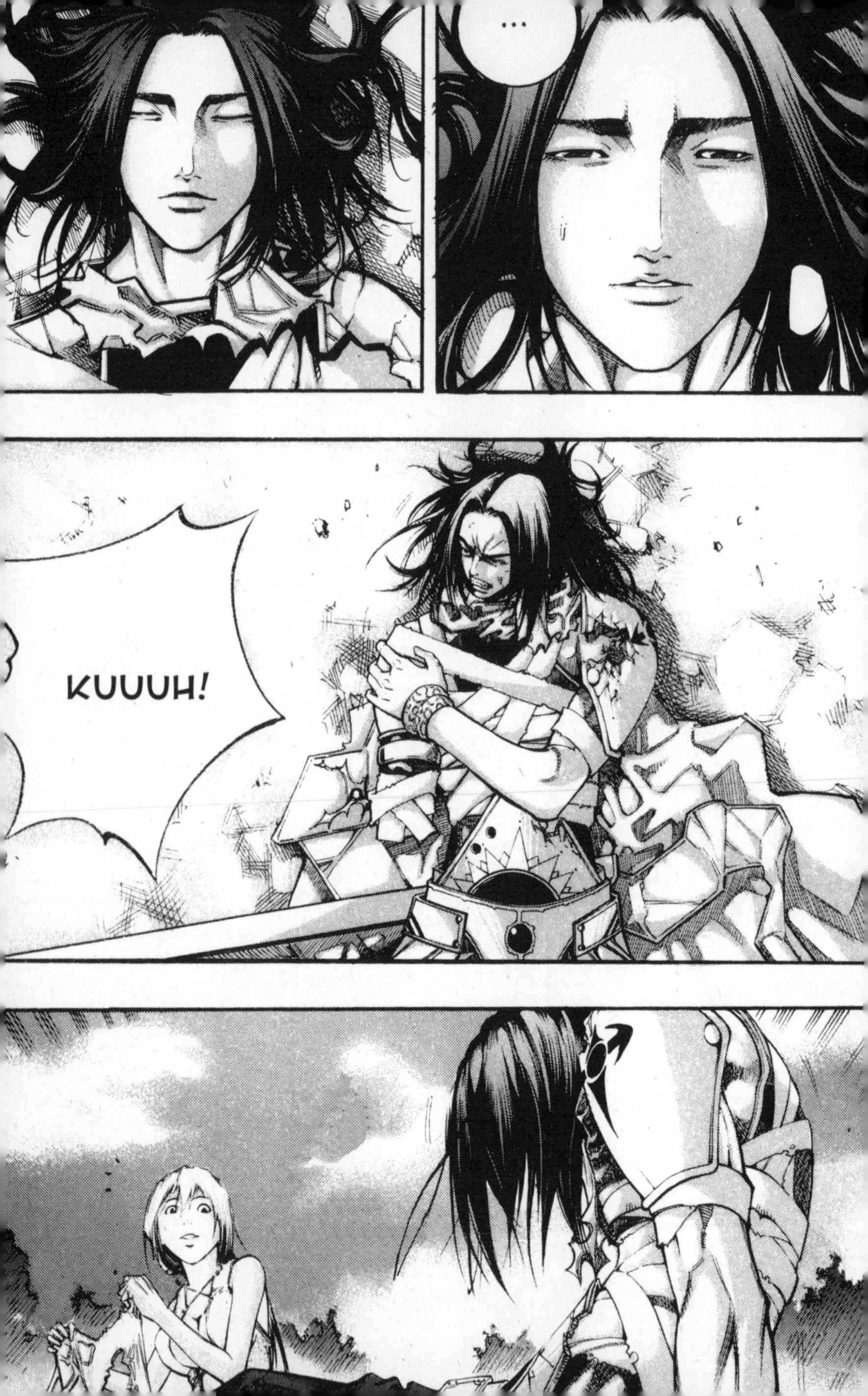
...
KUUUH!

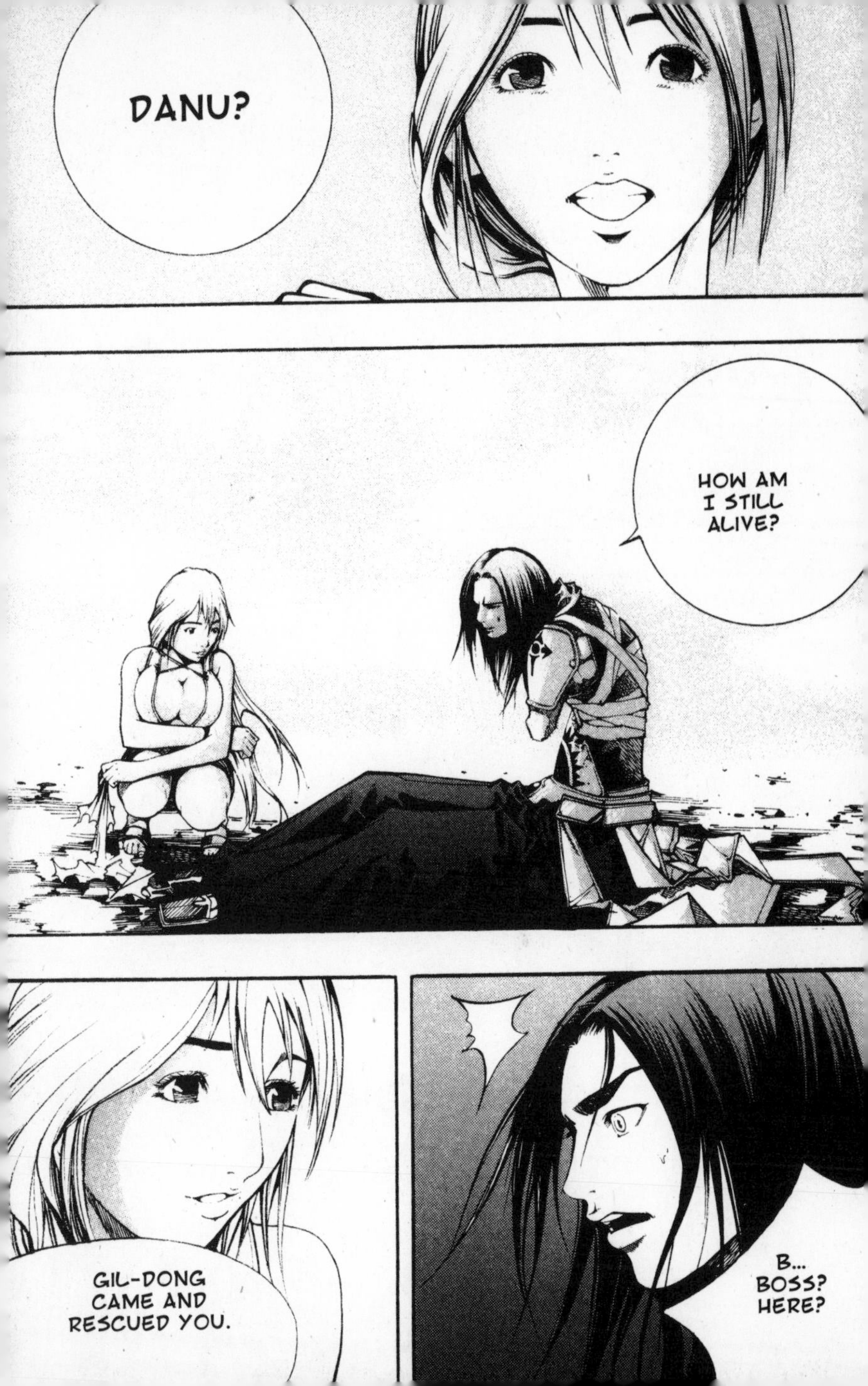
DANU?
HOW AM I STILL ALIVE?
GIL-DONG CAME AND RESCUED YOU.
B... BOSS? HERE?

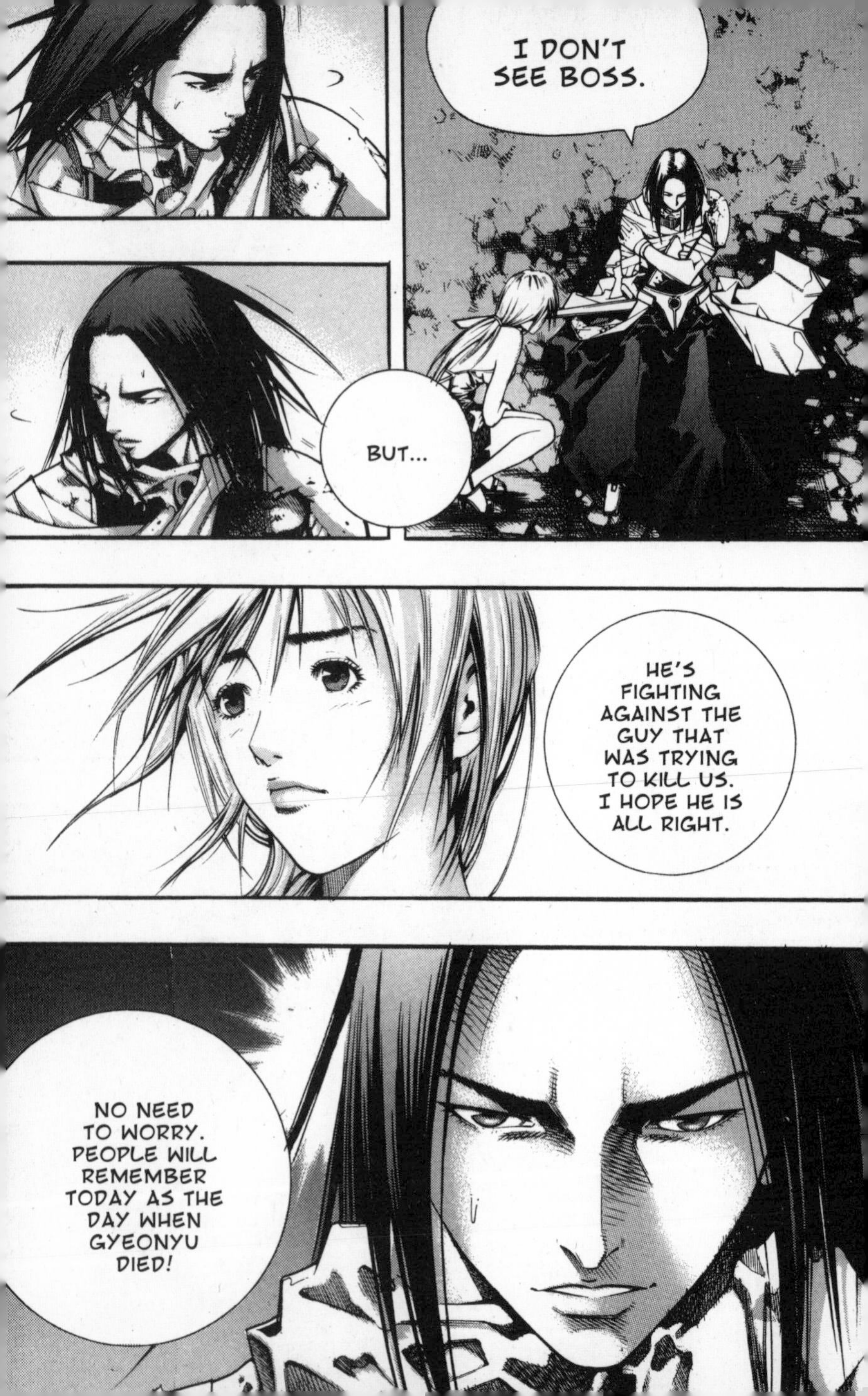
I DON'T SEE BOSS.
BUT...
HE'S FIGHTING AGAINST THE GUY THAT WAS TRYING TO KILL US. I HOPE HE IS ALL RIGHT.
NO NEED TO WORRY. PEOPLE WILL REMEMBER TODAY AS THE DAY WHEN GYEONYU DIED!

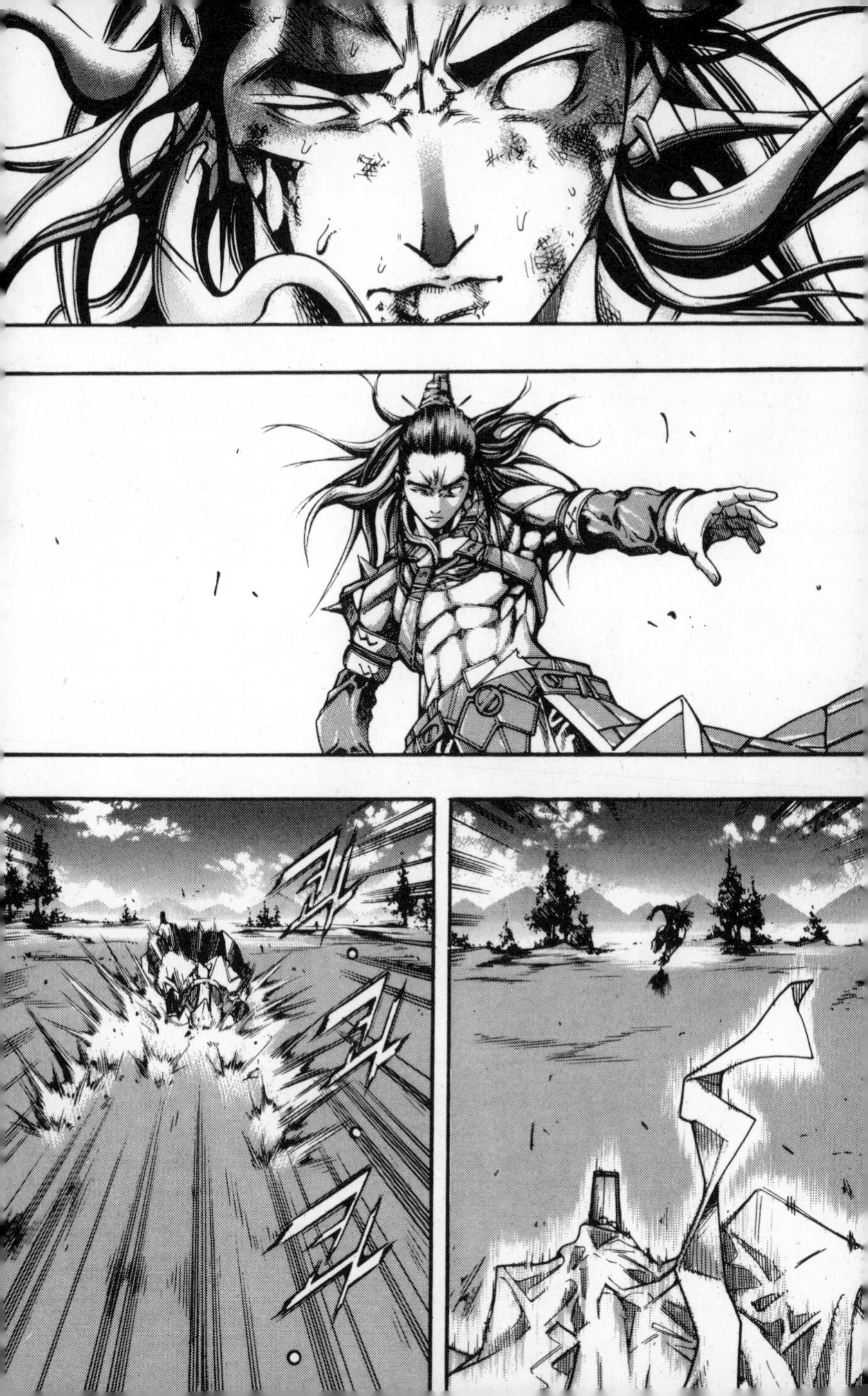

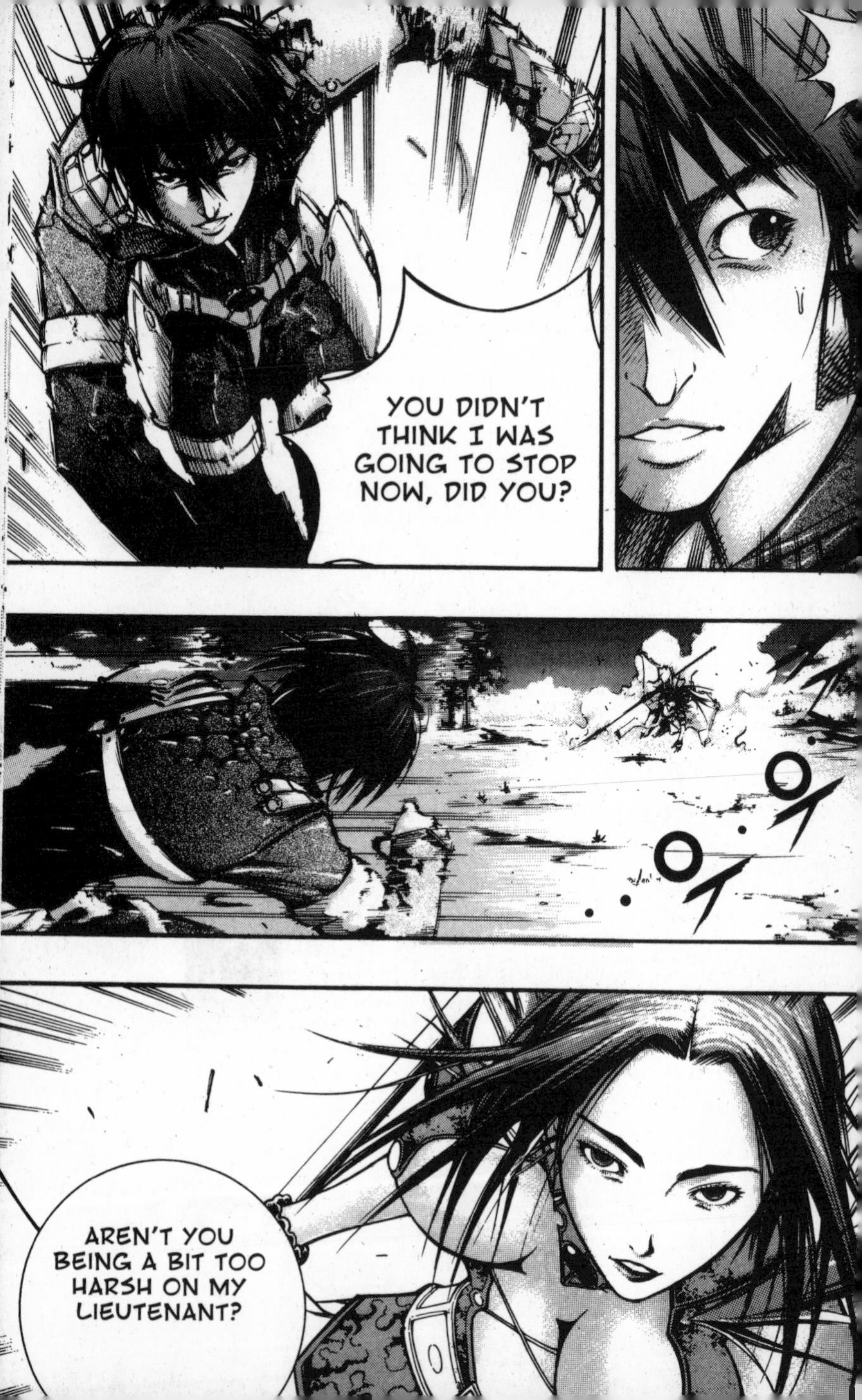
YOU DIDN'T THINK I WAS GOING TO STOP NOW, DID YOU?
AREN'T YOU BEING A BIT TOO HARSH ON MY LIEUTENANT?

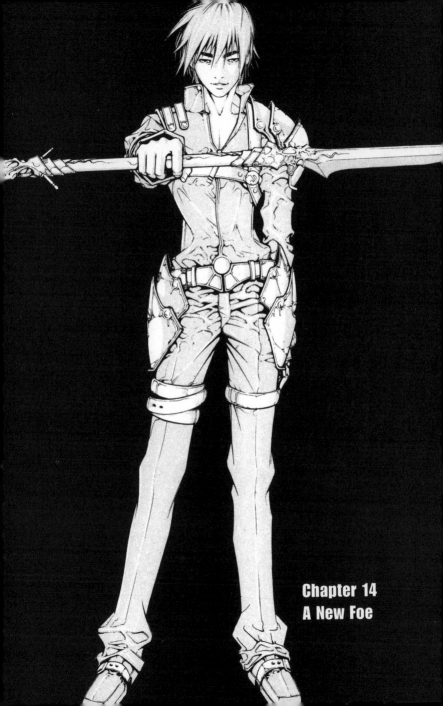

Chapter 14
A New Foe

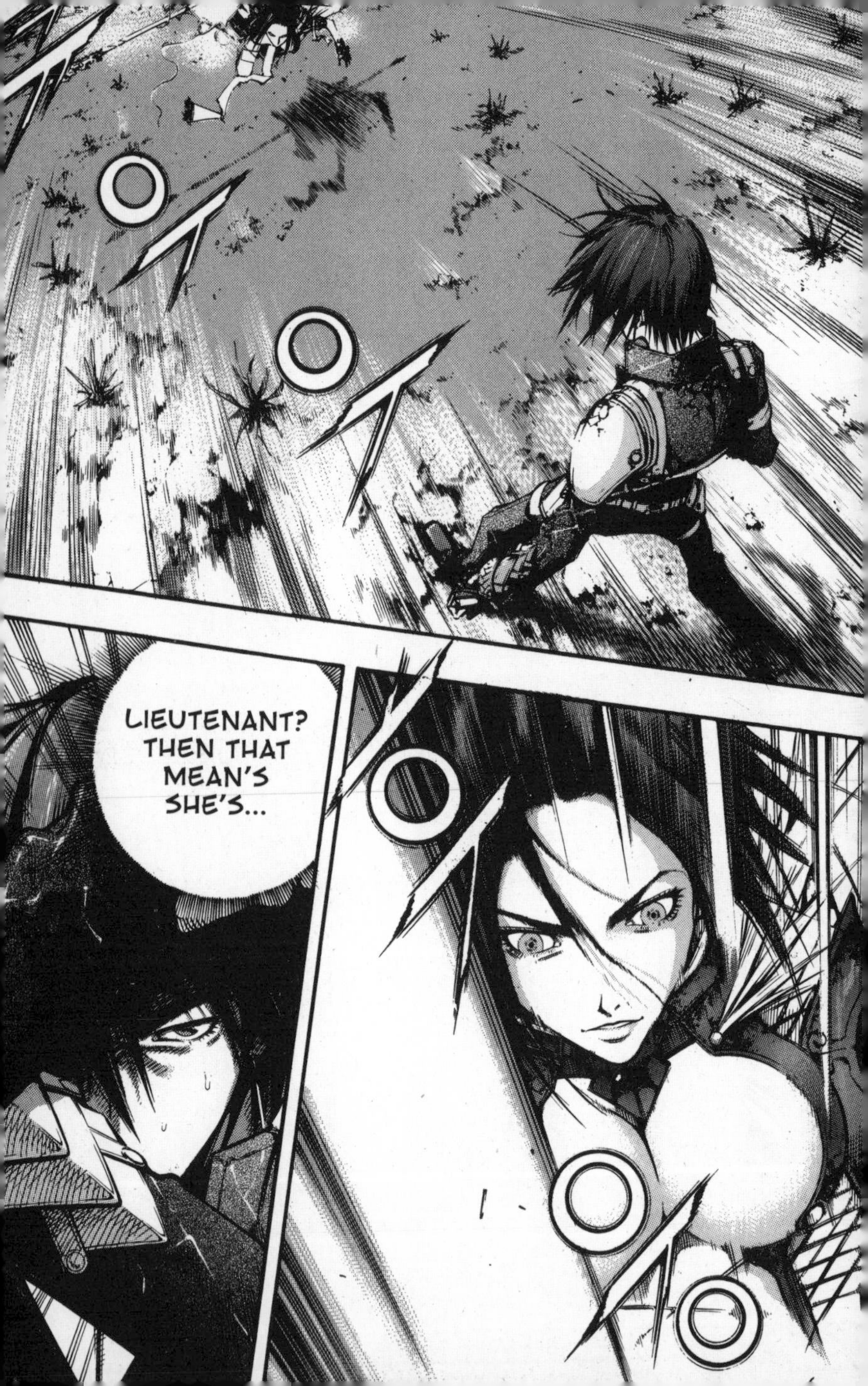
LIEUTENANT? THEN THAT MEAN'S SHE'S...

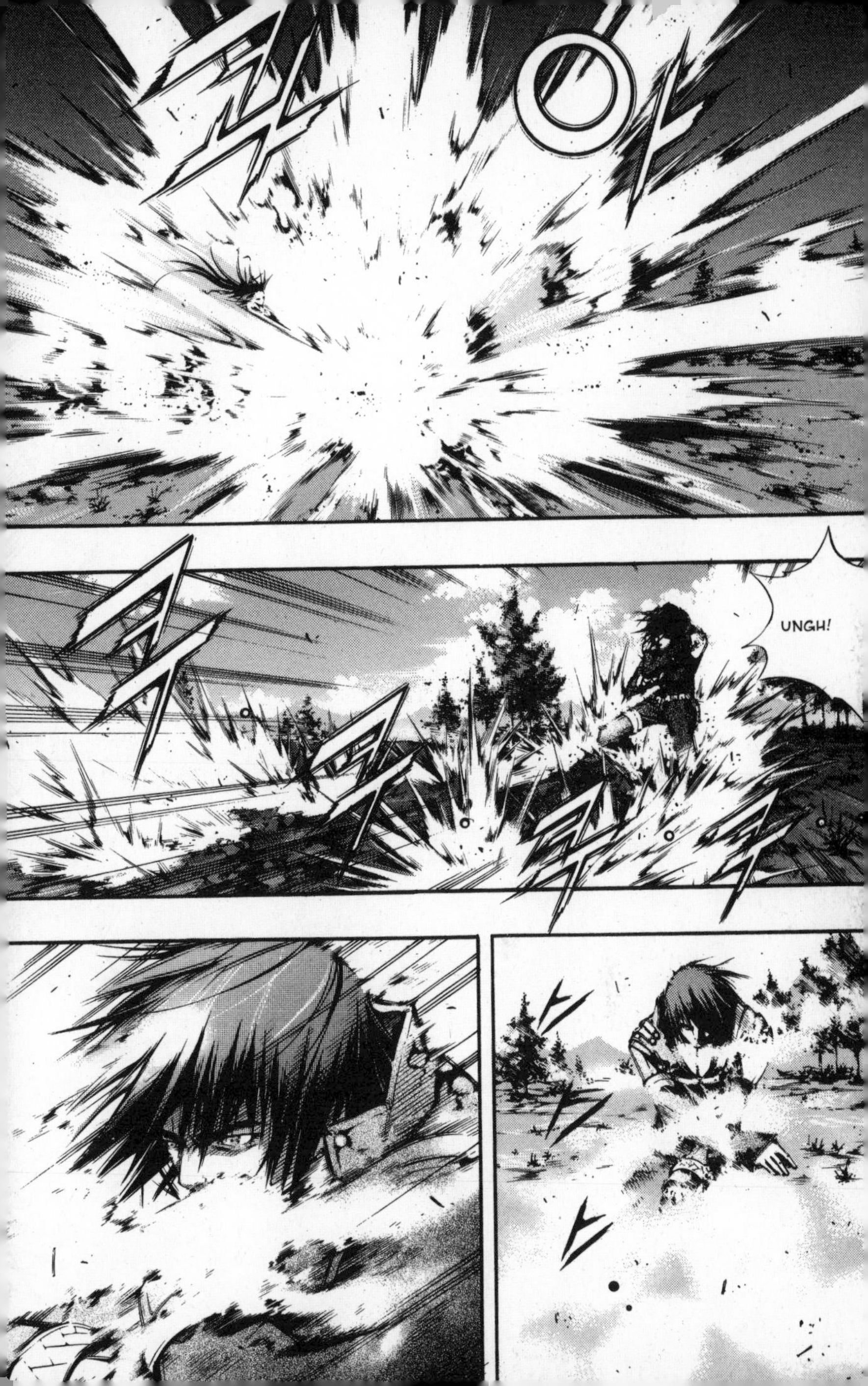
UNGH!

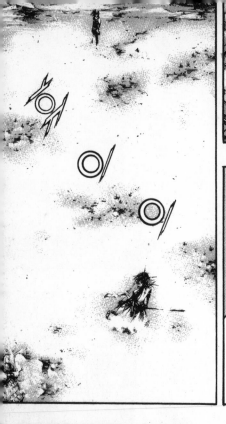

W-WHAT ARE YOU DOING HERE, MY CAPTAIN?

LOOK AT YOU!

I...I'M SORRY.

MASTER WILL BE MOST DISPLEASED WITH YOU, GYEONYU. YOU SHOULD PREPARE YOURSELF TO BE SCOLDED!

.....

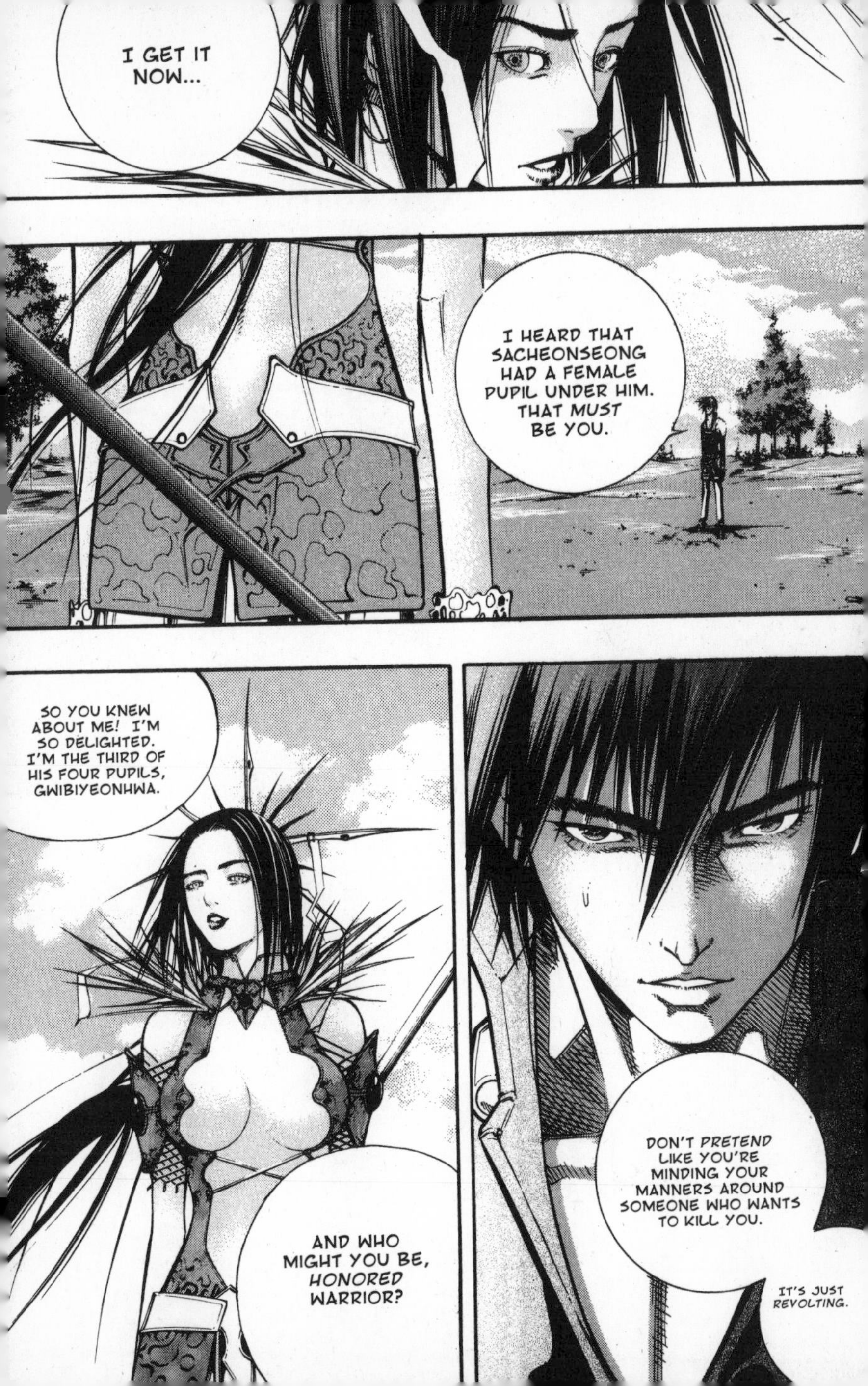
I GET IT NOW...
I HEARD THAT SACHEONSEONG HAD A FEMALE PUPIL UNDER HIM. THAT *MUST* BE YOU.
SO YOU KNEW ABOUT ME! I'M SO DELIGHTED. I'M THE THIRD OF HIS FOUR PUPILS, GWIBIYEONHWA.
AND WHO MIGHT YOU BE, *HONORED* WARRIOR?
DON'T *PRETEND* LIKE YOU'RE MINDING YOUR MANNERS AROUND SOMEONE WHO WANTS TO KILL YOU.
IT'S JUST REVOLTING.

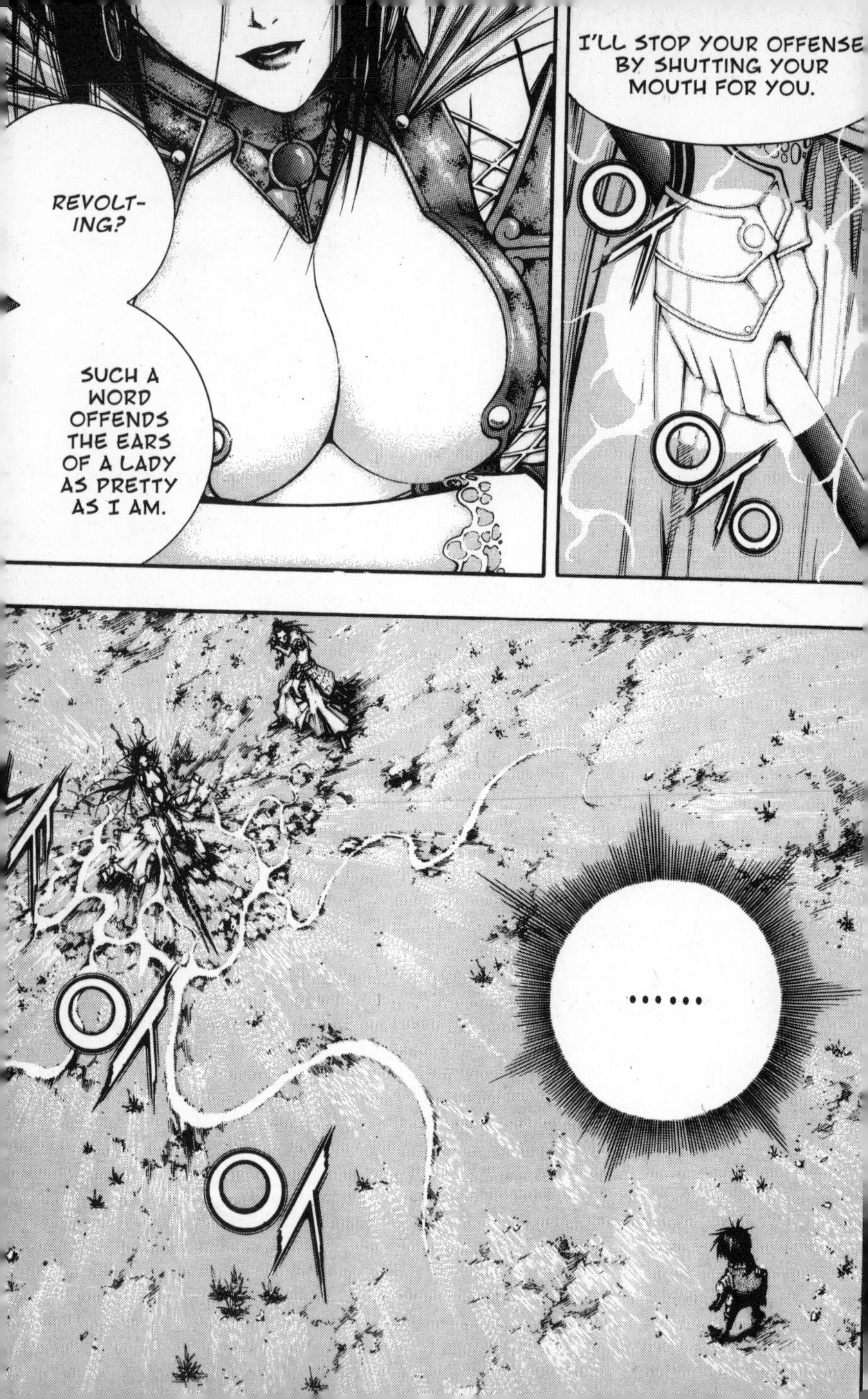
REVOLT-
ING?
SUCH A WORD OFFENDS THE EARS OF A LADY AS PRETTY AS I AM.
I'LL STOP YOUR OFFENSE BY SHUTTING YOUR MOUTH FOR YOU.
......

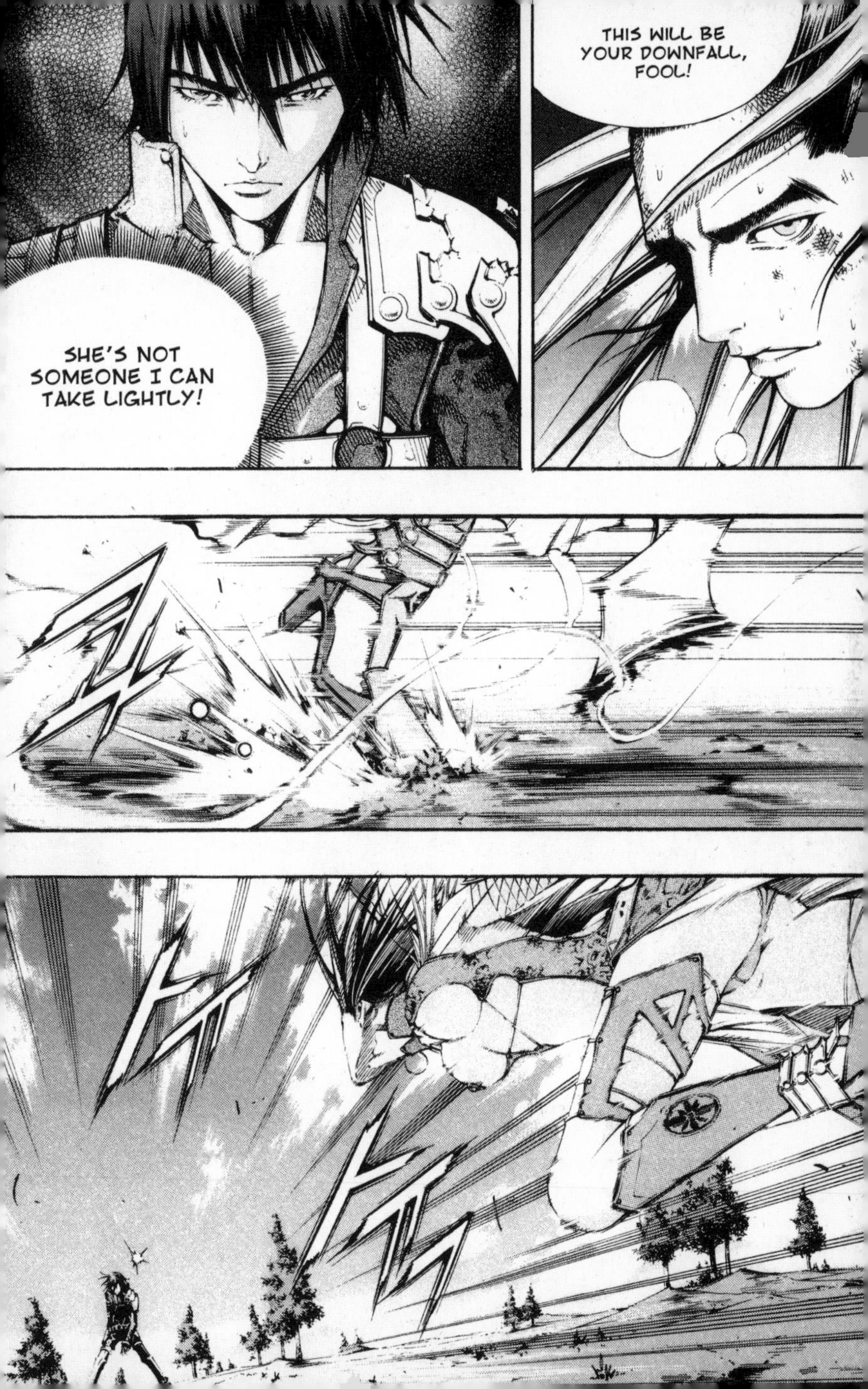
THIS WILL BE YOUR DOWNFALL, FOOL!
SHE'S NOT SOMEONE I CAN TAKE LIGHTLY!

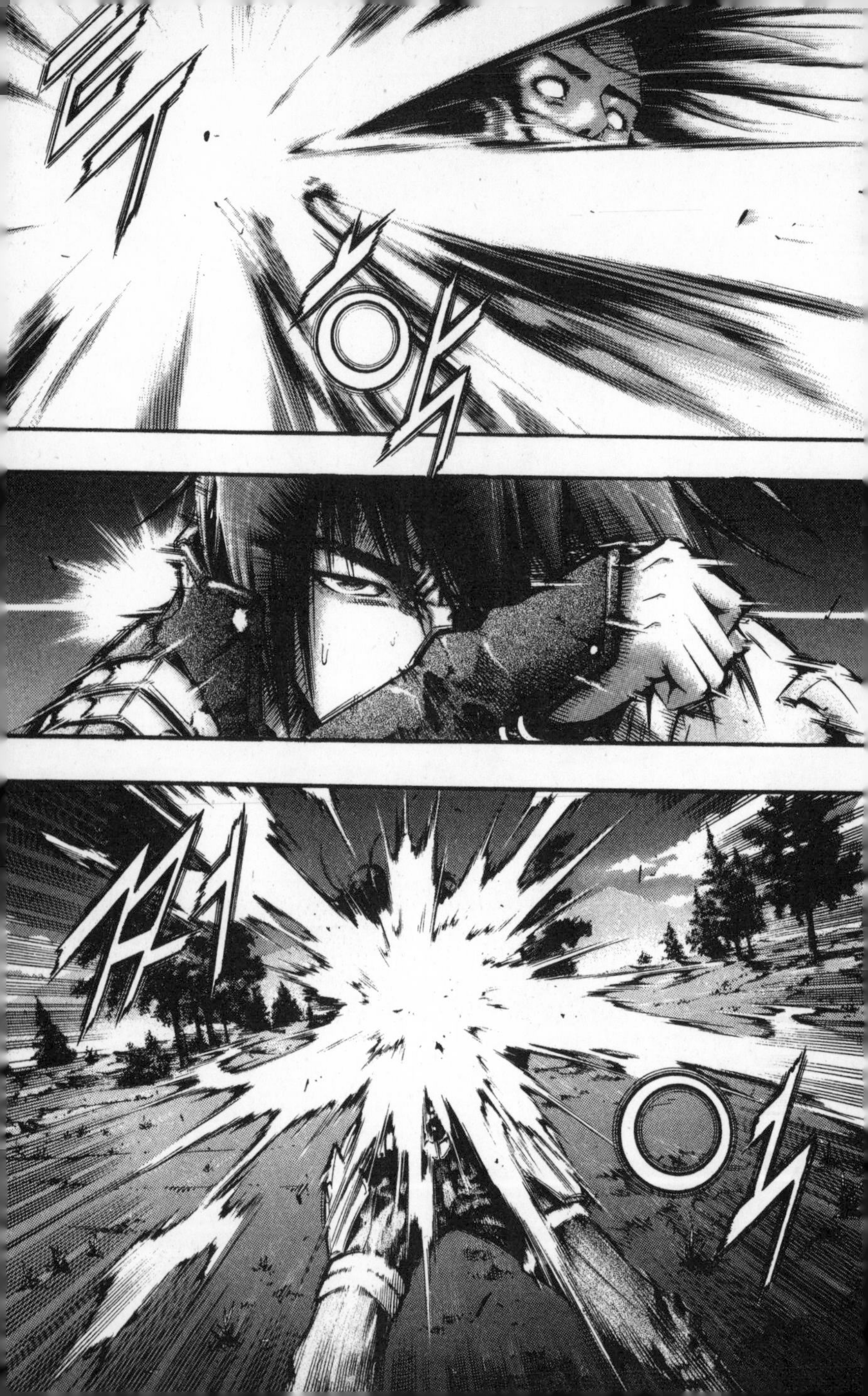

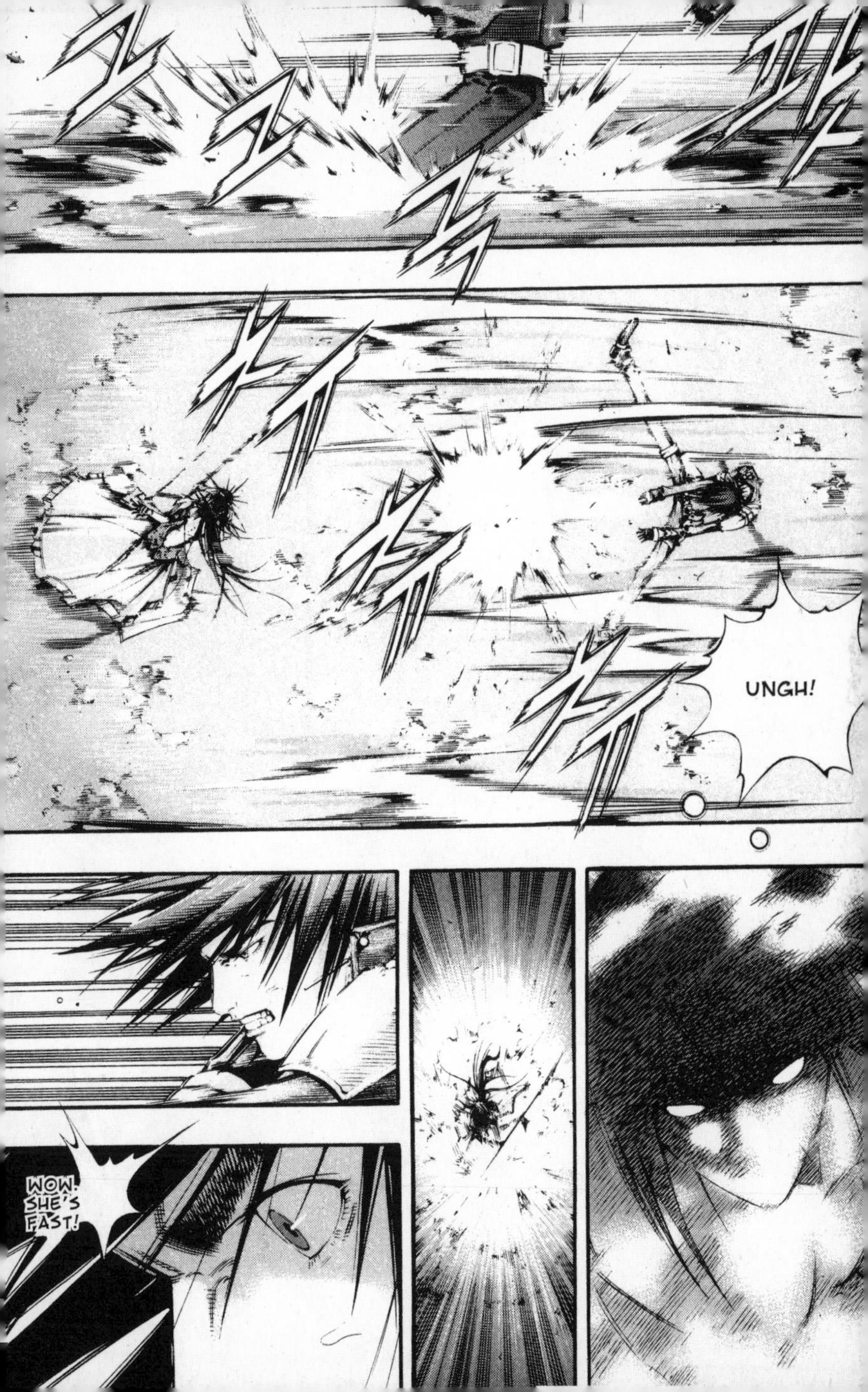
UNGH!
WOW. SHE'S FAST!

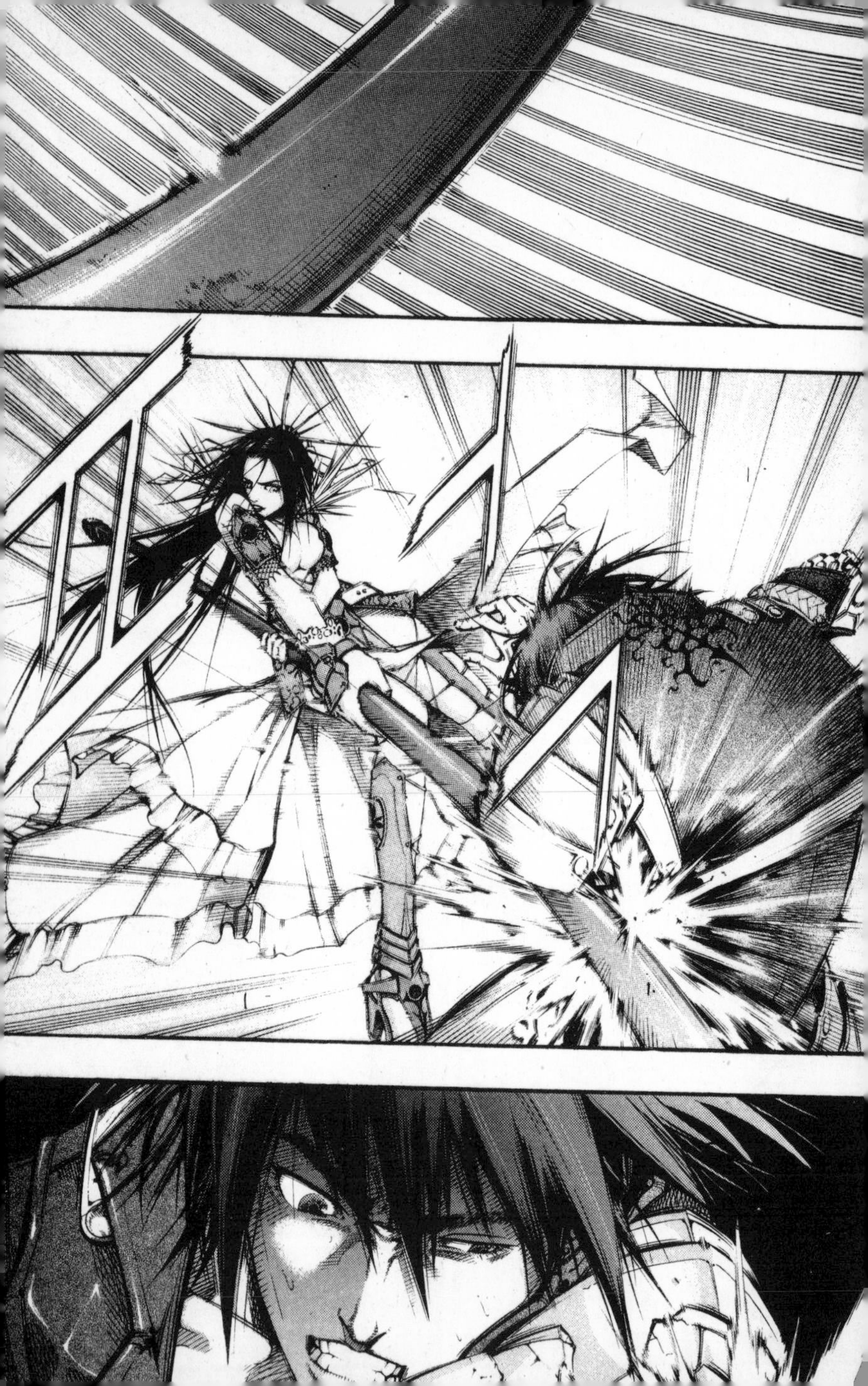

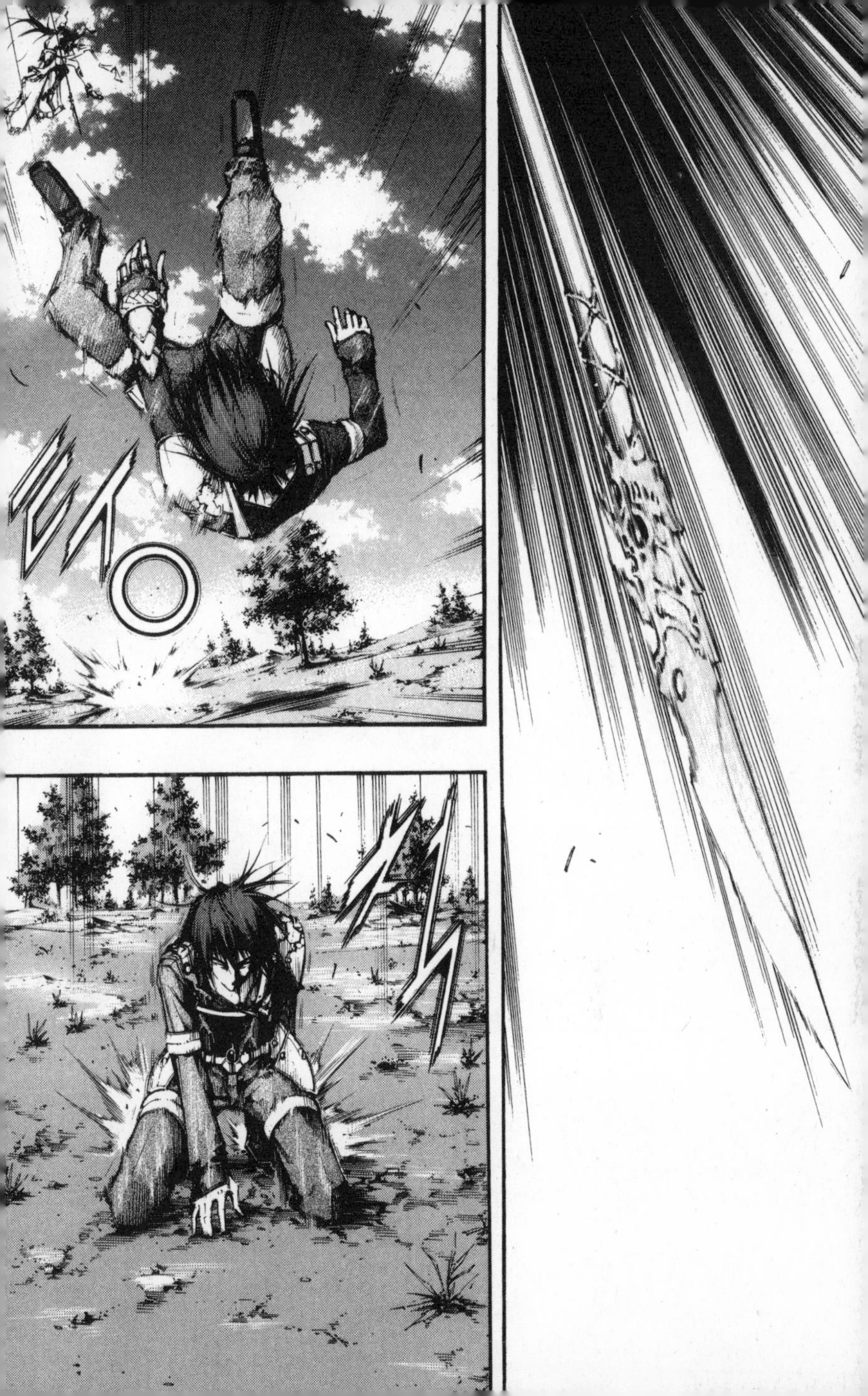

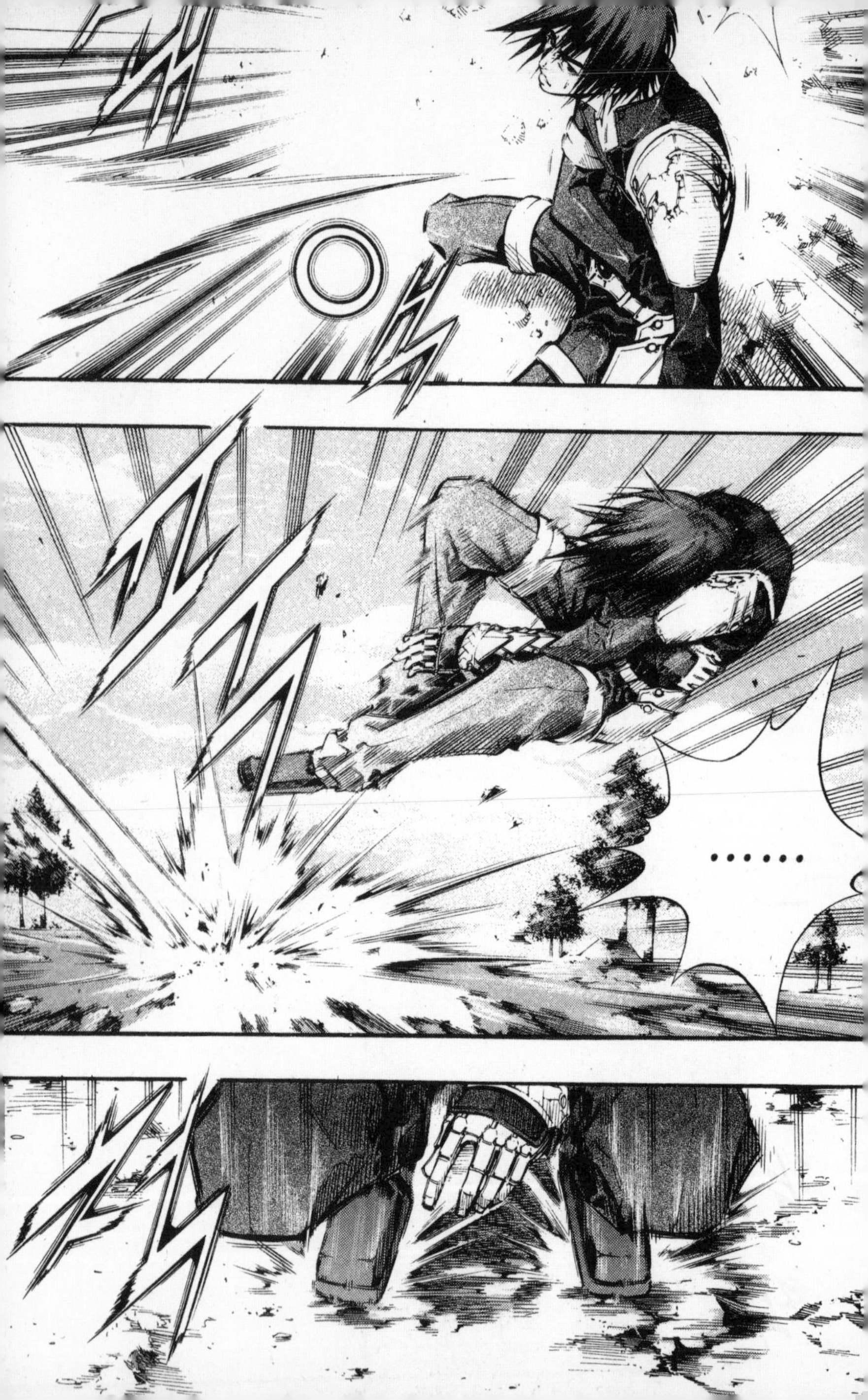
……

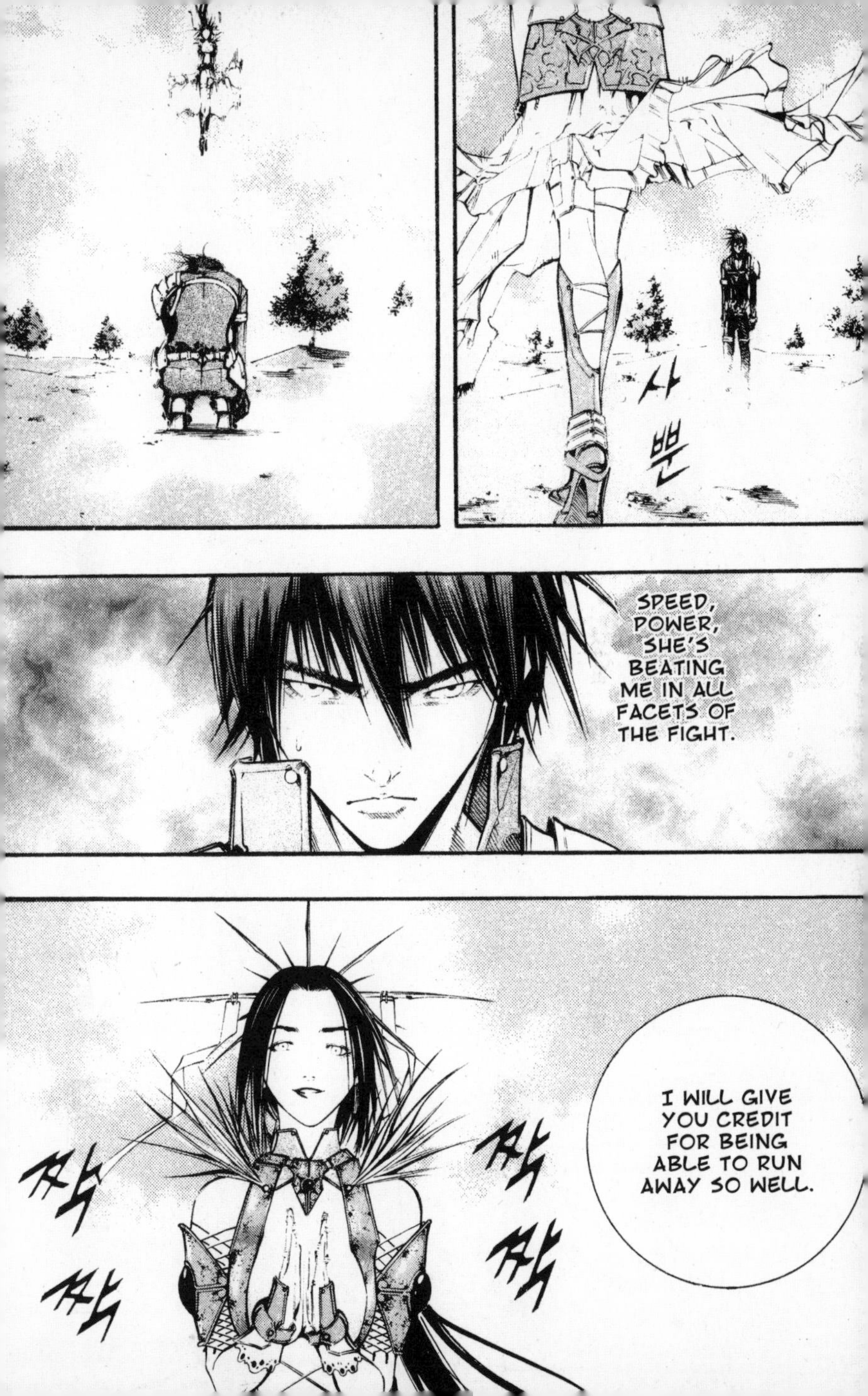
사뿐
SPEED, POWER, SHE'S BEATING ME IN ALL FACETS OF THE FIGHT.
I WILL GIVE YOU CREDIT FOR BEING ABLE TO RUN AWAY SO WELL.

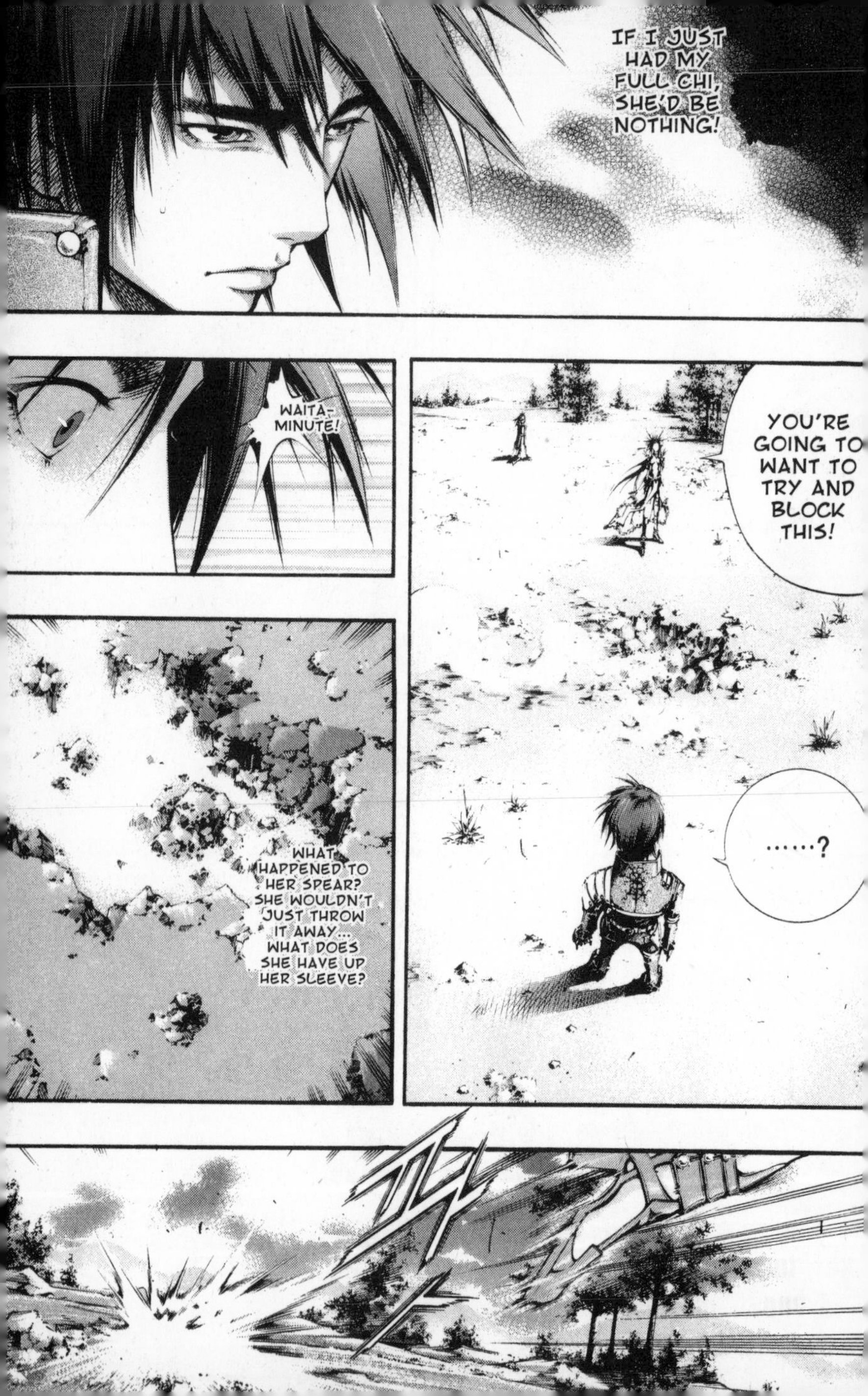
IF I JUST HAD MY FULL CHI, SHE'D BE NOTHING!
WAITA-MINUTE!
YOU'RE GOING TO WANT TO TRY AND BLOCK THIS!
......?
WHAT HAPPENED TO HER SPEAR? SHE WOULDN'T JUST THROW IT AWAY... WHAT DOES SHE HAVE UP HER SLEEVE?

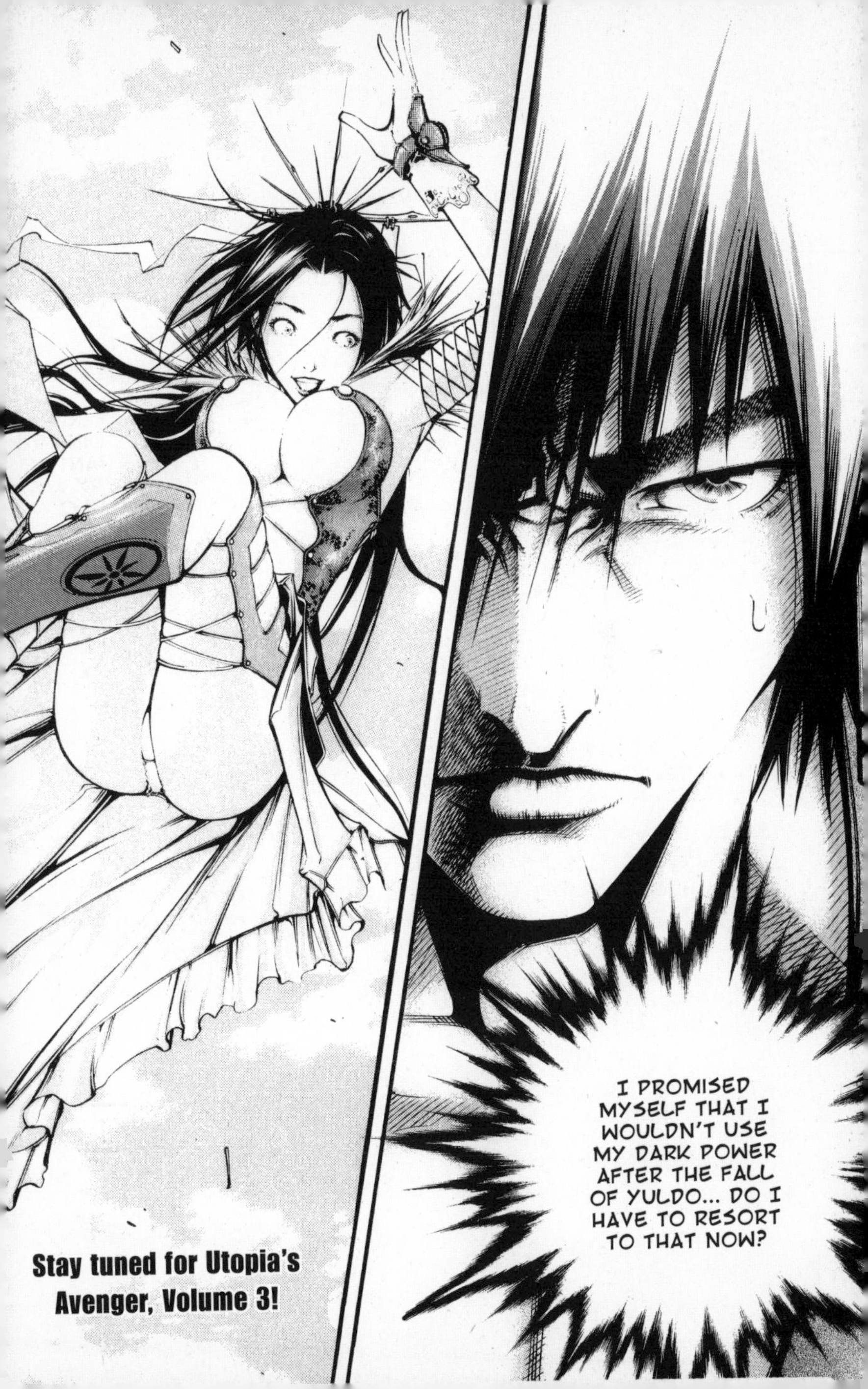
I PROMISED MYSELF THAT I WOULDN'T USE MY DARK POWER AFTER THE FALL OF YULDO... DO I HAVE TO RESORT TO THAT NOW?
Stay tuned for Utopia's Avenger, Volume 3!

**In the Next
Exciting Volume of**

WHAT MOVE COULD THE EVIL
GWIBIYEONHWA BE ABOUT TO
UNLEASH? AND WHAT IS THIS "DARK
POWER" THAT HONG GIL-DONG
HAD PROMISED NEVER AGAIN TO USE?
BUT HE MAY NOT HAVE A CHOICE IN THE
MATTER, WHEN HIS MORTALLY INJURED
COMRADE-IN-ARMS, DANU, ONCE AGAIN
RUSHES TO HIS SIDE IN THE HEAT OF BATTLE!
AND LATER, DURING A BRIEF RESPITE AT
SANGHUI'S HOME, WE LEARN A LITTLE MORE
ABOUT OUR HERO, GIL-DONG, AND THE
FRIGHTFUL SECRET HE HAS KEPT ALL
THESE YEARS...

BE HERE FOR VOLUME 3!

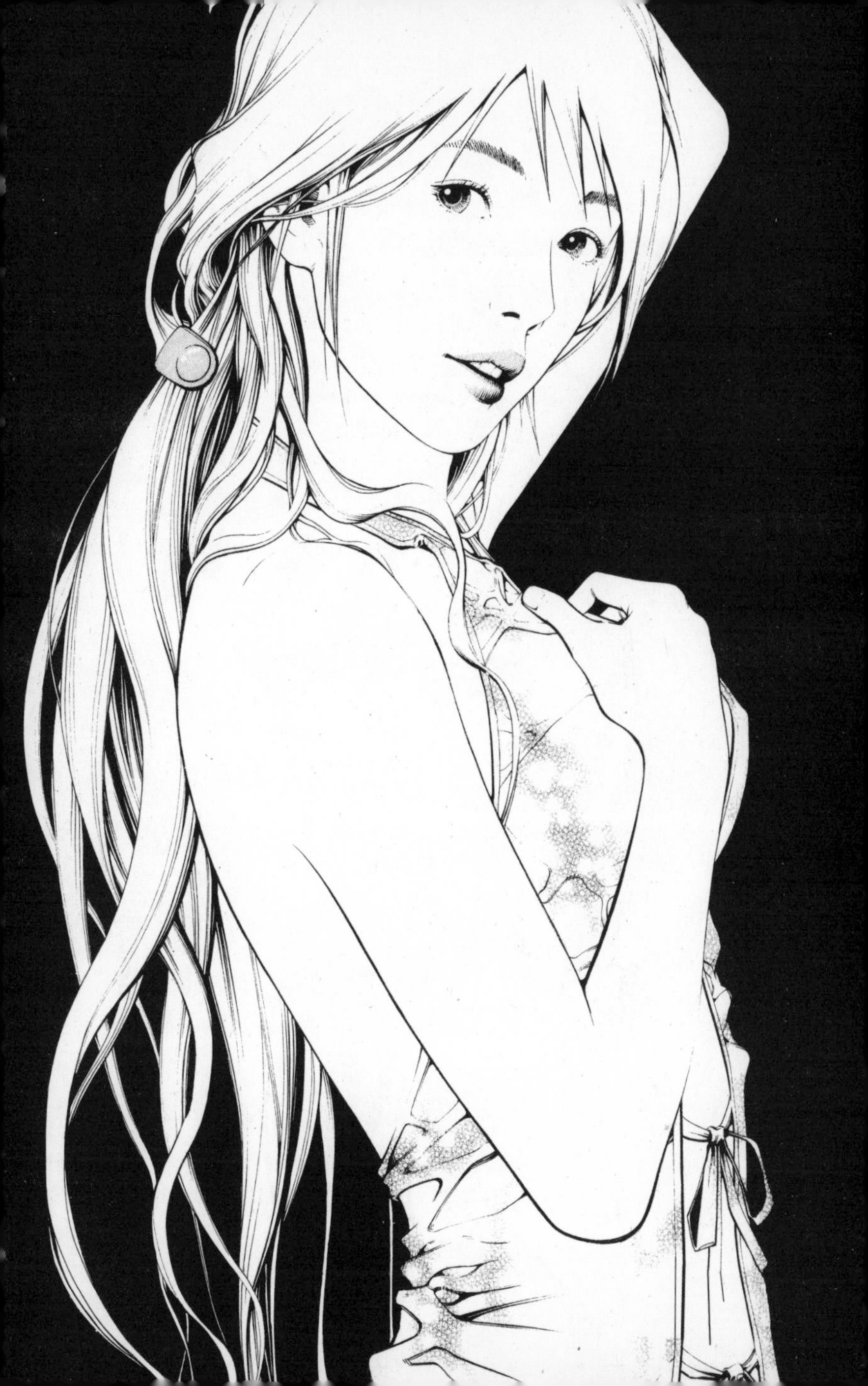

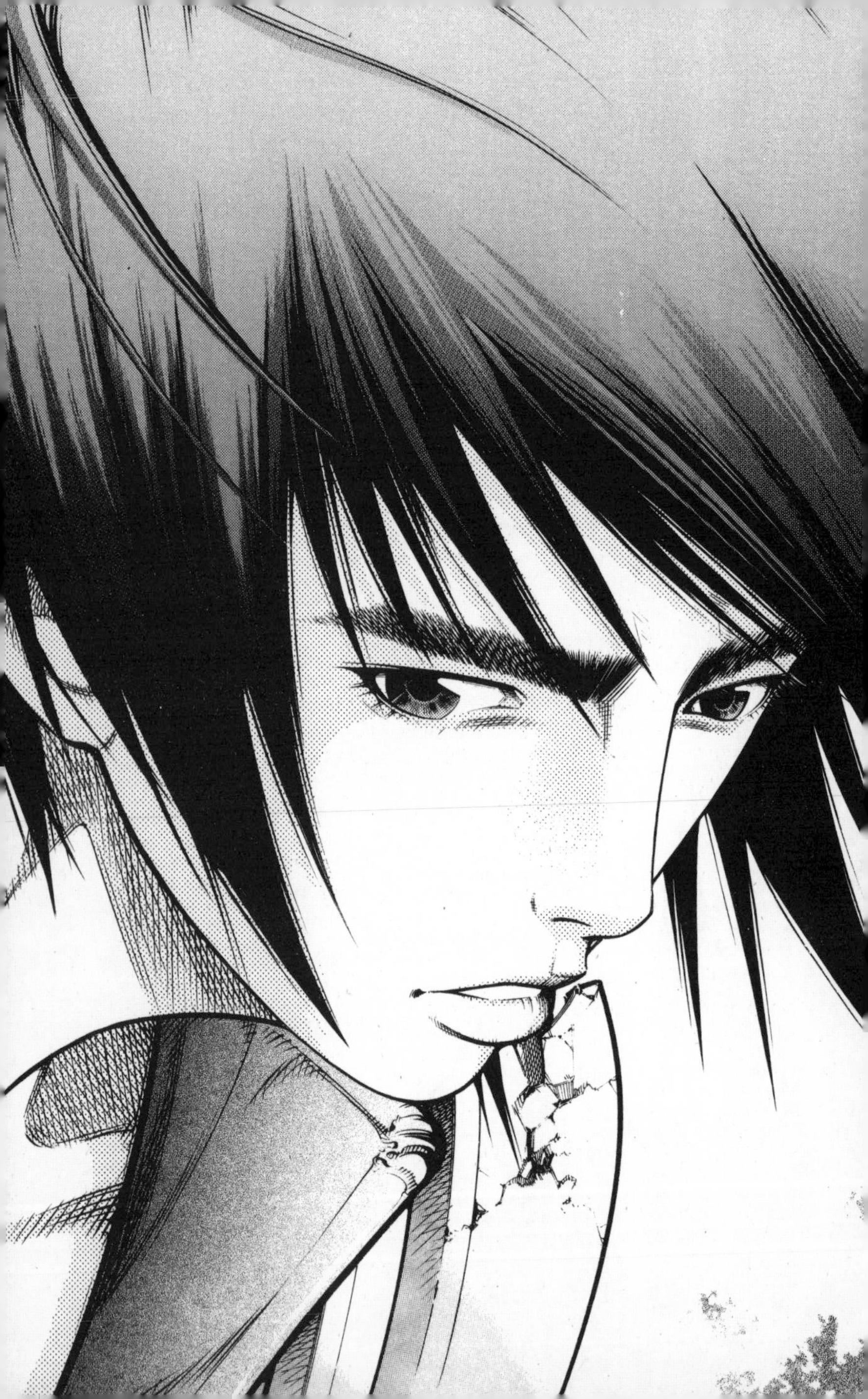

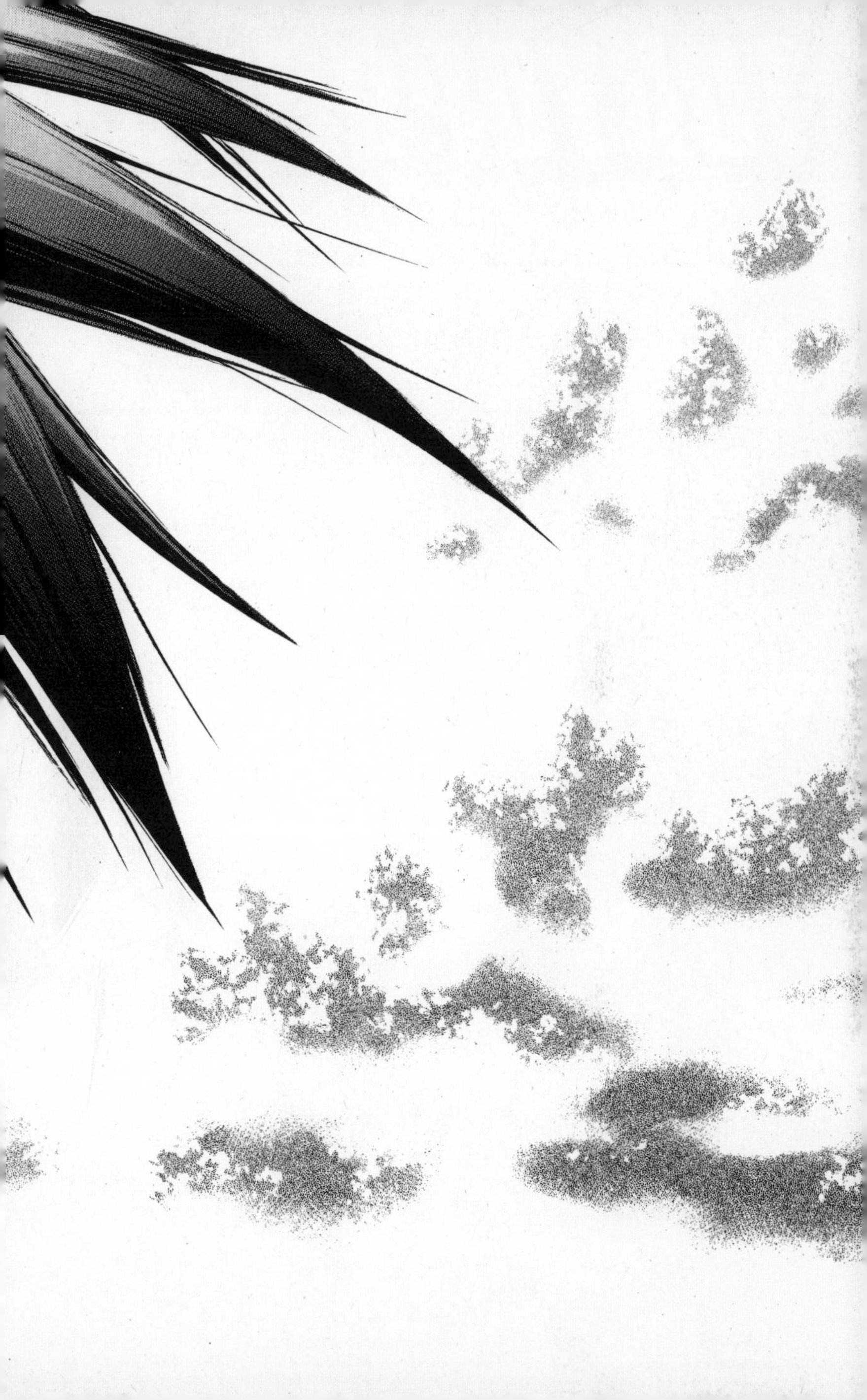

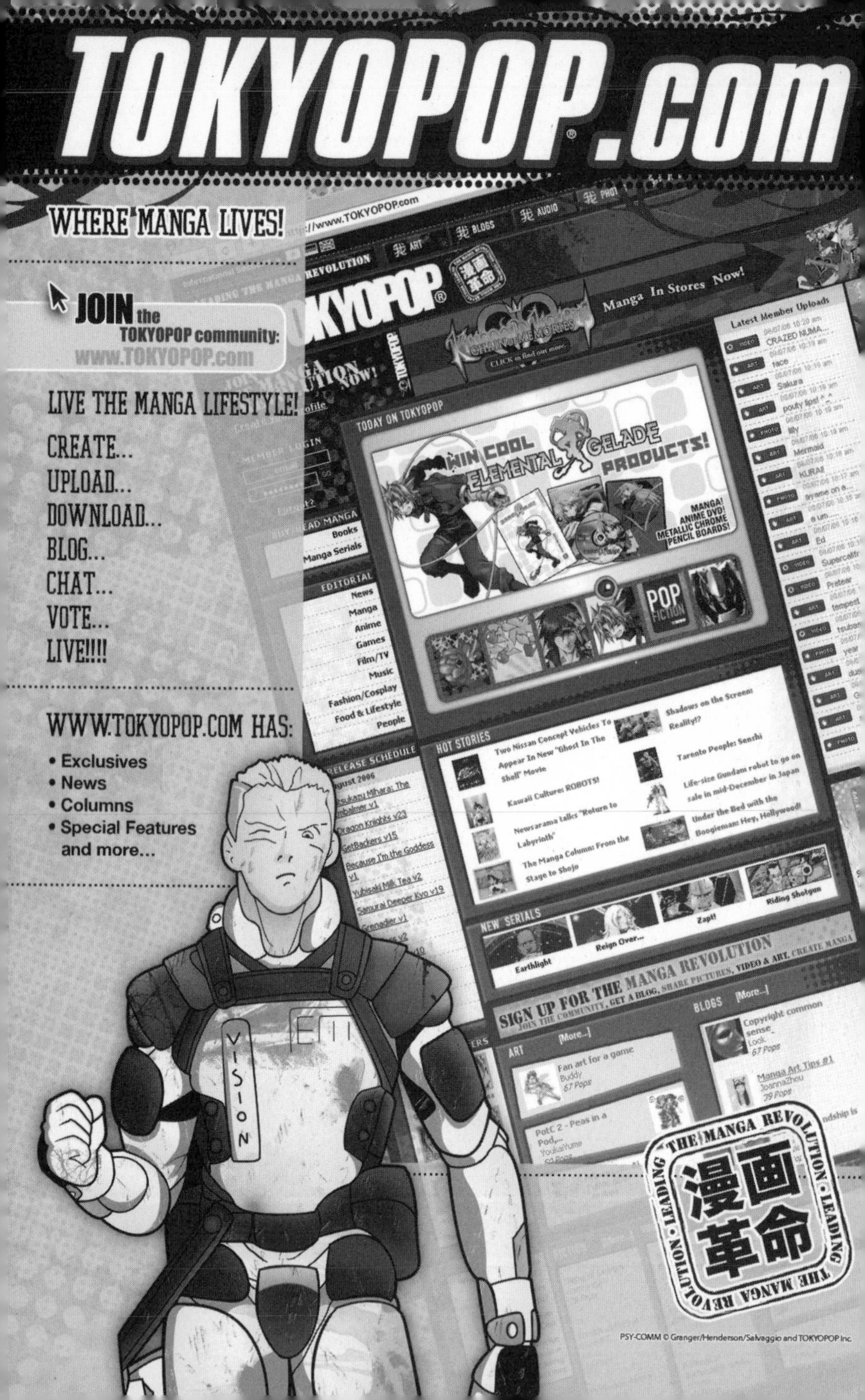

TOKYOPOP®.com
WHERE MANGA LIVES!
JOIN the TOKYOPOP community:
www.TOKYOPOP.com
LIVE THE MANGA LIFESTYLE!
CREATE...
UPLOAD...
DOWNLOAD...
BLOG...
CHAT...
VOTE...
LIVE!!!!
WWW.TOKYOPOP.COM HAS:
• Exclusives
• News
• Columns
• Special Features and more...
THE MANGA REVOLUTION
漫画革命
LEADING THE MANGA REVOLUTION
PSY-COMM © Granger/Henderson/Salvaggio and TOKYOPOP Inc.

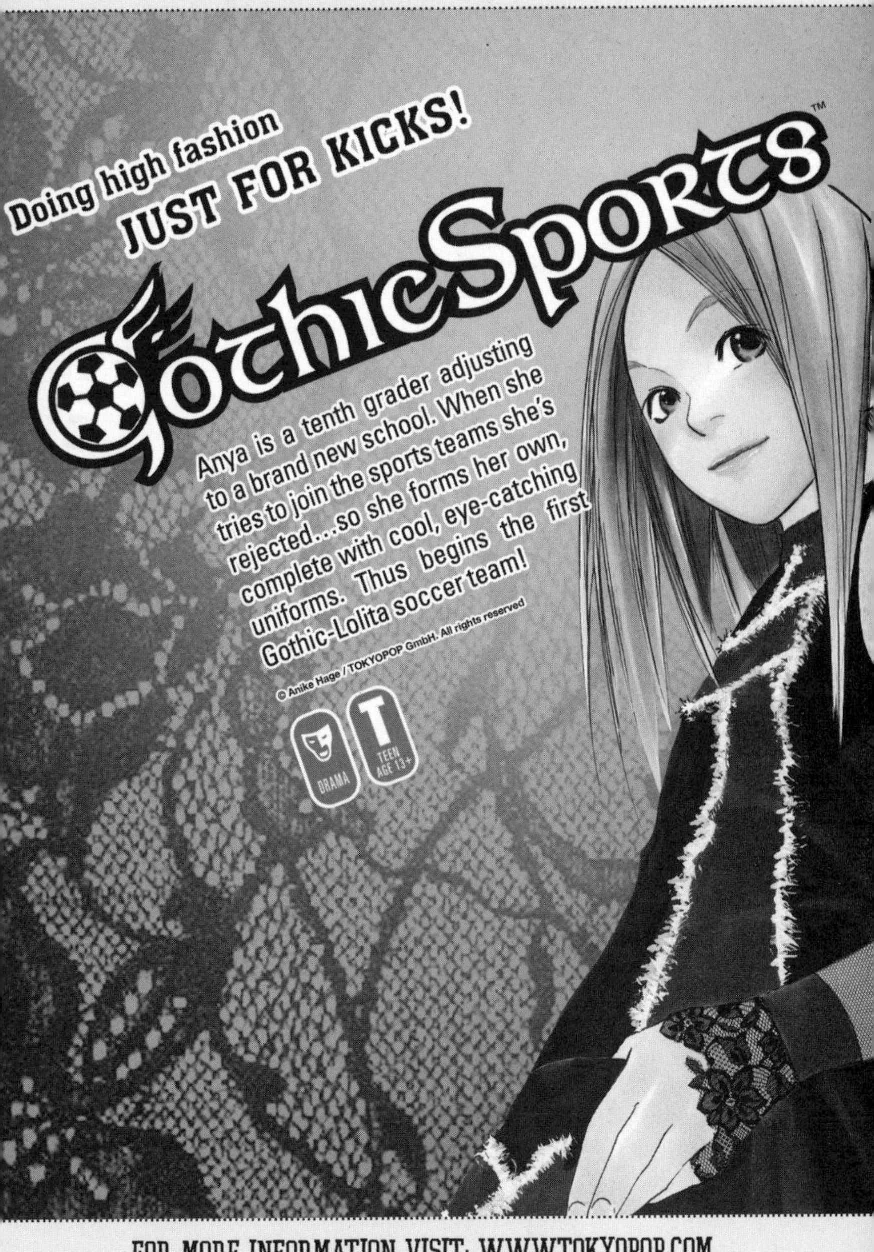
Doing high fashion
JUST FOR KICKS!
GothicSports™
Anya is a tenth grader adjusting to a brand new school. When she tries to join the sports teams she's rejected...so she forms her own, complete with cool, eye-catching uniforms. Thus begins the first Gothic-Lolita soccer team!
© Anike Hage / TOKYOPOP GmbH. All rights reserved
DRAMA
T
TEEN AGE 13+

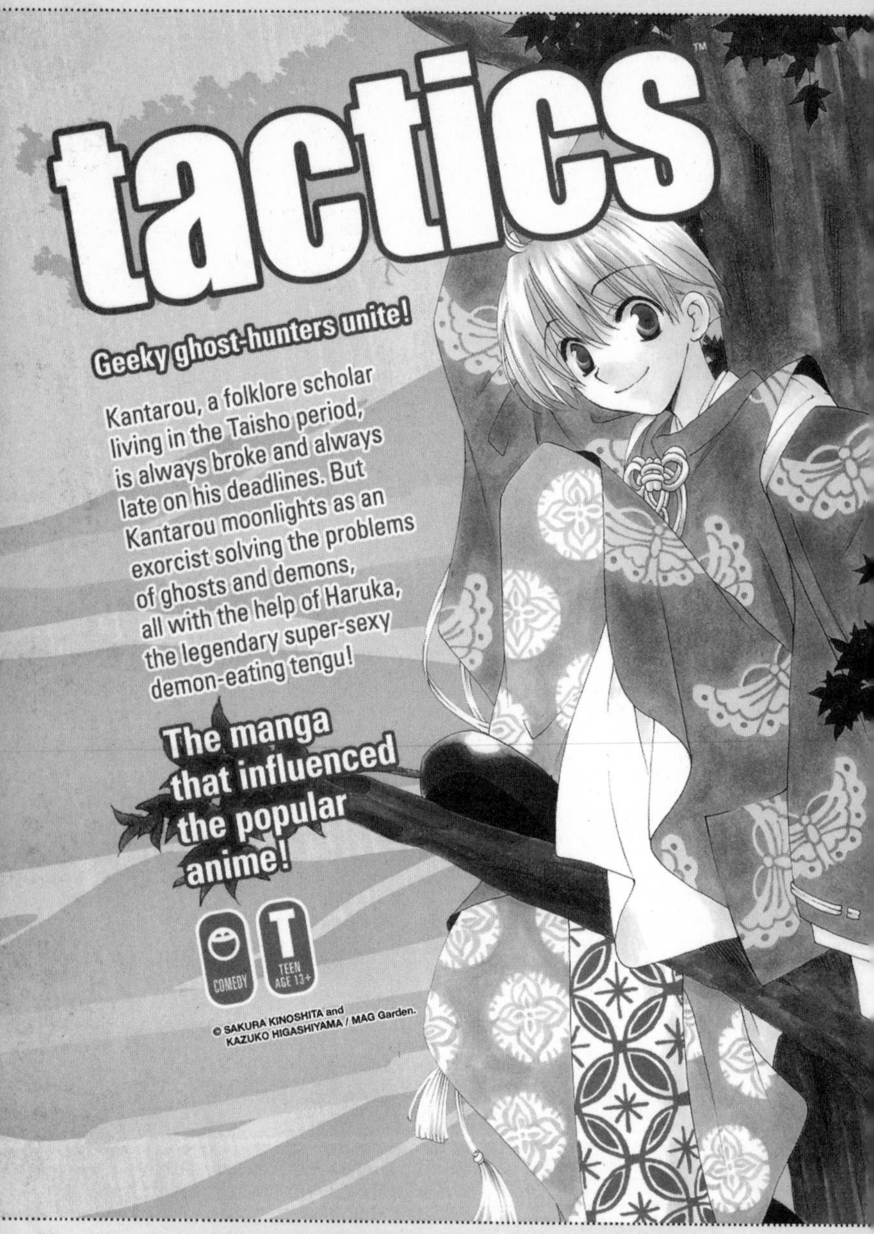
tactics™
Geeky ghost-hunters unite!
Kantarou, a folklore scholar living in the Taisho period, is always broke and always late on his deadlines. But Kantarou moonlights as an exorcist solving the problems of ghosts and demons, all with the help of Haruka, the legendary super-sexy demon-eating tengu!
The manga that influenced the popular anime!
COMEDY
T
TEEN AGE 13+
© SAKURA KINOSHITA and KAZUKO HIGASHIYAMA / MAG Garden.

Disney's Kilala Princess™

Meet Kilala, an ordinary girl who loves all the Disney Princesses!

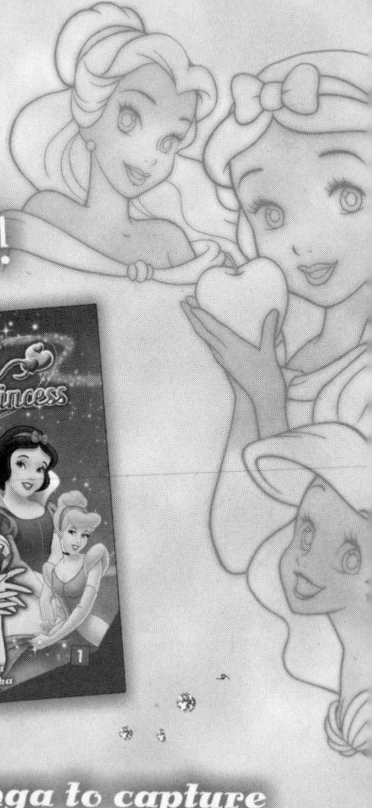

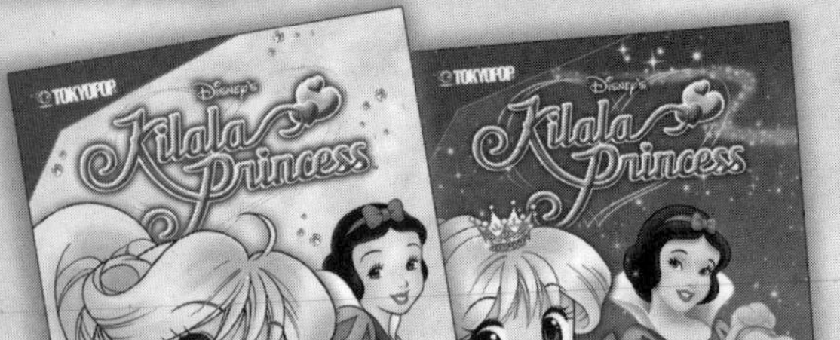
TOKYOPOP
Disney's Kilala Princess
2
Art by Nao Kodaka
Story by Rika Tanaka
TOKYOPOP
Disney's Kilala Princess
1

The first manga to capture the MAGIC of Disney's princesses!

FANTASY
A
ALL AGES

FOR MORE INFORMATION VISIT: WWW.TOKYOPOP.COM/KILALAPRINCESS

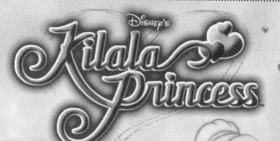

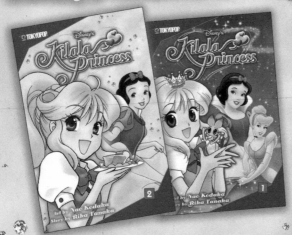

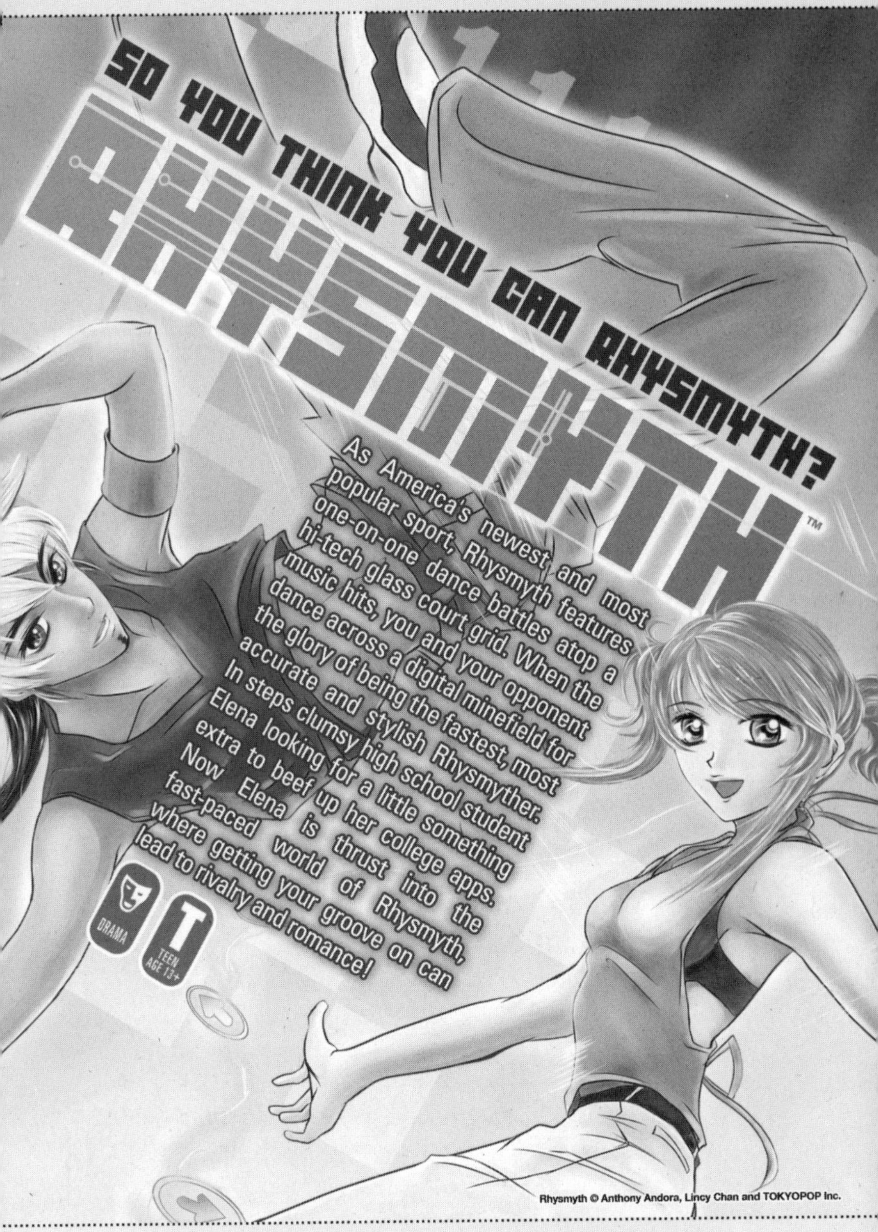
SO YOU THINK YOU CAN RHYSMYTH?
RHYSMYTH™
As America's newest and most popular sport, Rhysmyth features one-on-one dance battles atop a hi-tech glass court grid. When the music hits, you and your opponent dance across a digital minefield for the glory of being the fastest, most accurate and stylish Rhysmyther. In steps clumsy high school student Elena looking for a little something extra to beef up her college apps. Now Elena is thrust into the fast-paced world of Rhysmyth, where getting your groove on can lead to rivalry and romance!
DRAMA
T
TEEN AGE 13+
Rhysmyth © Anthony Andora, Lincy Chan and TOKYOPOP Inc.

TOKYOPOP MANGA SUPPLEMENT

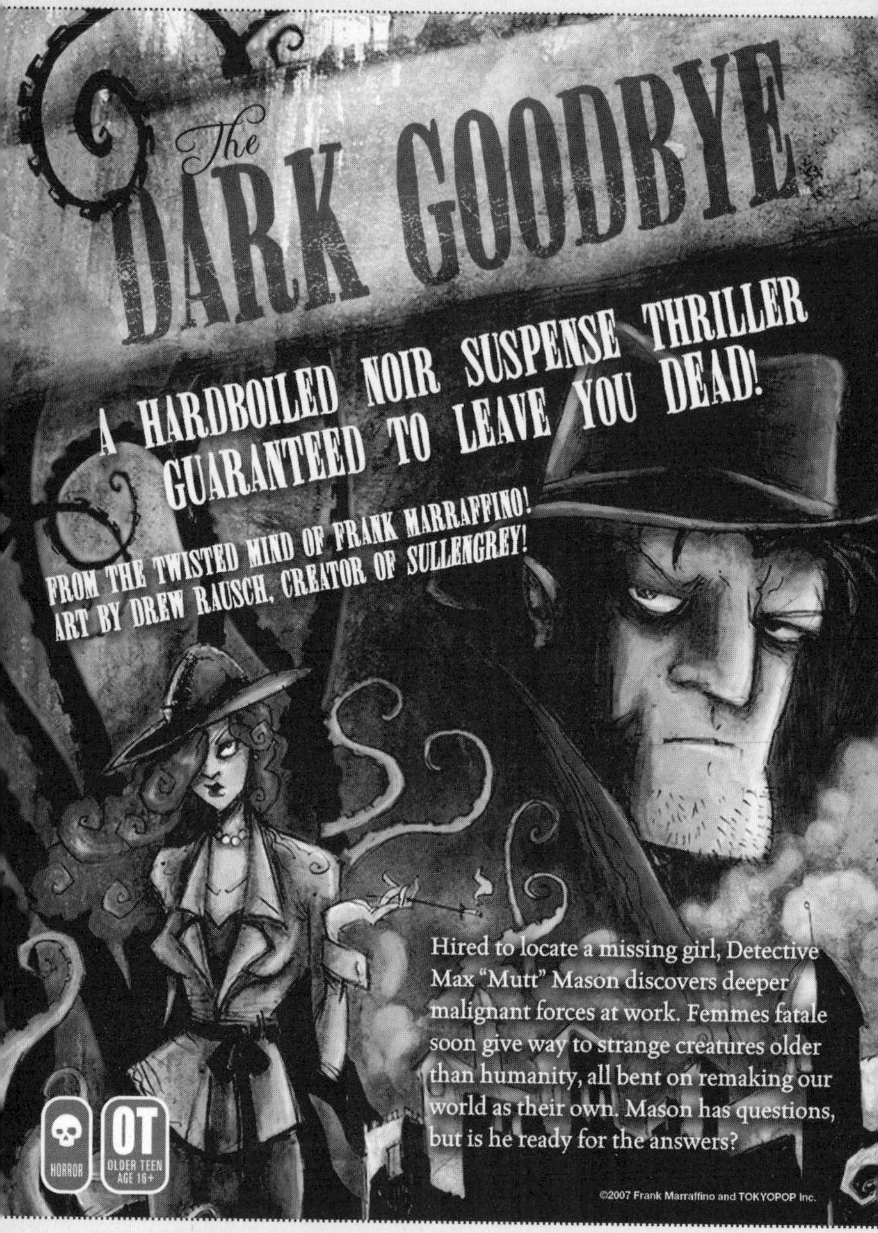
The DARK GOODBYE
A HARDBOILED NOIR SUSPENSE THRILLER GUARANTEED TO LEAVE YOU DEAD!
FROM THE TWISTED MIND OF FRANK MARRAFFINO!
ART BY DREW RAUSCH, CREATOR OF SULLENGREY!
Hired to locate a missing girl, Detective Max "Mutt" Mason discovers deeper malignant forces at work. Femmes fatale soon give way to strange creatures older than humanity, all bent on remaking our world as their own. Mason has questions, but is he ready for the answers?
HORROR
OT
OLDER TEEN AGE 16+
©2007 Frank Marraffino and TOKYOPOP Inc.

FOR MORE INFORMATION VISIT: WWW.TOKYOPOP.COM